HUMAN CULTURE

HUMAN CULTURE

HIGHLIGHTS OF
CULTURAL ANTHROPOLOGY

Carol R. Ember
Human Relations Area Files

Melvin Ember
Human Relations Area Files

PEARSON

Prentice
Hall

UPPER SADDLE RIVER, NEW JERSEY 07458

Library of Congress Cataloging-in-Publication Data

Ember, Carol R.
   Human culture: highlights of cultural anthropology/Carol R. Ember.
      p. cm.
   Includes bibliographical references and index.
   ISBN 978-0-13-603629-6
   1. Ethnology.   I. Ember, Melvin.   II. Cultural anthropology.   III. Title.
   GN316.E63 2009
   306—dc22   2008000242

Editorial Director: Leah Jewell
Publisher: Nancy Roberts
Editorial Assistant: Nart Varoqua
Director of Marketing: Brandy Dawson
Marketing Manager: Lindsey Prudhomme
Production Liaison: Barbara Reilly
Operations Specialist: Ben Smith
Director, Image Resource Center: Melinda Patelli
Manager, Rights and Permissions: Zina Arabia
Manager, Visual Research: Beth Brenzel
Manager, Cover Visual Research and Permissions: Karen Sanatar
Image Permission Coordinator: Fran Toepfer
Cover Art Director: Jayne Conte
Cover Design: Sue Behnke
Cover Photo: Chad Ehlers/The Stock Connection
Composition/Full-Service Project Management: Kari Callaghan Mazzola and John P. Mazzola/Big Sky Composition
Printer/Binder: Edwards Brothers, Inc.
Cover Printer: Phoenix Color Corp.

This book was set in 10/12 Adobe Garamond.

Pearson Education LTD.
Pearson Education Singapore, Pte. Ltd
Pearson Education, Canada, Ltd
Pearson Education—Japan
Pearson Education Australia PTY, Limited

Pearson Education North Asia Ltd
Pearson Educación de Mexico, S.A. de C.V.
Pearson Education Malaysia, Pte. Ltd
Pearson Education, Upper Saddle River, New Jersey

10 9 8 7 6 5 4 3 2 1
ISBN 13: 978-0-13-603629-6
ISBN 10:   0-13-603629-5

HUMAN CULTURE

HIGHLIGHTS OF
CULTURAL ANTHROPOLOGY

Carol R. Ember
Human Relations Area Files

Melvin Ember
Human Relations Area Files

PEARSON

Prentice
Hall

UPPER SADDLE RIVER, NEW JERSEY 07458

Library of Congress Cataloging-in-Publication Data

Ember, Carol R.
   Human culture: highlights of cultural anthropology/Carol R. Ember.
      p. cm.
   Includes bibliographical references and index.
   ISBN 978-0-13-603629-6
   1. Ethnology.   I. Ember, Melvin.   II. Cultural anthropology.   III. Title.
   GN316.E63 2009
   306—dc22   2008000242

Editorial Director: Leah Jewell
Publisher: Nancy Roberts
Editorial Assistant: Nart Varoqua
Director of Marketing: Brandy Dawson
Marketing Manager: Lindsey Prudhomme
Production Liaison: Barbara Reilly
Operations Specialist: Ben Smith
Director, Image Resource Center: Melinda Patelli
Manager, Rights and Permissions: Zina Arabia
Manager, Visual Research: Beth Brenzel
Manager, Cover Visual Research and Permissions: Karen Sanatar
Image Permission Coordinator: Fran Toepfer
Cover Art Director: Jayne Conte
Cover Design: Sue Behnke
Cover Photo: Chad Ehlers/The Stock Connection
Composition/Full-Service Project Management: Kari Callaghan Mazzola and John P. Mazzola/Big Sky Composition
Printer/Binder: Edwards Brothers, Inc.
Cover Printer: Phoenix Color Corp.

This book was set in 10/12 Adobe Garamond.

Pearson Education LTD.
Pearson Education Singapore, Pte. Ltd
Pearson Education, Canada, Ltd
Pearson Education—Japan
Pearson Education Australia PTY, Limited

Pearson Education North Asia Ltd
Pearson Educación de Mexico, S.A. de C.V.
Pearson Education Malaysia, Pte. Ltd
Pearson Education, Upper Saddle River, New Jersey

10 9 8 7 6 5 4 3 2 1
ISBN 13: 978-0-13-603629-6
ISBN 10:   0-13-603629-5

BRIEF CONTENTS

Part I Introduction

Chapter 1 The Importance of Anthropology   1

Chapter 2 The Study of Culture   22

Part II Cultural Variation

Chapter 3 Language and Communication   43

Chapter 4 Economics   68

Chapter 5 Social Stratification: Class, Ethnicity, and Racism   94

Chapter 6 Sex and Gender   115

Chapter 7 Marriage, Family, and Kinship   137

Chapter 8 Political Life   165

Chapter 9 Religion and Magic   187

Chapter 10 Culture Change and Globalization   206

Part III Using Anthropology

Chapter 11 Global Issues   227

Chapter 12 Applied and Practicing Anthropology   245

CONTENTS

Preface   xiii

About the Authors   xix

Part I   Introduction

Chapter 1   The Importance of Anthropology   1

The Scope of Anthropology   2

The Holistic Approach   3

The Anthropological Curiosity   3

Fields of Anthropology   4

Explanation and Evidence   10

   Science and Humanism   *12*

The Relevance of Anthropology   18

Summary   20

Glossary Terms   21

Critical Questions   21

Chapter 2   The Study of Culture   22

Defining Features of Culture   23

Attitudes That Hinder the Study of Cultures   26

Cultural Relativism   27

Increasing Cultural Diversity within the Countries of the World   28

Describing a Culture   29

Some Assumptions about Culture   34

Types of Research in Cultural Anthropology   37

Summary   41

Glossary Terms   42

Critical Questions   42

Part II   Cultural Variation

Chapter 3   Language and Communication   43

Communication   44

Origins of Language   48

Descriptive Linguistics   50

Historical Linguistics   54

Processes of Linguistic Divergence   56

Relationships between Language and Culture   57

Ethnography of Speaking   60

Writing and Literacy   63

Why Are "Mother Tongues" Retained, and for How Long?   64

Summary   65

Glossary Terms   66

Critical Questions   67

Chapter 4   Economics   68

Getting Food   69

The Origin, Spread, and Intensification of Food Production   78

Food on the Move   80

Allocation of Resources   81

Conversion of Resources   84

Distribution of Goods and Services   88

Summary   92

Glossary Terms   93

Critical Questions   93

Chapter 5   Social Stratification: Class, Ethnicity, and Racism   94

Variation in Degree of Social Inequality   95

Egalitarian Societies   96

Rank Societies   98

Class Societies   99

   Is Global Inequality Increasing?   *105*

Racism and Inequality   106

Ethnicity and Inequality   109

The Emergence of Stratification   111

Summary   113

Glossary Terms   114

Critical Questions   114

Chapter 6   Sex and Gender   115

Gender Concepts   116

Physique and Physiology   117

Gender Roles   118

Relative Contributions to Work   121

Political Leadership and Warfare   124

   Why Some Societies Let Women Participate in Combat   *125*

The Relative Status of Women   127

Personality Differences   129

Sexuality   132

Summary   135

Glossary Terms   136

Critical Questions   136

Chapter 7   Marriage, Family, and Kinship   137

Marriage   138

The Family   148

   One-Parent Families: Why the Recent Increase?   *150*

Marital Residence and Kinship   151

Summary   163

Glossary Terms   164

Critical Questions   164

Chapter 8   Political Life   165

Types of Political Organization   166

   The Growth of Cities   *172*

The Spread of State Societies   174

Variation in Political Process   175

Resolution of Conflict   178

Summary   185

Glossary Terms   186

Critical Questions   186

Chapter 9   Religion and Magic   187

Variation in Religious Beliefs   188

   The Usefulness of Religion: Taboos among New England Fishermen   *189*

Variation in Religious Practices   193

Religion and Adaptation   199

Summary   204

Glossary Terms   205

Critical Questions   205

Chapter 10   Culture Change and Globalization   206

How and Why Cultures Change   207

Culture Change and Adaptation   214

Types of Culture Change in the Modern World   215

   Obesity, Hypertension, and Diabetes: Health Consequences of Modernization?   *219*

Ethnogenesis: The Emergence of New Cultures   220

Globalization: Problems and Opportunities   221

Cultural Diversity in the Future   224

Summary   225

Glossary Terms   226

Critical Questions   226

Part III   Using Anthropology

Chapter 11   Global Issues   227

Natural Disasters and Famine   228

Inadequate Housing and Homelessness   230

   Global Warming, Air Pollution, and Our Dependence on Oil   *232*

Family Violence and Abuse   234

Crime   236

War   238

   Ethnic Conflicts: Ancient Hatreds or Not?   *240*

Terrorism   241

Making the World Better   243

Summary   244

Glossary Term   244

Critical Questions   244

Chapter 12   Applied and Practicing Anthropology   245

Motives for Applying and Practicing Anthropology   246

Ethics of Applied Anthropology   247

Evaluating the Effects of Planned Change   248

Difficulties in Instituting Planned Change   249

Cultural Resource Management   251

Forensic Anthropology   253

Medical Anthropology   254

   The Cultural Construction of Beauty   *232*

Summary   265

Glossary Terms   266

Critical Questions   266

Glossary   267

Notes   273

References   283

Photo Credits   307

Index   309

PREFACE

This book presents the highlights of the twelfth edition of our *Cultural Anthropology*. The size of the book makes it useful for quarter courses, as well as for courses that encourage a lot of supplemental reading.

The human species may be the most widespread species in the world today. Humans have been moving tremendous distances ever since *Homo erectus* moved out of Africa. In the past 100 years or so, the number of migrants has grown enormously. For example, between the 1880s and 1920s, 20 million people left China for other parts of Asia, the Americas, and many other places around the world. And the migrations continue today. With jet planes, cell phones, and the Internet, people can live global lives, and often move back and forth from one country to another. Anthropology increasingly studies immigrant populations and the flow of people and ideas across the globe. We have included feature boxes in several chapters to highlight this growing interest in migrants and immigrants—for example, why some immigrant groups retained their "mother tongues" longer than others and how foods have spread in recent times.

In preparing this book we try to go beyond descriptions, as always. We are interested not only in *what* humans are and were like, but also in *why* they got to be that way, in all their variety. To help students appreciate what it means to understand, we include an extended discussion of explanation and evidence in the first chapter. When alternative explanations are discussed subsequently, we try to communicate the necessity of evaluating them logically as well as on the basis of the available evidence. Throughout the book, we try to communicate that no idea, including ideas put forward in textbooks, should be accepted even tentatively without supporting tests that could have gone the other way.

Organization of the Text

Part I: Introduction

Chapter 1: The Importance of Anthropology Chapter 1 introduces the student to anthropology. We discuss what we think is distinctive about anthropology in general, and about each of its subfields in particular. We outline how each of the subfields is related to other disciplines such as biology, psychology, and sociology. We direct attention to the increasing importance of applied anthropology and the importance of understanding others in today's more globalized world. We discuss what it means to understand scientifically. In a feature box we explain the differences between scientific and humanistic understanding; we point out that the two approaches are not incompatible.

Chapter 2: The Study of Culture   This chapter introduces the concept of culture and includes an expanded discussion of the concept of society. We first try to convey a feeling for what culture is before dealing more explicitly with the concept and some assumptions about it. A section on cultural relativism puts the concept in its historical context and covers recent thinking on the subject. We discuss the fact that individual behavior varies in all societies and how such variation may be the beginning of new cultural patterns. The chapter's feature box discusses the increasing cultural diversity within the countries of the world because of immigration and migration.

Part II: Cultural Variation

In most of the chapters that follow, we try to convey the range of cultural variation with ethnographic examples from all over the world. Wherever we can, we discuss possible explanations of why societies may be similar or different in regard to some aspect of culture. If anthropologists have no explanation as yet for the variation, we say so. But if we have some idea of the conditions that may be related to a particular kind of variation, even if we do not know yet why they are related, we discuss that, too. If we are to train students to go beyond what we know now, we have to tell them what we do not know, as well as what we think we know.

Chapter 3: Language and Communication   Here we discuss communication in humans and other animals. We look at the debate over the degree of difference between human and nonhuman primate language abilities. We discuss the origins of language and how creoles and children's language acquisition can help us understand the origins, and we cover new research on infant understanding of language. We describe the fundamentals of descriptive linguistics and the processes of linguistic divergence. After discussing the interrelationships between language and other aspects of culture, we discuss the ethnography of speaking and the differences in speech according to status, gender, and ethnicity. We discuss interethnic or intercultural communication, indicating how linguists can play a role in helping people improve their cross-cultural communication, and we touch on the history of writing and literacy. The feature box discusses why some immigrant groups retain their "mother tongues" longer than others.

Chapter 4: Economics   Chapter 4 discusses how societies vary in getting their food, how they have changed over time, and how that variation seems to affect other kinds of cultural variation—including variation in social stratification and political life. We discuss how societies vary in the ways they allocate resources (what is "property" and what ownership may mean), convert or transform resources through labor into usable goods, and distribute and perhaps exchange goods and services. We describe recent experimental evidence on sharing and cooperation. The feature box explores where particular foods came from and how different foods and cuisines spread around the world as people migrated.

Chapter 5: Social Stratification: Class, Ethnicity, and Racism   This chapter explores the variation in degree of social stratification and how various forms of social inequality may develop. We discuss how egalitarian societies work hard to prevent dominance. We show how people in the United States often deny the existence of class. We end with an extensive discussion of "race," racism, and ethnicity and how they often relate to the inequitable distribution of resources. The feature box discusses social stratification on the global level: how the gap between rich and poor countries has been widening, and what may account for that trend.

Chapter 6: Sex and Gender   The first part of Chapter 6 focuses on gender concepts and how and why they vary cross-culturally. We discuss the gender division of labor in primary and secondary subsistence, and why females generally work harder. We include material on female hunting and discuss its impact on theories about the gender division of labor, and we discuss gender roles in warfare. In the second part of the chapter we discuss variation in sexual attitudes and practices, including marital sex and extramarital sex. We also discuss homosexuality, including female-female relationships. The feature box describes cross-cultural research on why some societies allow women to participate in combat.

Chapter 7: Marriage, Family, and Kinship   After discussing various theories about why marriage might be universal, we move on to discuss variation in marriage and restrictions on marriage: how one marries, whom one marries, and how many one marries. We explain variation in family form, including the phenomenon of couples choosing to live together without marriage. The feature box discusses why one-parent families are on the increase in the United States and other countries. In discussing variation in marital residence and kinship structure, we emphasize how understanding residence is important for understanding social life in all societies.

Chapter 8: Political Life   Here we look at how societies have varied in their levels of political organization, the various ways people become leaders, the degree to which they participate in the political process, and the peaceful and violent methods of resolving conflict. We discuss how colonialization has transformed legal systems and ways of making decisions, and we expand our discussion of states as empires. The feature box discusses the role of migrants in the growth of cities around the world.

Chapter 9: Religion and Magic   In this chapter, we focus on variation in religious belief and practice, including the character and hierarchy of supernatural beings and the intervention of gods in human affairs. We discuss religious change and the rise of fundamentalism. The feature box discusses research on New England fishermen that suggests how their taboos may reduce anxiety.

Chapter 10: Culture Change and Globalization   After discussing the ultimate sources of culture change—discovery and innovation—we explore some of what is known about the conditions under which people are likely to accept innovations. We discuss the costs and benefits of innovations, and types of external and internal pressures for culture change. We draw particular attention to processes of change in the modern world, including colonialization, commercialization, industrialization, and globalization. We also discuss the rise of new cultures, or ethnogenesis. We close with a discussion of the likelihood of cultural diversity in the future. We point out that globalization does not always result in similarity (e.g., McDonald's in Japan has become very Japanese). We discuss how worldwide communication can sometimes allow the less powerful to be heard. To convey that culture change often has biological consequences, the feature box discusses obesity, hypertension, and diabetes as health consequences of modernization.

Part III: Using Anthropology

Chapter 11: Global Issues   In this chapter we discuss the relationship between basic and applied research, and how research may suggest possible solutions to various global social problems, including natural disasters and famines, homelessness, crime, family violence, war, and terrorism. One feature box discusses global warming and our dependence on oil. A second feature box is on ethnic conflicts.

Chapter 12: Applied and Practicing Anthropology   This chapter looks at anthropological work outside of academia, the ethical issues involved in trying to improve people's lives, and the difficulties in evaluating whether a program is beneficial. We point out how applied anthropologists are playing more of a role in planning, rather than serving only as peripheral advisers to those programs already in place. The feature box discusses how medical anthropology views eating disorders and their relation to conceptions of beauty.

Features of This Book

Feature Boxes   Feature boxes appear in each chapter. These boxes focus on migrants and immigrants in recent times and on current issues in cultural anthropology.

Readability   We derive a lot of pleasure from trying to describe research findings, especially complicated ones, in ways that introductory students can understand. Thus, we try to minimize technical jargon, using only those terms that students must know to appreciate the achievements of anthropology and to take advanced courses. We think readability is important, not only because it may enhance the reader's understanding of what we write, but also because it should make learning about anthropology more enjoyable. When new terms are introduced, which of course must happen sometimes, they are set in boldface type and defined in the text (and in the Glossary at the end of the book).

Glossary   At the end of each chapter we list the new terms that have been introduced. These terms are set in boldface type and defined in the text. We deliberately do not repeat the definitions at the end of the chapter to allow students to ask themselves if they know the terms; however, we do provide page numbers to find the definitions and we also provide all the definitions again in the Glossary at the end of the book.

Outlines and Summaries   In addition to the outline provided at the beginning of each chapter, there is a detailed summary at the end of each chapter that will help students review the major concepts and findings discussed in the chapter.

Critical Questions   At the end of each chapter we provide three or four questions that may stimulate thinking about the implications of the chapter. The questions do not ask for repetition of what is in the text. We want students to imagine, to go beyond what we know or think we know.

End-of-Book Notes   Because we believe in the importance of documentation, we think it is essential to tell our readers, both professionals and students, what our conclusions are based on. Usually the basis is published research. The abbreviated notes at the end of the book provide information for finding the complete citation in the References section at the end of the book.

Supplements

This textbook is part of a complete teaching and learning package that has been carefully created to enhance the topics discussed in the text.

Instructor's Resource Manual with Tests   (0-13-603760-7) For each chapter in the text, this valuable resource provides a detailed outline, a list of objectives, discussion questions, and classroom activities. In addition, test questions in multiple-choice, true-false, and short-answer formats are available for each chapter; the answers to all questions are page-referenced to the text.

TestGEN-EQ   (0-13-603757-7) This computerized software allows instructors to create their own personalized exams, to edit any or all of the existing test questions, and to add new questions. Other special features of this program include random generation of test questions, creation of alternate versions of the same test, scrambling question sequence, and test preview before printing.

Prentice Hall Anthropology PowerPoint® Slides   (0-13-603768-2) These PowerPoint slides combine graphics and text for each chapter in a colorful format to help instructors convey anthropological principles in a new and exciting way. For easy access, they are available in the Instructor's Resource Center at <www.prenhall.com/anthropology>.

Strategies in Teaching Anthropology, Fifth Edition   (0-13-603466-7) Unique in focus and content, this book focuses on the "how" of teaching Anthropology across all of its sub-fields—Cultural Anthropology, Biological Anthropology, Archaeology, and Linguistics—to provide a wide array of associated learning outcomes and student activities. It is a valuable single-source compendium of strategies and "tricks of the trade" from a group of seasoned teaching anthropologists who are working in a variety of teaching settings and who share their pedagogical techniques, knowledge, and observations. Please see your local Pearson sales representative for more information.

MyAnthroKit   (0-13-603758-5) MyAnthroKit is an online resource that contains book-specific practice tests, chapter summaries, learning objectives, flashcards, Weblinks, Research Navigator, and media-rich activities that enhance topics covered in your textbook. For more information, please contact your local Pearson sales representative.

Discovering Anthropology: Researchers at Work—Cultural Anthropology   (0-13-219706-5) This collection of case studies provides examples of anthropologists working in a variety of settings. Please see your local Pearson sales representative for information about packaging this supplement with *Human Culture.*

Research Navigator™   Research Navigator™ can help students complete research assignments efficiently and with confidence by providing three exclusive databases of high-quality, scholarly, and popular articles accessed by easy-to-use search engines.

- **EBSCO's ContentSelect™ Academic Journal Database,** organized by subject, contains many of the leading academic journals for anthropology. Instructors and students can search the online journals by keyword, topic, or multiple topics. Articles include abstract and citation information and can be cut, pasted, e-mailed, or saved for later use.

- *The New York Times* **Search-by-Subject Archive** provides articles specific to Anthropology and is searchable by keyword or multiple keywords. Instructors and students can view full-text articles from the world's leading journalists writing for *The New York Times*.
- **Link Library** offers editorially selected "best of the Web" sites for Anthropology. Link Libraries are continually scanned and kept up-to-date, providing the most relevant and accurate links for research assignments.

Gain access to Research Navigator™ by using the access code found in the front of the brief guide called *The Prentice Hall Guide to Research Navigator*™ (0-13-600863-1).

The Dorling Kindersley/Prentice Hall Atlas of Anthropology   (0-13-191879-6) Beautifully illustrated by Dorling Kindersley, with narrative by leading archaeological author Brian M. Fagan, this striking atlas features 30 full-color maps, timelines, and illustrations to offer a highly visual but explanatory geographical overview of topics from all four fields of Anthropology. Please contact your Pearson representative for ordering information.

Acknowledgments

We thank the people at Prentice Hall for all of their help, particularly Nancy Roberts, Publisher for the Social Sciences, and we thank Kari Callaghan Mazzola and John Mazzola of Big Sky Composition for seeing the manuscript through the production process.

We also thank the following reviewers, whose comments directly influenced the creation of this new book: Carol Apt, South Carolina State University; Kristina Casper-Denman, American River College; Phyllisa Eisentraut, Shasta College; Risa Ellovich, North Carolina State University; Luther P. Gerlach, University of Minnesota; Mark J. Hartmann, University of Arkansas at Little Rock; Linda Keng, University of Houston; Patricia D. Mathews, Borough of Manhattan Community College; Michael D. Pool, Austin Community College; Juris Zarins, Southwest Missouri State University.

Thank you all, named and unnamed, who gave us advice.

Carol R. Ember and Melvin Ember

ABOUT THE AUTHORS

Carol R. Ember started at Antioch College as a chemistry major. She began taking social science courses because some were required, and she soon found herself intrigued with the subject matter. There were a lot of questions without answers, and she became excited about the possibility of a research career in social science. She spent a year in graduate school at Cornell studying sociology before continuing on to Harvard, where she studied anthropology primarily with John and Beatrice Whiting.

For her Ph.D. dissertation she worked among the Luo of Kenya. While she was there she noticed that many boys were assigned "girls' work," such as babysitting and household chores, because their mothers (who did most of the agriculture) did not have enough girls to help out. She decided to study the possible effects of task assignment on the social behavior of boys. Using systematic behavior observations, she compared girls, boys who did a great deal of "girls' work," and boys who did little such work. She found that boys assigned "girls' work" were intermediate in many social behaviors compared with the other boys and girls. Later, she did cross-cultural research on variation in marriage, family, descent groups, and war and peace, mainly in collaboration with Melvin Ember, whom she married in 1970. All of these cross-cultural studies tested theories on data for worldwide samples of societies.

From 1970 to 1996, she taught at Hunter College of the City University of New York. She has served as president of the Society of Cross-Cultural Research and was one of the directors of the Summer Institutes in Comparative Anthropological Research, which were funded by the National Science Foundation. Since 1996 she has served as executive director of the Human Relations Area Files, Inc., a nonprofit research agency at Yale University.

After graduating from Columbia College, Melvin Ember went to Yale University for his Ph.D. His mentor at Yale was George Peter Murdock, an anthropologist who was instrumental in promoting cross-cultural research and building a full-text database on the cultures of the world to facilitate cross-cultural hypothesis testing. This database came to be known as the Human Relations Area Files (HRAF) because it was originally sponsored by the Institute of Human Relations at Yale. Growing in annual installments and now distributed in electronic format, the HRAF database currently covers approximately 400 cultures, past and present, all over the world.

Melvin Ember did fieldwork for his dissertation in American Samoa, where he conducted a comparison of three villages to study the effects of commercialization on political life. In addition, he did research on descent groups and how they changed with the increase of buying and selling. His cross-cultural studies focused originally on variation in marital residence and descent groups. He has also done cross-cultural research on the relationship between economic and political development, the origin and extension of the incest taboo, the causes of polygyny, and how archaeological correlates of social customs can help us draw inferences about the past.

After four years of research at the National Institute of Mental Health, he taught at Antioch College and then Hunter College of the City University of New York. He has served as president of the Society for Cross-Cultural Research. Since 1987 he has been president of the Human Relations Area Files, Inc., a nonprofit research agency at Yale University.

THE IMPORTANCE OF ANTHROPOLOGY

Chapter Outline

- The Scope of Anthropology
- The Holistic Approach
- The Anthropological Curiosity
- Fields of Anthropology
- Explanation and Evidence
- The Relevance of Anthropology

What is **anthropology** and what can it do? By definition, anthropology is a discipline of infinite curiosity about human beings. The term comes from the Greek *anthropos* for "man, human" and *logos* for "study." Anthropologists seek answers to an enormous variety of questions about humans. They are interested in discovering when, where, and why humans appeared on the earth, how and why they have changed since then, and how and why modern human populations vary in certain physical features. Anthropologists are also interested in how and why societies in the past and present have varied in their customary ideas and practices. There is a practical side to anthropology, too. Applied and practicing anthropologists put anthropological methods, information, and results to use in efforts to solve practical problems.

But defining anthropology as the study of human beings is not completely satisfactory, for such a definition would appear to incorporate a whole catalog of disciplines: sociology, psychology, political science, economics, history, human biology, and perhaps even the humanistic disciplines of philosophy and literature. Needless to say, practitioners of the many other disciplines concerned with humans would not be happy to be regarded as being in subbranches of anthropology. After all, most of those disciplines have existed longer than anthropology, and each is somewhat distinctive. There must, then, be something unique about anthropology—a reason for its having developed as a separate discipline and for its having retained a separate identity over the last 100 years.

The Scope of Anthropology

Anthropologists are generally thought of as individuals who travel to little-known corners of the world to study exotic peoples or who dig deep into the earth to uncover the fossil remains or the tools and pots of people who lived long ago. These views, though clearly stereotyped, do indicate how anthropology differs from other disciplines concerned with humans. Anthropology is broader in scope, both geographically and historically. Anthropology is concerned explicitly and directly with all varieties of people throughout the world, not just those close at hand or within a limited area. It is also interested in people of all periods. Beginning with the immediate ancestors of humans, who lived a few million years ago, anthropology traces the development of humans until the present. Every part of the world that has ever contained a human population is of interest to anthropologists.

Anthropologists have not always been as global and comprehensive in their concerns as they are today. Traditionally, they concentrated on non-Western cultures and left the study of Western civilization and other complex societies to other disciplines. In recent years, however, this division of labor among the disciplines has begun to disappear. Now anthropologists work in their own and other complex societies.

What induces anthropologists to choose so broad a subject for study? In part, they are motivated by the belief that any suggested generalization about human beings, any possible explanation of some characteristic of human culture or biology, should be shown to apply to many times and places of human existence. If a generalization or explanation does not prove to apply widely, we are entitled or even obliged to be skeptical about it. The skeptical attitude, in the absence of persuasive evidence, is our best protection against accepting invalid ideas about humans.

For example, when American educators discovered in the 1960s that African-American schoolchildren rarely drank milk, they assumed that lack of money or education was the cause. But evidence from anthropology suggested a different explanation. Anthropologists had known for years that in many parts of the world where milking animals are kept, people do not drink fresh milk; rather, they sour it before they drink it, or they make it into cheese. Why they do so is now clear. Many people lack an enzyme, lactase, that is necessary for breaking down lactose, the sugar in milk. When such people drink regular milk, it actually interferes with digestion. Not only is the lactose in milk not digested but other nutrients are less likely to be digested as well; in many cases, drinking milk will cause cramps, stomach gas, diarrhea, and nausea. Studies indicate that milk intolerance is found in many parts of the world.[1] The condition is common in adulthood among Asians, southern Europeans, Arabs and Jews, West Africans, Inuit (Eskimos), North American Indians, and South American Indians, as well as African Americans. Because anthropologists are acquainted with human life in an enormous variety of geographic and historical settings, they are often able to correct mistaken beliefs about people.

The Holistic Approach

In addition to the worldwide as well as the historical scope of anthropology, another distinguishing feature of the discipline is its **holistic**, or multifaceted, approach to the study of human beings. Anthropologists study not only all varieties of people but many aspects of human experience as well. For example, when describing a group of people, an anthropologist might discuss the history of the area in which the people live, the physical environment, the organization of family life, the general features of their language, the group's settlement patterns, political and economic systems, religion, and styles of art and dress.

In the past, individual anthropologists tried to be holistic and cover many subjects. Today, as in many other disciplines, so much information has been accumulated that anthropologists tend to specialize in one topic or area. Thus, one anthropologist may investigate the physical characteristics of some of our prehistoric ancestors. Another may study the biological effect of the environment on a human population over time. Still another will concentrate on many customs of a particular group of people. Despite this specialization, however, the discipline of anthropology retains its holistic orientation in that its many different specialties, taken together, describe many aspects of human existence, both past and present.

The Anthropological Curiosity

Thus far we have described anthropology as being broader in scope, both historically and geographically, and more holistic in approach than other disciplines concerned with human beings. But this statement again implies that anthropology is the all-inclusive human science. How, then, is anthropology really different from those other disciplines? We suggest that anthropology's distinctiveness lies principally in the kind of curiosity it arouses.

In studying a human population anthropologists tend to focus on *typical* characteristics (traits, customs) of that population: People in many societies depend on agriculture. Why? And where, when, and why did people first start to farm? Why do some populations have lighter skin than others? Why do some languages contain more terms for color than others? Why do some societies have more political participation than others? The anthropological curiosity mostly focuses on the typical characteristics of human groups and how to explain them. Economists take a monetary system for granted and study how it operates. Anthropologists ask how frequently monetary systems are found, why they vary, and why only some societies during the last few thousand years used money. In short, anthropologists are curious about the typical characteristics of human groups—how and why populations and their characteristics have varied around the globe and throughout the ages.

Fields of Anthropology

Different anthropologists concentrate on different typical characteristics of societies. Some are concerned primarily with *biological* or *physical characteristics* of human populations; others are interested principally in what we call *cultural characteristics.* Hence, there are two broad classifications of subject matter in anthropology: **biological (physical) anthropology** and **cultural anthropology**. Biological anthropology is one major field of anthropology. Cultural anthropology is divided into three major subfields—archaeology, linguistics, and ethnology. Ethnology, the study of recent cultures, is now usually referred to by the parent name, cultural anthropology (see Figure 1.1). Crosscutting these four fields is a fifth, applied or practicing anthropology.

Biological Anthropology

Biological (physical) anthropology seeks to answer two distinct sets of questions. The first set includes questions about the emergence of humans and their later evolution (this focus is called **human paleontology** or **paleoanthropology**). The second set includes questions about how and why contemporary human populations vary biologically (this focus is called **human variation**).

In order to reconstruct human evolution, human paleontologists search for and study the buried, hardened remains or impressions—known as **fossils**—of humans, prehumans, and related animals. Paleontologists working in East Africa, for instance, have excavated the fossil remains of humanlike beings who lived more than 3 million years ago. These findings have suggested the approximate dates when our ancestors began to develop two-legged walking, very flexible hands, and a larger brain.

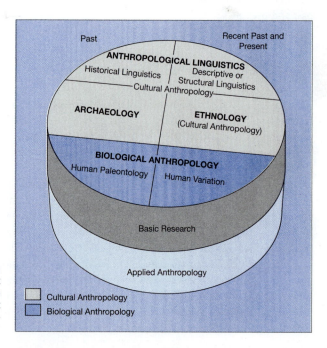

Figure 1.1 The Subdivisions of Anthropology

The four major subdisciplines of anthropology (in bold type) may be classified according to subject matter (biological or cultural) and according to the period with which each is concerned (distant past versus recent past and present). There are applications of anthropology in all four subdisciplines.

In attempting to clarify evolutionary relationships, human paleontologists may use not only the fossil record but also geological information on the succession of climates, environments, and plant and animal populations. Moreover, when reconstructing the past of humans, paleontologists are also interested in the behavior and evolution of our closest relatives among the mammals—the prosimians, monkeys, and apes, which, like ourselves, are members of the order of **Primates**. Anthropologists, psychologists, and biologists who specialize in the study of primates are called **primatologists**. The various species of primates are observed in the wild and in the laboratory. One especially popular subject of study is the chimpanzee, which bears a close resemblance to humans in behavior and physical appearance, has a similar blood chemistry, and is susceptible to many of the same diseases. It now appears that chimpanzees share as much as 99 percent of their genes with humans.[2]

From primate studies, biological anthropologists try to discover characteristics that are distinctly human, as opposed to those that might be part of the primate heritage. With this information, they may be able to infer what our prehistoric ancestors were like. The inferences from primate studies are checked against the fossil record. The evidence from the earth, collected in bits and pieces, is correlated with scientific observations of our closest living relatives. In short, biological anthropologists piece together bits of information obtained from different sources. They construct theories that explain the changes observed in the fossil record and then attempt to evaluate their theories by checking one kind of evidence against another. Human paleontology thus overlaps with disciplines such as geology, general vertebrate (and particularly primate) paleontology, comparative anatomy, and the study of comparative primate behavior.

The second major focus of biological anthropology, the study of human variation, investigates how and why contemporary human populations differ in biological or physical characteristics. All living people belong to one species, ***Homo sapiens***, for all can successfully interbreed. Yet there is much that varies among human populations. Investigators of human variation ask such questions as: Why are some peoples taller than others? How have human populations adapted physically to their environmental conditions? Are some peoples, such as Inuit (Eskimos), better equipped than other peoples to endure cold? Does darker skin pigmentation offer special protection against the tropical sun?

Birute Galdikas works with two orangutans in Borneo.

To understand the biological variations observable among contemporary human populations, biological anthropologists use the principles, concepts, and techniques of at least three other disciplines: human genetics (the study of human traits that are inherited), population biology (the study of environmental effects on, and interaction with, population characteristics), and epidemiology (the study of how and why diseases affect different populations in different ways). Research on human variation, therefore, overlaps research in other fields.

Cultural Anthropology

Cultural anthropology focuses on universals and variation in culture in the past and present. But what is culture? Because the concept of culture is so central to anthropology, we devote a whole chapter to it. To an anthropologist, the term *culture* refers to the customary ways of thinking and behaving of a particular population or society. The culture of a social group includes many things—its language, religious beliefs, food preferences, music, work habits, gender roles, how they rear their children, how they construct their houses, and many other learned behaviors and ideas that have come to be widely shared or customary among the group. The three main branches of cultural anthropology are **archaeology** (the study of past cultures, primarily through their material remains), **anthropological linguistics** (the anthropological study of languages), and **ethnology** (the study of existing and recent cultures), now usually referred to by the parent name, cultural anthropology.

Archaeology   The archaeologist seeks not only to reconstruct the daily life and customs of peoples who lived in the past but also to trace cultural changes and to offer possible explanations for those changes. This concern is similar to that of the historian, but the archaeologist reaches much farther back in time. The historian deals only with societies that left written records and is therefore limited to the last 5,000 years of human history. Human societies, however, have existed for more than a million years, and only a small proportion in the last 5,000 years had writing. For all those past societies lacking a written record, the archaeologist serves as historian. Lacking written records for study, archaeologists must try to reconstruct history from the remains of human cultures. Some of these remains are as grand as the Mayan temples discovered at Chichén Itzá in Yucatán, Mexico. More often they are as ordinary as bits of broken pottery, stone tools, and garbage heaps.

Most archaeologists deal with **prehistory**, the time before written records. But there is a specialty within archaeology, called **historical archaeology**, that studies the remains of recent peoples who left written records. This specialty, as its name implies, employs the methods of both archaeologists and historians to study recent societies for which there is both archaeological and historical information.

In trying to understand how and why ways of life have changed through time in different parts of the world, archaeologists collect materials from sites of human occupation. Usually, these sites must be unearthed. On the basis of materials they have excavated and otherwise collected, archaeologists ask various questions: Where, when, and why did the distinctive human characteristic of toolmaking first emerge? Where, when, and why did agriculture first develop? Where, when, and why did people first begin to live in cities?

To collect the data they need to suggest answers to these and other questions, archaeologists use techniques and findings borrowed from other disciplines, as well as what they can infer from anthropological studies of recent and contemporary cultures. For example, to guess where to dig for evidence of early toolmaking, archaeologists rely on geology to tell them where sites of early human occupation are likely to be found, because of erosion and uplifting, near the surface of the earth. To infer when agriculture first developed, archaeologists date the relevant excavated materials by a process originally developed by chemists. And to try to understand why cities first emerged, archaeologists may use information from historians, geographers, and others about how recent and contemporary cities are related economically and politically to their hinterlands. If we can discover what recent and contemporary cities have in common, we can speculate on why cities developed originally. Thus, archaeologists use information from the present and recent past in trying to understand the distant past.

Anthropological Linguistics   Anthropological linguistics is another branch of cultural anthropology. Linguistics, or the study of languages, is a somewhat older discipline than anthropology, but the early linguists concentrated on the study of languages that had been written for a long time—languages such as English that had been written for nearly a thousand years. Anthropological linguists began to do fieldwork in places where the language was not yet written. This meant that anthropologists could not consult a dictionary or grammar to help them learn the language. Instead, they first had to construct a dictionary and grammar, after which they could study the structure and history of the language.

Like biological anthropologists, linguists study changes that have taken place over time, as well as contemporary variation. Some anthropological linguists are concerned with the emergence of language and also with the divergence of languages over thousands of years. The study of how languages change over time and how they may be related is known as **historical linguistics**. Anthropological linguists are also interested in how contemporary languages differ, especially in how they construct words, phrases, and other features. This focus of linguistics is generally called **descriptive** or **structural linguistics**. The study of how language is used in social contexts is called **sociolinguistics**.

In contrast with the human paleontologist and archaeologist, who have physical remains to help them reconstruct change over time, the historical linguist deals only with languages—and usually unwritten ones at that. (Remember that writing is only about 5,000 years old, and most languages since then have not been written.) Because an unwritten language must be heard in order to be studied, it does not leave any trace once its speakers have died. Linguists interested in reconstructing the history of unwritten languages must begin in the present, with comparisons of contemporary languages. On the basis of these comparisons, they draw inferences about the kinds of change in language that may have occurred in the past and that may account for similarities and differences observed in the present. The historical linguist typically asks such questions as these: Did two or more contemporary languages diverge from a common ancestral language? If they are related, how far back in time did they begin to differ?

Unlike the historical linguist, the descriptive (or structural) linguist is typically concerned with discovering and recording the principles that determine how sounds and words are put together in speech. For example, a structural description of a particular language might tell us that the sounds *t* and *k* are interchangeable in a word without causing a difference in meaning. In American Samoa, one could say *Tutuila* or *Kukuila* as the name of the largest island, and everyone, except perhaps the tourist or the newly arrived anthropologist, would understand that the same island was being mentioned.

The sociolinguist is interested in the social aspects of language, including what people speak about and how they interact conversationally, their attitudes toward speakers of other dialects or languages, and how people speak differently in different social contexts. In English, for example, we do not address everyone we meet in the same way. "Hi, Sandy" may be the customary way a person greets a friend. But we would probably feel uncomfortable addressing a doctor by her or his first name; instead, we would probably say, "Good morning, Dr. Brown." Such variations in language use, which are determined by the social status of the persons being addressed, are significant for the sociolinguist.

Anthropologist Margaret Kieffer interviews a Mayan woman in Guatemala.

Ethnology (Cultural Anthropology)   Ethnologists seek to understand how and why peoples today and in the recent past differ in their customary ways of thinking and acting. Ethnology—now usually called *cultural anthropology*—is concerned with patterns of thought and behavior, such as marriage customs, kinship organization, political and economic systems, religion, folk art, and music, and with the ways in which these patterns differ in contemporary societies. Ethnologists also study the dynamics of culture—that is, how various cultures develop and change. In addition, they are interested in the relationship between beliefs and practices within a culture. Thus, the aim of ethnologists is largely the same as that of archaeologists. Ethnologists, however, generally use data collected through observation and interviewing of living peoples. Archaeologists, on the other hand, must work with fragmentary remains of past cultures, on the basis of which they can only make inferences about the customs of prehistoric peoples.

One type of ethnologist, the **ethnographer**, usually spends a year or so living with, talking to, and observing the people whose customs he or she is studying. This fieldwork provides the data for a detailed description (an **ethnography**) of customary behavior and thought. Ethnographers vary in the degree to which they strive for completeness in their coverage of cultural and social life. Earlier ethnographers tended to strive for holistic coverage; more recent ethnographers have tended to specialize or focus on narrower realms such as ritual healing or curing, interaction with the environment, effects of modernization or globalization, or gender issues. Ethnographies often go beyond description; they may address current anthropological issues or try to explain some aspect of a culture.

Because so many cultures have undergone extensive change in the recent past, it is fortunate that another type of ethnologist, the **ethnohistorian**, is prepared to study how the ways of life of a particular group of people have changed over time. Ethnohistorians investigate written documents (which may or may not have been produced by anthropologists). They may spend many years going through documents, such as missionary accounts, reports by traders and explorers, and government records, to try to establish the cultural changes that have occurred. Unlike ethnographers, who rely mostly on their own observations, ethnohistorians rely on the reports of others. Often, they must attempt to piece together and make sense of widely scattered, and even apparently contradictory, information. Thus, the ethnohistorian's research is very much like that of the historian, except that the ethnohistorian is usually concerned with the history of a people who did not themselves leave written records. The ethnohistorian tries to reconstruct the recent history of a people and may also suggest why certain changes in their way of life took place.

With the data collected and analyzed by the ethnographer and ethnohistorian, the work of a third type of ethnologist, the **cross-cultural researcher**, can be done. The cross-cultural researcher is interested in discovering general patterns about cultural traits—what is universal, what is variable, why traits vary, and what the consequences of the variability might be. Why, for example, is there more gender inequality in some societies than in others? Is family violence related to aggression in other areas of life? What are the effects of living in a very unpredictable environment? In testing possible answers to such questions, cross-cultural researchers use data from samples of cultures to try to arrive at explanations or relationships that hold across cultures. Archaeologists may find the results of cross-cultural research useful for making inferences about the past, particularly if researchers have discovered material indicators of cultural variation.

Because ethnologists may be interested in many aspects of customary behavior and thought—from economic behavior to political behavior to styles of art, music, and religion—ethnology overlaps with disciplines that concentrate on some particular aspect of human existence, such as sociology, psychology, economics, political science, art, music, and comparative religion. But the distinctive feature of cultural anthropology is its interest in how all these aspects of human existence vary from society to society, in all historical periods, and in all parts of the world.

Applied Anthropology

All knowledge may turn out to be useful. In the physical and biological sciences it is well understood that technological breakthroughs like DNA splicing, spacecraft docking in outer space, and the development of minuscule computer chips could not have taken place without an enormous amount of basic research to uncover the laws of nature in the physical and biological worlds. If we did not understand fundamental principles, the technological achievements we are so proud of would not be possible. Researchers are often simply driven by curiosity, with no thought as to where the research might lead, which is why such research is sometimes called *basic research*. The same is true of the social sciences. If a researcher finds out that societies with combative sports tend to have more wars, it may lead to other inquiries about the relationships between one kind of aggression and another. The knowledge acquired may ultimately lead to discovering ways to reduce social problems, such as family violence and war.

Whereas basic research may ultimately help to solve practical problems, applied research is more explicit in its practical goals. Today about half of all professional anthropologists are applied, or practicing, anthropologists. **Applied** or **practicing anthropology** is explicit in its concern with making anthropological knowledge useful.[3] Applied anthropologists may be trained in any or all of the subfields of anthropology. In contrast to basic researchers, who are almost always employed in colleges, universities, and museums, applied anthropologists are usually employed in settings outside traditional academia, including government agencies, international development agencies, private consulting firms, businesses, public health organizations, medical schools, law offices, community development agencies, and charitable foundations.

In urban areas before new construction begins, archaeologists may be called upon to excavate and record information on historical sites, as shown here in New York City.

Biological anthropologists may be called upon to give forensic evidence in court, or they may work in public health, or design clothes and equipment to fit human anatomy. Archaeologists may be involved in preserving and exhibiting artifacts for museums and in doing contract work to find and preserve cultural sites that might be damaged by construction or excavation. Linguists may work in bilingual educational training programs or may work on ways to improve communication. Ethnologists may work in a wide variety of applied projects ranging from community development, urban planning, health care, and agricultural improvement, to personnel and organizational management, and assessment of the impact of change programs on people's lives.[4] We discuss applied and practicing anthropology more fully in the final chapter of the book.

Explanation and Evidence

Anthropologists in the field try to arrive at accurate answers to descriptive questions. How do the people make a living? How do they marry? What gods do they believe in? But as important as accurate description is, it is not the ultimate goal of anthropology. Anthropologists want to *understand*—to know *why* people have certain customs or beliefs, not just to see that they *do* have them. As difficult as the *how* and *what* questions are to answer, the *why* questions are even harder. *Why* questions deal with explanations, which are harder to generate and harder to evaluate. In science, to understand is to explain, and so the major goal of science is to arrive at trustworthy explanations.[5]

For many anthropologists, the plausibility or persuasiveness of an explanation cannot be considered a sufficient reason to accept it. The explanation must also be tested and supported by objective evidence that could have falsified it. And even when it is supported, there still may be grounds for skepticism. According to the scientific orientation, all knowledge is uncertain and therefore subject to increasing or decreasing confirmation as new tests are made. This means that we will never arrive at absolute truth. On the other hand, and this is encouraging, we should be able to achieve more and more reliable understanding if we keep testing our theories.

But what is scientific understanding—what does it mean to explain, and what kinds of evidence are needed to evaluate an explanation?

Explanations

An **explanation** is an answer to a *why* question. There are many types of explanations, some more satisfying than others. For example, suppose we ask why a society thinks that a couple should abstain from sex for a year or so after the birth of a baby. If we say their tradition is to practice a long postpartum sex taboo, is this a satisfactory explanation? We would have to say no, because the thing to be explained (the taboo) is being explained by itself, by its prior existence. To explain something in terms of tradition is to say that people do it because they already do it, which is not informative. What kinds of explanations are more satisfactory, then? In science, there are two kinds of explanations that are sought: associations and theories.

Associations or Relationships

One way of explaining something (an observation, an action, a custom) is to say how it conforms to a general principle or relationship. So to explain why the water left outside in the basin froze, we say that it was cold last night and that water freezes at 32°F. The statement that water solidifies (becomes ice) at 32° is a statement of a relationship or association between two **variables**—things or quantities that vary. In this case, variation in the state of water (liquid versus solid) is related to variation in the temperature of the air (above versus below 32°F). The truth of the relationship is suggested by repeated observations. In the physical sciences, such relationships are called **laws** when they are accepted by almost all scientists. We find such explanations satisfactory because they allow us to predict what will happen in the future or to understand something that has happened regularly in the past.

In the social sciences, associations are usually stated *probabilistically*; that is, we say that two or more variables tend to be related in a predictable way, which means that there are usually some exceptions. For example, to explain why a society has a long postpartum sex taboo, we can point to the association (or correlation) that John Whiting found in a worldwide sample of societies: Societies with apparently low-protein diets tend to have long postpartum sex taboos.[6] We call the relationship between low-protein diets and the sex taboo a **statistical association**, which means that the observed relationship is unlikely to be due to chance. Why this association exists is a theoretical issue.

Theories

Even though laws and statistical associations explain by relating what is to be explained to other things, we want to know more: why those laws or associations exist. Why does water freeze at 32°F? Why do societies with low-protein diets tend to have long postpartum sex taboos? Therefore, scientists try to formulate theories that will explain the observed relationships (laws and statistical associations).[7] **Theories** are explanations of laws and statistical associations.

By way of example, let us consider why some societies have long postpartum sex taboos. We have already noted that an observed statistical association can be used to help explain it. In general (but not

SCIENCE AND HUMANISM

Some people question whether the scientific approach is desirable or possible when it comes to humans. They often describe themselves as humanists because they use the human capacity to intuit, empathize, evoke, interpret, and illuminate as ways to understand. This orientation offers a very different kind of understanding because, compared with that offered by science, it does not insist on objectivity, nor does it insist on putting insights to empirical tests as science does. This is not to say that scientists do not intuit or interpret. They often do in the process of deriving theories, which involves a creative leap of imagination. And scientists, like anyone else, may empathize with the plight of the people they study. But the crucial difference between the humanistic and scientific orientations lies in the end result. For humanists, interpretation or evocation is the goal; for scientists, the goal is testing interpretations to see if they may be wrong.

Is objectivity possible? Or, because we are humans observing other humans, can we only be subjective? Objectivity requires trying to get at the truth despite the observer's subjective desires or needs. Is that possible? Can any human be unbiased? In an absolute sense, no one can be completely free of bias. But science has ways to strive for objectivity; it does not need to assume that every human is completely unbiased. Remember that even when humans engage in physical science, they are often the observers or the creators of the instruments that do the observation. When an instrument points to a number, two persons may get slightly different readings because they look at the instrument from different angles. But neither person will be far off the mark, and the average of readings by two or more individuals will be very close to the "true" score.

But do we see other people objectively? Undoubtedly, some things about them are harder to "see" than others. It is easier to know objectively that wives and husbands usually sit down to dinner together, harder to "see" how they feel about one another. Suppose you are in a society where you never observe any obvious expression of affection between husbands and wives. At first, your own cultural bias might lead you to think that such couples don't care for each other much. Such an observation might indeed be biased (and not objective) if it turned out that couples privately express affection to each other but avoid public expressions. Or it might be that couples communicate their affection for each other in ways you didn't notice. But that doesn't mean that you wouldn't be able to figure this out eventually. In trying to understand the meaning of female-male relationships, you might very well try to establish close, personal relationships with some families. You might then ask people to tell you stories to try to see how they portrayed relations between husband and wife. In short, a humanistic approach might help you understand how couples really feel about each other. But a scientist might go through the same procedure too in order to come to a tentative understanding.

As this example illustrates, humanistic understanding and science are really not incompatible. Both the scientist and the humanist would agree on the need to convey what a culture is like (e.g., with regard to how couples feel about each other). But scientists would insist on more. First, they would try to verify, perhaps by systematic interviewing, how commonly a feeling is shared in the culture; second, they would want to explain why this feeling is common in some cultures but not in others. Therefore, they would have to create a theory to explain the variation and then collect evidence to test the theory to see if it might be wrong.

The poet Marianne Moore wrote that poetry gives us "imaginary gardens with real toads in them." Can imagination, humanistic or scientific, be meaningful without at least some real toads?

Sources: James Lett, "Scientific Anthropology," in David Levinson and Melvin Ember, eds., *Encyclopedia of Cultural Anthropology,* 4 vols. (New York: Henry Holt, 1996). The quote from Marianne Moore is from John Timpane, "Essay: The Poetry of Science," *Scientific American* (July 1991): 128.

always), if a society has a low-protein diet, it will have a long postpartum sex taboo. But most people would ask additional questions: Why does a low-protein diet explain the taboo? What is the mechanism by which a society with such a diet develops the custom of a long postpartum sex taboo? A theory is intended to answer such questions.

John Whiting's theory is that a long postpartum sex taboo may be an adaptation to certain conditions. Particularly in tropical areas, where the major food staples are low in protein, babies are vulnerable to the protein-deficiency disease called *kwashiorkor*. But if a baby could continue to nurse for a long time, it might have a better chance of surviving. The postpartum sex taboo might be adaptive, Whiting's theory suggests, because it increases the likelihood of a baby's survival. If a mother puts off having another baby for a while, the first baby might have a better chance to survive because it can be fed mother's milk for a longer time. Whiting suggests that parents may be aware, whether unconsciously or consciously, that having another baby too soon might jeopardize the survival of the first baby, and so they might decide that it would be a good idea to abstain from intercourse for more than a year after the birth of the first baby.

As this example of a theory illustrates, there are differences between a theory and an association. A theory is more complicated, containing a series of statements. An association usually states quite simply that there is a relationship between two or more measured variables. Another difference is that, although a theory may mention some things that are observable, such as the presence of a long postpartum sex taboo, parts of it are difficult or impossible to observe directly. For example, with regard to Whiting's theory, it would be difficult to find out if people had deliberately or unconsciously decided to practice a long postpartum sex taboo because they recognized that babies would thereby have a better chance to survive. Then, too, the concept of adaptation—that some characteristic promotes greater reproductive success—is difficult to verify because it is difficult to find out whether different individuals or groups have different rates of reproduction because they do or do not practice the supposedly adaptive custom. Thus, some concepts or implications in a theory are unobservable (at least at the present time), and only some aspects may be observable. In contrast, statistical associations or laws are based entirely on observations.[8]

Why Theories Cannot Be Proved

Many people think that the theories they learned in physics or chemistry courses have been proved. Unfortunately, many students get that impression because their teachers present "lessons" in an authoritative manner. It is now generally agreed by scientists and philosophers of science that although some theories may have considerable evidence supporting them, no theory can be said to be proved or unquestionably true. This is because many of the concepts and ideas in theories are not directly observable and therefore not directly verifiable. For example, scientists may try to explain how light behaves by postulating that it consists of particles called photons, but photons cannot be observed, even with the most powerful microscope. So exactly what a photon looks like and exactly how it works remain in the realm of the unprovable. The photon is a **theoretical construct**, something that cannot be observed or verified directly. Because all theories contain such constructs, theories cannot be proved entirely or with absolute certainty.[9]

Why should we bother with theories, then, if we cannot prove that they are true? Perhaps the main advantage of a theory as a kind of explanation is that it may lead to new understanding or knowledge. A theory can suggest new relationships or imply new predictions that might be supported or confirmed by new research. For example, Whiting's theory about long postpartum sex taboos has implications that could be investigated by researchers. Because the theory discusses how a long postpartum sex taboo might be adaptive, we would expect that certain changes would result in the taboo's disappearance. For example, suppose people adopted either mechanical birth-control devices or began to give supplementary high-protein foods to babies. With birth control, a family could space births without abstaining from sex, so we would expect the custom of postpartum abstinence to disappear. So, too, we would expect it to disappear with protein supplements for babies, because kwashiorkor would then be less likely to afflict the babies. Whiting's ideas might also prompt investigators to try to find out whether parents are consciously or unconsciously aware of the problem of close birth spacing in areas with low supplies of protein.

Although theories cannot be proved, they are rejectable. The method of *falsification,* which shows that a theory seems to be wrong, is mainly how theories are judged.[10] Scientists derive implications or predictions that should be true if the theory is correct. So, for example, Whiting predicted that societies with long postpartum sex taboos would be found more often in the tropics than in temperate regions and that they would be likely to have low-protein food supplies. Such predictions of what might be found are called **hypotheses**. If the predictions turn out not to be correct, the researcher is obliged to conclude that there may be something wrong with the theory or something wrong with the test of the theory. Theories that are not falsified are accepted for the time being because the available evidence seems to be consistent with them. But remember that no matter how much the available evidence seems to support a theory, we can never be certain it is true. There is always the possibility that some implication of it, some hypothesis derivable from it, will not be confirmed in the future.

Evidence: Testing Explanations

In any field of investigation, theories are generally the most plentiful commodity, apparently because of the human predisposition to try to make sense of the world. It is necessary, then, for us to have procedures that enable us to select from among the many available theories those that are more likely to be correct. "Just as mutations arise naturally but are not all beneficial, so hypotheses [theories] emerge naturally but are not all correct. If progress is to occur, therefore, we require a superfluity of hypotheses and also a mechanism of selection."[11] In other words, generating a theory or interpretation is not enough. We need some reliable method of testing whether or not that interpretation is likely to be correct. If an interpretation is not correct, it may detract from our efforts to achieve understanding by misleading us into thinking the problem is already solved.

The strategy in all kinds of testing in science is to predict what one would expect to find if a particular interpretation were correct, and then to conduct an investigation to see if the prediction is generally consistent with the data. If the prediction is not supported, the investigator is obliged to accept the possibility that the interpretation is wrong. If, however, the prediction holds true, then the investigator is entitled to say that there is evidence to support the theory. Thus, conducting research designed to test expectations derived from theory allows researchers to eliminate some interpretations and to accept others, at least tentatively.

Operationalization and Measurement

To transform theoretical predictions into statements that might be verified, a researcher provides an **operational definition** of each of the concepts or variables mentioned in the prediction. An operational definition is a description of the procedure that is followed to measure the variable.[12]

Whiting predicted that societies with a low-protein diet would have a long postpartum sex taboo. Amount of protein in the diet is a variable; some societies have more, others have less. Length of the

The Yanomamö Indians of Brazil (*left*) depend on root crops. The Masai pastoralists of Kenya (*right*) depend largely on milk and other products of their cattle.

postpartum sex taboo is a variable; a society may have a short taboo or a long taboo. Whiting operationally defined the first variable, *amount of protein,* in terms of staple foods.[13] If a society depended mostly on root and tree crops (cassava, bananas), Whiting rated the society as having low protein. If the society depended mostly on cereal crops (wheat, barley, corn, oats), he rated it as having moderate protein, because cereal crops have more protein by weight than root and tree crops. If the society depended mostly on hunting, fishing, or herding for food, he rated it as having high protein. The other variable in Whiting's prediction, *length of postpartum sex taboo,* was operationalized as follows: A society was rated as having a long taboo if couples customarily abstained from sex for more than a year after the birth of a baby; abstention for a year or less was considered a short taboo.

Specifying an operational definition for each variable is extremely important because it allows other investigators to check a researcher's results.[14] Science depends on *replication,* the repetition of results. Only when many researchers observe a particular association can we call that association or relationship a law. Providing operational definitions is also extremely important because it allows others to evaluate whether a measure is appropriate. Only when we are told exactly how something was measured can we judge whether the measure reflects what it is supposed to reflect. Specifying measures publicly is so important in science that we are obliged to be skeptical of any conclusions that involve variables that were not measured.

To **measure** something is to say how it compares with other things on some scale of variation.[15] People often assume that a measuring device is always a physical instrument, such as a scale or a ruler, but physical devices are not the only way to measure something. *Classification* is also a form of measurement. When we classify persons as male or female or employed versus unemployed, we are dividing them into *sets.* Deciding which set they belong to is a kind of measurement because doing so allows us to compare them. We can also measure things by deciding which cases or examples have more or less of something (e.g., more or less protein in the diet). The measures employed in physical science are usually based on

A thermometer provides a way of comparing or measuring the "heat" of different locations or over different time periods. While the physical sciences often use physical instruments and the social sciences often use humans to observe, all measurements compare things on some scale of variation.

scales that allow us to assign numbers to each case; we measure height in meters and weight in grams, for example. However we measure our variables, the fact that we can measure them means that we can test our hypotheses to see if the predicted relationships actually exist, at least most of the time.

Sampling

After deciding how to measure the variables in some predicted relationship, the investigator must decide how to select which cases to study to see if the predicted relationship holds. If the prediction is about the behavior of people, the sampling decision involves which people to observe. If the prediction is about an association between societal customs, the sampling decision involves which societies to study. Investigators must decide not only which cases to choose but also how many to choose. No researcher can investigate all the possible cases, so choices must be made. Some choices are better than others. The best is some kind of random sample. A random sample is one in which all cases selected had an equal chance of being included in the sample. Almost all statistical tests used to evaluate the results of research require random sampling, because only results based on a random sample can be assumed to be probably true for some larger set or universe of cases.

Statistical Evaluation

When researchers have measured the variables of interest for all the sample cases, they are ready to see if the predicted relationship actually exists in the data. Remember, the results may not turn out to be what the theory predicts. Sometimes researchers construct a *contingency table,* like that shown in Table 1.1, to

Table 1.1 Association between Availability of Protein and Duration of Postpartum Sex Taboo			
	Duration of Postpartum Sex Taboo		
Availability of Protein	**Short (0–1 Year)**	**Long (More Than 1 Year)**	**Total**
High	47	15	62
Medium	38	25	63
Low	20	27	47
Total	105	67	172

Source: Adapted from John W. M. Whiting, "Effects of Climate on Certain Cultural Practices," in Ward H. Goodenough, ed., *Explorations in Cultural Anthropology* (New York: McGraw-Hill, 1964), p. 520.

see if the variables are associated as predicted. In Whiting's sample of 172 societies, each case is assigned to a box, or cell, in the table, depending on how the society is measured on the two variables of interest. For example, a society that has a long postpartum sex taboo and a low-protein diet is placed in the third row of the Long Duration column. (In Whiting's sample [see Table 1.1] there are 27 such societies.) A society that has a short postpartum sex taboo and a low-protein diet is placed in the third row in the Short Duration column. (There are 20 such societies in the sample.) The statistical question is: Does the way the cases are distributed in the six cells of the table generally support Whiting's prediction? If we looked just at the table, we might not know what to answer. Many cases appear to be in the expected places. For example, most of the high-protein cases (47 of 62) have short taboos, and most of the low-protein cases (27 of 47) have long taboos. But there are also many exceptions (e.g., 20 cases have low protein and a short taboo). So, although many cases appear to be in the expected places, there are also many exceptions. Do the exceptions invalidate the prediction? How many exceptions would compel us to reject the hypothesis? Here is where we resort to *statistical tests of significance.*

Statisticians have devised various tests that tell us how "perfect" a result has to be for us to believe that there is probably an association between the variables of interest, that one variable generally predicts the other. Essentially, every statistical result is evaluated in the same objective way. We ask: What is the chance that this result (the numbers in the cells of the table) is purely accidental, that there is no association at all between the two variables? Although some of the mathematical ways of answering this question are complicated, the answer always involves a *probability value* (or *p-value*)—the likelihood that the observed result or a stronger one could have occurred by chance. The statistical test used by Whiting gives a *p*-value of less than .01 ($p < .01$) for the table. In other words, there is less than 1 chance out of 100 that the cell numbers are purely accidental. A *p*-value of less than .01 is a fairly low probability; most social scientists conventionally agree to call any result with a *p*-value of .05 or less (5 or fewer chances out of 100) a *statistically significant,* or probably true, result. When we describe relationships or associations in the rest of this book, we are almost always referring to results that have been found to be statistically significant.

But why should a probably true relationship have any exceptions? If a theory is really correct, shouldn't *all* the cases fit? There are many reasons why we can never expect a perfect result. First, even if a theory is correct (e.g., if a low-protein diet really does favor the adoption of a long postpartum sex taboo), there may still be other causes that we have not investigated. Some of the societies could have a long taboo even though they have high protein. For example, societies that depend mostly on hunting for their food, and would therefore be classified as having a high-protein diet, may have a problem carrying infants from one campsite to another and may practice a long postpartum sex taboo so that two infants will not have to be carried at the same time.

Exceptions to the predicted relationship might also occur because of *cultural lag*.[16] Culture lag occurs when change in one aspect of culture takes time to produce change in another aspect. Suppose that a society recently changed crops and is now no longer a low-protein society but still practices the taboo. This society would be an exception to the predicted relationship, but it might fit the theory if it stopped practicing the taboo in a few years. Measurement inaccuracy is another source of exceptions. Whiting's measure of protein, which is based on the major sources of food, is not a very precise measure of protein in the diet. It does not take into account the possibility that a "tree-crop" society might get a lot of protein from fishing or raising pigs. So it might turn out that some supposedly low-protein societies have been misclassified, which may be one reason why there are 20 cases in the lowest cell in the left-hand column of Table 1.1. Measurement error usually produces exceptions.

Significant statistical associations that are predictable from a theory offer tentative support for the theory. But much more is needed before we can be fairly confident about the theory. Replication is needed to confirm whether the predictions can be reproduced by other researchers using other samples. Other predictions should be derived from the theory to see if they too are supported. The theory should be pitted against alternative explanations to see which theory works better. The research process in science thus requires time and patience. Perhaps most important, it requires that researchers be humble. No matter how wonderful one's own theory seems, it is important to acknowledge that it may be wrong.

The Relevance of Anthropology

The idea that it is impossible to account for human behavior scientifically, either because our actions and beliefs are too individualistic and complex or because human beings are understandable only in other-worldly terms, is a self-fulfilling notion. We cannot discover principles explaining human behavior if we neither believe such principles exist nor bother to look for them. If we are to increase our understanding of human beings, we first have to believe it is possible to do so.

If we aim to understand humans, it is essential that we study humans in all times and places. We must study ancient humans and modern humans. We must study their cultures and their biology. How else can we understand what is true of humans generally or how they are capable of varying? If we study just our own society, we may come up only with explanations that are culture-bound, not general or applicable to most or all humans. Anthropology is useful, then, to the degree that it contributes to our understanding of human beings everywhere.

In addition, anthropology is relevant because it helps us avoid misunderstandings between peoples. If we can understand why other groups are different from ourselves, we might have less reason to condemn them for behavior that appears strange to us. We may then come to realize that many differences between peoples are products of physical and cultural adaptations to different environments. For example, someone who first finds out about the !Kung as they lived in the Kalahari Desert of southern Africa in the 1950s might assume that the !Kung were "backward." (The exclamation point in the name !Kung

A large number of emigrants from the former Soviet Union, particularly from Black Sea cities and towns such as Odessa, live in the Brighton Beach neighborhood of Brooklyn. Migrant and immigrant communities such as "Little Odessa" are an increasing focus of anthropological study.

signifies one of the clicking sounds made with the tongue by speakers of the !Kung language.) The !Kung wore little clothing, had few possessions, lived in meager shelters, and enjoyed none of our technological niceties like radio and computers. But let us reflect on how a typical North American community might react if it awoke to find itself in an environment similar to that in which the !Kung lived. The people would find that the arid land makes both agriculture and animal husbandry impossible, and they might have to think about adopting a nomadic existence. They might then discard many of their material possessions so that they could travel easily, in order to take advantage of changing water and food supplies. Because of the extreme heat and the lack of extra water for laundry, they might find it more practical to be almost naked than to wear clothes. They would undoubtedly find it impossible to build elaborate homes. For social security, they might start to share the food brought into the group. Thus, if they survived at all, they might end up looking and acting far more like the !Kung looked than like typical North Americans.

As the world becomes increasingly interconnected or globalized, the importance of understanding and trying to respect cultural and physical differences becomes necessary. Misunderstandings can cause people to go to war, and war with modern weapons of mass destruction can kill more people than ever before. The gap between rich and poor countries has widened and anthropologists have been increasingly concerned with the effects of inequality. Even when the powerful countries want to help others, they often try to impose their ways of life, which they consider superior. But anthropologists may not think that particular ways of life are generally superior. What's good for some may not be good for other people in different circumstances.

Knowledge of our past may bring both a feeling of humility and a sense of accomplishment. If we are to attempt to deal with the problems of our world, we must be aware of our vulnerability so we do not think that problems will solve themselves. But we also have to think enough of our accomplishments to believe that we can find solutions to problems. Much of the trouble we get into may be a result of feelings of self-importance and invulnerability—in short, our lack of humility. Knowing something about our evolutionary past may help us to understand and accept our place in the biological world. Just as for any other form of life, there is no guarantee that any particular human population, or even the entire human species, will perpetuate itself indefinitely. The earth changes, the environment changes, and humanity itself changes. What survives and flourishes in the present might not do so in the future.

Yet our vulnerability should not make us feel powerless. There are many reasons to feel confident about the future. Consider what we have accomplished so far. By means of tools and weapons fashioned from sticks and stones, we were able to hunt animals larger and more powerful than ourselves. We discovered how to make fire, and we learned to use it to keep ourselves warm and to cook our food. As we domesticated plants and animals, we gained greater control over our food supply and were able to establish more permanent settlements. We mined and smelted ores to fashion more durable tools. We built cities and irrigation systems, monuments and ships. We made it possible to travel from one continent to another in a single day. We conquered some illnesses and prolonged human life.

In short, human beings and their cultures have changed considerably over the course of history. Human populations have often been able to adapt to changing circumstances. Let us hope that humans continue to adapt to the challenges of the present and future.

Summary

1. Anthropology is literally the study of human beings. It differs from other disciplines concerned with people in that anthropology is: (a) concerned with humans in all places of the world and it traces human evolution and cultural development from millions of years ago to the present day; (b) holistic, that is, studies all aspects of peoples' experiences; (c) concerned with identifying and explaining typical characteristics (traits, customs) of particular human populations.

2. Biological anthropology, one of the major fields of anthropology, studies the emergence of humans and their later physical evolution (human paleontology) and how and why contemporary human populations vary biologically (human variation).

3. Cultural anthropology has three subfields—archaeology, anthropological linguistics, and ethnology (now usually referred to by the parent name, cultural anthropology). All the subfields deal with aspects of human culture, that is, with the customary ways of thinking and behaving of particular societies.

4. Archaeologists seek to reconstruct and explain the daily life and customs of prehistoric peoples from the remains of human cultures.

5. Anthropological linguists are concerned with the emergence of language and with the divergence of languages over time (historical linguistics) as well as how contemporary languages differ, both in construction (descriptive or structural linguistics) and in actual speech (sociolinguistics).

6. The ethnologist (now often called a cultural anthropologist) seeks to understand how and why peoples of today and the recent past differ in their customary ways of thinking and acting. There are three major types of cultural anthropologists: ethnographers, ethnohistorians, and cross-cultural researchers.

7. In all four major subdisciplines of anthropology, there are applied anthropologists, people who apply anthropological knowledge to achieve more practical goals.

8. Scientists try to achieve two kinds of explanations—associations and theories. Theories are falsified by deriving hypotheses or predictions that should be true if the theory is correct.

9. By showing us why other people are the way they are, both culturally and physically, anthropology may make us more tolerant. Knowledge of our past may bring us both a feeling of humility and a sense of accomplishment.

Glossary Terms

anthropological linguistics (p. 6)
anthropology (p. 2)
applied (practicing) anthropology (p. 9)
archaeology (p. 6)
biological (physical) anthropology (p. 4)
cross-cultural researcher (p. 9)
cultural anthropology (p. 4)
descriptive (structural) linguistics (p. 7)
ethnographer (p. 8)
ethnography (p. 8)
ethnohistorian (p. 8)
ethnology (p. 6)
explanation (p. 11)
fossils (p. 4)
historical archaeology (p. 6)
historical linguistics (p. 7)
holistic (p. 3)

Homo sapiens (p. 5)
human paleontology (p. 4)
human variation (p. 4)
hypotheses (p. 14)
laws (p. 11)
measure (p. 15)
operational definition (p. 14)
paleoanthropology (p. 4)
prehistory (p. 6)
Primates (p. 5)
primatologists (p. 5)
sociolinguistics (p. 7)
statistical association (p. 11)
theoretical construct (p. 13)
theories (p. 11)
variables (p. 11)

Critical Questions

1. Why study anthropology? What are its goals and how is it useful?

2. How does anthropology differ from other fields of study you've encountered that deal with humans? (Compare with psychology, sociology, political science, history, or biology, among others.)

3. Can a unique event be explained? Explain your answer.

4. Why is scientific understanding always uncertain?

THE STUDY OF CULTURE

Chapter Outline

- Defining Features of Culture
- Attitudes That Hinder
  the Study of Cultures
- Cultural Relativism

- Describing a Culture
- Some Assumptions
  about Culture

We all consider ourselves to be unique individuals with our own set of personal opinions, preferences, habits, and quirks. Indeed, all of us are unique; and yet most of us share the feeling that it is wrong to eat dogs, the belief that bacteria or viruses cause illness, the habit of sleeping on a bed. We share many such feelings, beliefs, and habits with most of the people who live in our society. We hardly ever think about the ideas and customs we share, but they constitute what anthropologists refer to as "North American culture."

We tend not to think about our culture because it is so much a part of us that we take it for granted. But when we become aware that other peoples have different feelings from ours, different beliefs, and different habits, we are becoming aware that our culture is different. Most North Americans would never even think of the possibility of eating dog meat if we did not know that people in some other societies commonly do so. We would not realize that our belief in germs was cultural if we were not aware that people in some societies think that illness is caused by witchcraft or evil spirits. We could not become aware that it is our custom to sleep on beds if we were not aware that people in many societies sleep on the floor or on the ground. It is only when we compare ourselves with people in other societies that we become aware of cultural differences and similarities. This is, in fact, the way that anthropology as a profession began. When Europeans began to explore and move to faraway places, they were forced to confront the sometimes striking facts of cultural variation.

Defining Features of Culture

In everyday usage, the word *culture* refers to a desirable quality we can acquire by attending a sufficient number of plays and concerts and visiting art museums and galleries. The anthropologist, however, has a different definition, as Ralph Linton noted:

> *Culture* refers to the total way of life of any society, not simply to those parts of this way which the society regards as higher or more desirable. Thus culture, when applied to our own way of life, has nothing to do with playing the piano or reading Browning. For the social scientist such activities are simply elements within the totality of our culture. This totality also includes such mundane activities as washing dishes or driving an automobile, and for the purposes of cultural studies these stand quite on a par with "the finer things of life." It follows that for the social scientist there are no uncultured societies or even individuals. Every society has a culture, no matter how simple this culture may be, and every human being is cultured, in the sense of participating in some culture or other.[1]

Culture, then, refers to innumerable aspects of life. Some anthropologists think of culture as the rules or ideas behind behavior.[2] Most anthropologists focus on how people behave customarily, including how they interact with others and the habits they share with others. In this view, **culture** is the set of learned behaviors and ideas (including beliefs, attitudes, values, and ideals) that are characteristic of a particular society or other social group. It should be noted that some anthropologists also include *material culture* in culture—things like houses, musical instruments, and tools that are the products of customary behavior.

Different kinds of groups can have cultures. People come to share behaviors and ideas because they communicate with and observe each other. While groups from families to societies share cultural traits, anthropologists have traditionally been concerned with the cultural characteristics of *societies*. Many anthropologists define **society** as a group of people who occupy a particular territory and speak a common language not generally understood by neighboring peoples. By this definition, societies may or may not correspond to countries or nations. There are many countries, particularly the newer ones, that have within their boundaries different peoples speaking mutually unintelligible languages. By our definition of society, such countries are composed of many different societies and therefore many cultures. And most societies have recently become more multicultural because of immigration and migration. Also, by our definition of society, some societies may even include more than one country or nation. For example, we would have to say that Canada and the United States form a single society because the two groups generally speak English, live next to each other, and share many common ideas and behaviors. That is why we refer to "North American culture" in this chapter. Not everyone would agree that Canada and the United States form a single society; some would prefer to consider the United States and Canada two different societies because they are separate political entities.

Culture Is Commonly Shared

If only one person thinks or does a certain thing, that thought or action represents a personal habit, not a pattern of culture. For a thought or action to be considered cultural, it must be commonly shared by some population or group of individuals. Even if some behavior is not commonly practiced, it is cultural if most people think it is appropriate. The idea that marriage should involve only two people is cultural in North American society. Most North Americans share this idea and act accordingly when they marry. The role of president or prime minister is not widely shared—after all, there is only one such person at a time—but the role is cultural because most inhabitants of a country with such a position agree that it should exist, and its occupant is generally expected to exhibit certain behaviors. We usually share many behaviors and ideas with our families and friends (although anthropologists are not particularly concerned with this type of cultural group). We commonly share cultural characteristics with segments of our population whose ethnic or regional origins, religious affiliations, and occupations are the same as or similar to our own. We share certain practices and ideas with most North Americans. And we share some cultural traits with people beyond our society who have similar interests (such as rules for international sporting events) or similar roots (as do the various English-speaking nations).

When we talk about the commonly shared customs of a society, which constitute the central concern of cultural anthropology, we are referring to *a* culture. When we talk about the commonly shared customs of a group within a society, which are a central concern of sociology, we are referring to a **subculture**. And when we study the commonly shared customs of some group that includes different societies, we are talking about a phenomenon for which we do not have a single word—for example, as when we refer to *Western culture* (the cultural characteristics of societies in or derived from Europe) or the *culture of poverty* (the presumed cultural characteristics of poor people the world over).

We must remember that even when anthropologists refer to something as cultural, there is always individual variation, which means that not everyone in a society shares a particular cultural characteristic of that society. For example, it is cultural in North American society for adults to live apart from their parents. But not all adults in our society do so, nor do all adults wish to do so. The custom of living apart from parents is considered cultural because most adults practice that custom. As Edward Sapir noted in the late 1930s, in every society studied by anthropologists—in the simplest as well as the most complex—individuals do not all think and act the same.[3] As we discuss later, individual variation is the source of new culture.[4]

Culture Is Learned

Not all things shared generally by a population are cultural. The typical hair color of a population is not cultural, nor is eating. For something to be considered cultural, it must be learned as well as shared. A typical hair color (unless dyed) is not cultural because it is genetically determined. Humans eat because they must; but what and when and how they eat are learned and vary from culture to culture. Most North Americans do not consider dog meat edible, and indeed the idea of eating dogs horrifies us. But in China, as in some other societies, dog meat is considered delicious. In our society, many people consider a baked ham to be a holiday dish. In several societies of the Middle East, however, including those of Egypt and Israel, eating the meat of a pig is forbidden by sacred writings.

To some extent, all animals exhibit learned behaviors, some of which may be shared by most individuals in a population and may therefore be considered cultural. But different animal species vary in the degree to which their shared behaviors are learned or are instinctive. The sociable ants, for instance, despite all their patterned social behavior, do not appear to have much, if any, culture. They divide their labor, construct their nests, form their raiding columns, and carry off their dead—all without having been taught to do so and without imitating the behavior of other ants. In contrast, much of the behavior of humans appears to be culturally patterned.

We are increasingly discovering that our closest biological relatives, the monkeys and the apes, not only learn a wide variety of behaviors on their own, they also learn from each other. Some of their learned responses are as basic as those involved in maternal care; others are as frivolous as the taste for candy. Frans de Waal reviewed seven long-term studies of chimpanzees and identified at least 39 behaviors that were clearly learned from others.[5] When shared and socially learned, these behaviors could be described as cultural.

Most human learned behavior is probably acquired with the aid of spoken, symbolic language. All people known to anthropologists, regardless of their kind of society, have had a complex system of spoken, symbolic communication, what we call *language.*

Language is *symbolic* in that a word or phrase can represent what it stands for, *whether or not that thing is present.* The symbolic quality of language has tremendous implications for the transmission of culture. It means that a human parent can tell a child that a snake, for example, is dangerous and should be avoided. The parent can then describe the snake in great detail—its length, diameter, color, texture, shape, and means of locomotion. The parent can also predict the kinds of places where the child is likely to encounter snakes and explain how the child can avoid them. Should the child encounter a snake, he or she will probably recall the symbolic word for the animal, remember as well the related information, and so avoid danger.

To sum up, we may say that something is cultural if it is a learned behavior or idea (belief, attitude, value, ideal) that is generally shared by the members of a society or other social group.

Much of culture is learned by children imitating their parents and other role models.

Attitudes That Hinder the Study of Cultures

Many of the Europeans who first traveled to faraway places were revolted or shocked by customs they observed. Such reactions are not surprising. People commonly feel that their own behaviors and attitudes are the correct ones and that people who do not share those patterns are immoral or inferior. The person who judges other cultures solely in terms of his or her own culture is **ethnocentric**—that is, he or she holds an attitude called **ethnocentrism**. Most North Americans would think that eating dogs or insects is disgusting, but they clearly do not feel the same way about eating beef. Similarly, they would react negatively to child betrothal, lip plugs, or digging up the bones of the dead.

Our own customs and ideas may appear bizarre or barbaric to an observer from another society. Hindus in India, for example, would consider our custom of eating beef both primitive and disgusting. In their culture, the cow is a sacred animal and may not be slaughtered for food. In many societies a baby is almost constantly carried by someone, in someone's lap, or asleep next to others.[6] People in such societies may think it is cruel of us to leave babies alone for long periods of time, often in devices that resemble cages (cribs and playpens). Even our most ordinary customs—the daily rituals we take for granted—might seem thoroughly absurd when viewed from an outside perspective. An observer of our society might take notes on certain strange behaviors that seem quite ordinary to us, as the following description shows:

> The daily body ritual performed by everyone includes a mouth-rite. Despite the fact that these people are so punctilious about the care of the mouth, this rite involves a practice which strikes the uninitiated stranger as revolting. It was reported to me that the ritual consists of inserting a small bundle of hog hairs into the mouth, along with certain magical powders, and then moving the bundle in a highly formalized series of gestures. In addition to the private mouth-rite, the people seek out a holy-mouth man once or twice a year. These practitioners have an impressive set of paraphernalia, consisting of a variety of augers, awls, probes, and prods. The use of these objects in the exorcism of the evils of the mouth involves almost unbelievable ritual torture of the client. The holy-mouth man opens the client's mouth and, using the above mentioned tools, enlarges any holes which decay may have created in teeth. Magical materials are put into these holes. If there are no naturally occurring holes in the teeth, large sections of one or more teeth are gouged out so that the supernatural substance can be applied. In the client's view, the purpose of these ministrations is to arrest decay and to draw friends. The extremely sacred and traditional character of the rite is evident in the fact that the natives return to the holy-mouth man year after year, despite the fact that their teeth continue to decay.[7]

We are likely to protest that to understand the behaviors of a particular society—in this case, our own—the observer must try to find out what the people in that society say about why they do things. For example, the observer might find out that periodic visits to the "holy-mouth man" are for medical, not magical, purposes. Indeed, the observer, after some questioning, might discover that the "mouth-rite" has no sacred or religious connotations whatsoever. Actually, Horace Miner, the author in the 1950s of the passage on the "daily mouth ritual," was not a foreigner. An American, he described the "ritual" the way he did to show how the behaviors involved might be interpreted by an outside observer.

Ethnocentrism hinders our understanding of the customs of other people and, at the same time, keeps us from understanding our own customs. If we think that everything we do is best, we are not likely to ask why we do what we do or why "they" do what "they" do.

We may not always glorify our own culture. Other ways of life may sometimes seem more appealing. For instance, a North American who has two or three jobs just to make a living might briefly be attracted to the lifestyle of the !Kung of the Kalahari Desert in the 1950s. The !Kung shared their food and therefore were free to engage in leisure activities during the greater part of the day. They obtained all their food by men hunting animals and women gathering wild plants. They had no facilities for refrigeration, so

Because we are ethnocentric about many things, it is often difficult to criticize our own customs, some of which might seem shocking to a member of another society. The elderly in America often spend their days alone. In contrast, the elderly in Japan often live in a three-generational family.

sharing a large freshly killed animal was clearly more sensible than hoarding meat that would soon rot. More-over, the sharing provided a kind of social security system for the !Kung. If a hunter was unable to catch an animal on a certain day, he could obtain food for himself and his family from someone else in his band. Then, at some later date the game he caught would provide food for the family of another, unsuccessful hunter. This system of sharing also ensured that persons too young or too old to help with the collecting of food would still be fed.

Could we learn from the !Kung? Perhaps we could in some respects, but we must not glorify their way of life either or think that their way of life might be easily imported into our own society. Other aspects of !Kung life would not appeal to many North Americans. For example, when the nomadic !Kung de-cided to move their camps, they had to carry all the family possessions, substantial amounts of food and water, and all young children below age four or five. This is a sizable burden to carry for any distance. The !Kung traveled about 1,500 miles in a single year.[8] Thus, for them being nomadic meant that fam-ilies could not have many possessions. It is unlikely that most North Americans would find the !Kung way of life enviable in this respect.

Both ethnocentrism and its opposite, the glorification of other cultures, hinder effective anthropolog-ical study.

Cultural Relativism

A hundred years ago, some evolutionists thought of Western cultures as being at the highest or most progressive stage of evolution, and non-Western cultures were often believed to represent earlier stages of evolution. Not only were these early ideas based on very poor evidence of the details of world ethnog-raphy, they were also based on a good deal of ethnocentrism.

INCREASING CULTURAL DIVERSITY
WITHIN THE COUNTRIES OF THE WORLD

The modern world is culturally diverse in two ways. There are native cultures in every part of the world, and there are migrant or immigrant cultures in most countries. (Migrants are people who have left one place to settle in another, often because they are forced by persecution or genocide to migrate; immigrants are people who have come into a new country, often because they have chosen to.) Parts of populations have moved away from their native places since the dawn of humanity. The first modern-looking humans moved out of Africa only in the last 100,000 years. People have been moving ever since. The people we call Native Americans were actually the first migrants to the New World; most anthropologists think they came from northeast Asia. In the last 200 years the United States and Canada have experienced more extensive immigration. As is commonly said, they have become nations of migrants and immigrants, and Native Americans are now vastly outnumbered by the people and their descendants who came from Europe, Africa, Asia, Latin America, and elsewhere. North America not only has native and regional subcultures, but also ethnic, religious, and occupational subcultures, each with its own distinctive set of culture traits. Thus, North American culture is partly a "melting pot" and partly a mosaic of cultural diversity. Many of us, not just anthropologists, like this diversity. We like to go to ethnic restaurants regularly. We like salsa, sushi, and spaghetti. We compare and enjoy the different geographic varieties of coffee. We like music and artists from other countries. We often choose to wear clothing that may have been manufactured halfway around the world. We like all of these things not only because they may be affordable. We like them mostly, perhaps, because they are different.

Many of the population movements in the world today, as in the past, are responses to persecution and war. The word *diaspora* is often used nowadays to refer to these major dispersions. Most were and are involuntary: people fleeing danger and death. But not always. Scholars distinguish different types of diaspora, including "victim," "labor," "trade," and "imperial" diasporas. The Africans who were sold into slavery, the Armenians who fled genocide in the early twentieth century, the Jews who fled persecution and genocide in various places over the centuries, the Palestinians who fled to the West Bank, Gaza, Jordan, and Lebanon in the mid-twentieth century, and the Rwandans who fled genocide toward the end of the twentieth century were mostly victims. The Chinese, Italians, and the Poles may have mostly moved to take advantage of job opportunities, the Lebanese to trade, and the British to extend and service their empire. Often these categories overlap; population movements can and have occurred for more than one reason. Some of the recent diasporas are less one-way than in the past. People are more "transnational," just as economics and politics are more "globalized." The new global communications have facilitated the retention of homeland connections—socially, economically, and politically. Some diasporic communities play an active role in the politics of their homelands, and some nation-states have begun to recognize their far-flung emigrants as important constituencies.

As cultural anthropologists increasingly study migrant and immigrant groups, they focus on how the groups have adapted their cultures to new surroundings, what they have retained, how they relate to the homeland, how they have developed an ethnic consciousness, and how they relate to other minority groups and the majority culture.

Sources: Melvin Ember, Carol R. Ember, and Ian Skoggard, eds., *Encyclopedia of Diasporas: Immigrant and Refugee Cultures around the World,* 2 vols. (New York: Kluwer Academic/Plenum Publishers, 2004); David Levinson and Melvin Ember, eds., *American Immigrant Cultures: Builders of a Nation,* 2 vols. (New York: Macmillan Reference, 1997).

Franz Boas and many of his students—like Ruth Benedict, Melville Herskovits, and Margaret Mead—challenged the attitude that Western cultures were obviously superior. The anthropological attitude that a society's customs and ideas should be described objectively and understood in the context of that society's problems and opportunities became known as **cultural relativism**. Does cultural relativism mean that the actions of another society, or of our own, should not be judged? Does our insistence on objectivity mean that anthropologists should not make moral judgments about the cultural phenomena they observe and try to explain? Does it mean that anthropologists should not try to bring about change? Not necessarily. While the concept of cultural relativism remains an important anthropological tenet, anthropologists differ in their interpretation of the principle of cultural relativism.

Many anthropologists are now uncomfortable with the strong form of cultural relativism advocated by Benedict and Herskovits in the 1930s and 1940s, that all patterns of culture are equally valid. What if the people practice slavery, torture, or genocide? If the strong doctrine of relativism is adhered to, then cultural practices such as these are not to be judged, and we should not try to eliminate them. A weaker form of cultural relativism asserts that anthropologists should strive for objectivity in describing a people, and in their attempts to understand the reasons for cultural behavior they should be wary of superficial or quick judgment. Tolerance should be the basic mode unless there is strong reason to behave otherwise.[9] The weak version of cultural relativity does not preclude anthropologists from making judgments or from trying to change behavior they think is harmful. But judgments need not, and should not, preclude accurate description and explanation in spite of any judgments we might have.

But now that we have defined what is cultural, we must ask a further question: How does an anthropologist go about deciding which particular behaviors, values, and beliefs of individuals are cultural?

Describing a Culture

Individual Variation

Describing a particular culture might seem relatively uncomplicated at first. You simply observe what the people in that society do and then record their behavior. But consider the substantial difficulties you might encounter. How would you decide which people to observe? And what would you conclude if each of the first dozen people you observed or talked to behaved quite differently in the same situation?

To understand better how an anthropologist might make sense of diverse behaviors, let us examine the diversity at a professional football game in the United States. When people attend a football game, various members of the crowd behave differently while "The Star-Spangled Banner" is being played. As they stand and listen, some people remove their hats; a child munches popcorn; a veteran of the armed forces stands at attention; a teenager searches the crowd for a friend; and the coaches take a final opportunity to intone secret chants and spells designed to sap the strength of the opposing team. Yet, despite these individual variations, most of the people at the game respond in a basically similar manner: Nearly everyone stands silently, facing the flag. Moreover, if you go to several football games, you will observe that many aspects of the event are similar. Although the plays will vary from game to game, the rules of the game are never different, and although the colors of the uniforms of the teams are different, the players never appear on the field dressed in swimsuits.

Although the variations in individual reactions to a given stimulus are theoretically limitless, they tend to fall within socially acceptable limits. The child listening to the anthem may continue to eat popcorn but will probably not do a rain dance. Similarly, it is unlikely that the coaches will run onto the field and embrace the singer. It is part of the anthropologist's goal to find out what those limits are. She or he may note, for example, that some limitations on behavior have a practical purpose: A spectator who disrupts the game by wandering onto the field would be required to leave. Other limitations are purely traditional. In our society it is considered proper for a man to remove his overcoat if he becomes overheated, but others would undoubtedly frown upon his removing his trousers even if the weather were quite warm. Using such observations, the anthropologist discovers the customs and the ranges of acceptable behavior that characterize the society under study.

By focusing on the range of customary behavior, discovered by observing or asking about individual variation, the anthropologist is able to describe cultural characteristics of a group. An anthropologist interested in describing courtship and marriage in our society would initially encounter variety. The anthropologist may note that one couple prefers to go to a movie on a first date, whereas another couple chooses to go bowling; some couples have very long engagements, and others never become engaged at all; some couples emphasize religious rituals in the marriage ceremony, but others are married by civil authorities; and so on. Despite this variability, the anthropologist might begin to detect certain regularities in courting practices. Couples nearly always arrange the dates by themselves; they try to avoid their parents when on dates; they often manage to find themselves alone at the end of a date; they put their lips together frequently; and so forth. After a series of more and more closely spaced encounters, a man and woman may decide to declare themselves publicly as a couple, either by announcing that they are engaged or by revealing that they are living together or intend to do so. Finally, if the two of them decide to marry, they must in some way have their union recorded by the civil authorities.

In our society a person who wishes to marry cannot disregard the customary patterns of courtship. If a man saw a woman on the street and decided he wanted to marry her, he could conceivably choose a quicker and more direct form of action than the usual dating procedure. He could get on a horse, ride to the woman's home, snatch her up in his arms, and gallop away with her. In Sicily, until the last few decades such a couple would have been considered legally married, even if the woman had never met the man before or had no intention of marrying. But in our society, any man who acted in such a fashion would be arrested and jailed for kidnapping and would probably have his sanity challenged. Such behavior would not be acceptable in our society. Although individual behaviors may vary, most social behavior falls within culturally acceptable limits.

In deciding what is cultural behavior, anthropologists look for commonalities, understanding that there is always considerable variation. In North American culture, unmarried couples are allowed and even encouraged to spend time with each other, but how they spend their time may vary from activities such as eating in restaurants to activities such as bike riding.

Cultural Constraints

The French sociologist Emile Durkheim stressed that culture is something *outside* us exerting a strong coercive power on us. We do not always feel the constraints of our culture because we generally conform to the types of conduct and thought it requires. Standards or rules about what is acceptable behavior are referred to by social scientists as **norms**. The importance of a norm usually can be judged by how members of a society respond when the norm is violated.

Cultural constraints are of two basic types, *direct* and *indirect.* Naturally, the direct constraints are the more obvious. If you choose to wear a casual shorts outfit to a wedding, you will probably be subject to some ridicule and a certain amount of social isolation. But if you choose to wear nothing, you may be exposed to a stronger, more direct cultural constraint—arrest for indecent exposure.

Although indirect forms of cultural constraint are less obvious than direct ones, they are no less effective. Durkheim illustrated this point when he wrote, "I am not obliged to speak French with my fellow-countrymen, nor to use the legal currency, but I cannot possibly do otherwise. If I tried to escape this necessity, my attempt would fail miserably."[10] In other words, if Durkheim had decided he would rather speak Serbo-Croatian than French, nobody would have tried to stop him. But no one may have understood him either. And although he would not have been put into prison for trying to buy groceries with Icelandic money, he would have had difficulty convincing the local merchants to sell him food.

In a series of classic experiments on conformity, Solomon Asch revealed how strong cultural constraints can be. Asch coached the majority of a group of college students to give deliberately incorrect answers to questions involving visual stimuli. A "critical subject," the one student in the room who was not so coached, had no idea that the other participants would purposely misinterpret the evidence presented to them. Asch found that in one-third of the experiments, the critical subjects consistently allowed their own correct perceptions to be distorted by the obviously incorrect statements of the others. And in another 40 percent of the experiments, the critical subject yielded to the opinion of the group some of the time.[11]

The existence of social or cultural constraints, however, is not necessarily incompatible with individuality. Cultural constraints are usually exercised most forcefully around the limits of acceptable behavior. Thus, there is often a broad range of behavior within which individuals can exercise their uniqueness. And individuals do not always give in to the wishes of the majority. In the Asch experiments, many individuals, about one-fourth of the critical subjects, consistently retained their independent opinions in the face of complete disagreement with the majority.

Ideal versus Actual Cultural Patterns

Every society has ideas (values and norms) about how people in particular situations ought to feel and behave. In everyday terms we speak of these ideas as *ideals;* in anthropology we refer to them as *ideal cultural patterns.* These patterns tend to be reinforced through cultural constraints. But we all know that people do not always behave according to the standards they express. If they did, there would be no need for direct or indirect constraints. Some of our ideal patterns differ from actual behavior because the ideal is outmoded—that is, it is based on the way society used to be. (Consider the ideal of "free enterprise," that industry should be totally free of governmental regulation.) Other ideal patterns may never have been actual patterns and may represent merely what people would like to see as correct behavior.

To illustrate the difference between ideal and actual culture, consider the idealized belief, long cherished in North America, that everybody is "equal before the law," that everybody should be treated in the same way by the police and courts. Of course, we know that this is not always true. The rich, for example, may receive less jail time and be sent to nicer prisons. Nevertheless, the ideal is still part of our culture; most of us continue to believe that the law should be applied equally to all.

How to Discover Cultural Patterns

There are two basic ways in which an anthropologist can discover cultural patterns. When dealing with customs that are overt or highly visible within a society—for example, our custom of sending children to school—the investigator can determine the existence of such practices by direct observation and by interviewing some knowledgeable people. When dealing with a particular sphere of behavior that encompasses many individual variations, or when the people studied are unaware of their pattern of behavior, the anthropologist should collect information from a sample of individuals in order to establish what the cultural pattern is.

One example of a cultural pattern that most people in a society are not aware of is how far apart people stand when they are having a conversation. Yet there is considerable reason to believe that unconscious cultural rules govern such behavior. These rules become obvious when we interact with people who have different rules. We may experience considerable discomfort when another person stands too close (indicating too much intimacy) or too far (indicating unfriendliness). Edward Hall reported that Arabs customarily stand quite close to others, close enough to be able to smell the other person. In interactions between Arabs and North Americans, then, the Arabs will move closer at the same time that the North Americans back away.[12]

If we wanted to arrive at the cultural rule for conversational distance between casual acquaintances, we could study a sample of individuals from a society and determine the *modal response,* or *mode.* The mode is a statistical term that refers to the most frequently encountered response in a given series of responses. So, for the North American pattern of casual conversational distance, we would plot the actual distance for many observed pairs of people. Some pairs may be 2 feet apart, some 2.5, and some 4 feet apart. If we count the number of times every particular distance is observed, these counts provide what we call a *frequency distribution.* The distance with the highest frequency is the *modal pattern.* Very often the frequency distribution takes the form of a *bell-shaped curve*, as shown in Figure 2.1.

There the characteristic being measured is plotted on the horizontal axis (in this case, the distance between conversational pairs), and the number of times each distance is observed (its frequency) is plotted

Distance between people conversing varies cross-culturally. The faces of the Rajput Indian men on the left are much closer than the faces of the American women on the right.

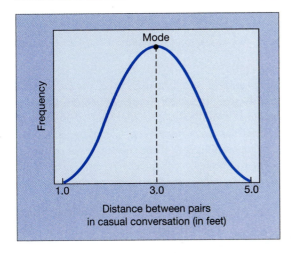

Mode

Frequency

1.0   3.0   5.0

Distance between pairs
in casual conversation (in feet)

Figure 2.1   Frequency Distribution Curve

on the vertical axis. If we were to plot how a sample of North American casual conversational pairs is distributed, we would probably get a bell-shaped curve that peaks at around 3 feet.[13] Is it any wonder, then, that we sometimes speak of keeping others "at arm's length"?

Frequency distributions may be calculated on the basis of behaviors exhibited or responses given by all the members of a particular population. But studying everybody is rarely necessary. Instead, most social scientists rely on a subset, or sample, that is believed to be representative of the larger population. As we noted in the first chapter, the best way to ensure that a sample is representative is to choose a *random sample.*

Because it is relatively easy to make generalizations about public aspects of a culture, such as the existence of executive, legislative, and judicial branches in the U.S. government, or about widely shared norms or behaviors, which almost anyone can identify correctly, random sampling is often not necessary. But in dealing with aspects of culture that are more private, difficult to put into words, or unconscious, the investigator may have to observe or interview a sample of people in order to generalize correctly about whether or not there are cultural patterns. The reason is that most people may not be aware of others' private behavior and thoughts, such as sexual attitudes and behavior, nor are they aware of unconscious cultural patterns, such as conversational distance. The fact that something is less readily observed publicly or harder to put into words does not imply that it is less likely to be shared. However, it is harder to discover those aspects of culture.

Although we may be able to discover by interviews and observation that a behavior, thought, or feeling is widely shared within a society, how do we establish that something commonly shared is learned, so that we can call it cultural? Establishing that something is or is not learned may be difficult. Because children are not reared apart from adult caretakers, the behaviors they exhibit as part of their genetic inheritance are not clearly separated from those they learn from others around them. We suspect that particular behaviors and ideas are learned if they vary from society to society. And we suspect purely genetic determinism when particular behaviors or ideas are found in all societies. For example, as we will see in the chapter on language and communication, children the world over seem to acquire language at about the same age, and the structure of their early utterances seems to be similar. These facts suggest that human children are born with an innate grammar. However, although early childhood language seems similar the world over, the particular languages spoken by adults in different societies show considerable variability. This variability suggests that particular languages have to be learned.

Some Assumptions about Culture

Culture Is Generally Adaptive

There are some cultural behaviors that, if carried to an extreme, would decrease the chances of survival of a particular society. For example, certain tribes in New Guinea view women as unclean and dangerous individuals with whom physical contact should be as limited as possible. Suppose the men in one such tribe decided to avoid contact, including sexual contact, with women. Clearly, we would not expect such a society to survive for long. Either the people clinging to those customs will become extinct, taking the customs with them, or the customs will be replaced, thereby possibly helping the people to survive. By either process, **maladaptive customs**—those that diminish the chances of survival and reproduction—are likely to disappear. The customs of a society that enhance survival and reproductive success are **adaptive** and are likely to persist. Hence, we assume that if a society has survived long enough to be described in the annals of anthropology (the "ethnographic record"), much, if not most, of its cultural repertoire is adaptive, or was at one time.

When we say that a custom is adaptive, we mean it is adaptive only with respect to a specific physical and social environment. What may be adaptive in one environment may not be adaptive in another. Therefore, when we ask why a society may have a particular custom, we really are asking if that custom makes sense as an adaptation to that society's particular environmental conditions. Many cultural behaviors that would otherwise appear incomprehensible to us may be understandable as a society's response to its environment. Witness the long postpartum sex taboo we discussed in the first chapter.

Just as culture may be an adjustment to the physical environment and to biological demands, it may also represent an adjustment to the social environment. For example, we do not know for sure why the Hopi Indians of what is now the state of Arizona began building their settlements on the tops of mesas. They must have had strong reasons for doing so, because there are many difficulties in building on such sites, not the least of which is the problem of hauling water long distances. It is possible that the Hopi chose to locate their villages on mesa tops for defensive reasons when Athapaskan-speaking groups of Indians (the Navajo and Apache) moved into the Hopi area.

A given custom represents one society's adaptation to its environment; it does not represent all possible adaptations. Different societies may choose different means of adjusting to the same situation. Thus, among some South American Indian societies where people's diets are low in protein, there is no long postpartum sex taboo, but induced abortion is reported to be a common practice. This practice may serve the same function of spacing out live births and thereby preventing too early weaning of children.

Although we may assume that societies surviving long enough to be described have had many more adaptive culture traits than maladaptive traits, that does not mean that all culture traits are adaptive. Some, if not many, traits may be neutral in terms of adaptation. That is, they may have no direct relationship to reproductive success. Consider, for example, rules about what to wear at weddings and funerals, how to set the table, and how far to stand from someone. Perhaps someone will uncover survival and reproductive consequences of these shared behaviors, but probably they are neutral in terms of survival. Such neutral traits may once have had adaptive consequences, or they may never have had any.

We must remember that a society is not forced to adapt its culture to changing environmental circumstances. Even in the face of changed circumstances, people may choose not to change their customs. For example, the Tapirapé of central Brazil did not alter their custom of limiting the number of births, even though they suffered severe population losses after contact with Europeans and their diseases. The Tapirapé population fell to fewer than 100 people from over 1,000. Clearly they were on the way to extinction, yet they continued to value small families. Not only did they believe that a woman should have no more than three children, but they took specific steps to achieve this limitation. They practiced infanticide if twins were born, if the third child was of the same sex as the first two children, and if the possible fathers broke certain taboos during pregnancy or in the child's infancy.[14]

Of course, it is also possible that a people will behave maladaptively even if they try to alter their behavior. After all, although people may alter their behavior according to what they perceive will be helpful to them, what they perceive to be helpful may not prove to be adaptive.

Culture Is Mostly Integrated

When we hear of an unfamiliar cultural pattern, our natural response is to try to imagine how that pattern would work in our own society. We might wonder, for example, what would happen if North American women adopted a long postpartum sex taboo—say, one year of abstinence after the birth of a baby. Such a question is purely whimsical, for the customs of one culture cannot easily be grafted onto another culture. A long postpartum sex taboo presupposes a lack of effective birth-control methods, but our society already has many such methods. Moreover, a long postpartum sex taboo could conceivably affect important aspects of our culture, such as the idea that a happy marriage is a sexy one. The point is that with such a taboo imposed on it, our culture would no longer be the same. Too many aspects of the culture would have to be changed to accommodate the new behavior. This is so because our culture is mostly integrated.

In saying that a culture is mostly *integrated,* we mean that the elements or traits that make up that culture are not just a random assortment of customs but are mostly adjusted to or consistent with one another. One reason anthropologists believe that culture tends to be integrated is that culture is generally adaptive. If certain customs are more adaptive in particular settings, then those "bundles" of traits will generally be found together under similar conditions. For example, the !Kung, as we have mentioned, subsisted by hunting wild animals and gathering wild plants. They were also nomadic, had very small communities, had few material possessions, and shared food within their bands. As we will see, these cultural traits usually occur together when people depend on hunting and gathering for their food.

A culture may also tend to be integrated for psychological reasons. The ideas of a culture—attitudes, values, ideals, and rules for behavior—are stored, after all, in the brains of individuals. Research in social psychology has suggested that people tend to modify beliefs or behaviors that are not cognitively or conceptually consistent with other information.[15] We do not expect cultures to be completely integrated, just as we do not expect individuals to be completely consistent. But if a tendency toward cognitive consistency is found in humans, we might expect that at least some aspects of a culture would tend to be integrated for that reason.

Humans are also capable of rational decision making; they can usually figure out that certain things are not easy to do because of other things they do. For example, if a society has a long postpartum sex taboo, we might expect that most people in the society could figure out that it would be easier to observe the taboo if husband and wife did not sleep in the same bed. Or if people drive on the left side of the road, as in England, it is easier and less dangerous to drive a car with a steering wheel on the right because that placement allows you to judge more accurately how close you are to cars coming at you from the opposite direction.

The tendency for a culture to be integrated, then, may be cognitively and emotionally, as well as adaptively, induced.

Culture Is Always Changing

When you examine the history of a society, it is obvious that its culture has changed over time. Some of the shared behaviors, beliefs, and values that were common at one time are modified or replaced at another time. In North American society, we only have to consider our attitudes toward sex and marriage to realize that a lot of our culture has changed recently. The impetus for change may come from within the society or from without. From within, the unconscious or conscious pressure for consistency will produce culture change if enough people adjust old behavior and thinking to new. Change can also occur if people try to invent better ways of doing things.

A good deal of culture change may be stimulated by changes in the external environment. If agricultural people move into an arid area, they will either have to give up farming or develop a system of irrigation. In the modern world, changes in the social environment may be stimuli for culture change, not just changes in the physical environment. Many North Americans, for example, started to think seriously about conserving energy and about using sources of energy other than oil only after oil supplies from the Middle East were curtailed in 1973 and 1974. Different societies have often affected each other, and a significant amount of the radical and rapid culture change that has occurred in the last few hundred years has been due to the imperial expansion of Western societies into other areas of the world. Native Americans, for instance, were forced to alter their lifestyles drastically when they were driven off their lands and confined to reservations. In the chapter on culture change and globalization, we discuss the major patterns of culture change in the modern world, much of it affected by the expansion of the West.

If we assume that cultures are more than random collections of behaviors, beliefs, and values—that they tend to be adaptive, integrated, and changing—then the similarities and differences between them should be understandable. That is, we can expect that similar circumstances within or outside the culture will give rise to, or favor, similar cultural responses. In the chapters that follow, we hope to convey the highlights of what anthropologists know about aspects of cultural variation and what they do not know.

This painting of a beach scene in the early 1900s reminds us of how much cultural ideas about modesty have changed over time.

We frequently describe particular cultures to illustrate aspects of cultural variation. When we do so, the reader should understand that the description of a particular culture or cultural trait always pertains to a particular time period and sometimes to a specific subgroup. For example, the !Kung of the 1950s were mostly dependent on the collection of wild plants and animals and moved their camp sites frequently, but later they became more sedentary and engaged in wage labor.

Types of Research in Cultural Anthropology

Cultural anthropologists use several methods to conduct research. The types of research in cultural anthropology can be classified according to two criteria. One is the spatial scope of the study—analysis of a single society, analysis of societies in a region, or analysis of a worldwide sample of societies. The other criterion is the temporal scope of the study—historical versus nonhistorical. Combinations of these criteria are shown in Table 2.1.

Ethnography

Around the beginning of the twentieth century, anthropologists started to live among the people they were studying. They observed, and even took part in, the important events of those societies and carefully questioned the people about their native customs. This method is known as **participant-observation**. Participant-observation always involves **fieldwork**, which is firsthand experience with the people being studied, but fieldwork may also involve other methods, such as conducting a census or a survey.[16]

Fieldwork, the cornerstone of modern anthropology, is the means by which most anthropological information is obtained. Regardless of other methods that anthropologists may use, participant-observation is regarded as fundamental. In contrast to the casual descriptions of travelers and adventurers, anthropologists' descriptions record, describe, analyze, and eventually formulate a picture of the culture, or at least part of it.[17] After doing fieldwork, an anthropologist may prepare an *ethnography*, a description and analysis of the society studied.

How an anthropologist goes about doing participant-observation in another culture depends on the person, the culture, and the interaction between the two. Without a doubt, the experience is physically and psychologically demanding. Although it helps enormously to learn the local language before one goes, often it is not possible to do so, and so most anthropologists find themselves struggling to communicate in addition to trying to figure out how to behave properly. Participant-observation involves a

Table 2.1 Types of Research in Cultural Anthropology		
Scope	**Nonhistorical**	**Historical**
Single society	Ethnography Within-culture comparison	Ethnohistory Within-culture comparison
Region	Controlled comparison	Controlled comparison
Worldwide sample	Cross-cultural research	Cross-historical research

dilemma. Participation implies living like the people you have come to study, trying to understand subjectively what they think and feel by doing what they do, whereas observation implies a certain amount of objectivity and detachment.[18] Because participant-observation is such a personal experience, anthropologists have begun to realize that *reflecting* on their experiences and their personal interaction with the people they live with is an important part of the enterprise.

An essential part of the participant-observation process is finding some knowledgeable people who are willing to work with you (anthropologists call them *informants*), to help you interpret what you observe and tell you about aspects of the culture that you may not have a chance to see, or may not be entitled to see. For example, it is not likely that you will see many weddings in a village of 200 people in a year of fieldwork. So how can you know who will be a good informant? It is obviously important to find people who are easy to talk to and who understand what information you need. But how do you know who is knowledgeable? You can't just assume that the people you get along with have the most knowledge. (Besides, knowledge is often specialized; one person may know a whole lot more about some subjects than others.) At a minimum, you have to try out a few different people to compare what they tell you about a subject. What if they disagree? How do you know who is more trustworthy or accurate? Fortunately, formal methods have been developed to help select the most knowledgeable informants. One method called the "cultural consensus model" relies on the principle that those things that most informants agree on are probably cultural. After you establish which things appear to be cultural by asking a sample of informants the same questions about a particular cultural domain, it will be easy to discover which informants are very likely to give answers that closely match the cultural consensus. These individuals are your best bets to be the most knowledgeable in that domain.[19] It may seem paradoxical, but the most knowledgeable and helpful individuals are not necessarily "typical" individuals. Many anthropologists have pointed out that key informants are likely to feel somewhat marginal in their culture. After all, why would they want to spend so much time with the visiting anthropologist?[20]

Ethnohistorians need to analyze pieces of information from a variety of sources, such as the accounts of explorers in the Pacific. Pictured here is a painting of the arrival of a French explorer in Maui, Hawaii in the late 1700s.

Participant-observation is valuable for understanding some aspects of culture, particularly the things that are the most public, readily talked about, and most widely agreed upon. But more systematic methods are important too: mapping, house-to-house censuses, behavior observations (e.g., to determine how people spend their time), as well as focused interviews with a sample of informants.

Ethics in Fieldwork   Anthropologists have many ethical obligations—to the people they study, to their anthropological colleagues, to the public and world community. But anthropologists agree that should a conflict arise in ethical obligations, the most important obligation is to protect the interests of the people they study. According to the profession's code of ethics, anthropologists should tell people in the field site about the research and they should respect the right of people to remain anonymous if they so choose.[21] It is for this reason that informants are often given "pseudonyms" or fake names; many anthropologists have extended this principle to using a fake name for the community as well. But the decision to create a fake name for a community is questionable in many circumstances.[22] First, anthropologists "stick out" and it is not hard for anyone interested to figure out where they lived and worked. Governments may have to be asked for research clearance, which means that they know where the anthropologist is going to do the fieldwork. Second, people who are studied are often proud of their place and their customs and they may be insulted if their community is called something else. Third, important geographic information is often vital to understanding the community. You have to reveal if it is located at the confluence of two major rivers, or if it is the trading center of the region. And lastly, it may be difficult for a future anthropologist to conduct a follow-up study if the community is disguised.

Honest, objective reporting is also an obligation to the anthropological profession and to the public at large. But suppose a custom or trait that appears perfectly reasonable to the observed community is considered objectionable by outsiders? Such customs could range from acts that outsiders consider criminal, such as infanticide, to those that are considered repugnant, such as eating dogs. An anthropologist may believe that publication of the information could bring harm to the population. Kim Hill and Magdalena Hurtado faced this situation when they realized that infanticide rates were high in the group they studied in South America. They did not want to play up their findings, nor did they want to dissimulate. After they met with community leaders to discuss the situation, they agreed not to publish their findings in Spanish to minimize the possibility that the local media or neighboring groups might learn of their findings.[23]

Everyday decisions like how to compensate people for their time are not easy either. Nowadays, many if not most informants expect to be paid or receive gifts. But in the early days of anthropology, in places where money was not an important part of the native economy, the decision to pay people was not a clear ethical choice. Payments or nonmonetary gifts can increase inequalities or create jealousies. On the other hand, doing nothing by way of compensation doesn't seem right either. As an alternative some anthropologists try to find some community project that they can help with. This is not to say that the anthropologist is necessarily a burden on the community. People often like to talk about their customs, and they may want others to appreciate their way of life. And anthropologists are often amusing. They may ask "funny" questions, and when they try to say or do customary things they often do them all wrong. Probably every anthropologist has been laughed at sometimes in the field.

Within-Culture Comparisons

Ethnographers could test a theory within one society if they decide to compare individuals, families, households, communities, or districts. The natural variability that exists can be used to make a comparison. Suppose we want to verify Whiting's assumption that in a society with a low-protein diet, longer postpartum taboos enhance the survival of babies. Although almost all couples might practice a long postpartum sex taboo because it is customary, some couples might not adhere to the taboo consistently and some couples might not conceive quickly after the taboo is lifted. So we would expect some variation in spacing between births. If we collected information on the births of each mother and the survival outcome of each birth, we would be able to compare the survival rates of children born a short time after the mother's last pregnancy with those of children born after longer intervals. A significantly higher survival rate for the births after longer intervals would support Whiting's theory. What if some communities within the society had access to more protein than others? If Whiting's theory is correct, those communities with more protein should also have a higher survival rate for babies. If there were variation in the length of the postpartum sex taboo, the communities with more protein should have shorter taboos.

Whether or not we can design intracultural tests of hypotheses depends on whether we have sufficient variability in the variables in our hypotheses. More often than not we do, and we can make use of that variation to test hypotheses within a culture.

Regional Controlled Comparisons

In a regional controlled comparison, the anthropologist compares ethnographic information obtained from societies found in a particular region—societies that presumably have similar histories and occupy similar environments. The anthropologist who conducts a regional comparison is apt to be familiar with the complex of cultural features associated with that region. These features may provide a good understanding of the context of the phenomenon that is to be explained. Because some of the societies being compared will have the characteristic that is to be explained and some will not, the anthropologist can determine whether the conditions hypothesized to be related are in fact related, at least in that region. We must remember, however, that two or more conditions may be related in one region for reasons peculiar to that region. Therefore, an explanation supported in one region may not fit others.

Cross-Cultural Research

The most common use of worldwide comparisons has been to test explanations. An example is Whiting's test of his theory about the adaptive functions of a long postpartum sex taboo. Recall that Whiting hypothesized that if his theory is correct, variation in protein supplies in the adult diet should predict variation in the duration of the postpartum sex taboo. Cross-cultural researchers first identify conditions that should generally be associated if a particular theory is correct. Then they look at a worldwide sample of societies to see if the expected association generally holds true. Most cross-culturalists choose a published sample of societies that was not constructed for any specific hypothesis test. Two of the most widely used samples are the Standard Cross-Cultural (SCCS) sample of 186 societies and the *Human Relations Area Files (HRAF) Collection of Ethnography,* an annually growing collection of original ethnographic books and articles on approximately 400 cultures, past and present, around the world.[24] Since the HRAF collection actually contains full-text ethnographies that are subject-indexed by paragraph, a researcher can quickly find the information to code a variable across a large number of societies. In contrast, the SCCS sample contains pointers to ethnography, not ethnographies themselves. But thousands of variables have now been coded by researchers for this sample, so those researchers who want to use the data coded by others tend to use this sample.

The advantage of cross-cultural research is that the conclusion drawn from it is probably applicable to most societies, if the sample used for testing has been more or less randomly selected and therefore is representative of the world. In other words, in contrast with the results of a regional comparison, which may or may not be applicable to other regions, the results of a cross-cultural study are probably applicable to most societies and most regions.

Historical Research

Ethnohistory consists of studies based on descriptive materials about a single society at more than one point in time. It provides the essential data for historical studies of all types, just as ethnography provides the essential data for all nonhistorical types of research. Ethnohistorical data may consist of sources other than the ethnographic reports prepared by anthropologists—accounts by explorers, missionaries, traders, and government officials. Ethnohistorians, like historians, cannot simply assume that all the documents they find are simply descriptions of fact; they were written by very different kinds of people with very different goals and purposes. So they need to separate carefully what may be fact from what may be speculative interpretation. To reconstruct how a culture changed over hundreds of years, where the natives left few or no written accounts, anthropologists have to seek out travelers' accounts and other historical documents that were written by non-natives.

The goal of theory in cultural anthropology is to explain variation in cultural patterns, that is, to specify what conditions will favor one cultural pattern rather than another. Such specification requires us to assume that the supposed causal, or favoring, conditions antedated the pattern to be explained. Theories or explanations, then, imply a sequence of changes over time, which are the stuff of history. Therefore, if we want to come closer to an understanding of the reasons for the cultural variations we are investigating, we should examine historical sequences. They will help us determine whether the conditions we think caused various phenomena truly antedated those phenomena and thus might more reliably be said to have caused them. In the chapters that follow, we discuss not only what we strongly suspect about the determinants of cultural variation but also what we do not know or only dimly suspect. We devote a lot of our discussion to what we do not know—what has not yet been the subject of research that tests hypotheses and theories—because we want to convey a sense of what cultural anthropology might discover in the future.

Summary

1. Culture may be defined as the learned behaviors and ideas (beliefs, attitudes, values, and ideals) generally shared by the members of a society or other social group.

2. When anthropologists refer to *a* culture, they are usually referring to the cultural patterns of a particular society—that is, a particular territorial population speaking a language not generally understood by neighboring territorial populations.

3. Ethnocentrism, judging other cultures in terms of your own, and its opposite—the glorification of other cultures—impede anthropological inquiry. An important tenet in anthropology is the principle of cultural relativism: the attitude that a society's customs and ideas should be studied objectively and understood in the context of that society's culture.

4. Anthropologists seek to discover the customs and ranges of acceptable behavior that constitute the culture of a society under study. In doing so, they focus on general or shared patterns of behavior rather than on individual variations.

5. One important factor that limits the range of individual variation is the culture itself, which acts directly or indirectly as a constraint on behavior. The existence of cultural constraints, however, is not necessarily incompatible with individuality.

6. Several assumptions are frequently made about culture. First, culture is generally adapted to the particular conditions of its physical and social environment. What may be adaptive in one environment may not be adaptive in another. Second, culture is mostly integrated, in that the elements or traits that make up the culture are mostly adjusted to or consistent with one another. Third, culture is always changing.

7. Cultural anthropologists use several different methods to conduct research. The types of research in cultural anthropology can be classified according to two criteria: the spatial scope of the study (analysis of a single society, analysis of several or more societies in a region, or analysis of a worldwide sample of societies) and the temporal scope of the study (historical versus nonhistorical). The basic research methods, then, are ethnography and ethnohistory, within-culture comparisons, historical and nonhistorical regional controlled comparisons, and historical and nonhistorical cross-cultural research.

Glossary Terms

adaptive customs (p. 34)
cultural relativism (p. 29)
culture (p. 23)
ethnocentric (p. 26)
ethnocentrism (p. 26)
fieldwork (p. 37)

maladaptive customs (p. 34)
norms (p. 31)
participant-observation (p. 37)
society (p. 23)
subculture (p. 24)

Critical Questions

1. Would it be adaptive for a society to have everyone adhere to the cultural norms? Why do you think so?

2. Why does culture change more rapidly in some societies than in others? What external and internal factors might affect the rapidity of culture change?

3. Does the concept of cultural relativism promote international understanding, or does it hinder attempts to have international agreement on acceptable behavior, such as human rights?

CHAPTER 3

LANGUAGE AND COMMUNICATION

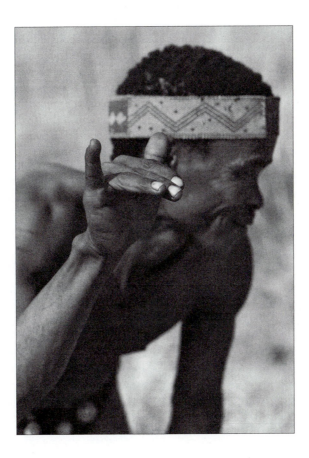

Chapter Outline

- Communication
- Origins of Language
- Descriptive Linguistics
- Historical Linguistics
- Processes of Linguistic Divergence

- Relationships between Language and Culture
- Ethnography of Speaking
- Writing and Literacy

Few of us can remember when we first became aware that words signified something. Yet that moment was a milestone for us, not just in the acquisition of language but in becoming acquainted with all the complex, elaborate behavior that constitutes our culture. Without language, the transmission of complex traditions would be virtually impossible, and each person would be trapped within his or her own world of private sensations.

Helen Keller, left deaf and blind by illness at the age of 19 months, gives a moving account of the afternoon she first established contact with another human being through words:

> [My teacher] brought me my hat, and I knew I was going out into the warm sunshine. This thought, if a wordless sensation may be called a thought, made me hop and skip with pleasure.
>
> We walked down the path to the well house, attracted by the fragrance of the honeysuckle with which it was covered. Someone was drawing water and my teacher placed my hand under the spout. As the cool stream gushed over one hand she spelled into the other the word water, first slowly, then rapidly. Suddenly I felt a misty consciousness as of something forgotten—a thrill of returning thought; and somehow the mystery of language was revealed to me. I knew then that w-a-t-e-r meant the wonderful cool something that was flowing over my hand. That living word awakened my soul, gave it light, hope, joy, set it free! There were barriers still, it is true, barriers that could in time be swept away. I left the well house eager to learn. Everything had a name, and each name gave birth to a new thought. As we returned to the house every object which I touched seemed to quiver with life. That was because I saw everything with the strange, new sight that had come to me.[1]

Communication

Against all odds, Helen Keller had come to understand the essential function that language plays in all societies—namely, that of communication. The word *communicate* comes from the Latin verb *communicare,* "to impart," "to share," "to make *common.*" We communicate by agreeing, consciously or unconsciously, to call an object, a movement, or an abstract concept by a common name. For example, speakers of English have agreed to call the color of grass *green,* even though we have no way of comparing precisely how two persons actually experience this color. What we share is the agreement to call similar sensations *green.* Any system of language consists of publicly accepted symbols by which individuals try to share private experiences. Spoken or vocal language is probably the major transmitter of culture, allowing us to share and pass on our complex configuration of attitudes, beliefs, and patterns of behavior.

Nonverbal Human Communication

As we all know from experience, the spoken word does not communicate all that we know about a social situation. We can usually tell when someone says, "It was good to meet you," whether he or she really means it. We can tell if people are sad from their demeanor, even if they say, "I'm fine," in response to the question "How are you?" Obviously, our communication is not limited to spoken language. We communicate directly through facial expression, body stance, gesture, and tone of voice and indirectly through systems of signs and symbols, such as writing, algebraic equations, musical scores, dancing, painting, code flags, and road signs. As Anthony Wilden put it, "every act, every pause, every movement in living and social systems is also a message; silence is communication; short of death it is impossible for an organism or person not to communicate."[2] How can silence be a communication? Silence may reflect companionship, as when two people work side by side on a project, but silence can also communicate unfriendliness. An anthropologist can learn a great deal from what people in a society do not talk about. For example, in India, sex is not supposed to be talked about. HIV infection is spreading very fast in India, so the unwillingness of people to talk about sex makes it extraordinarily difficult for medical anthropologists and health professionals to do much to reduce the rate of spread.[3]

Some nonverbal communication appears to be universal in humans. For example, humans the world over appear to understand facial expression in the same way; that is, they are able to recognize a happy, sad, surprised, angry, disgusted, or afraid face. But nonverbal communication is also culturally variable. Different cultures have different rules about the emotions that are acceptable to express. One study compared how Japanese and Americans express emotion. Individuals from both groups were videotaped while they were shown films intended to evoke feelings of fear and disgust. When the subjects saw the films by themselves, without other people present, they showed the same kinds of facial expressions of fear and disgust. But culture could affect expression too. When an authority figure was present during the videotaping, the Japanese subjects tried to mask their negative feelings with a half-smile more often than did the Americans.[4]

Nonverbal communication can even involve the voice. Consider how we might know that a person is not fine even though she just said "I'm fine." A depressed person might speak very quietly and use a flat tone of voice. If a person thought about explaining what was really wrong but thought better of it, a significant pause or silence might come before the words "I'm fine." A person's **accent** (differences in pronunciation) can tell a lot about the person's background, such as place of origin and education. There are also nonverbal (nonword) sounds that people make—grunts, laughs, giggles, moans, and sighs.

Nonhuman Communication

Systems of communication are not unique to human beings, nor is communication by sound. Other animal species communicate in a variety of ways. One way is by sound. A bird may communicate by a call that "this is my territory"; a squirrel may utter a cry that leads other squirrels to flee from danger. Another means of animal communication is odor. An ant releases a chemical when it dies, and its fellows then carry it away to the compost heap. Apparently the communication is highly effective; a healthy ant painted with the death chemical will be dragged to the funeral heap again and again. Another means of communication, body movement, is used by bees to convey the location of food sources. Karl von Frisch discovered that the black Austrian honeybee—by choosing a round dance, a wagging dance, or a short, straight run—can communicate not only the precise direction of the source of food but also its distance from the hive.[5]

One of the biggest scholarly debates is the degree to which nonhuman animals, particularly nonhuman primates, differ from humans in their capacity for language. Some scholars see so much discontinuity that they postulate that humans must have acquired (presumably through mutation) a specific genetic capability for language. Others see much more continuity between humans and nonhuman primates and point to research that shows much more cognitive capacity in nonhuman primates than previously thought possible. They point out that the discontinuity theorists are constantly raising the standards for the capacities thought necessary for language.[6] For example, in the past, only human communication was thought to be symbolic. But recent research suggests that some monkey and ape calls in the wild are also symbolic.

When we say that a call, word, or sentence is **symbolic communication**, we mean at least two things. First, the communication has meaning even when its *referent* (whatever is referred to) is not present. Second, the meaning is arbitrary; the receiver of the message could not guess its meaning just from the sound(s) and does not know the meaning instinctively. In other words, symbols have to be learned. There is no compelling or "natural" reason that the word *dog* in English should refer to a smallish four-legged omnivore that is sometimes the bane of letter carriers.

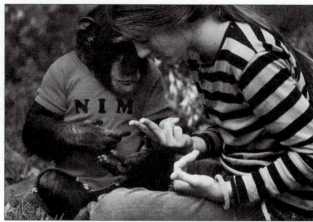

Apes lack the human capacity for speech, so researchers have explored the capacity of chimpanzees and other apes to communicate with hand gestures. A variety of signs from American Sign Language, used by the hearing impaired, are shown on the left. On the right, researcher Joyce Butler teaches Nim, a chimpanzee, a sign for "drink."

Vervet monkeys in Africa are not as closely related to humans as are African apes. Nevertheless, scientists who have observed vervet monkeys in their natural environment consider at least three of their alarm calls to be symbolic because each of them *means* (refers to) a different kind of predator—eagles, pythons, or leopards—and monkeys react differently to each call. For example, they look up when they hear the "eagle" call. Experimentally, in the absence of the referent, investigators have been able to evoke the normal reaction to a call by playing it back electronically. Another indication that the vervet alarm calls are symbolic is that infant vervets appear to need some time to learn the referent for each. When they are very young, infants apply a particular call to more animals than adult vervets apply the call to. So, for example, infant vervets will often make the eagle warning call when they see any flying bird. The infants learn the appropriate referent apparently through adult vervets' repetition of infants' "correct" calls; in any case, the infants gradually learn to restrict the call to eagles.[7]

How is human vocalization different? Since monkeys and apes appear to use symbols at least some of the time, it is not appropriate to emphasize symbolism as the distinctive feature of human language. However, there is a significant quantitative difference between human language and other primates' systems of vocal communication. All human languages employ a much larger set of symbols.

Another often-cited difference between human and nonhuman vocalizations is that the other primates' vocal systems are *closed*—that is, different calls are not combined to produce new, meaningful utterances. In contrast, human languages are *open* systems, governed by complex rules about how sounds and sequences of sounds can be combined to produce an infinite variety of meanings.[8] For example, an English speaker can combine *care* and *full* (*careful*) to mean one thing, then use each of the two elements in other combinations to mean different things. *Care* can be used to make *carefree, careless,* or *caretaker; full* can be used to make *powerful* or *wonderful.* And because language is a system of shared symbols, it can be re-formed into an infinite variety of expressions and be understood by all who share these symbols. In this way, for example, T. S. Eliot could form a sentence never before formed—"In the room the women come and go/talking of Michelangelo"[9]—and the sense of his sentence, though not necessarily his private meaning, could be understood by all speakers of English.

While no primatologist disputes the complexity and infinite variety with which human languages can combine sounds, the closed versus open distinction has been called into question by research on cotton-top tamarins, pygmy marmosets, capuchin monkeys, and rhesus macaques. These nonhuman primates also combine calls in orderly sequences,[10] but not nearly as much as humans do.

Another trait thought to be unique to humans is the ability to communicate about past or future events. But Sue Savage-Rumbaugh has observed wild bonobos leaving what appear to be messages to other bonobos to follow a trail. They break off vegetation where trails fork and point the broken plants in the direction to follow.

Perhaps most suggestive are the successful attempts to teach apes to communicate with humans and with each other using human-created signs. These successes have led many scholars to question the traditional assumption that the gap between human and other animal communication is enormous. Even a parrot, which has a small brain, has been taught to communicate with a human trainer in ways once thought impossible. Alex (the parrot) could correctly answer questions in English about what objects are made of, how many objects of a particular type there are, and even what makes two objects the same or different.[11] When he was not willing to continue a training session, Alex said: "I'm sorry . . . Wanna go back."[12] Chimpanzees Washoe and Nim and the gorilla Koko were taught hand signs based on American Sign Language (ASL, used by the hearing impaired in the United States). Subsequently, many chimpanzees were trained on symbol keyboards connected to computers. For example, Sherman and Austin began to communicate with each other about actions they were intending to do, such as the types of tools they needed to solve a problem. And they were able to classify items into categories, such as "food" and "tools."

Some of the best examples of linguistic ability come from a chimpanzee named Kanzi. In contrast to other apes, Kanzi initially learned symbols just by watching his mother being taught, and he spontaneously began using the computer symbols to communicate with humans, even indicating his intended actions. Kanzi did not need rewards or to have his hands put in the right position. And he understood a great deal of what was spoken to him in English. For example, when he was 5 years old, Kanzi heard someone talk about throwing a ball in the river, and he turned around and did so. Kanzi has come close to having a primitive English grammar when he strings symbols together.[13] If chimpanzees and other primates have the capacity to use nonspoken language and even to understand spoken language, then the difference between humans and nonhumans may not be as great as people used to think.

Are these apes really using language in some minimal way? Many investigators agree about one thing—nonhuman primates have the ability to "symbol," to refer to something (or a class of things) with an arbitrary "label" (gesture or sequence of sounds).[14] The gorilla Koko (with a repertoire of about 375 signs) extended the sign for *drinking straw* to plastic tubing, hoses, cigarettes, and radio antennae. Washoe originally learned the sign *dirty* to refer to feces and other soil and then began to use it insultingly, as in "dirty Roger," when her trainer Roger Fouts refused to give her things she wanted. Even the mistakes made by the apes suggest that they are using signs symbolically, just as words are used in spoken language. For example, the sign *cat* may be used for dog if the animal learned *cat* first (just as our daughter Kathy said "dog" to all pictures of four-footed animals, including elephants, when she was 18 months old).

When we discuss the structure of sounds (phonology) later in this chapter, we will see that every human language has certain ways of combining sounds and ways of not combining those sounds. Apes do not have anything comparable to linguistic rules for allowed and not allowed combinations of sounds. In addition, humans have many kinds of discourse. We make lists and speeches, tell stories, argue, and recite poetry. Apes do none of these things.[15] But apes do have at least some of the capacities for language. Therefore, understanding their capacities may help us better understand the evolution of human language.

Origins of Language

How long humans have had spoken language is not known. Some think that the earliest *Homo sapiens,* perhaps 100,000 years ago, may have had the beginnings of language. Others believe that language developed only in the last 40,000 years or so, with the emergence of modern humans. Because the only unambiguous remains of language are found on written tablets, and the earliest stone tablets date back only about 5,000 years,[16] pinpointing the emergence of earliest languages remains speculative. Theories about when language developed are based on nonlinguistic information such as when cranial capacity expanded dramatically, when complex technology and symbolic artifacts (such as art) started to be made, and when the anatomy of the throat, as inferred from fossil remains, began to resemble what we see in modern humans.

Noam Chomsky and other theoreticians of grammar suggest that there is an innate *language-acquisition device* in the human brain, as innate to humans as call systems are to other animals.[17] If humans are unique in having an innate capacity for language, then some mutation or series of mutations had to be favored in human evolution, not before the human line separated from apes. Whether such a mechanism in fact exists is not clear. But we do know that the actual development of individual language is not completely biologically determined; if it were, all human beings would speak the same brain-generated language. Instead, about 4,000 to 5,000 mutually unintelligible languages have been identified. More than 2,000 of them were still spoken as of recently, most by peoples who did not traditionally have a system of writing.

Can we learn anything about the origins of language by studying the languages of nonliterate (no writing) and technologically simpler societies? The answer is no, because such languages are not simpler or less developed than ours. The sound systems, vocabularies, and grammars of technologically simpler peoples are in no way inferior to those of peoples with more complex technology.[18] Of course, people in other societies, and even some people in our own society, will not be able to name the sophisticated machines used in our society. All languages, however, have the potential for doing so. As we will see later in this chapter, all languages possess the amount of vocabulary their speakers need, and all languages expand in response to cultural changes. A language that lacks terminology for some of our conveniences may have a rich vocabulary for events or natural phenomena that are of particular importance to the people in that society.

If there are no primitive languages, and if the earliest languages have left no traces that would allow us to reconstruct them, does that mean we cannot investigate the origins of language? Some linguists think that understanding the way children acquire language, which we discuss shortly, can help us understand the origins of language. Other linguists have suggested that an understanding of how creole languages develop will also tell us something about the origins of language.

Creole Languages

Some languages developed in various areas where European colonial powers established commercial enterprises that relied on imported labor, generally slaves. The laborers in one place often came from several different societies and in the beginning would speak with their masters and with each other in some kind of *pidgin* (simplified) version of the masters' language. Pidgin languages lack many of the building blocks found in the languages of whole societies, building blocks such as prepositions (*to, on,* and so forth) and auxiliary verbs (designating future and other tenses). Many pidgin languages developed into and were replaced by so-called *creole languages,* which incorporate much of the vocabulary of the masters' language but also have a grammar that differs from it and from the grammars of the laborers' native languages.[19]

Derek Bickerton argues that there are striking grammatical similarities in creole languages throughout the world. This similarity, he thinks, is consistent with the idea that some grammar is inherited by all humans. Creole languages, therefore, may resemble early human languages. All creoles use intonation instead of a change in word order to ask a question. The creole equivalent of the question "Can you fix this?" would be "You can fix this?" The creole version puts a rising inflection at the end; in contrast, the English version reverses the subject and verb without much inflection at the end. All creoles express the future and the past in the same grammatical way, by the use of particles (such as the English *shall*) between subject and verb, and they all employ double negatives, as in the Guyana English creole "Nobody no like me."[20]

It is possible that many other things about language are universal, that all languages are similar in many respects, because of the way humans are "wired" or because people in all societies have similar experiences. For example, names for frogs may usually contain *r* sounds because frogs make them.[21]

Children's Acquisition of Language

Apparently a child is equipped from birth with the capacity to reproduce all the sounds used by the world's languages and to learn any system of grammar. Research on 6-months-old infants finds that they can distinguish sounds of approximately 600 consonants and 200 vowels—all the sounds of all the languages of the world. But by about the time of their first birthdays, babies become better at recognizing the salient sounds and sound clusters of their parents or caretakers and become less adept at distinguishing those of other languages.[22]

Children's acquisition of the structure and meaning of language has been called the most difficult intellectual achievement in life. If that is so, it is pleasing to note that they accomplish it with relative ease and vast enjoyment. Many believe that this "difficult intellectual achievement" may in reality be a natural response to the capacity for language that is one of humans' genetic characteristics. All over the world children begin to learn language at about the same age, and in no culture do children wait until they are 7 or 10 years old. By 12 or 13 months of age, children are able to name a few objects and actions, and by 18 to 20 months they can make one key word stand for a whole sentence: "Out!" for "Take me out for a walk right now"; "Juice!" for "I want some juice now." Evidence suggests that children acquire the concept of a word as a whole, learning sequences of sounds that are stressed or at the ends of words (e.g., "raffe" for giraffe). Even hearing-impaired children learning signs in ASL tend to acquire and use signs in a similar fashion.[23]

A lot of language instruction is by pointing to something and saying what it is called.

Children the world over tend to progress to two-word sentences at about 18 to 24 months of age. In their sentences they express themselves in "telegraph" form—using nounlike words and verblike words but leaving out the seemingly less important words. So a two-word sentence such as "Shoes off" may stand for "Take my shoes off," or "More milk" may stand for "Give me more milk, please."[24] They do not utter their two words in random order, sometimes saying "off" first, other times saying "shoes" first. If a child says "Shoes off," then he or she will also say "Clothes off" and "Hat off." They seem to select an order that fits the conventions of adult language, so they are likely to say "Daddy eat," not "Eat Daddy." In other words, they tend to put the subject first, as adults do. And they tend to say "Mommy coat" rather than "Coat Mommy" to indicate "Mommy's coat."[25] Adults do not utter sentences such as "Daddy eat," so children seem to know a lot about how to put words together with little or no direct teaching from their caretakers.

If there is a basic grammar imprinted in the human mind, we should not be surprised that children's early and later speech patterns seem to be similar in different languages. We might also expect children's later speech to be similar to the structure of creole languages. And it is, according to Derek Bickerton.[26] The "errors" children make in speaking are consistent with the grammar of creoles. For example, English-speaking children three to four years old tend to ask questions by intonation alone, and they tend to use double negatives, such as "I don't see no dog," even though the adults around them do not speak that way and consider the children's speech "wrong."

But some linguists argue that the evidence for an innate grammar is weak because children the world over do not develop the same grammatical features at similar ages. For example, word order is a more important determinant of meaning in English than in Turkish; the endings of words are more important in Turkish. The word at the beginning of the sentence in English is likely to be the subject. The word with a certain ending in Turkish is the likely subject. Consistent with this difference, English-speaking children learn word order earlier than Turkish children do.[27]

Future research on children's acquisition of language and on the structure of creole languages may bring us closer to an understanding of the origins of human language. But even if much of grammar is universal, we still need to understand how and why the thousands of languages in the world vary, which brings us to the conceptual tools linguists have had to invent in order to study languages.

Descriptive Linguistics

In every society children do not need to be taught "grammar" to learn how to speak. They begin to grasp the essential structure of their language at a very early age, without direct instruction. If you show English-speaking children a picture of one "gork" and then a picture of two of these creatures, they will say there are two "gorks." Somehow they know that adding an *s* to a noun means more than one. But they do not know this consciously, and adults may not either. One of the most surprising features of human language is that meaningful sounds and sound sequences are combined according to rules that often are not consciously known by the speakers.

These rules should not be equated with the "rules of grammar" you were taught in school so that you would speak "correctly." Rather, when linguists talk about rules, they are referring to the patterns of speaking that are discoverable in actual speech. Needless to say, there is some overlap between the actual rules of speaking and the rules taught in school. But there are rules that children never hear about in school, because their teachers are not linguists and are not aware of them. When linguists use the term *grammar,* they are *not* referring to the prescriptive rules that people are supposed to follow in speaking. Rather, *grammar* to the linguist consists of the actual, often unconscious principles that predict how most people talk. As we have noted, young children may speak two-word sentences that conform to a linguistic rule, but their speech is hardly considered "correct."

Discovering the mostly unconscious rules operating in a language is a very difficult task. Linguists have had to invent special concepts and methods of transcription (writing) to permit them to describe: (1) the rules or principles that predict how sounds are made and how they are used (slightly varying sounds are often used interchangeably in words without creating a difference in meaning—this aspect of language is called **phonology**); (2) how sound sequences (and sometimes even individual sounds) convey meaning and how meaningful sound sequences are strung together to form words (this aspect is called **morphology**); and (3) how words are strung together to form phrases and sentences (this aspect is called **syntax**).

Phonology

Most of us have had the experience of trying to learn another language and finding that some sounds are exceedingly difficult to make. Although the human vocal tract theoretically can make a very large number of different sounds—**phones**, to linguists—each language uses only some of them. It is not that we cannot make the sounds that are strange to us; we just have not acquired the habit of making those sounds. And until the sounds become habitual for us, they continue to be difficult to form.

Finding it difficult to make certain sounds is only one of the reasons we have trouble learning a "foreign" language. Another problem is that we may not be used to combining certain sounds or making a certain sound in a particular position in a word. Thus, English speakers find it difficult to combine *z* and *d*, as Russian speakers often do (because we never do so in English), or to pronounce a word in Samoan, a South Pacific language, that begins with the sound English speakers write as *ng*, even though we have no trouble putting that sound at the end of words, as in the English *sing* and *hitting*.

In order to study the patterning of sounds, linguists who are interested in *phonology* have to write down speech utterances as sequences of sound. This task would be almost impossible if linguists were restricted to using their own alphabet (say, the one we use to write English), because other languages use sounds that are difficult to represent with the English alphabet or because the alphabet we use in English can represent a particular sound in different ways. (English writing represents the sound *f* by *f* as in *food*, but also as *gh* in *tough* and *ph* in *phone*.) In addition, in English different sounds may be represented by the same letter. English has 26 letters but more than 40 significant sounds (sounds that can change the meaning of a word).[28] To overcome these difficulties in writing sounds with the letters of existing writing systems, linguists have developed systems of transcription with special alphabets in which each symbol represents only one particular sound.

Once linguists have identified the sounds or phones used in a language, they try to identify which sounds affect meaning and which sounds do not. One way is to start with a simple word like *lake* and change the first sound to *r* to make the word *rake*. The linguist will ask if this new combination of sounds means the same thing. An English speaker would say *lake* means something completely different from *rake*. These minimal contrasts enable linguists to identify a **phoneme** in a language—a sound or set of sounds that makes a difference in meaning in that language.[29] So the sound *l* in *lake* is different phonemically from the sound *r* in *rake*. The ways in which sounds are grouped together into phonemes vary from language to language. We are so used to phonemes in our own language that it may be hard to believe that the contrast between *r* and *l* may not make a difference in meaning in some languages. For example, in Samoan, *l* and *r* can be used interchangeably in a word without changing the meaning (therefore, these two sounds belong to the same phoneme in Samoan). So Samoan speakers may say "Leupena" sometimes and "Reupena" at other times when they are referring to someone who in English would be called "Reuben."

English speakers may joke about languages that "confuse" *l* and *r*, but they are not usually aware that we do the same thing with other sets of sounds. For example, in English, the word we spell *and* may be pronounced quite differently by two different English speakers without changing the meaning, and no one would think that a different word was spoken. We can pronounce the *a* in *and* as in the beginning of the word *air,* or we can pronounce it as the *a* in *bat.* If you say those varying *a* sounds and try to think about how you are forming them in your mouth, you will realize that they are two different sounds. English speakers might recognize a slight difference in pronunciation but pay little or no attention to it because the two ways to pronounce the *a* in *and* do not change the meaning. Now think about *l* and *r.* If you form them in your mouth, you will notice that they are only slightly different with respect to how far the tongue is from the ridge behind the upper front teeth. Languages do tend to consider sounds that are close as belonging to the same phoneme, but why they choose some sounds and not others to group together is not yet fully understood.

Why, for example, are two or more consonants strung together in some languages, whereas in other languages vowels are *almost* always put between consonants? The Samoan language now has a word for "Christmas" borrowed from English, but the borrowed word has been changed to fit the rules of Samoan. In the English word, two consonants come first, *k* and *r,* which we spell as *ch* and *r.* The Samoan word is *Kerisimasi* (pronounced as if it were spelled Keh-ree-see-mah-see). It has a vowel after each consonant, or five consonant-vowel syllables.

Why do some languages like Samoan alternate consonants and vowels more or less regularly? Recent cross-cultural research suggests three predictors of this variation. One predictor is a warmer climate. Where people live in warmer climates, the typical syllable is more likely to be a consonant-vowel syllable. Linguists have found that consonant-vowel syllables provide the most contrast in speech. Perhaps when people converse outdoors at a distance, which they are likely to do in a warmer climate, they need more contrast between sounds to be understood. A second predictor of consonant-vowel alternation is literacy. Languages that are written have fewer consonant-vowel syllables. If communication is often in written form, meaning does not have to depend so much on contrast between adjacent sounds. A third (indeed the strongest) predictor of consonant-vowel alternation is the degree to which babies are held by others. Societies with a great deal of baby-holding have a lot of consonant-vowel syllables. A cross-cultural study relates baby-holding to a societal preference for regular rhythm in music. The theory is that when babies are held on a person much of the day, they begin to associate regular rhythm with pleasurable experiences. The baby senses the regular rhythm of the caretaker's heartbeats or the caretaker's rhythmic work, and the reward value of that experience generalizes to a preference for all regular rhythms in adult life, including apparently a regular consonant-vowel alternation in adult speech. Compare the rhythm of the Samoan word *Kerisimasi* with the English word *Christmas.*[30]

Morphology

A phoneme in a language usually does not mean something by itself. Usually phonemes are combined with other phonemes to form a meaningful sequence of sounds. *Morphology* is the study of sequences of sounds that have meaning. Often these meaningful sequences of sounds make up what we call *words,* but a word may be composed of a number of smaller meaningful units. We take our words so much for granted that we do not realize how complicated it is to say what words are. People do not usually pause very much between words when they speak; if we did not know our language, a sentence would seem like a continuous stream of sounds. This is how we first hear a foreign language. It is only when we understand the language and write down what we say that we separate (by spaces) what we call words. But a word is really only an arbitrary sequence of sounds that has a meaning; we would not "hear" words as separate units if we did not understand the language spoken.

Because anthropological linguists traditionally investigated unwritten languages, sometimes without the aid of interpreters, they had to figure out which sequences of sounds conveyed meaning. And because words in many languages can often be broken down into smaller meaningful units, linguists had to invent special words to refer to those units. Linguists call the smallest unit of language that has a meaning a **morph**. Just as a phoneme may have one or more phones, one or more morphs with the same meaning may make up a **morpheme**. For example, the prefix *in-,* as in *indefinite,* and the prefix *un-,* as in *unclear,* are morphs that belong to the morpheme meaning *not.* Although some words are single morphs or morphemes (e.g., *for* and *giraffe* in English), many words are a combination of morphs, generally prefixes, roots, and suffixes. Thus *cow* is one word, but the word *cows* contains two meaningful units—a root (*cow*) and a suffix (pronounced like *z*) meaning more than one. The **lexicon** of a language, which a dictionary approximates, consists of words and morphs and their meanings.

In English, the meaning of an utterance (containing a subject, verb, object, and so forth) usually depends on the order of the words. "The dog bit the child" is different in meaning from "The child bit the dog." But in many other languages, the grammatical meaning of an utterance does not depend much, if at all, on the order of the words. Rather, meaning may be determined by how the morphs in a word are ordered. For example, in Luo, a language of East Africa, the same bound morpheme may mean the subject or object of an action. If the morpheme is the prefix to a verb, it means the subject; if it is the suffix to a verb, it means the object. Another way that grammatical meaning may be conveyed is by altering or adding a bound morpheme to a word to indicate what part of speech it is. For example, in Russian, the word for "mail" when it is the subject of a sentence is pronounced something like "pawchtah." When "mail" is used as the object of a verb, as in "I gave her the mail," the ending of the word changes to "pawchtoo." And if I say, "What was in the mail?" the word becomes "pawchtyeh."

Some languages have so many bound morphemes that they might express as a complex but single word what is considered a sentence in English. For example, the English sentence "He will give it to you" can be expressed in Wishram, a Chinookan dialect that was spoken along the Columbia River in the Pacific Northwest, as *acimluda* (a-c-i-m-l-ud-a, literally "will-he-him-thee-to-give-will"). Note that the pronoun *it* in English is gender-neutral; Wishram requires that *it* be given a gender, in this case, "him."[31]

Syntax

Because language is an open system, we can make up meaningful utterances that we have never heard before. We are constantly creating new phrases and sentences. The rules or syntax that predict how phrases and sentences are generally formed may be partly learned in school, but children know many of them even before they get to school. In adulthood, our understanding of morphology and syntax is so intuitive that we can even understand a nonsense sentence, such as this famous one from Lewis Carroll's *Through the Looking Glass:*

'Twas brillig, and the slithy toves
Did gyre and gimble in the wabe

Simply from the ordering of the words in the sentence, we can surmise which part of speech a word is, as well as its function in the sentence. *Brillig* is an adjective; *slithy* an adjective; *toves* a noun and the subject of the sentence; *gyre* and *gimble* verbs; and *wabe* a noun and the object of a prepositional phrase. Of course, an understanding of morphology helps too. The *-y* ending in *slithy* is an indication that the latter is an adjective, and the *-s* ending in *toves* tells us that we most probably have more than one of these creatures. In addition to producing and understanding an infinite variety of sentences, speakers of a language can tell when a sentence is not "correct" without consulting grammar books. Speakers of a language know these implicit rules of syntax but are not usually consciously aware of them. The linguist's description of the syntax of a language tries to make these rules explicit.

Historical Linguistics

The field of historical linguistics focuses on how languages change over time. Written works provide the best data for establishing such changes. For example, the following short passage from Chaucer's *Canterbury Tales,* written in the English of the fourteenth century, has recognizable elements but is different enough from modern English to require a translation.

> A Frere ther was, a wantowne and a merye,
> A lymytour, a ful solempne man.
> In alle the ordres foure is noon that kan
> So muche of daliaunce and fair language.
> He hadde maad ful many a mariage
> Of yonge wommen at his owene cost.

> A friar there was, wanton and merry,
> A limiter [a friar limited to certain districts], a very important man.
> In all the orders four there is none that knows
> So much of flirting and engaging language.
> He had arranged many a marriage
> Of young women at his own cost.[32]

In this passage we can recognize several changes. Many words are spelled differently today, and in some cases, meaning has changed: *Full,* for example, would be translated today as *very.* What is less evident is that changes in pronunciation have occurred. For example, the *g* in *mariage* (marriage) was pronounced *zh,* as in the French from which it was borrowed, whereas now it is usually pronounced like either *g* in *George.*

Because languages spoken in the past leave no traces unless they were written, and most of the languages known to anthropology were not written by their speakers, you might think that historical linguists can study linguistic change only by studying written languages such as English. But that is not the case. Linguists can reconstruct changes that have occurred by comparing contemporary languages that are similar. Such languages show phonological, morphological, and syntactical similarities because they usually derive from a common ancestral language. For example, Romanian, Italian, French, Spanish, and Portuguese have many similarities. On the basis of these similarities, linguists can reconstruct what the ancestral language was like and how it changed into what we call the Romance languages. Of course, these reconstructions can easily be tested and confirmed because we know from many surviving writings what the ancestral language, Latin, was like; and we know from documents how Latin diversified as the Roman Empire expanded. Thus, common ancestry is frequently the reason why neighboring, and sometimes even separated, languages show patterns of similarity.

But languages can be similar for other reasons too. Contact between speech communities, often with one group dominant over another, may lead one language to borrow from the other. For example, English borrowed a lot of vocabulary from French after England was conquered by the French-speaking Normans in A.D. 1066. Languages may also show similarities even though they do not derive from a common ancestral language and even though there has been no contact or borrowing between them. Such similarities may reflect common or universal features of human cultures or human brains or both. (As we noted

This reproduced page dates from a 1433 book authored by John Lydgate. The language is described by linguists as Middle English, spanning approximately 1100–1500.

earlier in the chapter, the grammatical similarities exhibited by creole languages may reflect how the human brain is "wired.") Finally, even unrelated and separated languages may show some similarities because of the phenomenon of convergence; similarities can develop because some processes of linguistic change may have only a few possible outcomes.

Language Families and Culture History

Latin is the ancestral language of the Romance languages. We know this from documentary (written) records. But if the ancestral language of a set of similar languages is not known from written records, linguists still can reconstruct many features of that language by comparing the derived languages. (Such a reconstructed language is called a **protolanguage**.) That is, by comparing presumably related languages, linguists can become aware of the features that many of them have in common, features that were probably found in the common ancestral language. The languages that derive from the same protolanguage are called a *language family.* The language family that English belongs to is called *Indo-European,* because it includes most of the languages of Europe and some of the languages of India. About 50 percent of the world's more than 6 billion people speak Indo-European languages.[33] Another very large language family, now spoken by more than a billion people, is Sino-Tibetan, which includes the languages of northern and southern China as well as those of Tibet and Burma.

The field of historical linguistics got its start in 1786, when a British scholar living in India, Sir William Jones, noticed similarities between Sanskrit (a language spoken and written in ancient India) and classical Greek, Latin, and more recent European languages.[34] In 1822, Jakob Grimm, one of the brothers

Grimm of fairytale fame, formulated rules to describe the sound shifts that had occurred when the various Indo-European languages diverged from each other. So, for example, in English and the other languages in the Germanic branch of the Indo-European family, *d* regularly shifted to *t* (compare the English *two* and *ten* with the Latin *duo* and *decem*) and *p* regularly shifted to *f* (English *father* and *foot,* Latin *pater* and *pes*). Scholars generally agree that the Indo-European languages derive from a language spoken 5,000 to 6,000 years ago.[35] The ancestral Indo-European language, many of whose features have now been reconstructed, is called *proto-Indo-European.*

The Bantu languages in Africa (spoken by perhaps 100 million people) form a subfamily of the larger Niger-Congo family of languages. Bantu speakers currently live in a wide band across the center of Africa and down the eastern and western sides of southern Africa. All of the Bantu languages presumably derive from people who spoke proto-Bantu. But where was their homeland? Most historical linguists now agree with Joseph Greenberg's suggestion that the origin of Bantu was in what is now the Middle Benue area of eastern Nigeria.[36] The point of origin is presumably where there is the greatest diversity of related languages and *dialects* (varying forms of a language); it is assumed that the place of origin has had the most time for linguistic diversity to develop, compared with an area only recently occupied by a related language. For example, England has more dialect diversity than New Zealand or Australia.

Why were the Bantu able to spread so widely over the last few thousand years? Anthropologists have only begun to guess.[37] Initially, the Bantu probably kept goats and practiced some form of agriculture and thereby were able to spread, displacing hunter-gatherers in the area. As the Bantu speakers expanded, they began to cultivate certain cereal crops and herd sheep and cattle. Around this time, after 1000 B.C., they also began to use and make iron tools, which may have given them significant advantages. In any case, by 1,500 to 2,000 years ago, Bantu speakers had spread throughout central Africa and into the northern reaches of southern Africa. But speakers of non-Bantu languages still live in eastern, southern, and southwestern Africa.

Processes of Linguistic Divergence

The historical or comparative linguist hopes to do more than record and date linguistic divergence. Just as the physical anthropologist may attempt to develop explanations for human variation, so the linguist investigates the possible causes of linguistic variation. Some of the divergence undoubtedly comes about gradually. When groups of people speaking the same language lose communication with one another because they become separated, either physically or socially, they begin to accumulate small changes in phonology, morphology, and syntax (which occur continuously in any language). These variant forms of language are considered **dialects** when the differences in phonology, morphology, and syntax are not great enough to produce unintelligibility. Eventually, if the separation continues, the former dialects of the same language will become separate languages; that is, they will become mutually unintelligible, as German and English now are. Geographic barriers, such as large bodies of water, deserts, and mountains, may separate speakers of what was once the same language, but distance by itself can also produce divergence. For example, if we compare dialects of English in the British Isles, it is clear that the regions farthest away from each other are the most different linguistically (compare the northeast of Scotland and London).[38]

Whereas isolation brings gradual divergence between speech communities, contact results in greater resemblance. This effect is particularly evident when contact between mutually unintelligible languages introduces borrowed words, which usually name some new item borrowed from the other culture—*tomato, canoe, sushi,* and so on. Bilingual groups within a culture may also introduce foreign words, especially when the mainstream language has no real equivalent. Thus, *salsa* has come into English, and *le weekend* into French.

Conquest and colonization often result in extensive and rapid borrowing, if not linguistic replacement. The Norman conquest of England introduced French as the language of the new aristocracy. It was 300 years before the educated classes began to write in English. During this time the English borrowed words from French and Latin, and the two languages—English and French—became more alike than they would otherwise have been. About 50 percent of the English general vocabulary originated in French. Different social classes may react to language contact differentially. For example, English aristocrats eventually called their meat "pork" and "beef" (derived from the French words), but the people who raised the animals and prepared them for eating continued (at least for a while) to refer to the meat as "pig" and "bull," the original Anglo-Saxon words.

In those 300 years of extensive contact, the grammar of English remained relatively stable. English lost most of its inflections or case endings, but it adopted little of the French grammar. In general, the borrowing of words, particularly free morphemes,[39] is much more common than the borrowing of grammar.[40] As we might expect, borrowing by one language from another can make the borrowing language more different from its *sibling languages* (those derived from a common ancestral language) than it would otherwise be. Partly as a result of the French influence, the English vocabulary looks quite different from the languages to which it is actually most similar in terms of phonology and grammar—German, Dutch, and the Scandinavian languages.

Relationships between Language and Culture

Some attempts to explain the diversity of languages have focused on the possible interactions between language and other aspects of culture. On the one hand, if it can be shown that a culture can affect the structure and content of its language, then it would follow that linguistic diversity derives at least in part from cultural diversity. On the other hand, the direction of influence between culture and language might work in reverse: Linguistic features and structures might affect other aspects of the culture.

Cultural Influences on Language

One way a society's language may reflect its corresponding culture is in **lexical content**, or vocabulary. Which experiences, events, or objects are singled out and given words may be a result of cultural characteristics.

Basic Words for Colors, Plants, and Animals   Early in the twentieth century many linguists pointed to the lexical domain (vocabulary) of color words to illustrate the supposed truth that languages vary arbitrarily or without apparent reason. Different languages not only had different numbers of basic color words (from 2 to 12 or so; for example, the words *red, green,* and *blue* in English), but they also, it was thought, had no consistency in the way they classified or divided the colors of the spectrum. But findings from a comparative (cross-linguistic) study contradicted these traditional presumptions about variation in the number and meaning of basic color words. On the basis of their study of at first 20 and later over 100 languages, Brent Berlin and Paul Kay found that languages did not encode color in completely arbitrary ways.[41]

Although different languages do have different numbers of basic color words, most speakers of any language are very likely to point to the same color chips as the best representatives of particular colors. For example, people the world over mean more or less the same color when they are asked to select the best "red." Moreover, there appears to be a nearly universal sequence by which basic color words are added to a language.[42] If a language has just two basic color words, its speakers will always refer to "black" (or dark) hues and "white" (or light) hues. If a language has three basic color words, the third word will nearly always be "red." The next category to appear is either "yellow" or "grue" (green/blue); then different words for green and blue; and so on. To be sure, we usually do not see the process by which basic color words are added to a language. But we can infer the usual sequence because, for example, if a language has a word for "yellow," it will almost always have a word for "red," whereas having a word for "red" does not mean that the language will have a word for "yellow."

What exactly is a *basic* color word? All languages, even the ones with only two basic color terms, have many different ways of expressing how color varies. For example, in English we have words such as turquoise, blue-green, scarlet, crimson, and sky blue. Linguists do not consider these to be basic color words. In English the basic color words are *white, black, red, green, yellow, blue, brown, pink, purple, orange,* and *gray.* One feature of a basic color word is that it consists of a single morph; it cannot include two or more units of meaning. This feature eliminates combinations such as *blue-green* and *sky blue.* A second feature of a basic color word is that the color it represents is not generally included in a higher-order color term. For example, scarlet and crimson are usually considered variants of red, turquoise a variant of blue. A third feature is that basic terms tend to be the first-named words when people are asked for color words. Finally, for a word to be considered a basic color word, many individual speakers of the language have to agree on the central meaning (in the color spectrum) of the word.[43]

Why do different societies (languages) vary in number of basic color terms? Berlin and Kay suggest that the number of basic color terms in a language increases with technological specialization as color is used to decorate and distinguish objects.[44] Cross-linguistic variation in the number of basic color terms does not mean that some languages make more color distinctions than others. Every language could make a particular distinction by combining words (e.g., "fresh leaf" for green); a language need not have a separate basic term for that color.

There may also be many basic color terms because of a biological factor.[45] Peoples with darker (more pigmented) eyes seem to have more trouble distinguishing colors at the dark (blue-green) end of the spectrum than do peoples with lighter eyes. It might be expected, then, that peoples who live nearer the equator (who tend to have darker eyes, presumably for protection against damaging ultraviolet radiation) would tend to have fewer basic color terms. And they do.[46] Moreover, it seems that both cultural and biological factors are required to account for cross-linguistic variation in the number of basic color terms. Societies tend to have six or more such terms (with separate terms for blue and green) only when they are relatively far from the equator and only when their cultures are more technologically specialized.[47] As we will see in later chapters, technological specialization tends to go with larger communities, more centralized governments, occupational specialization, and more social inequality. Societies with such traits are often referred to in a shorthand way as more "complex," which should not be taken to mean "better."

Cecil Brown has found what seem to be developmental sequences in other lexical domains. Two such domains are general, or *life-form,* terms for plants and for animals. Life-form terms are higher-order classifications. All languages have lower-order terms for specific plants and animals. For example, English has words such as *oak* and *pine, sparrow,* and *salmon.* English speakers make finer distinctions too—*pin oak* and *white pine, white-throated sparrow,* and *red salmon.* But why in some languages do people have a larger number of general terms such as *tree, bird,* and *fish?* It seems that these general terms show a universal developmental sequence too. That is, general terms seem to be added in a somewhat consistent order. After "plant" comes a term for "tree"; then one for "grerb" (small, green, leafy, nonwoody plant); then "bush" (for plants between tree and grerb in size); then "grass"; then "vine."[48] The life-form terms for animals also seem to be added in sequence; after "animal" comes a term for "fish," then "bird," then "snake," then "wug" (for small creatures other than fish, birds, and snakes—for example, worms and bugs), then "mammal."[49]

More complex societies tend to have a larger number of general, or life-form, terms for plants and animals than do simpler societies, just as they tend to have a larger number of basic color terms. Do all realms or domains of vocabulary increase in size as social complexity increases? If we look at the total vocabulary of a language (as can be counted in a dictionary), more complex societies do have larger vocabularies.[50] But we have to remember that complex societies have many kinds of specialists, and dictionaries will include the terms used by such specialists. If we look instead at the nonspecialist **core vocabulary** of languages, it seems that all languages have a core vocabulary of about the same size.[51] Indeed, although some domains increase in size with social complexity, some remain the same and still others decrease. An example of a smaller vocabulary domain in complex societies is that of specific names for plants. Urban North Americans may know general terms for plants, but they know relatively few names for specific plants. The typical individual in a small-scale society can commonly name 400 to 800 plant species; a typical person in our own and similar societies may be able to name only 40 to 80.[52] The number of life-form terms is larger in societies in which ordinary people know less about particular plants and animals.[53]

The evidence now available strongly supports the idea that the vocabulary of a language reflects the everyday distinctions that are important in the society. Those aspects of environment or culture that are of special importance will receive greater attention in the language. For example, many languages lack the possessive transitive verb we write as "have," as in "I have." Instead, the language may say something such as "it is to me." A cross-cultural study has suggested that a language may develop the verb "have" after the speakers of that language have developed a system of private property or personal ownership of resources.[54]

Linguistic Influences on Culture: The Sapir–Whorf Hypothesis

There is general agreement that culture influences language. But there is less agreement about the opposite possibility—that language influences other aspects of culture. Edward Sapir and Benjamin Lee Whorf suggested that language is a force in its own right, that it affects how individuals in a society perceive and conceive reality. This suggestion is known as the *Sapir–Whorf hypothesis*.[55] In comparing the

The word *sushi* has been borrowed in North America to identify a Japanese style of food.

English language with Hopi, Whorf pointed out that English-language categories convey discreteness with regard to time and space, but Hopi does not. English has a discrete past, present, and future, and things occur at a definite time. Hopi expresses things more as ongoing processes without time being apportioned into fixed segments. According to Ronald Wardhaugh, Whorf believed that these language differences lead Hopi and English speakers to see the world differently.[56]

As intriguing as that idea is, the relevant evidence is mixed. Linguists today do not generally accept the view that language coerces thought, but some suspect that particular features of language may facilitate certain patterns of thought.[57] The influences may be clearest in poetry and metaphors, where words and phrases are applied to other than their ordinary subjects, as in "all the world's a stage."[58] One of the serious problems in testing the Sapir–Whorf hypothesis is that researchers need to figure out how to separate the effects of other aspects of culture from the effects of language.

One approach that may reveal the direction of influence between language and culture is to study how children in different cultures (speaking different languages) develop concepts as they grow up. If language influences the formation of a particular concept, we might expect that children will acquire that concept earlier in societies where the languages emphasize that concept. For example, some languages make more of gender differences than others. Do children develop gender identity earlier when their language emphasizes gender? (Very young girls and boys seem to believe they can switch genders by dressing in opposite-sex clothes, suggesting that they have not yet developed a stable sense that they are unchangeably girls or boys.) Alexander Guiora and his colleagues have studied children growing up in Hebrew-speaking homes (Israel), English-speaking homes (the United States), and Finnish-speaking homes (Finland). Hebrew has the most gender emphasis of the three languages; all nouns are either masculine or feminine, and even second-person and plural pronouns are differentiated by gender. English emphasizes gender less, differentiating by gender only in the third-person singular (*she* or *her* or *hers*, *he* or *him* or *his*). Finnish emphasizes gender the least; although some words, such as *man* and *woman*, convey gender, differentiation by gender is otherwise lacking in the language. Consistent with the idea that language may influence thought, Hebrew-speaking children acquire the concept of stable gender identity the earliest on the average, Finnish-speaking children the latest.[59]

Another approach is to predict from language differences how people may be expected to perform in experiments. Comparing the Yucatec Mayan language and English, John Lucy predicted that English speakers might recall the *number* of things presented more than Yucatec Mayan speakers. For most classes of nouns, English requires a linguistic way of indicating whether something is singular or plural. You cannot say "I have dog" (no indication of number), but must say "I have a dog," "I have dogs," or "I have one (two, three, several, many) dogs." Yucatec Maya, like English, can indicate a plural, but allows the noun to be neutral with regard to number. In a number of experiments, Yucatec Mayan and American English speakers were equally likely to recall the objects in a picture, but they differed in how often they described the number of a particular object in the picture. Yucatec Mayan speakers did so less often, consistent with their language's lack of insistence on indicating number.[60] So the salience of number in the experiments was probably a consequence of how the languages differ.

Ethnography of Speaking

Many linguists are concerned with the *ethnography of speaking*—that is, with cultural and subcultural patterns of speech variation in different social contexts.[61] The sociolinguist might ask, for example, what kinds of things one talks about in casual conversation with a stranger. A foreigner may know English vocabulary and grammar well but may not know that one typically chats with a stranger about the weather or where one comes from, and not about what one ate that day or how much money one earns.

A foreigner may be familiar with much of the culture of a North American city, but if that person divulges the real state of his or her health and feelings to the first person who says, "How are you?" he or she has much to learn about "small talk" in North American English.

Similarly, North Americans tend to get confused in societies where greetings are quite different from ours. People in some other societies may ask as a greeting, "Where are you going?" or "What are you cooking?" Some Americans may think such questions are rude; others may try to answer in excruciating detail, not realizing that only vague answers are expected, just as we don't really expect a detailed answer when we ask people how they are.

Social Status and Speech

That a foreign speaker of a language may know little about the small talk of that language is but one example of the sociolinguistic principle that what we say and how we say it are not wholly predictable by the rules of our language. Who we are socially and whom we are talking to may greatly affect what we say and how we say it.

In a study interviewing children in a New England town, John Fischer noted that in formal interviews, children were likely to pronounce the ending in words such as *singing* and *fishing,* but in informal conversations they said *"singin'"* and *"fishin'."* Moreover, he noted that the phenomenon also appeared to be related to social class; children from higher-status families were less likely to drop the ending than were children from lower-status families. Subsequent studies in English-speaking areas tend to support Fischer's observations with regard to this speech pattern.[62]

Status can also influence the way people speak to each other. Terms of address are a good example. In English, forms of address are relatively simple. One is called either by a first name or by a title (such as *Doctor, Professor, Ms.,* or *Mister*) followed by a last name. Terms of address in English vary with the nature of the relationship between the speakers.[63] The reciprocal use of first names generally signifies an informal or intimate relationship between two persons. A title and last name used reciprocally usually indicates a more formal or businesslike relationship between individuals who are roughly equal in status. Nonreciprocal use of first names and titles in English is reserved for speakers who recognize a marked difference in status between them. This status difference can be a function of age, as when a child refers to her mother's friend as Mrs. Miller and is in turn addressed as Sally, or can be due to occupational hierarchy, as when a person refers to his boss as Ms. Ramirez and is in turn addressed as Joe.

Strangers in North America shake hands when they meet; friends touch each other more warmly. How we speak to others also differs according to the degree of friendship.

Gender Differences in Speech

In many societies the speech of men differs from the speech of women. The variation can be slight, as in our own society, or more extreme, as with the Carib Indians in the Lesser Antilles of the West Indies, among whom women and men use different words for the same concepts.[64] In Japan, males and females use entirely different words for numerous concepts (e.g., the male word for water is *mizu*, the female version is *ohiya*), and females often add the polite prefix *o-* (females tend to say *ohasi* for chopsticks; males tend to say *hasi*).[65] In the United States and other Western societies, there are differences in the speech of females and males, but they are not as dramatic as in the Carib and Japanese cases. For example, earlier we noted the tendency for the *g* to be dropped in words such as *singing* when the situation is informal and when the social class background is lower. Women are more likely than men to keep the *g* sound and less likely than men to drop the *h* in words such as *happy*.[66] Gender differences occur in intonation and in phrasing of sentences as well. Robin Lakoff found that, in English, women tend to answer questions with sentences that have rising inflections at the end instead of a falling intonation associated with a firm answer. Women also tend to add questions to statements, such as "They caught the robber last week, didn't they?"[67]

One explanation for the gender differences, particularly with regard to pronunciation, is that women in many societies may be more concerned than men with being "correct."[68] In societies with social classes, what is considered more correct by the average person may be what is associated with the upper class. In other societies, what is older may be considered more correct. Gender differences in speech may parallel some of the gender differences noted in other social behavior (as we will see in the chapter on sex and gender): Girls are more likely than boys to behave in ways that are acceptable to adults.

There are not enough studies to know just how common it is for women to exhibit more linguistic "correctness." We do know of some instances where it is not the case. For example, in a community in Madagascar where people speak Merina, a dialect of Malagasy, it is considered socially correct to avoid explicit directives. So instead of directly ordering an action, a Merina speaker will try to say it indirectly. Also, it is polite to avoid negative remarks, such as expressing anger toward someone. In this community, however, it is women, not men, who often break the rules; women speak more directly and express anger more often.[69] This difference may be related to the fact that women are more involved in buying and selling in the marketplace.

Men and women typically differ in what they talk about, or do not talk about. Deborah Tannen offers some examples. When women hear about someone else's troubles they are likely to express understanding of the other's feelings; in contrast, men are likely to offer solutions. Men tend not to ask for directions; women do. Women tend to talk a lot in private settings; men talk more in public settings. These and other differences can cause friction and misunderstanding between the genders. When women express their troubles and men offer solutions, women feel that their feelings are not understood; men are frustrated that the women do not take their solutions seriously. Men may prefer to sit at home quietly and feel put-upon to have to engage in conversation; women feel slighted when men avoid extended conversations with them. Why these differences? Tannen suggests that misunderstanding between men and women arises because boys and girls grow up in somewhat different cultures. Girls typically play in small groups, talk frequently, and are intimate with others. Boys more often play in large groups in which jockeying for status and attention are more of a concern. Higher-status individuals give directions and solutions; they do not seek directions or solutions. So asking for directions is like acknowledging lower status. But large play groups resemble public settings, and so later in life men feel more comfortable speaking in public. Women, in contrast, are more comfortable speaking in small, intimate groups.[70]

Multilingualism and Codeswitching

For many people the ability to speak more than one language is a normal part of life. One language may be spoken at home and another in school, the marketplace, or government. Or more than one language may be spoken at home if family members come from different cultures and still other languages are spoken outside. Some countries explicitly promote multilingualism. For example, Singapore has four official languages—English, Mandarin (one of the Chinese languages), Tamil, and Malay. English is stressed for trade, Mandarin as the language of communication with most of China, Malay as the language of the general region, and Tamil as the language of an important ethnic group. Moreover, most of the population speaks Hokkien, another Chinese language. Education is likely to be in English and Mandarin.[71]

What happens when people who know two or more languages communicate with each other? Very often you find them **codeswitching**, using more than one language in the course of conversing.[72] Switching can occur in the middle of a Spanish-English bilingual sentence, as in "No van a bring it up in the meeting" ("They are not going to bring it up in the meeting").[73] Or switching can occur when the topic or situation changes, such as from social talk to schoolwork. Codeswitching involves a great deal of knowledge of two or more languages and an awareness of what is considered appropriate or inappropriate in the community. For example, in the Puerto Rican community in New York City, codeswitching within the same sentence seems to be common in speech among friends, but if a stranger who looks like a Spanish speaker approaches, the language will shift entirely to Spanish.[74]

Codeswitching may need to be understood in terms of the broader political and historical context. For example, German speakers in Transylvania, where Romanian is the national language, hardly ever codeswitch to Romanian. Perhaps the reason is that, before the end of World War II, German speakers were a privileged economic group who looked down upon landless Romanians and their language. Under socialism, the German speakers lost their economic privilege, but they continued to speak German among themselves. In the rare cases that Romanian is used among German speakers, it tends to be associated with low-status speech, such as singing bawdy songs. The opposite situation occurred in a Hungarian region of German-speaking Austria. The people of this agricultural region, annexed to Austria in 1921, were fairly poor peasant farmers. After World War II, business expansion began to attract labor from rural areas, so many Hungarians eagerly moved into jobs in industry. German was seen by the younger generations as a symbol of higher status and upward mobility; not surprisingly, codeswitching between Hungarian and German became part of their conversations. Indeed, in the third generation, German has become the language of choice, except when speaking to the oldest Hungarians. The Hungarian-Austrian situation is fairly common in many parts of the world, where the language of the politically dominant group ends up being "linguistically dominant."[75]

Writing and Literacy

Most of us have come to depend on writing for so many things that it is hard to imagine a world without it. Yet humans spent most of their history on earth without written language and many, if not most, important human achievements predate written language. Parents and other teachers passed on their knowledge by oral instruction and demonstration. Stories, legends, and myths abounded—the stuff we call oral literature—even in the absence of writing. This is not to say that writing is not important. Far more information and far more literature can be preserved for a longer period of time with a writing system. The earliest writing systems are only about 6,000 years old and are associated with early cities and

WHY ARE "MOTHER TONGUES" RETAINED, AND FOR HOW LONG?

The longer an immigrant group lives in another country, the more they incorporate the culture of their new home. At some point the original language is no longer even partially understood. Consider people who originally came from Wales, the region west of England in Great Britain. In that region, until about 100 years ago, most people spoke the Welsh language, which belongs to the Celtic subfamily of Indo-European along with Irish and Scottish Gaelic and Breton. (Celtic is a different subfamily from the one English belongs to, which is Germanic.) In 1729, the Welsh in Philadelphia established the Welsh Society, the oldest ethnic organization in the United States. Many of the members, if not all, spoke Welsh in addition to English at that time, but by the twentieth century hardly any of their descendants did.

If immigrant groups eventually lose their "mother tongues" in many if not most countries, this doesn't mean that the process occurs at the same speed in every group. Why is that? Why do some immigrant groups lose their language faster than others? Is it because they do not live in tightly knit ethnic enclaves? Or because they marry outside their ethnic group? Or because they do not have traditional festivals or celebrations marking their separate identity? A comparative study by Robert Schrauf discovered the most likely reasons. First, Schrauf assessed the degree to which immigrant groups coming to North America retained their native language over time. The greatest retention was defined as when the third generation (the grandchildren of immigrants) continued to use the native language. Examples were Chicanos, Puerto Ricans, Cubans, and Haitians. On the other hand, in some groups the third generation had no comprehension of the native language except for isolated words. Even the second generation (the children of immigrants) mostly spoke and understood only English. Examples were Italians, Armenians, and Basques. Chinese and Koreans were in the middle, with some evidence that the third generation understands a little of the native language. Schrauf then measured seven social factors that might explain longer versus shorter retention of the mother tongue. He looked at whether the group lived in tightly knit communities, retained religious rituals from the old country, had separate schools and special festivals, visited their homeland, did not intermarry, or worked with others of their ethnic group.

Schrauf used data on 11 North American ethnic groups drawn from the HRAF Collection of Ethnography. The major advantage of the HRAF materials is that ethnographies written for more general purposes, or for purposes other than linguistic ones, contain a wealth of information concerning sociocultural features of ethnic groups that may be tested for their possible effects on language retention and loss.

We might suspect that all of the factors measured by Schrauf would lead people to retain their native language (and presumably other native cultural patterns). But not all do, apparently. Only living in tightly knit communities and retaining religious rituals strongly predict retention of the mother tongue in the home into the third generation. Why? Possibly because living in an ethnic community and religious ritual are experienced early in life. Conditions associated with early socialization might have more lasting effects than conditions experienced later in life, such as schooling, visits to the homeland, marriage, and work. Participation in celebrations and festivals is probably important, too, but it does not have quite as strong an effect, perhaps because celebrations and festivals are not everyday experiences.

As always, in the case of research, this study raises questions for future research. Would the same effects be found outside of North America? Would the results be the same if we looked also at other immigrant groups in North America? Do some immigrant groups live in close-knit communities because of discrimination or choice? If choice, are some groups more interested in assimilating than others? And if so, why?

Sources: D. Douglas Caulkins, "Welsh," in David Levinson and Melvin Ember, eds., *American Immigrant Cultures: Builders of a Nation,* 2 vols. (New York: Macmillan Reference, 1997), vol. 2, pp. 935–41; Robert W. Schrauf, "Mother Tongue Maintenance among North American Ethnic Groups," *Cross-Cultural Research,* 33 (1999): 175–92.

Children do not need help learning the language spoken in their homes. However, reading and writing cannot usually be learned without instruction. Nowadays children in most cultures are expected to learn to read and write in school. These Trobriand children from Papua New Guinea are allowed to wear their traditional clothes to school once a week.

states. Early writing is associated with systematic record-keeping—keeping of ledgers for inventorying goods and transactions. In early times probably only the elite could read and write—indeed it is only recently that universal literacy (the ability to read and write) has become the goal of most countries. But in most countries the goal of universal literacy is far from achieved. Even in countries with universal education the quality of education and the length of education varies considerably between subcultures and genders. Just as some ways of speaking are considered superior to others, a high degree of literacy is usually considered superior to illiteracy.[76] But literacy in what language or languages? Recent efforts to preserve languages have encouraged writing of texts in languages that were only spoken previously. Obviously, there will be few texts in those languages; other languages have vast numbers of written texts. As more and more accumulated knowledge is written and stored in books, journals, and databases, attainment of literacy in those written languages will be increasingly critical to success. And texts do not only convey practical knowledge—they may also convey attitudes, beliefs, and values that are characteristic of the culture associated with the language in which the texts are written.

Summary

1. The essential function language plays in all societies is that of communication. Although human communication is not limited to spoken language, such language is of overriding importance because it is the primary vehicle through which culture is shared and transmitted.

2. Systems of communication are not unique to humans. Other animal species communicate in a variety of ways—by sound, odor, body movement, and so forth. The ability of chimpanzees and gorillas to learn and use sign language suggests that symbolic communication is not unique to humans. Still, human language is distinctive as a communication system in that its spoken and symbolic nature permits an infinite number of combinations and recombinations of meaning.

3. Nonverbal human communication includes posture, mannerisms, body movement, facial expressions, and signs and gestures. Nonverbal human communication also includes tone of voice, accent, nonword sounds, and all the optional vocal features that communicate meaning apart from the language itself.

4. Descriptive (or structural) linguists try to discover the rules of phonology (the patterning of sounds), morphology (the patterning of sound sequences and words), and syntax (the patterning of phrases and sentences) that predict how most speakers of a language talk.

5. By comparative analysis of cognates (words similar in sound and meaning) and grammar, historical linguists test the notion that certain languages derive from a common ancestral language, or protolanguage. The goals are to reconstruct the features of the protolanguage, to hypothesize how the offspring languages separated from the protolanguage or from each other, and to establish the approximate dates of such separations.

6. When two groups of people speaking the same language lose communication with each other because they become separated either physically or socially, they begin to accumulate small changes in phonology, morphology, and syntax. If the separation continues, the two former dialects of the same language will eventually become separate languages—that is, they will become mutually unintelligible.

7. Whereas isolation brings about divergence between speech communities, contact results in greater resemblance. This effect is particularly evident when contact between mutually unintelligible languages introduces borrowed words, most of which name some new item borrowed from the other culture.

8. Some attempts to explain the diversity of languages have focused on the possible interaction between language and other aspects of culture. On the one hand, if it can be shown that a culture can affect the structure and content of its language, then it would follow that linguistic diversity derives at least in part from cultural diversity. On the other hand, the direction of influence between culture and language might work in reverse; the linguistic structures might affect other aspects of the culture.

9. In recent years, some linguists have begun to study variations in how people actually use language when speaking. This type of linguistic study, called sociolinguistics, is concerned with the ethnography of speaking—that is, with cultural and subcultural patterns of speaking in different social contexts.

10. In bilingual or multilingual populations, codeswitching (using more than one language in the course of conversing) has become increasingly common.

11. Written language dates back only about 6,000 years, but writing and written records have become increasingly important; literacy is now a major goal of most countries.

Glossary Terms

accent (p. 45)
codeswitching (p. 63)
core vocabulary (p. 59)
dialects (p. 56)
lexical content (p. 57)
lexicon (p. 53)
morph (p. 53)
morpheme (p. 53)

morphology (p. 51)
phones (p. 51)
phoneme (p. 51)
phonology (p. 51)
protolanguage (p. 55)
syntax (p. 51)
symbolic communication (p. 45)

Critical Questions

1. Why might natural selection have favored the development of true language in humans but not in apes?

2. Would the world be better off with many different languages spoken or with just one universal language? Why do you think so?

3. Discuss some new behavior or way of thinking that led people to adopt or invent new vocabulary or some new pattern of speech.

CHAPTER 4

ECONOMICS

Chapter Outline

- Getting Food
- The Origin, Spread, and Intensification of Food Production
- Allocation of Resources
- Conversion of Resources
- Distribution of Goods and Services

When we think of economics, we think of things and activities involving money. We think of the costs of goods and services, such as food, rent, haircuts, and movie tickets. We may also think of factories, farms, and other enterprises that produce the goods and services we need, or think we need. In industrial societies, workers may stand before a moving belt for eight hours, tightening identical bolts that glide by. For this task they are given bits of paper that may be exchanged for food, shelter, and other goods or services. But many societies—indeed, most that are known to anthropology—did not have money or the equivalent of the factory worker. Still, all societies have economic systems, whether or not they involve money. All societies have customary ways to get food. They also have rules specifying how people gain access to natural resources and ways of transforming or converting those resources, through labor, into necessities and other goods and services. Finally, all societies have customs for distributing goods and services.

As we shall see in this chapter, a great deal of the cross-cultural variation in economic systems is related to how a society gets its food.

Getting Food

For most people in our society, getting food is a trip to the supermarket. Within an hour, we can gather enough food from the shelves to last us a week. Seasons don't daunt us. Week after week, we know food will be there. But we do not think of what would happen if the food were not delivered to the supermarket. We wouldn't be able to eat, and without eating for a while, we would die. Despite the old adage "Man [or woman] does not live by bread alone," without bread or the equivalent we could not live at all. Food-getting activities, then, take precedence over other activities important to survival. Reproduction, social control (the maintenance of peace and order within a group), defense against external threat, and the transmission of knowledge and skills to future generations—none could take place without energy derived from food. But it is not merely energy that is required for survival and long-term reproduction. Food-getting strategies need to provide the appropriate combination of nutrients throughout varying seasons and changing environmental conditions.

In this section we look first at the ways different societies get food and discuss some of the features associated with the different patterns.

Food Collection

Food collection may be generally defined as a food-getting strategy that obtains wild plant and animal resources through gathering, hunting, scavenging, or fishing. Although this was the way humans got their food for most of human history, food collectors in the world today, also referred to as **foragers** or **hunter-gatherers**, are not very numerous and most of them live in what have been called the *marginal areas* of the earth—deserts, the Arctic, and dense tropical forests—habitats that do not allow easy exploitation by modern agricultural technologies. In the last few hundred years only about 5 million people are or were foragers.[1]

Anthropologists are interested in studying the relatively few food-collecting societies still available for observation because these groups may help us understand some aspects of human life in the past, when all people were foragers. But we must be cautious in drawing inferences about the past from our observations of recent and contemporary food collectors, for three reasons. First, early foragers lived in almost all types of environments, including some very bountiful ones. Therefore, what we observe among recent and contemporary food collectors, who generally live in deserts, the Arctic, and tropical forests, may not be comparable to what would have been observable in more favorable environments in the past.[2] Second, contemporary foragers are not relics of the past. Like all contemporary societies, they have evolved and are still evolving. Third, recent and contemporary foragers have been interacting with kinds of societies that did not exist until after 10,000 years ago—agriculturalists, pastoralists, and intrusive, powerful state societies.[3] Many foraging people increasingly depend on agriculture, trade, or commercial activities, so what we see recently may be very different from the past. Let us examine one area of the world where recent food collectors were the only inhabitants until about 200 years ago.

Australian Aborigines   Before Europeans came to the Australian continent, all the people who lived there (who are referred to as *aborigines*) depended on food collection. Although the way of life of Australian aborigines is now considerably altered, we consider the life of the Ngatatjara as described by Richard Gould in the 1960s, when they still lived by gathering wild plants and hunting wild animals in the Gibson Desert of western Australia.[4]

The desert environment of the Ngatatjara averages less than 8 inches of rain per year, and the temperature in summer may rise to 118°F. The few permanent waterholes are separated by hundreds of square miles of sand, scrub, and rock. Even before Europeans arrived in Australia, the area was sparsely populated—fewer than one person per 35 to 40 square miles. Now there are even fewer people, because the aboriginal population was decimated by introduced diseases and mistreatment after the Europeans arrived.

On a typical day, the camp begins to stir just before sunrise, while it is still dark. Children are sent to fetch water, and the people breakfast on water and food left over from the night before. In the cool of the early morning, the adults talk and make plans for the day. The talking goes on for a while. Where should they go for food—to places they have been to recently or to new places? Sometimes there are other considerations. For example, one woman may want to search for plants whose bark she needs to make new sandals. When the women decide which plants they want to collect and where they think those plants are most likely to be found, they take up their digging sticks and set out with large wooden bowls of drinking water on their heads. Their children ride on their hips or walk alongside. Meanwhile, the men may have decided to hunt emus, 6-foot-tall ostrichlike birds that do not fly. The men go to a creekbed where they will wait to ambush any game that may come along. They lie patiently behind a screen of brush they have set up, hoping for a chance to throw a spear at an emu or even a kangaroo. They can throw only once, because if they miss, the game will run away.

By noon, the men and women are usually back at camp, the women with their wooden bowls each filled with up to 15 pounds of fruit or other plant foods, the men more often than not with only some small game, such as lizards and rabbits. The men's food-getting is less certain of success than the women's, so most of the Ngatatjara aborigines' diet is plant food. The daily cooked meal is eaten toward evening, after an afternoon spent resting, gossiping, and making or repairing tools.

The aborigines traditionally were nomadic, moving their campsites fairly frequently. The campsites were isolated and inhabited by only a small number of people, or they were clusters of groups including as many as 80 persons. The aborigines never established a campsite right next to a place with water. If they were too close, their presence would frighten game away and might cause tension with neighboring bands, who also would wait for game to come to the scarce watering spots.

Today many aborigines live in small settled villages. For example, in the 1980s, Victoria Burbank worked in a village she calls "Mangrove" in the Northern Territory of Australia. The once-nomadic aborigines live in a village of about 600, which was founded in the 1950s around a Protestant mission.

Their houses have stoves, refrigerators, toilets, washing machines, and even television sets. Their children attend school full time, and there is a health clinic for their medical needs. They still do some foraging, but most of their food comes from the store. Some earn wages, but many subsist on government welfare checks.[5]

General Features of Food Collectors   Despite the differences in terrain and climate under which they live and the different food-collecting technologies they use, Australian aborigines, Inuit (Eskimo), and most other recent foragers had certain characteristic cultural patterns (see Table 4.1). Most lived in small communities in sparsely populated territories and followed a nomadic lifestyle, forming no permanent settlements. As a rule, they did not recognize individuals' land rights. Their communities generally did not have different classes of people and tended to have no specialized or full-time political officials.[6] Division of labor in food-collecting societies was based largely on age and gender: Men exclusively hunted large marine and land animals and usually did most of the fishing, and women usually gathered wild plant foods.[7]

  When we say that food collectors tend to have certain traits, this does not mean that all of them have those traits. There is considerable variability among societies that depend on foraging. Food-collecting societies that depend heavily on fishing (such as on the Pacific Coast of the northwestern United States

Table 4.1 Variation in Food-Getting and Associated Features				
	Food Collectors		**Food Producers**	
	Foragers	**Horticulturalists**	**Pastoralists**	**Intensive Agriculturalists**
Population density	Lowest	Low-moderate	Low	Highest
Maximum community size	Small	Small-moderate	Small	Large (towns and cities)
Nomadism/ permanence of settlements	Generally nomadic or seminomadic	More sedentary: communities may move after several years	Generally nomadic or seminomadic	Permanent communities
Food shortages	Infrequent	Infrequent	Frequent	Frequent
Trade	Minimal	Minimal	Very important	Very important
Full-time craft specialists	None	None or few	Some	Many (high degree of craft specialization)
Individual differences in wealth	Generally none	Generally minimal	Moderate	Considerable
Political leadership	Informal	Some part-time political officials	Part- and full-time political officials	Many full-time political officials

and Canada or on the south coast of New Guinea) are more likely to have bigger and more permanent communities and somewhat more social inequality than do those societies elsewhere who mostly forage for game and plants.[8] The Pacific Coast and New Guinea coastal people also tend to have higher population densities, food storage,[9] occupational specialization, resource ownership, slavery, and competitiveness.[10] For example, two foraging groups that depended heavily on annual salmon runs were the Tlingit of southeastern Alaska and the Nimpkish of British Columbia. Both groups had a three-tiered class system with a high class, commoners, and slaves. The high-status individuals were obliged to stage competitive elaborate feasts with distributions of valuables.[11] This type of inequality and competitiveness was very different from what we find in typical food collectors, who generally show little social differentiation.

Is there a typical pattern of food-getting among food collectors? Many anthropologists have assumed that foragers typically get their food more from gathering than from hunting, and that women contribute more than men to subsistence, because women generally do the gathering.[12] Although gathering is the most important food-getting activity for some food collectors (e.g., the Ngatatjara aborigines and the !Kung of southern Africa), this is not true for most food-collecting societies known to us. A survey of 180 such societies indicates that there is a lot of variation with regard to which food-getting activity is most important to the society. Gathering is the most important activity for 30 percent of the surveyed societies, hunting for 25 percent, and fishing for 38 percent. (Perhaps, then, we should call most recent food collectors fisher-gatherer-hunters.) In any case, because men generally do the fishing as well as the hunting, the men usually contribute more to food-getting than do the women among recent food collectors.[13]

Because food collectors move their camps often and walk great distances, it may seem that the food-collecting way of life is difficult. Although we do not have enough quantitative studies to tell us what is typical of most food collectors, studies of two Australian aborigine groups[14] and of one !Kung group[15] indicate that those food collectors do not spend many hours getting food. For example, !Kung adults spend an average of about 17 hours per week collecting food. Even when you add the time spent making tools (about 6 hours a week) and doing housework (about 19 hours a week), the !Kung seem to have more leisure time than many agriculturalists, as we discuss later.

Food Production

Beginning about 10,000 years ago, certain peoples in widely separated geographic locations made the revolutionary changeover to **food production**. That is, they began to cultivate and then domesticate plants and animals. (Domesticated plants and animals are different from the ancestral wild forms.) With domestication of these food sources, people acquired control over certain natural processes, such as animal breeding and plant seeding. Today, most peoples in the world depend for their food on some combination of domesticated plants and animals.

Anthropologists generally distinguish three major types of food production systems—horticulture, intensive agriculture, and pastoralism.

Horticulture   The word **horticulture** may conjure up visions of people with "green thumbs" growing orchids and other flowers in greenhouses. But to anthropologists, the word means the growing of crops of all kinds with relatively simple tools and methods, in the absence of permanently cultivated fields. The tools are usually hand tools, such as the digging stick or hoe, not plows or other equipment pulled by animals or tractors. And the methods used do not include fertilization, irrigation, or other ways to restore soil fertility after a growing season.

There are two kinds of horticulture. The more common one involves a dependence on **extensive or shifting cultivation**. The land is worked for short periods and then left idle for some years. During the years when the land is not cultivated, wild plants and brush grow; when the fields are later cleared by *slash-and-burn techniques,* nutrients are returned to the soil. The other kind of horticulture involves a dependence on long-growing tree crops. The two kinds of horticulture may be practiced in the same society, but in neither case is there permanent cultivation of field crops.

Most horticultural societies do not rely on crops alone for food. Many also hunt or fish; a few are nomadic for part of the year. For example, the Kayapo of the Brazilian Amazon leave their villages for as long as three months at a time to trek through the forest in search of game. The entire village participates in a trek, carrying large quantities of garden produce and moving their camp every day.[16] Other horticulturalists raise domestic animals, but these are usually not large animals, such as cattle and camels.[17] More often than not, the animals raised by horticulturalists are smaller ones, such as pigs, chickens, goats, and sheep.

Let us look now at a recent horticultural society, the Yanomamö of the Brazilian-Venezuelan Amazon.

THE YANOMAMÖ   Dense tropical forest covers most of Yanomamö territory. From the air, the typical village is located in a forest clearing and looks like a single, large, circular lean-to with its inner side open to the central plaza. Each individual family has its own portion of the lean-to under the common roof. Each family's portion of the lean-to has a back wall (part of the closed back wall around the circular village structure), but the portions are open on the sides to each other as well as onto the central plaza of the village. The Yanomamö get most of their calories from garden produce, but according to Raymond Hames, the Yanomamö actually spend most of their time foraging.[18]

Before the people can plant, the forest must be cleared of trees and brush. Like most shifting cultivators, the Yanomamö use a combination of techniques: slashing the undergrowth, felling trees, and using controlled burning to clear a garden spot—in other words, **slash-and-burn** horticulture. Before the 1950s, the Yanomamö had only stone axes, so felling trees was quite difficult. Now they have steel machetes and axes given or traded to them by missionaries.

A Yanomamö boy peels cassava.

Because of the work involved in clearing a garden, the Yanomamö prefer to make use of forest patches that have little thorny brush and not too many large trees.[19] After the ground is cleared, the Yanomamö plant plantains, manioc, sweet potatoes, taro, and a variety of plants for medicine, condiments, and craft materials. Men do the heavy clearing work to prepare a garden, and they as well as women plant the crops. Women usually go to the gardens daily to weed and harvest. After two or three years the yields diminish and the forest starts growing back, making continued cultivation less desirable and more difficult, so they abandon the garden and clear a new one. If they can, they clear adjacent forest, but if gardens are far from the village they will move the village to a new location. Villages are moved about every five years because of gardening needs and warfare. There is a great deal of intervillage raiding, so villages are often forced to flee to another location.

Extensive cultivation requires a lot of territory because new gardens are not cleared until the forest grows back. What is often misunderstood is why it is so important to shift gardens. Not only is a burned field easier to plant, but the organic matter that is burned provides necessary nutrients for a good yield. If horticulturalists come back too quickly to a spot with little plant cover, a garden made there will not produce a satisfactory yield.

The Yanomamö crops do not provide much protein, so hunting and fishing are important to their diet. Men hunt birds, peccaries, monkeys, and tapir with bows and arrows. Fishing is enjoyed by women, men, and children. They catch fish by hand, with small bows and arrows, and by stream poisoning. Everybody gathers honey, hearts of palm, Brazil nuts, and cashews, although the men usually climb trees to shake down the nuts. Much of the foraging is done from the village base, but the Yanomamö, like the Kayapo, may go on treks to forage from time to time.

General Features of Horticulturalists   In most horticultural societies, simple farming techniques have tended to yield more food from a given area than is generally available to food collectors. Consequently, horticulture is able to support larger, more densely populated communities. The way of life of horticulturalists is more sedentary than that of food collectors, although communities may move after some years to farm a new series of plots. (Some horticulturalists have permanent villages because they depend mostly on food from trees that keep producing for a long time.) In contrast with most recent food-collecting groups, horticultural societies exhibit the beginnings of social differentiation. For example, some individuals may be part-time craftworkers or part-time political officials, and certain members of a kin group may have more status than other individuals in the society.

Intensive Agriculture   People engaged in **intensive agriculture** use techniques that enable them to cultivate fields permanently. Essential nutrients may be put back in the soil through the use of fertilizers, which may be organic material (most commonly dung from humans or other animals) or inorganic (chemical) fertilizers. But there are other ways to restore nutrients. The Luo of western Kenya plant beans around corn plants. Bacteria growing around the roots of the bean plant replace lost nitrogen, and the corn plant conveniently provides a pole for the bean plant to wind around as it grows. Some intensive agriculturalists use irrigation from streams and rivers to ensure an adequate supply of waterborne nutrients. Crop rotation and plant stubble that has been plowed under also restore nutrients to the soil.

In general, the technology of intensive agriculturalists is more complex than that of horticulturalists. Plows rather than digging sticks are generally employed. But there is enormous variation in the degree to which intensive agriculturalists rely on mechanization rather than hand labor. In some societies the most complex machine is an animal-drawn plow; in the corn and wheat belts of the United States, huge tractors till, seed, and fertilize 12 rows at a time.[20]

Let's look at one group of intensive agriculturalists, those of the Mekong Delta in Vietnam.

RURAL VIETNAM: THE MEKONG DELTA   The village of Khanh Hau, situated along the flat Mekong Delta, comprised about 600 families when it was described by Gerald Hickey in the late 1950s, before the Vietnam War.[21] The delta area has a tropical climate, with a rainy season that lasts from May to November. As a whole, the area has been made habitable only through extensive drainage.

Wet rice cultivation is the principal agricultural activity of Khanh Hau. It is part of a complex, specialized arrangement that involves three interacting components: (1) a complex system of irrigation and water control; (2) a variety of specialized equipment, including plows, waterwheels, threshing sledges, and winnowing machines; and (3) a clearly defined set of socioeconomic roles—from those of landlord, tenant, and laborer to those of rice miller and rice merchant.

In the dry season, the farmer decides what sort of rice crop to plant, whether of long (120 days) or short (90 days) maturation. The choice depends on the capital at his disposal, the current cost of fertilizer, and the anticipated demand for rice. The seedbeds are prepared as soon as the rains have softened the ground in May. The soil is turned over (plowed) and broken up (harrowed) as many as six separate times, with two-day intervals for "airing" between operations. During this time, the rice seeds are soaked in water for at least two days to stimulate sprouting. Before the seedlings are planted, the paddy is plowed once more and harrowed twice in two directions at right angles.

Planting is a delicate, specialized operation that must be done quickly and is performed most often by hired male laborers. But efficient planting is not enough to guarantee a good crop. Proper fertilization and irrigation are equally important. In the irrigating, steps must be taken to ensure that the water level remains at exactly the proper depth over the entire paddy. Water is distributed by means of scoops, wheels, and mechanical pumps. Successive crops of rice ripen from late September to May; all members of the family may be called upon to help with the harvest. After each crop is harvested, it is threshed, winnowed, and dried. Normally, the rice is sorted into three portions: One is set aside for use by the household in the following year; one is for payment of hired labor and other services (such as loans from agricultural banks); and one is for cash sale on the market. Aside from the harvesting, women do little work in the fields, spending most of their time on household chores. In families with little land, however, young daughters help in the fields and older daughters may hire themselves out to other farmers.

The villagers also cultivate vegetables, raise pigs, chickens, and the like, and frequently engage in fishing. The village economy usually supports three or four implement makers and a much larger number of carpenters.

Extensive drainage has made the Mekong Delta region of Vietnam able to support intensive agriculture.

General Features of Intensive Agricultural Societies   Societies with intensive agriculture are more likely than horticulturalists to have towns and cities, a high degree of craft specialization, complex political organization, and large differences in wealth and power. Studies suggest that intensive agriculturalists work longer hours than horticulturalists.[22] For example, men engaged in intensive agriculture average nine hours of work a day, seven days a week; women average almost eleven hours of work per day. Most of the work for women in intensive agricultural societies involves food processing and work in and around the home, but they also spend a lot of time working in the fields. We discuss some of the implications of the work patterns for women in the chapter on sex and gender.

Intensive agricultural societies are more likely than horticultural societies to face famines and food shortages, even though intensive agriculture is generally more productive than horticulture.[23] Why, if more food can be produced per acre, is there more risk of shortage among intensive agriculturalists? Intensive agriculturalists may be more likely to face food shortages because they are often producing crops for a market. Producing for a market pushes farmers to cultivate plants that give them the highest yield rather than cultivating plants that are drought-resistant or that require fewer nutrients. Farmers producing for a market also tend to concentrate on one crop. Crop diversity is often a protection against total crop failure because fluctuations in weather, plant diseases, or insect pests are not likely to affect all the crops. There are also fluctuations in market demand. If the market demand drops and the price falls for a particular crop, farmers may not have enough cash to buy the other food they need.

The Commercialization and Mechanization of Agriculture   Some intensive agriculturalists produce very little for sale; most of what they produce is for their own use. But there is a worldwide trend for intensive agriculturalists to produce more and more for a market. This trend is called **commercialization**, which may occur in any area of life and which involves increasing dependence on buying and selling, usually with money as the medium of exchange.

The increasing commercialization of agriculture is associated with several other trends. One is that farm work is becoming more and more mechanized as hand labor becomes scarce, because of migration to industrial and service jobs in towns and cities, or too expensive. A second trend is the emergence and spread of *agribusiness,* large corporation-owned farms that may be operated by multinational companies and worked by hired, as opposed to family, labor. For example, consider how cotton farming has changed in the southeastern United States. In the 1930s, mules and horses used in plowing were replaced by tractors. This change allowed some landowners to evict their sharecroppers and expand their holdings. After World War II, mechanical cotton pickers replaced most of the harvest laborers. But a farmer had to have a good deal of money or be a corporation to acquire those machines, each of which cost many tens of thousands of dollars.[24] So the mechanization of cotton farming sent many rural farm laborers off to the cities of the North in search of employment, and the agricultural sector increasingly became big business. A third trend associated with the commercialization of agriculture, including animal raising, is a reduction in the proportion of the population engaged in food production. In the United States today, for example, less than 1 percent of the total population work on farms.[25]

Later, in the chapter on culture change and globalization, we more fully discuss some of the apparent consequences of the worldwide changeover to commercial or market economies.

Pastoralism   Most agriculturalists keep and breed some animals (practice animal husbandry), but a small number of societies depend mostly for their living on domesticated herds of animals that feed on natural pasture.[26] We call such a system **pastoralism**. We might assume that pastoralists breed animals to eat their meat, but most do not. Pastoralists more often get their animal protein from live animals in the form of milk, and some pastoralists regularly take blood, which is rich in protein, from their animals to mix with other foods. The herds often indirectly provide food because many pastoralists trade animal products for plant foods and other necessities. In fact, a large proportion of their food may actually come from trade with agricultural groups.[27] For example, some pastoral groups in the Middle East derive much of their livelihood from the sale of what we call oriental rugs, which are made on hand looms from the wool of their sheep. One pastoral society we shall examine are the Lapps or Saami of Scandinavia.

THE LAPPS   The Lapps or Saami practice reindeer herding in northwestern Scandinavia where Finland, Sweden, and Norway share common frontiers. It is a typical Arctic habitat: cold, windswept, with long, dark days for half the year. Considerable change has occurred recently, so we first discuss the food-getting strategy in the 1950s, as described by Ian Whitaker and T. I. Itkonen.[28]

The Lapps herd their reindeer either intensively or, more often, extensively. In the *intensive system,* the herd is constantly under observation within a fenced area for the whole year. Intensively herded reindeer and other animals are accustomed to human contact. Hence, the summer corralling of the females for milking and the breaking in of the ox-reindeer for use as work animals are not difficult tasks. The *extensive system* involves allowing the animals to migrate over a large area. It requires little surveillance and encompasses large herds. Under this system, the reindeer are allowed to move through their seasonal feeding cycles watched by only one or two scouts. The other Lapps stay with the herd only when it has settled in its summer or winter habitat. But milking, breaking in, and corralling are harder in the extensive than in the intensive system because the animals are less accustomed to humans.

Even under the extensive system, which theoretically permits Lapps to engage in subsidiary economic activities such as hunting and fishing, the reindeer herd is the essential, if not the only, source of income. A family might possess as many as 1,000 reindeer, but usually the figure is half that number. Studies show 200 to be the minimum number of reindeer needed to provide for a family of four or five adults. Women may have shared the herding chores in the past under the intensive system, but now, under the extensive system, men do the herding. Women still do the milking. The Lapps eat the meat of the bull reindeer; the female reindeer are kept for breeding purposes. Bulls are slaughtered in the fall, after the mating season. Meat and hides are frequently sold or bartered for other food and necessities.

Reindeer are still herded nowadays, but snowmobiles, all-terrain vehicles, and even helicopters (instead of sleds) are used for herding. Ferries move reindeer to and from different pastures, and the herders

A Saami reindeer herder feeds two of her animals in the snow.

may be killed by community agreement; this behavior was reported among the !Kung and the Hadza. Finally, particularly among more nomadic groups, people may just move away from a leader they don't like. The active attempts to put down upstarts in many egalitarian societies prompts Christopher Boehm to suggest that dominance comes naturally to humans. Egalitarian societies work hard to reverse that tendency.[3] The Mbuti provide an example of a society almost totally equal: "Neither in ritual, hunting, kinship nor band relations do they exhibit any discernible inequalities of rank or advantage."[4] Their hunting bands have no leaders, and recognition of the achievement of one person is not accompanied by privilege of any sort. Economic resources such as food are communally shared, and even tools and weapons are frequently passed from person to person. Only within the family are rights and privileges differentiated.

Rank Societies

Most societies with social *ranking* practice agriculture or herding, but not all agricultural or pastoral societies are ranked. Ranking is characterized by social groups with unequal access to prestige or status but *not* significantly unequal access to economic resources or power. Unequal access to prestige is often reflected in the position of chief, a rank to which only some members of a specified group in the society can succeed.

Unusual among rank societies were the nineteenth-century Native Americans who lived along the northwestern coast of the United States and the southwestern coast of Canada. An example were the Nimpkish, a Kwakiutl group.[5] These societies were unusual because their economy was based on food collecting. But huge catches of salmon—which were preserved for year-round consumption—enabled them to support fairly large and permanent villages. These societies were similar to food-producing societies in many ways, not just in their development of social ranking. Still, the principal means of proving one's high status was to give wealth away. The tribal chiefs celebrated solemn rites by grand feasts called *potlatches* at which they gave gifts to every guest.[6]

In rank societies, the position of chief is at least partly hereditary. The criterion of superior rank in some Polynesian societies, for example, was genealogical. Usually the eldest son succeeded to the position of chief, and different kinship groups were differentially ranked according to their genealogical distance from the chiefly line. In rank societies, chiefs are often treated with deference by people of lower rank. For example, among the Trobriand Islanders of Melanesia, people of lower rank must keep their heads lower than a person of higher rank. So, when a chief is standing, commoners must bend low. When commoners have to walk past a chief who happens to be sitting, he may rise and they will bend. If the chief chooses to remain seated, they must crawl.[7]

While there is no question that chiefs in a rank society enjoy special prestige, there is some controversy over whether they really do not also have material advantages. Chiefs may sometimes look as if they are substantially richer than commoners, for they may receive many gifts and have larger storehouses. In some instances, the chief may even be called the "owner" of the land. However, Marshall Sahlins maintains that the chief's storehouses only house temporary accumulations for feasts or other redistributions. And although the chief may be designated the "owner" of the land, others have the right to use the land. Furthermore, Sahlins suggests that the chief in a rank society lacks power because he usually cannot make people give him gifts or force them to work on communal projects. Often the chief can encourage production only by working furiously on his own cultivation.[8]

This picture of economic equality in rank societies is beginning to be questioned. Laura Betzig studied patterns of food sharing and labor on Ifaluk, a small atoll in the Western Carolines.[9] Chiefly status

In societies with rank and class, deference is usually shown to political leaders, as in the case of this Fon chief in the lowlands of Cameroon, Africa.

is inherited geneaologically in the female line, although most chiefs are male. (In the sex and gender chapter, we discuss why political leaders are usually male, even in societies structured around women.) As in other chiefly societies, Ifaluk chiefs are accorded deference. For example, during collective meals prepared by all the island women, chiefs were served first and were bowed to. The Ifaluk chiefs are said to control the fishing areas. Were the catches equitably distributed? Betzig measured the amount of fish each household got. All the commoners received an equal share, but the chiefs got extra fish; their households got twice as much per person as other households. Did the chiefs give away more later?

Theoretically, it is generosity that is supposed to even things out, but Betzig found that the gifts from chiefs to other households did not equal the amount the chiefs received from others. Furthermore, while everyone gave to the chiefs, the chiefs gave mostly to their close relatives. On Ifaluk, the chiefs did not work harder than others; in fact, they worked less. Is this true in other societies conventionally considered to be rank societies? We do not know. However, we need to keep in mind that the chiefs in Ifaluk were not noticeably better off either. If they lived in palaces with servants, had elaborate meals, or were dressed in fine clothes and jewelry, we would not need measures of food received or a special study to see if the chiefs had greater access to economic resources, because their wealth would be obvious. But rank societies may not have had as much economic equality as we used to think.

Class Societies

In class societies, as in rank societies, there is unequal access to prestige. But, unlike rank societies, class societies are characterized by groups of people that have substantially greater or lesser access to economic resources and power. That is, not every social group has the same opportunity to obtain land, animals, money, or other economic benefits or the same opportunity to exercise power that other groups have. Fully stratified or class societies range from somewhat open to virtually closed class, or caste, systems.

Open Class Systems

A **class** is a category of persons who all have about the same opportunity to obtain economic resources, power, and prestige. Different classes have differing opportunities. We call class systems *open* if there is some possibility of moving from one class to another. Although class status is not fully determined at birth in open class societies, there is a high probability that most people will stay close to the class into which they were born and will marry within that class. Classes tend to perpetuate themselves through the inheritance of wealth. John Brittain suggested that, in the United States, the transfer of money through bequests accounts for much of the wealth of the next generation. As we might expect, the importance of inheritance seems to increase at higher levels of wealth. That is, the wealth of richer people comes more from inheritance than does the wealth of not-so-rich people.[10]

Other mechanisms of class perpetuation may be more subtle, but they are still powerful. In the United States there are many institutions that make it possible for an upper-class person to have little contact with other classes. Private day and boarding schools put upper-class children in close contact mostly with others of their class. Attending these schools makes it more likely they will get into universities with higher prestige. Debutante balls and exclusive private parties ensure that young people meet the "right people." Country clubs, exclusive city clubs, and service in particular charities continue the process of limited association. People of the same class also tend to live in the same neighborhoods. Before 1948, explicit restrictions kept certain groups out of particular neighborhoods, but after the U.S. Supreme Court ruled such discrimination unconstitutional, more subtle methods were developed. For instance, zoning restrictions may prohibit multiple-family dwellings in a town or neighborhood and lots below a certain acreage.[11]

Identification with a social class begins early in life. In addition to differences in occupation, wealth, and prestige, social classes vary in many other ways, including religious affiliation, closeness to kin, ideas about child rearing, job satisfaction, leisure-time activities, style of clothes and furniture, and (as noted in the chapter on language and communication) even in styles of speech.[12] People from each class tend to be more comfortable with those from the same class; they talk similarly and are more likely to have similar interests and tastes.

People of the same social class tend to socialize together, where they live or where they vacation. Pictured here is an upscale hotel in Victoria, British Columbia.

Degree of Openness   Some class systems are more open than others; that is, it is easier in some societies to move from one class position to another. Social scientists typically compare the class of a person with the class of his or her parent or parents to measure the degree of mobility. Although most people aspire to move up, mobility also includes moving down. Obtaining more education, particularly a university education, is one of the most effective ways to move upward in contemporary societies. For example, in the United States, college-educated individuals have on average 60 percent more income than those without a college education.[13] In fact, in many countries educational attainment predicts one's social class better than parents' occupation does.[14]

How do the United States and Canada compare with other countries in degree of class mobility? Canada and Sweden have more mobility than the United States, France, and Britain. Japan and Italy have less mobility. If we focus on the ease of moving into the highest class, Italy, France, Spain, Germany, and Japan are more difficult than Britain and the United States.[15]

Class openness also varies over time. In "Paradise," Ontario, Barrett found that the rigid stratification system of the 1950s opened up considerably as new people moved into the community. No one disputed who belonged to the elite in the past. They were of British background, lived in the largest houses, had new cars, and vacationed in Florida. Moreover, they controlled all the leadership positions in the town. By the 1980s, though, the leaders came mostly from the middle and working classes.[16]

Degree of Inequality   Degree of class mobility, however, is not the same as degree of economic inequality. For example, Japan, Italy, and Germany have less mobility than the United States, but less inequality. Degree of inequality can vary considerably over time. In the United States, inequality has fluctuated considerably from the 1900s to the present. The greatest inequality was just before the 1929 stock market crash, when the top 1 percent had 42.6 percent of all the wealth. The least inequality was in the mid-1970s after the stock market declined by 42 percent. Then the top 1 percent controlled 17.6 percent of the wealth.

Change over time in the degree of inequality sometimes appears to have economic causes; for example, the 1929 crash made the wealthy less wealthy. But some of the change over time is due to shifts in public policy. During the New Deal of the 1930s, tax changes and work programs shifted more income to ordinary people; in the 1980s, tax cuts for the wealthy helped the rich get richer. In the 1990s, the rich continued to get richer and the poor got poorer.[17] One way of calculating the disparity between rich and poor is to use the ratio of income held by the top fifth of the households divided by the income held by the bottom fifth. Comparatively speaking, the United States presently has more inequality than any of the countries in western Europe, with a ratio of 9 to 1 (see Figure 5.1 on page 102). That is, the top 20 percent of U.S. households controls nine times the wealth controlled by the bottom 20 percent. Norway, on the other hand, has a ratio of about 3.5 to 1. And Germany has a ratio of about 4.5 to 1. The degree of inequality in the United States exceeds that of India, with a ratio of about 5.5 to 1. South Africa and Brazil are among the most unequal countries, with ratios of 22 to 1 and 24 to 1, respectively.

Recognition of Class

Societies that have open class systems vary in the degree to which members of the society recognize that there are classes, albeit somewhat open classes. The United States is unusual. Despite objective evidence of multiple social classes, many people in the United States deny their existence. The ideology that hard work and strong character can transform anyone into a success appears to be so powerful that it masks the realities of social inequality.[18] A recent poll found that more people in the United States now believe that the chance of moving up has improved in the last few decades when in reality mobility has declined.[19] When we were growing up we were told that "Anyone can be President of the United States." As "proof"

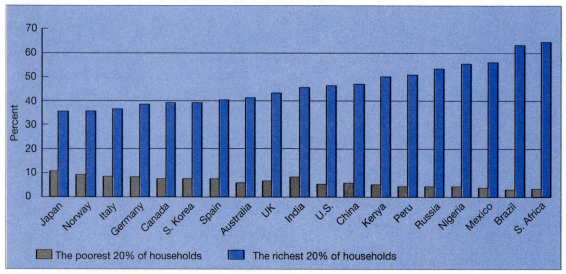

Figure 5.1   Proportion of National Income Earned by the Richest 20 Percent of Households Compared with the Poorest 20 Percent: Selected Country Comparisons

Source: These data are abstracted from *2001 World Development Indicators* (Washington, D.C.: The World Bank, 2001), pp. 70–73.

people pointed to a few individuals who rose from humble beginnings. But consider the odds. How many presidents have come from poor families? How many were not European in background? How many were not Protestant? (And, as we discuss in the next chapter, how many were not male?) So far, all of the presidents of the United States have been European in ancestry, all but one have been Protestant, and all have been male. And only a handful came from humble beginnings. In the Canadian town of "Paradise" the ideology of "classlessness" became more prevalent over time, paralleling the trend in the United States where most people see themselves as "middle class."[20] To move up the social ladder people seem to have to believe that it is possible to do so. However, it is one thing to believe in mobility; it is another thing to deny the existence of classes. Why would people deny that classes exist?

Caste Systems

Some societies have classes that are virtually closed. They are called castes. A **caste** is a ranked group in which membership is determined at birth, and marriage is restricted to members of one's own caste. The only way you can belong is by being born into the group; and since you cannot marry outside the group, your children cannot acquire another caste status either. In India, for example, there are several thousand hereditary castes. Although the precise ranking of these thousands of groups is not clear, there appear to be four main levels of hierarchy. The castes in India are often thought to be associated with different oc-cupations, but that is not quite true. Most Indians live in rural areas and have agricultural occupations, but their castes vary widely.[21]

Castes may exist in conjunction with a more open class system. Indeed, in India today, members of a low caste who can get wage-paying jobs, chiefly those in urban areas, may improve their social stand-ing in the same ways available to people in other class societies. In general, however, they still cannot marry someone in a higher caste, so the caste system is perpetuated.

India has witnessed a marked increase in service and high technology jobs as companies around the world outsource many of their service activities to India. Caste is less important now for jobs.

Questions basic to all stratified societies, and particularly to a caste society, were posed by John Ruskin, a nineteenth-century British essayist: "Which of us . . . is to do the hard and dirty work for the rest—and for what pay? Who is to do the pleasant and clean work, and for what pay?"[22] In India those questions have been answered by the caste system, which mainly dictates how goods and services are exchanged, particularly in rural areas.[23]

Japan also had a caste group within a class society. Now called *burakumin* (instead of the pejorative *Eta*), this group traditionally had occupations that were considered unclean.[24] Comparable to India's Untouchables, they were a hereditary, endogamous (in-marrying) group. Their occupations were traditionally those of farm laborer, leatherworker, and basket weaver; their standard of living was very low. The burakumin are physically indistinguishable from other Japanese.[25] Discrimination against the burakumin was officially abolished by the Japanese government in 1871, but it was not until the twentieth century that the burakumin began organizing to bring about change. These movements appear to be paying off as more active steps have been taken recently by the Japanese government to alleviate discrimination and poverty. As of 1995, 73 percent of burakumin marriages were with non-burakumin. In public opinion polls, two-thirds of burakumin now said that they had not encountered discrimination. However, most burakumin still live in segregated neighborhoods where unemployment, crime, and alcoholism rates are high.[26]

In Rwanda, a country in east-central Africa, a longtime caste system was overthrown, first by an election and then by a revolution in 1959 to 1960. Three castes had existed, each distinguished from the others by physical appearance and occupation.[27] It is believed that the three castes derived from three different language groups that came together through migration and conquest. Later, however, they began to use a common language, although remaining endogamous and segregated by hereditary occupations. The taller and leaner ruling caste, the Tutsi, constituted about 15 percent of the population. They were the landlords and practiced the prestigious occupation of herding. The shorter and stockier agricultural caste, the Hutu, made up about 85 percent of the population. As tenants of the Tutsi, they produced most of the country's food. The much shorter Twa, accounting for less than 1 percent of the population, were foragers who formed the lowest caste.

Colonial rule, first by the Germans and then by the Belgians after World War I, strengthened Tutsi power. When the Hutu united to demand more of the rewards of their labor in 1959, the king and many of the Tutsi ruling caste were driven out of the country. The Hutu then established a republican form of government and declared independence from Belgium in 1962. In this new government, however, the forest-dwelling Twa were generally excluded from full citizenship. In 1990, Tutsi rebels invaded from

Uganda, and attempts were made to negotiate a multiparty government. However, civil war continued, and in 1994 alone over a million people, mostly Tutsi, were killed. Almost 2 million refugees, mostly Hutu, fled to Zaire (now Congo) as the Tutsi-led rebels established a new government.[28]

In the United States, African Americans used to have more of a castelike status determined partly by the inherited characteristic of skin color. Until recently, some states even had laws prohibiting an African American from marrying a European American. When interethnic marriage did occur, children of the union were often regarded as having lower status than European-American children, even though they may have had blond hair and light skin. In the South, where treatment of African Americans as a caste was most apparent, European Americans refused to eat with African Americans or sit next to them at lunch counters, on buses, and in schools. Separate drinking fountains and toilets reinforced the idea of ritual uncleanness. The economic advantages and gains in prestige enjoyed by European Americans are well documented.[29] In the following sections, on slavery, racism, and inequality, we discuss the social status of African Americans in more detail.

Slavery

Slaves are persons who do not own their own labor, and as such they represent a class. We may associate slavery with a few well-known examples, such as ancient Egypt, Greece, and Rome or the southern United States, but slavery has existed in some form in almost every part of the world at one time or another, in simpler as well as in more complex societies. Slaves are often obtained from other cultures directly: kidnapped, captured in war, or given as tribute. Or they may be obtained indirectly as payment in barter or trade. Slaves sometimes come from the same culture; one became a slave as payment of a debt, as a punishment for a crime, or even as a chosen alternative to poverty. Slave societies vary in the degree to which it is possible to become freed from slavery.[30] Sometimes the slavery system has been a closed class, or caste, system, sometimes a relatively open class system. In different slave-owning societies, slaves have had different, but always some, legal rights.[31]

In ancient Greece, slaves often were conquered enemies. Because city-states were constantly conquering one another or rebelling against former conquerors, slavery was a threat to everyone. After the Trojan War, the transition of Hecuba from queen to slave was marked by her cry, "Count no one happy, however fortunate, before he dies."[32] Nevertheless, Greek slaves were considered human beings, and they could even acquire some higher-class status along with freedom. Andromache, Hecuba's daughter-in-law, was taken as a slave and concubine by one of the Greek heroes. When his legal wife produced no children, Andromache's slave son became heir to his father's throne. Although slaves had no rights under law, once they were freed, either by the will of their master or by purchase, they and their descendants could become assimilated into the dominant group. In other words, slavery in Greece was not seen as the justified position of inferior people. It was regarded, rather, as an act of fate—"the luck of the draw"—that relegated one to the lowest class in society.

Among the Nupe, a society in central Nigeria, slavery was of quite another type.[33] The methods of obtaining slaves—as part of the booty of warfare and, later, by purchase—were similar to those of Europeans, but the position of the slaves was very different. Mistreatment was rare. Male slaves were given the same opportunities to earn money as other dependent males in the household—younger brothers, sons, or other relatives. A slave might be given a garden plot of his own to cultivate, or he might be given a commission if his master was a craftsman or a tradesman. Slaves could acquire property, wealth, and even slaves of their own. But all of a slave's belongings went to the master at the slave's death.

Manumission—the granting of freedom to slaves—was built into the Nupe system. If a male slave could afford the marriage payment for a free woman, the children of the resulting marriage were free; the man himself, however, remained a slave. Marriage and concubinage were the easiest ways out of bondage

When people support themselves by what they collect and produce, as most did until a few thousand years ago, it's difficult to compare the standards of living of different societies because we cannot translate what people have into market or monetary value. It's only when people are at least partly involved in the world market economy that we can measure the standard of living in monetary terms. Today this comparison is possible for most of the world. Many in most societies depend on buying and selling for a living, and the more who depend on international exchange, the more possible it is to compare them in terms of standard economic indicators. We don't have such indicators for all different societies, but we do have them for many countries. Those indicators suggest that the degree of economic inequality in the world is not only very substantial but has generally increased over time.

This conveys just how economically unequal the world is: Surveying households in 91 countries, Branko Milanovic calculated that the richest 1 percent of people in the world have as much total income as 57 percent of the people at the bottom. Over one billion people on earth live on less than one U.S. dollar a day. This level of inequality exceeds the degree of inequality within any individual country. The disparities are not just in terms of income; there are vast inequalities in literacy, access to clean water, and mortality from a wide range of diseases.

Global inequality has increased substantially in the last three decades. To measure the changes, we can compare the ratio between the richest and poorest fifths over time across countries. In 1997, the ratio was 70.4 to 1, which is calculated by dividing the income for the top fifth by the income for the bottom fifth. That ratio has increased since the 1970s, when the ratio was 33.7 to 1. Higher inequality over time does not necessarily mean that the poor are worse off than before; it is possible that the rich can get much richer and the poor remain the same. However, it does seem that the poor have gotten poorer and the rich have gotten richer in the countries of the world. Between 1988 and 1993 Milanovic calculated that the real incomes of the bottom 5 percent dropped by 25 percent, while the incomes of the richest 20 percent grew by about 12 percent.

If the world as a whole is seeing improvements in technology and economic development, why is inequality in the world increasing? As we shall see in the chapter on culture change and globalization, it is often the rich within a society who benefit most from new technology, at least initially. They are not only the most likely to be able to afford it, but also the only ones who can afford to take the risks that it involves. The same may be true for nations. Those that already have capital are more likely than the poorer nations to take advantage of improvements in technology. Also, the poorer countries generally have the highest rates of population growth, so income per capita can fall if population increases faster than the rate of economic development. Economists tell us that a developing country may, at least initially, experience an increase in inequality, but the inequality often decreases over time. Will the inequalities among countries also decrease as the world economy develops further?

The prospect is not entirely bleak. It's true that the disparity between rich and poor countries has increased in recent years, but it's also true that the world economy has improved in some respects. The United Nations has computed a "human development index" for 114 countries, combining measures of life expectancy, literacy, and a measure of per capita purchasing power. According to this index, all countries but Zambia have improved over a period of 30 years, many of them substantially. A child in the world today can expect to live 8 more years than 30 years ago. Literacy has increased from 47 percent in 1970 to 73 percent in 1999. The most progress has occurred in East Asia and the Pacific, the least in sub-Saharan Africa. World leaders at the United Nations Millennium Declaration have committed themselves to a number of goals by the year 2015, including halving the proportion of people living in extreme poverty and halving the proportion of people suffering from hunger. Even if those goals are achieved, much more will remain to be done if we are to achieve a more equal world.

Sources: Human Development Report, UN Development Programme (New York: Oxford University Press, 2001), pp. 9–25; Branko Milanovic, *The Economic Journal,* 112 (2002): 51–92; *State of the World* (New York: Norton, 1994), pp. 1–8; Peter Donaldson, *Worlds Apart* (London: British Broadcasting Corporation, 1971); Philips Foster, *The World Food Problem* (Boulder: Lynne Rienner, 1992), pp. 149–51.

for a slave woman. Once she had produced a child by her master, both she and the child had free status. The woman, however, was only figuratively free; if a concubine, she had to remain in that role. As might be expected, the family trees of the nobility and the wealthy were liberally grafted with branches descended from slave concubines.

The most fortunate slaves among the Nupe were the house slaves. They could rise to positions of power in the household as overseers and bailiffs, charged with law enforcement and judicial duties. (Recall the Old Testament story of Joseph, who was sold into slavery by his brothers. Joseph became a household slave of the pharaoh and rose to the position of second in the kingdom because he devised an ingenious system of taxation.) There was even a titled group of Nupe slaves, the Order of Court Slaves, who were trusted officers of the king and members of an elite. Slave status in general, though, placed one at the bottom of the social ladder. In the Nupe system, few slaves, mainly princes from their own societies, ever achieved membership in the titled group. Nupe slavery was abolished at the beginning of the twentieth century.

In the United States, slavery originated as a means of obtaining cheap labor, but the slaves soon came to be regarded as deserving of their low status because of their alleged inherent inferiority. Because the slaves were from Africa and dark-skinned, some European Americans justified slavery and the belief in "black" people's inferiority by quoting Scripture out of context ("They shall be hewers of wood and drawers of water"). Slaves could not marry or make any other contracts, nor could they own property. In addition, their children were also slaves, and the master had sexual rights over the female slaves. Because the status of slavery was determined by birth in the United States, slaves constituted a caste. During the days of slavery, therefore, the United States had both a caste and a class system. And even after the abolition of slavery, as we have noted, some castelike elements remained. It is important to note that these castelike elements were not limited to the American South where slavery had been practiced. For example, although Indiana was established as a "free" state in 1816, in its first constitution "Negros" did not have the right to vote nor could they intermarry with "Whites." In the constitution of 1851 Indiana did not allow "Negros" to come into the state, nor did it allow the existing African-American residents to attend public schools even though they had to pay school taxes.[34] In Muncie, Indiana, in the first half of the twentieth century, there was customary segregation in shows, restaurants, and parks. It was not until the 1950s that the public swimming pool was desegregated.[35]

As to why slavery may have developed in the first place, cross-cultural research is as yet inconclusive. We do know, however, that slavery is not an inevitable stage in economic development, contrary to what some have assumed. In other words, slavery is not found mainly in certain economies, such as those dependent on intensive agriculture. Unlike the United States until the Civil War, many societies with intensive agriculture did not develop any variety of slavery. Also, the hypothesis that slavery develops where available resources are plentiful but labor is scarce is not supported by the cross-cultural evidence. All we can say definitely is that slavery does not occur in developed or industrial economies; either it disappears or it was never present in them.[36]

Racism and Inequality

Racism is the belief that some "races" are inferior to others. In a society composed of people with noticeably different physical features, such as differences in skin color, racism is almost invariably associated with social stratification. Those "races" considered inferior make up a larger proportion of the lower social classes or castes. Even in more open class systems, where individuals from all backgrounds can achieve higher status positions, individuals from "racial" groups deemed inferior may be subject to discrimination in housing or may be more likely to be searched or stopped by the police.

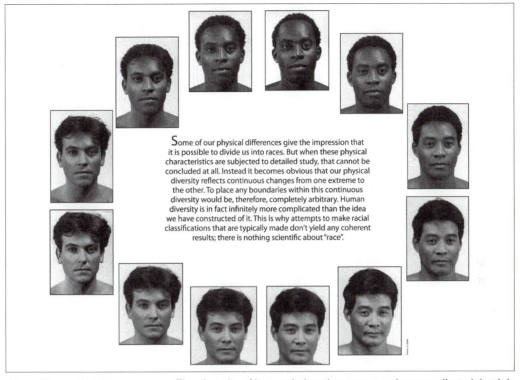

Some of our physical differences give the impression that it is possible to divide us into races. But when these physical characteristics are subjected to detailed study, that cannot be concluded at all. Instead it becomes obvious that our physical diversity reflects continuous changes from one extreme to the other. To place any boundaries within this continuous diversity would be, therefore, completely arbitrary. Human diversity is in fact infinitely more complicated than the idea we have constructed of it. This is why attempts to make racial classifications that are typically made don't yield any coherent results; there is nothing scientific about "race".

It is an illusion that there are races. The diversity of human beings is so great and so complicated that it is impossible to classify the 5.8 billions of individuals into discrete "races."

In some societies, such as the United States, the idea that humans are divided into "races" is taken so much for granted that people are asked for their "race" on the census. Most Americans probably assume that "races" are real, meaningful categories, reflecting important biological variation. But that is not necessarily the case. You may have noticed that we put "races" in quotes. We have done so deliberately because most anthropologists are persuaded that "race" is a meaningless concept as applied to humans. To understand why we say that, we first need to consider what the concept of *race* means in biology.

Race as a Construct in Biology

While all members of a species can potentially interbreed with others, most reproduction takes place within smaller groups or breeding populations. Through time, populations inhabiting different geographic regions may develop some differences in biological traits. Biologists may then classify different geographic populations into different *varieties,* or **races**. If the term *race* is understood to be just a shorthand or classificatory way in which biologists describe variation within a species from one population to the next, the concept of race would probably not be controversial. But, as applied to humans, racial classifications have often been thought to imply that some "races" are innately inferior to others.

The misuse and misunderstanding of the term *race,* and its association with racist thinking, are two of the reasons that anthropologists and others have suggested that the concept of race may hinder the search to explain the development of biological differences in humans. In any case, racial classifications are not scientifically useful in that search because different populations are not clearly classifiable into discrete groups that can be defined in terms of the presence or absence of particular sets of biological traits.[37] Population A may have a higher frequency of trait X than population B, but the frequency of trait Y in the two populations may be the same. So biological characteristics in humans often vary from one population to another in uncorrelated ways. This situation makes racial classification a very arbitrary undertaking when it comes to humans. Compare the number of "races" that different classifiers have come up with. The number of supposed racial categories has varied from as few as 3 to more than 37 categories.[38]

How can groups be clearly divided into "races" if most adaptive biological traits show gradual, but not always correlated, differences from one region to a neighboring region?[39] Skin color is a good example. Darker skin appears to protect the body from damaging ultraviolet radiation, and natural selection seems to have favored individuals with darker skin in environments that have more sunlight. In the area around Egypt, there is a gradient of skin color as you move from north to south in the Nile Valley. Skin generally becomes darker closer to the equator (which is south) and lighter closer to the Mediterranean. Other adaptive traits may not have north-south gradients, because the environmental predictors may be distributed differently. Nose shape varies with humidity, but **clines**, or gradients of varying frequencies, in humidity do not particularly correspond to variation in latitude. So the gradient for nose shape is not the same as the gradient for skin color.

Because individual adaptive traits tend to be distributed in clines that do not always coincide, there is no line you could draw on a world map that would separate "white" from "black" people, or "whites" from "Asians."[40] Only traits that are neutral in terms of adaptation or natural selection will tend to cluster in regions.[41] It should also be noted that the traits we have mentioned are superficial surface features. Human populations do vary biologically in some ways, but it is important to realize that few of these ways are correlated with each other. And under the skin humans are nearly alike genetically. Indeed, humans are not very different genetically from chimpanzees! The two species share as much as 99 percent of their genes.[42]

Race as a Social Category

If race, in the opinion of many biological anthropologists, is not a particularly useful device for classifying humans, why is it so widely used as a category in various societies? Anthropologists suggest the reasons are social. That is, racial classifications are social categories to which individuals are assigned, by themselves and others, to separate "our" group from others. We have seen that people tend to be *ethnocentric,* to view their culture as better than other cultures. Racial classifications may reflect the same tendency to divide "us" from "them," except that the divisions are supposedly based on biological differences.[43] The "them" are almost always viewed as inferior to "us."

We know that racial classifications have often been, and still are, used by certain groups to justify discrimination, exploitation, or even genocide. The "Aryan race" was supposed to be the group of blond-haired, blue-eyed, white-skinned people whom Adolf Hitler wanted to dominate the world, to which end he and others attempted to destroy as many members of the Jewish "race" as they could. (It is estimated that 6 million Jews and others were murdered in what is now called the Holocaust.[44]) But who were the Aryans? Technically, Aryans are any people, including the German-speaking Jews in Hitler's Germany, who speak one of the Indo-European languages. The Indo-European languages include such disparate modern tongues as Greek, Spanish, Hindi, Polish, French, Icelandic, German, Gaelic, and English. And many Aryans speaking these languages have neither blond hair nor blue eyes. Similarly, all kinds of people may be Jews, whether or not they descend from the ancient Near Eastern population that spoke the Hebrew language. There are light-skinned Danish Jews and darker Jewish Arabs. One of the most orthodox Jewish groups in the United States is based in New York City and is composed entirely of African Americans.

The arbitrary and social basis of most racial classifications becomes apparent when you compare how they differ from one place to another. Consider, for example, what used to be thought about the "races" in South Africa. Under apartheid, which was a system of racial segregation and discrimination, someone with mixed "white" and "black" ancestry was considered "colored." However, when important people of African ancestry (from other countries) would visit South Africa, they were often considered "white." Chinese were considered "Asian"; but the Japanese, who were important economically to South Africa, were considered "white."[45] In some parts of the United States, laws against interracial marriage continued in force through the 1960s. You would be considered a "negro" if you had an eighth or more "negro" ancestry (if one or more of your eight grandparents were "negro"). So only a small amount of "negro" ancestry made a person "negro." But a small amount of "white" ancestry did not make a person "white." Biologically speaking, this makes no sense, but socially it was another story.[46]

If people of different "races" are viewed as inferior, they are almost inevitably going to end up on the bottom of the social ladder in a socially stratified society. Discrimination will keep them out of the better-paying or higher-status jobs and in neighborhoods that are poorer.

Ethnicity and Inequality

If "race" is not a scientifically useful category because people cannot be clearly divided into different "racial" categories based on sets of physical traits, then racial classifications such as "black" and "white" in the United States might better be described as *ethnic* classifications. How else can we account for the following facts? Groups in the United States that are now thought of as "white" were earlier thought of as belonging to inferior "races." For example, in the latter half of the nineteenth century, newspapers would often talk about the new immigrants from Ireland as belonging to the Irish "race." Similarly, before World War II, Jews were thought of as a separate "racial" group, and only became "white" afterward.[47] It is hard to escape the idea that changes in "racial" classification occurred as the Irish, Jews, and other immigrant groups became more accepted by the majority in the United States.[48]

It is apparent that *ethnic groups* and *ethnic identities* emerge as part of a social and political process. Defining **ethnicity** usually separates a group of people with common origins and language, shared history, and selected cultural difference such as a difference in religion. Those doing the defining can be outside or inside the ethnic group. Outsiders and insiders often perceive ethnic groups differently. In a country with one large core majority group, often the majority group doesn't think of itself as an ethnic group. Rather, they consider only the minority groups to have ethnic identities. For example, in the United States it is not common for the majority to call themselves European Americans, but other groups may be called African Americans, Asian Americans, or Native Americans. The minority groups, on the other hand, may have different named identities.[49] Asian Americans may identify themselves more specifically as Japanese Americans, Korean Americans, Chinese Americans, or Hmong. The majority population often uses derogatory names to identify people who are different. The majority may also tend to lump people of diverse ethnicities together. Naming a group establishes a social boundary between it and other ethnic groups.[50]

Ethnic identity may be manipulated, by insiders and by outsiders, in different situations. A particularly repressive regime that emphasizes nationalism and loyalty to the state may not only suppress the assertiveness of ethnic claims; it may also act to minimize communication among people who might otherwise embrace the same ethnic identity.[51] More democratic regimes may allow more expression of difference and celebrate ethnic difference. However, manipulation of ethnicity does not come just from the top. It may be to the advantage of minority groups to lobby for more equal treatment as a larger entity, such as Asian American, rather than as Japanese, Chinese, Hmong, Filipino, or Korean American.

Members of minority ethnic groups are more often at the bottom of the socioeconomic "ladder," but not always, as these pictures from the United States illustrate.

Similarly, even though there are hundreds of American Indian groups, originally speaking different languages, there may be political advantages for all if they are treated as Native Americans.

In many multiethnic societies, ethnicity and diversity are things to be proud of and celebrated. Shared ethnic identity often makes people feel comfortable with similar people and gives them a strong sense of belonging. Still, ethnic differences in multiethnic societies are usually associated with inequities in wealth, power, and prestige. In other words, ethnicity is part of the system of *stratification*.

Although there are some people who believe that inequities are deserved, the origins of ethnic stereotypes, prejudice, and discrimination usually follow from historical and political events that give some groups dominance over others. For example, even though there were many early stories of help given by native peoples to the English settlers in the seventeenth century in the land now known as North America, the English were the invaders, and negative stereotypes about native peoples developed to justify taking their land and their lives. Referring to the negative stereotypes of Native Americans that developed, J. Milton Yinger said: "One would almost think that it had been the Indian who had invaded Europe, driven back the inhabitants, cut their population to one-third of its original size, unilaterally changed treaties, and brought the dubious glories of firewater and firearms."[52]

Similarly, as we noted in the section on slavery, African slaves were initially acquired as cheap labor, but inhumane treatment of slaves was justified by beliefs about their inferiority. Unfortunately, stereotypes can become self-fulfilling prophesies, especially if those discriminated against come to believe the stereotypes. It is easy to see how this can happen. If there is a widespread belief that a group is inferior, and that group is given inferior schools and little chance for improvement or little chance for a good job, the members of that group may acquire few skills and not try hard. The result is often a vicious cycle.[53]

And yet, the picture is not all bleak. Change has occurred. The ethnic identity forged by a minority group can help promote political activism, such as the nonviolent civil rights movement in the United States in the 1960s. That activism, helped by some people in the more advantaged groups, helped break down many of the legal barriers and segregationist practices that reinforced inequality.

The traditional barriers in the United States have mostly been lifted in recent years, but the "color line" has not disappeared. African Americans are found in all social classes, but they remain underrepresented in the wealthiest group and overrepresented at the bottom. Discrimination may be lessened, but it is still not gone. In research done with matched pairs of "whites" and "blacks" applying for jobs or for housing, discrimination is still evident.[54] Thus, African Americans may have to be better than others to get promoted, or it may be assumed that they got ahead just because they were African American and were hired because of affirmative action programs. European Americans often expect African Americans to be "ambassadors," to be called on mainly for knowledge about how to handle situations involving other African Americans. African Americans may work with others, but they usually go home to African American neighborhoods. Or they may live in mixed neighborhoods and experience considerable isolation. Few African Americans can completely avoid the anguish of racism.[55]

The Emergence of Stratification

Anthropologists are not certain why social stratification developed. Nevertheless, they are reasonably sure that higher levels of stratification emerged relatively recently in human history. Archaeological sites dating before about 8,000 years ago do not show extensive evidence of inequality. Houses do not appear to vary much in size or content, and different communities of the same culture are similar in size and otherwise. Signs of inequality appear first in the Near East, about 2,000 years after agriculture emerged in that region. Inequality in burial suggests inequality in life. Particularly telling are unequal child burials. It is unlikely that children could achieve high status by their own achievements. So when archaeologists find statues and ornaments only in some children's tombs, as at the 7,500-year-old site of Tell es-Sawwan in Iraq,[56] the grave goods suggest that those children belonged to a higher-ranking family or a higher class.

Another indication that stratification is a relatively recent development in human history is the fact that certain cultural features associated with stratification also developed relatively recently. For example, most societies that depend primarily on agriculture or herding have social classes.[57] Agriculture and herding developed within the past 10,000 years, so we may assume that most food collectors in the distant past lacked social classes. Other recently developed cultural features associated with class stratification include fixed settlements, political integration beyond the community level, the use of money as a medium of exchange, and the presence of at least some full-time specialization.[58]

In 1966, the comparative sociologist Gerhard Lenski suggested that the trend since 8,000 years ago toward increasing inequality was reversing. He argued that inequalities of power and privilege in industrial societies—measured in terms of the concentration of political power and the distribution of income—are less pronounced than inequalities in complex preindustrial societies. Technology in industrialized societies is so complex, he suggested, that those in power are compelled to delegate some authority to subordinates if the system is to work. In addition, a decline in the birth rate in industrialized societies, coupled with the need for skilled labor, has pushed the average wage of workers far above the subsistence level, resulting in greater equality in the distribution of income. Finally, Lenski also suggested that the spread of the democratic ideology, and particularly its acceptance by elites, has significantly broadened the political power of the lower classes.[59] A few studies have tested and supported Lenski's hypothesis that inequality has decreased with industrialization. In general, nations that are highly industrialized exhibit a lower level of inequality than nations that are only somewhat industrialized.[60] But, as we have seen, even the most industrialized societies may still have an enormous degree of inequality.

Why did social stratification develop in the first place? On the basis of his study of Polynesian societies, Marshall Sahlins suggested that an increase in agricultural productivity results in social stratification.[61] According to Sahlins, the degree of stratification is directly related to the production of a surplus, which is made possible by greater technological efficiency. The higher the level of productivity and the larger the agricultural surplus, the greater the scope and complexity of the distribution system. The status of the chief, who serves as redistributing agent, is enhanced. Sahlins argued that the differentiation between distributor and producer inevitably gives rise to differentiation in other aspects of life:

> First, there would be a tendency for the regulator of distribution to exert some authority over production itself—especially over productive activities which necessitate subsidization, such as communal labor or specialist labor. A degree of control of production implies a degree of control over the utilization of resources, or, in other words, some preeminent property rights. In turn, regulation of these economic processes necessitates the exercise of authority in interpersonal affairs; differences in social power emerge.[62]

Sahlins later rejected the idea that a surplus leads to chiefships, postulating instead that the relationship may be the other way around—that is, leaders encourage the development of a surplus so as to enhance their prestige through feasts, potlatches, and other redistributive events.[63] Of course, both trajectories are possible—surpluses may generate stratification, and stratification may generate surpluses; they are not mutually exclusive.

Lenski's theory of the causes of stratification is similar to Sahlins's original idea. Lenski, too, argued that production of a surplus is the stimulus in the development of stratification, but he focused primarily on the conflict that arises over control of that surplus. Lenski concluded that the distribution of the surplus will be determined on the basis of power. Thus, inequalities in power promote unequal access to economic resources and simultaneously give rise to inequalities in privilege and prestige.[64]

The "surplus" theories of Sahlins and Lenski do not really address the question of why the redistributors or leaders will want, or be able, to acquire greater control over resources. After all, the redistributors or leaders in many rank societies do not have greater wealth than others, and custom seems to keep things that way. One suggestion is that as long as followers have mobility, they can vote with their feet by moving away from leaders they do not like. But when people start to make more permanent "investments" in land or technology (e.g., irrigation systems or weirs for fishing), they are more likely to put up with a leader's aggrandizement in exchange for protection.[65] Another suggestion is that access to economic resources becomes unequal only when there is population pressure on resources in rank or chiefdom societies.[66] Such pressure may be what induces redistributors to try to keep more land and other resources for themselves and their families.

C. K. Meek offered an example of how population pressure in northern Nigeria may have led to economic stratification. At one time, a tribal member could obtain the right to use land by asking permission of the chief and presenting him with a token gift in recognition of his higher status. But by 1921, the reduction in the amount of available land had led to a system under which applicants offered the chief large payments for scarce land. As a result of these payments, farms came to be regarded as private property, and differential access to such property became institutionalized.[67]

Future research by archaeologists, sociologists, historians, and anthropologists should provide more understanding of the emergence of social stratification in human societies and how and why it varies in degree.

Summary

1. Without exception, recent and modern industrial and postindustrial societies such as our own are socially stratified—that is, they contain social groups such as families, classes, or ethnic groups that have unequal access to important advantages, such as economic resources, power, and prestige. Anthropologists, based on firsthand observations, would say that such inequality has not always existed among the societies they have studied. While even the simplest societies (in the technological sense) have some differences in advantages based on age, ability, or gender—adults have higher status than children, the skilled more than the unskilled, men more than women (we discuss gender stratification in the next chapter)—anthropologists would argue that egalitarian societies exist where social groups (e.g., families) have more or less the same access to rights or advantages.

2. The presence or absence of customs or rules that give certain groups unequal access to economic resources, power, and prestige can be used to distinguish three types of societies. In egalitarian societies, social groups do not have unequal access to economic resources, power, or prestige; they are unstratified. In rank societies, social groups do not have very unequal access to economic resources or power, but they do have unequal access to prestige. Rank societies, then, are partially stratified. In class societies, social groups have unequal access to economic resources, power, and prestige. They are more completely stratified than are rank societies.

3. Stratified societies range from somewhat open class systems to caste systems, which are extremely rigid, since caste membership is fixed permanently at birth.

4. Slaves are persons who do not own their own labor; as such, they represent a class and sometimes even a caste. Slavery has existed in various forms in many times and places, regardless of "race" and culture. Sometimes slavery is a rigid and closed, or caste, system; sometimes it is a relatively open class system.

5. Within a society composed of people from widely divergent backgrounds and different physical features, such as skin color, racism is almost invariably associated with social stratification. Those "races" considered inferior make up a larger proportion of the lower social classes or castes. In the opinion of many biological anthropologists, "race" is not a scientifically useful device for classifying humans. "Racial" classifications should be recognized for what they mostly are—social categories to which individuals are assigned, by themselves and others, on the basis of supposedly shared biological traits.

6. In multiethnic societies, ethnic differences are usually associated with inequities in wealth, power, and prestige. In other words, ethnicity is part of the system of stratification.

7. Social stratification appears to have emerged relatively recently in human history, about 8,000 years ago. This conclusion is based on archaeological evidence and on the fact that certain cultural features associated with stratification developed relatively recently.

8. One theory suggests that social stratification developed as productivity increased and surpluses were produced. Another suggestion is that stratification can develop only when people have "investments" in land or technology and therefore cannot move away from leaders they do not like. A third theory suggests that stratification emerges only when there is population pressure on resources in rank societies.

Glossary Terms

caste (p. 102)
class (p. 100)
class societies (p. 96)
clines (p. 108)
economic resources (p. 95)
egalitarian societies (p. 96)
ethnicity (p. 109)

manumission (p. 104)
power (p. 95)
prestige (p. 96)
races (p. 107)
racism (p. 106)
rank societies (p. 96)
slaves (p. 104)

Critical Questions

1. What might be some of the social consequences of large differences in wealth? Explain your reasoning.

2. Is an industrial or a developed economy incompatible with a more egalitarian distribution of resources? Why or why not?

3. In a multiethnic society, does ethnic identity help or hinder social equality? Explain your answer.

4. Why do you suppose the degree of inequality has decreased in some countries in recent years?

SEX AND GENDER

Chapter Outline

- Gender Concepts
- Physique and Physiology
- Gender Roles
- Relative Contributions to Work
- Political Leadership and Warfare
- The Relative Status of Women
- Personality Differences
- Sexuality

We all know that humans come in two major varieties—female and male. The contrast between them is one of the facts of life we share with most animal species. But the fact that males and females always have different organs of reproduction does not explain why males and females may also differ in other physical ways. After all, there are many animal species—such as pigeons, gulls, and laboratory rats—in which the two sexes differ little in appearance.[1] Thus, the fact that we are a species with two sexes does not really explain why human females and males typically look different. Also, the fact that humans reproduce sexually does not explain why human males and females should differ in behavior or be treated differently by society. Yet no society we know of treats females and males in exactly the same way; indeed, females usually have fewer advantages than males. That is why in Chapter 5 we were careful to say that egalitarian societies have no *social groups* with unequal access to resources, power, and prestige. But within social groups (e.g., families), even egalitarian societies usually allow males greater access to economic resources, power, and prestige.

Because many of the differences between females and males may reflect cultural expectations and experiences, many researchers now prefer to speak of **gender differences**, reserving the term **sex differences** for purely biological differences.[2] Unfortunately, biological and cultural influences are not always clearly separable, so it is sometimes hard to know which term to use. As long as societies treat males and females differently, we may not be able to separate the effects of biology from the effects of culture, and both kinds of effect may be present. As we focus our discussion on differences and similarities between females and males, keep in mind that not all cultures conceive of gender as including just two categories. Sometimes "maleness" and "femaleness" are thought of as opposite ends of a continuum, or there might be three or more categories of gender, such as "female," "male," and "other."[3]

In this chapter we discuss what we know cross-culturally about how and why females and males may differ physically, in gender roles, and in personality. We also discuss how and why sexual behavior and attitudes about sex vary from culture to culture. First we focus on culturally varying concepts about gender.

Gender Concepts

In the United States and many Western societies your gender is thought of as female or male. There is no other category. In the instances where the baby's genitalia are ambiguous or when an adult desires a sex-change operation, there is a strong value on having the individual fit clearly into one or the other category. Many societies around the world share the male/female dichotomy when it comes to gender concepts. But a strict dichotomy is far from universal.

Some societies, like the Cheyenne Native Americans of the Great Plains, recognized male, female, and a third gender, referred to by the Cheyennes as "two-spirits." "Two-spirit" persons were usually young males. Their status as "two-spirit" persons was often recognized after their preadolescent vision quest. A two-spirit person would then wear women's dress and take on many of the activities of women. A two-spirit might even be taken as a second wife by a man, but whether the man and the two-spirit engaged in sex is not known. Europeans referred to a two-spirit individual as a *berdache*.[4] Accounts of "two-spirit" biological females who take on the role of men are relatively rare, but they do occur in a number of native North American societies, such as the Kaska of Yukon Territory, the Klamath of southern Oregon, and the Mohave of the Colorado River area in the southwestern United States. These biologically female "two-spirits" could marry women and such relationships were known to be lesbian relationships.[5]

In Oman there is a third gender role called *xanith*. Anatomically male, *xaniths* speak of themselves as "women." However, *xaniths* have their own distinctive dress—they wear clothes that are neither male nor female. In fact, their clothes and dress seem in-between. Men wear white clothes, women bright patterns, and *xaniths* wear unpatterned pastels. Men have short hair, women long, and *xaniths* are medium-length. Women are generally secluded in their houses and can only go out with permission from their husbands, but the *xanith* is free to come and go and works as a servant and/or a homosexual prostitute. But the *xanith* gender role is not necessarily forever. A *xanith* may decide to marry, and if he is able to have intercourse with his bride he becomes a "man." An older *xanith* who is no longer attractive may decide to become an "old-man."[6]

Physique and Physiology

As we noted at the outset, biological males and females of many animal species cannot readily be distinguished. Although they differ in chromosome makeup and in their external and internal organs of reproduction, they do not differ otherwise. In contrast, humans are **sexually dimorphic**—that is, the females and males of our species are generally different in size and appearance. Females have proportionately wider pelvises. Males typically are taller and have heavier skeletons. Females have a larger proportion of their body weight in fat; males have a larger proportion of body weight in muscle. Males typically have greater grip strength, proportionately larger hearts and lungs, and greater aerobic capacity (greater intake of oxygen during strenuous activity).

There is a tendency in our society to view "taller" and "more muscled" as better, which may reflect the bias toward males in our culture. Natural selection may have favored these traits in males but different ones in females. For example, because females bear children, selection may have favored earlier cessation of growth, and therefore less ultimate height, in females so that the nutritional needs of a fetus would not compete with a growing mother's needs.[7] (Females achieve their ultimate height shortly after puberty, but boys continue to grow for years after puberty.) Similarly, there is some evidence that females are less affected than males by nutritional shortages, presumably because they tend to be shorter and have proportionately more fat.[8] Natural selection may have favored those traits in females because they resulted in greater reproductive success.

Training can greatly increase muscle strength and aerobic capacity.

Both female and male athletes can build up their muscle strength and increase their aerobic work capacity through training. Given that fact, cultural factors, such as how much a society expects and allows males and females to engage in muscular activity, could influence the degree to which females and males differ muscularly and in aerobic capacity. Similar training may account for the recent trend toward decreasing differences between females and males in certain athletic events, such as marathons and swim meets. Even when it comes to female and male physique and physiology, then, what we see may be the result of both culture and genes.[9]

Gender Roles

Productive and Domestic Activities

In the chapter on economics, we noted that all societies assign or divide labor somewhat differently between females and males. Because role assignments have a clear cultural component, we speak of them as **gender roles**. What is of particular interest here about the gender division of labor is not so much that every society has different work for males and females but rather that so many societies divide up work in similar ways. The question, then, is why there are universal or near-universal patterns in such assignments.

Table 6.1 summarizes the worldwide patterns. We note which activities are performed by which gender in all or almost all societies, which activities are usually performed by one gender, and which activities are commonly assigned to either gender or both. Does the distribution of activities in the table suggest why females and males generally do different things?

One possible explanation may be labeled the **strength theory**. The greater strength of males and their superior capacity to mobilize their strength in quick bursts of energy (because of their greater aerobic work capacity) have commonly been cited as the reasons for the universal or near-universal patterns in the division of labor by gender. Certainly, activities that require lifting heavy objects (hunting large animals, butchering, clearing land, working with stone, metal, or lumber), throwing weapons, and running with great speed (as in hunting) may generally be performed best by males. And none of the activities females usually perform, with the possible exception of collecting firewood, seems to require the same degree of physical strength or quick bursts of energy. But the strength theory is not completely convincing, if only because it cannot readily explain all the observed patterns. For example, it is not clear that the male activities of trapping small animals, collecting wild honey, or making musical instruments require much physical strength.

Another possible explanation of the worldwide patterns in division of labor can be called the **compatibility-with-child-care theory**. The argument here is that women's tasks tend to be those that are compatible with child care. Although males can take care of infants, most traditional societies rely on breast-feeding of infants, which men cannot do. (In most societies, women breast-feed their children for two years on the average.) Women's tasks may be those that do not take them far from home for long periods, that do not place children in potential danger if they are taken along, and that can be stopped and resumed if an infant needs care.[10]

The compatibility theory may explain why *no* activities other than infant care are listed in the right-hand column of Table 6.1. That is, it may be that there are practically no universal or near-universal women-only activities because until recently most women have had to devote much of their time to nursing and caring for infants, as well as caring for other children. The compatibility theory may also explain why men usually perform tasks such as hunting, trapping, fishing, collecting honey, lumbering, and mining. Those tasks are dangerous for infants to be around, and in any case would be difficult to coordinate with infant care.[11]

Table 6.1   Worldwide Patterns in the Division of Labor by Gender

Type of Activity	Males Almost Always	Males Usually	Either Gender or Both	Females Usually	Females Almost Always
Primary subsistence activities	Hunt and trap animals, large and small	Fish Herd large animals Collect wild honey Clear land and prepare soil for planting	Collect shellfish Care for small animals Plant crops Tend crops Harvest crops Milk animals	Gather wild plants	
Secondary subsistence and household activities		Butcher animals	Preserve meat and fish	Care for children Cook Prepare vegetable foods drinks dairy products Launder Fetch water Collect fuel	Care for infants
Other	Lumber Mine and quarry Make boats musical instruments bone, horn, and shell objects Engage in combat	Build houses Make nets rope Exercise political leadership	Prepare skins Make leather products baskets mats clothing pottery	Spin yarn	

Sources: Mostly adapted from George P. Murdock and Caterina Provost, "Factors in the Division of Labor by Sex: A Cross-Cultural Analysis," *Ethnology,* 12 (1973): 203–25. The information on political leadership and warfare comes from Martin K. Whyte, "Cross-Cultural Codes Dealing with the Relative Status of Women," *Ethnology,* 17 (1978): 217. The information on child care comes from Thomas S. Weisner and Ronald Gallimore, "My Brother's Keeper: Child and Sibling Caretaker," *Current Anthropology,* 18 (1977): 169–80.

Finally, the compatibility theory may also explain why men seem to take over certain crafts in societies with full-time specialization. Although the distinction is not shown in Table 6.1, crafts such as making baskets, mats, and pottery are women's activities in noncommercial societies but tend to be men's activities in societies with full-time craft specialists.[12] Similarly, weaving tends to be a female activity unless it is produced for trade.[13] Why should commercial activities change the gender division of labor? Full-time specialization and production for trade may increase incompatibility with child care. Cooking is a good example in our own society. Women may be fine cooks, but chefs and bakers tend to be men, even though

In many farming societies, women can do some agriculture and take care of their young children at the same time, as this mother in Zambia demonstrates.

women traditionally do most of the cooking at home. Women might be more likely to work as cooks and chefs if they could leave their babies and young children in safe places to be cared for by other people.

But the compatibility theory does not explain why men usually prepare soil for planting, make objects out of wood, or work bone, horn, and shell. All of those tasks could probably be stopped to tend to a child, and none of them is any more dangerous to children nearby than is cooking. Why, then, do males tend to do them? The **economy-of-effort theory** may help explain patterns that cannot readily be explained by the strength and compatibility theories. For example, it may be advantageous for men to make musical instruments because men generally collect the hard materials involved (e.g., by lumbering).[14] And because they collect those materials, men may be more knowledgeable about the physical properties of the materials and so more likely to know how to work with them. The economy-of-effort interpretation also suggests that it would be advantageous for one gender to perform tasks that are located near each other. Thus, if women have to be near home to take care of young children, it would be economical for them to perform other chores that are located in or near the home.

A fourth explanation of division of labor is the **expendability theory**. This theory suggests that men, rather than women, will tend to do the dangerous work in a society because men are more expendable, because the loss of men is less disadvantageous reproductively than the loss of women. If some men lose their lives in hunting, deep-water fishing, mining, quarrying, lumbering, and the like, reproduction need not suffer as long as most fertile women have sexual access to men—for example, if the society permits two or more women to be married to the same man.[15] When would anybody, male or female, be willing to do dangerous work? Perhaps only when society glorifies those roles and endows them with high prestige and other rewards.

Although the various theories, singly or in combination, seem to explain much of the division of labor by gender, there are some unresolved problems. Critics of the strength theory have pointed out that in some societies women do engage in very heavy labor.[16] If women in some societies can develop the strength to do such work, perhaps strength is more a function of training than traditionally has been believed.

The compatibility theory also has some problems. It suggests that labor is divided to conform to the requirements of child care. But sometimes it seems the other way around. For example, women who spend a good deal of time in agricultural work outside the home often ask others to watch and feed their infants while they are unavailable to nurse.[17] Consider, too, the mountain areas of Nepal, where agricultural work is incompatible with child care; heavy loads must be carried up and down steep slopes, fields are far apart, and labor takes up most of the day. Yet women do this work anyway and leave their infants with others for long stretches of time.[18]

Furthermore, in some societies women hunt—one of the activities most incompatible with child care and generally not done by women. Many Agta women of the Philippines regularly hunt wild pig and deer; women alone or in groups kill almost 30 percent of the large game.[19] The women's hunting does not seem to be incompatible with child care. Women take nursing babies on hunting trips, and the women who hunt do not have lower reproductive rates than the women who choose not to hunt. Agta women may find it possible to hunt because the hunting grounds are only about a half-hour from camp, the dogs that accompany the women assist in the hunting and protect the women and babies, and the women generally hunt in groups, so others can help carry babies as well as carcasses. Hunting by women is also fairly common among the Aka, forest foragers in the Central African Republic. Aka women participate in and sometimes lead in organizing cooperative net-hunting, in which an area is circled and animals are flushed out and caught in nets. Women spend approximately 18 percent of their time net-hunting, which is more than men do.[20]

As the cases just described suggest, we need to know a lot more about labor requirements. More precisely, we need to know exactly how much strength is required in particular tasks, how dangerous those tasks are, and whether a person could stop working at a task to care for a child. So far, we have mostly guesses. When there is more systematically collected evidence on such aspects of particular tasks, we will be in a better position to evaluate the theories we have discussed. In any case, it should be noted that none of the available theories implies that the worldwide patterns of division of labor shown in Table 6.1 will persist. As we know from our own and other industrial societies, when machines replace human strength, when women have fewer children, and when women can assign child care to others, a strict gender division of labor begins to disappear.

Relative Contributions to Work

In the United States there has been a tendency to equate "work" with a job that brings in income. Until relatively recently, being a "homemaker" was not counted as an occupation. Anthropologists have not been immune from ignoring household work; indeed, most of the research on division of labor by gender has focused on **primary subsistence activities**—gathering, hunting, fishing, herding, and farming—and relatively less attention has been paid to gender contributions to **secondary subsistence activities** that involve the processing and preparation of food for eating or storing.

Overall Work

If we count all kinds of economic work, whether it be for primary subsistence, secondary subsistence, manufacturing, crafts, or for maintenance of the household, the studies that have been done largely suggest that women typically work more total hours per day than men in both intensive agricultural and horticultural societies.[21] We do not have that many studies yet—so we do not know if this is a cross-cultural universal. We do know though that in many societies, where women earn wages, they are still responsible for the bulk of household work as well as child care at home.

Subsistence Work

Researchers have focused mostly on primary subsistence activities, and they usually measure how much each gender's work in these primary activities contributes to the diet in terms of caloric intake. Alternatively, contribution to primary subsistence activities—generally outside activities, away from the home—can also be measured in terms of time spent doing them. Measures of caloric versus time contribution can yield different results. As we saw in the chapter on economics, more time is spent by the Yanomamö in hunting than in horticulture, but horticulture yields more calories.

In some societies women traditionally have contributed more to the economy than men by any measure. For example, among the Tchambuli of New Guinea in the 1930s, the women did all the fishing—going out early in the morning by canoe to their fish traps and returning when the sun was hot. Some of the catch was traded for sago (a starch) and sugarcane, and it was the women who went on the long canoe trips to do the trading.[22]

In contrast, men did almost all of the primary subsistence work among the Toda of India. As they were described early in the twentieth century, they depended for subsistence almost entirely on the dairy products of their water buffalo, either by using the products directly or by selling them for grain. Women were not allowed to have anything to do with dairy work; only men tended the buffalo and prepared the dairy products. Women's work was largely household work. Women prepared the purchased grain for cooking, cleaned house, and decorated clothing.[23]

A worldwide survey of a wide variety of societies has revealed that both women and men typically contribute to primary food-getting activities, but men usually contribute more in terms of calories.[24] Women are almost always occupied with infant-and child-care responsibilities in most societies, so it is not surprising that usually do most of the primary food-getting work, which generally has to be done away from the home.

Some of the variation in gender contribution to primary subsistence relates directly to the type of food-getting activities in the society. In societies that depend on hunting, fishing, and herding—generally male activities—for most of their calories, men usually contribute more than women.[25] For example, among the Inuit, who traditionally depended mostly on hunting and fishing, and among the Toda, who depended mostly on herding, men did most of the primary subsistence work. In societies that depend on gathering,

Grinding corn is very time-consuming and is hard work. Women near Lake Titicaca in Peru grind corn between two large stones.

primarily women's work, women tend to do most of the food-getting in terms of calories. The !Kung are an example. But the predominant type of food-getting is not always predictive. Among the Tchambuli, who depended mostly on fishing, women did most of the work. Most societies known to anthropology depend primarily on plant cultivation for their calories, not on hunting, gathering, fishing, or herding. And, with the exception of clearing land, preparing the soil, and herding large animals, which are usually men's tasks, the work of planting, crop tending (weeding, irrigating), and harvesting is done by men, women, or both (see Table 6.1). So we need some explanation of why women do most of the farming work in some societies but men do it in others. Different patterns predominate in different areas of the world. In Africa south of the Sahara, women generally do most of the farming. But in much of Asia and Europe and the areas around the Mediterranean, men do more.[26]

One explanatory factor is the kind of plant cultivation. With intensive agriculture, particularly plow agriculture, men's caloric contribution to primary subsistence tends to be much higher than women's. In horticultural societies, in contrast, women's contribution is relatively high compared with men's. Women usually contribute the most when horticulture is practiced, either root and tree crop horticulture or shifting/slash-and-burn cultivation. According to Ester Boserup, when population increases and there is pressure to make more intensive use of the land, cultivators begin to use the plow and irrigation, and males start to do more.[27] But it is not clear why.

Why should women not continue to contribute a lot to farming just because plows are used? In trying to answer this question, most researchers shift to considering how much time males and females spend in various farming tasks, rather than estimating the total caloric contribution of females versus males. The reason for this shift is that gender contribution to farming varies substantially over the various phases of the production sequence, as well as from one crop to another. Thus, the total amount of time females versus males work at farming tasks is easier to estimate than how much each gender contributes to the diet in terms of calories. How would caloric contribution be judged, for example, if men do the clearing and plowing, women do the planting and weeding, and both do the harvesting?

One suggestion about why males contribute more to agriculture when the plow is used is that plow agriculture involves a great deal of labor input in the clearing and preparation phases of cultivation and at the same time minimizes subsequent weeding time. Men usually clear land anyway, but clearing is a more time-consuming process if intensive agriculture is practiced. It has been estimated that in one district in Nigeria, 100 days of work are required to clear one acre of virgin land for plowing by tractor; only 20 days are required to prepare the land for shifting cultivation. Weeding is a task that probably can be combined with child care, and perhaps for that reason it may have been performed mostly by women previously.[28] But the fact that men do the plowing, which may take a lot of time, does not explain why women do relatively fewer farming tasks, including weeding, in societies that have the plow.[29]

Another explanation for why women contribute less time than men to intensive agriculture is that household chores increase with intensive agriculture and thus limit the time women can spend in the fields. Intensive agriculturalists typically rely heavily on grain crops, which take much more work to make edible. Cereal grains (corn, rice, wheat, oats, millet) are usually dried before storing and thus take a long time to cook if they are left whole. More cooking requires more time to collect water and firewood (usually women's work) and more time to clean pots and utensils. A variety of techniques can reduce cooking time (such as soaking, grinding, or pounding), but the process that speeds up cooking the most—grinding—is itself time-consuming (unless done by machine).[30] Finally, household work may increase substantially with intensive agriculture because women in such societies have more children than women in horticultural societies.[31] If household work increases in these ways, it is easy to understand why women cannot contribute more time than men, or as much time as men, to intensive agriculture. But women's contribution, although less than men's, is nonetheless substantial; they seem to work outside the home four and a half hours a day, seven days a week, on the average.[32]

We still have not explained why women contribute so much to horticulture in the first place. They may not have as much household work as intensive agricultural women, but neither do the men. Why, then, don't men do relatively more in horticulture also? One possibility is that in horticultural societies men are often drawn away from cultivation into other types of activities. There is evidence that if males are engaged in warfare when primary subsistence work has to be done, the women must do that work.[33] Men may also be withdrawn from primary subsistence work if they have to work in distant towns and cities for wages or if they periodically go on long-distance trading trips.[34]

When women contribute a lot to primary food-getting activities, we might expect their behavior and attitudes concerning children to be affected. Several cross-cultural studies suggest that this expectation is correct. In societies with a high female contribution to primary subsistence (in terms of contributing calories), infants are fed solid foods earlier (so that other persons besides mothers can feed them) than in societies with a low female contribution.[35] Girls are likely to be trained to be industrious (probably to help their mothers), and girl babies are more valued.[36]

Political Leadership and Warfare

In almost every known society, men rather than women are the leaders in the political arena. One cross-cultural survey found that, in about 85 percent of the surveyed societies, only men were leaders. In the societies in which some women occupied leadership positions, the women were either outnumbered by or less powerful than the male leaders.[37] If we look at countries, not cultures, women on the average make up only around 10 percent of the representatives in national parliaments or legislative bodies.[38] Whether or not we consider warfare to be part of the political sphere of life, we find an almost universal dominance of males in that arena. In 87 percent of the world's societies, women never participate actively in war.[39] (See the box "Why Some Societies Let Women Participate in Combat" for a discussion of women in combat in the remaining 13 percent of societies.)

Even in *matrilineal* societies, which seem to be oriented around women (see the chapter on marriage, family, and kinship), men usually occupy political positions. For example, among the Iroquois of what is now New York State, women had control over resources and a great deal of influence, but men, not women, held political office. The highest political body among the League of the Iroquois, which comprised five tribal groups, was a council of 50 male chiefs. Although women could not serve on the council, they could nominate, elect, and impeach their male representatives. Women also could decide between life and death for prisoners of war, forbid the men of their households to go to war, and intervene to bring about peace.[40]

Why have men (at least so far) almost always dominated the political sphere of life? Some scholars have suggested that men's role in warfare gives them the edge in all kinds of political leadership, particularly because they control weapons, an important resource.[41] But evidence suggests that force is rarely used to obtain leadership positions;[42] superior strength is not the deciding factor. Still, warfare may be related to political leadership for another reason. Warfare clearly affects survival, and it occurs regularly in most societies. Therefore, decision making about war may be among the most important kinds of politics in most societies. If so, then the persons who know the most about warfare should be making the decisions about it.

To explain why males and not females usually engage in fighting, let us refer to three of the possible explanations of the worldwide patterns in the gender division of labor. Warfare, like hunting, requires strength (for throwing weapons) and quick bursts of energy (for running). And certainly combat is one of the most dangerous and uninterruptible activities imaginable, hardly compatible with child care. Also, even if they do not at the time have children, women may generally be kept out of combat because their

Women can serve in the U.S. military but are not usually in units directly engaged in combat. Some women feel that such exclusion is unfair and decreases their chances of promotion in the military. Other people, including some women, insist that female participation in combat would be detrimental to military performance or is inappropriate for women. Women in the U.S. military have been attacked in the course of their duties in Iraq and some have died. Some countries currently allow women to engage in combat. And in the eighteenth and nineteenth centuries women made up one wing of the standing army in the West African Kingdom of Dahomey and at one point constituted one-third of the armed forces. Most societies, however, have excluded women from combat and some have excluded women from any involvement in military activities or planning.

Why, then, do some societies allow women to be warriors? Psychologist David Adams compared about 70 societies studied by anthropologists to try to answer that question. Although most societies exclude women from war, Adams found that women are active warriors, at least occasionally, in 13 percent of the sample societies. In native North America, such societies included the Comanche, Crow, Delaware, Fox, Gros Ventre, and Navajo. In the Pacific, there were active warrior women among the Maori of New Zealand, on Majuro Atoll in the Marshall Islands, and among the Orokaiva of New Guinea. In none of these societies were the warriors usually women, but women were allowed to engage in combat if they wanted to.

Societies with women warriors differ from those that exclude women from combat in one of two ways: Either they conduct war only against people in other societies (i.e., "purely external" war) or they marry within their own community. Adams argues that these two conditions, which are not particularly common, preclude the possibility of conflicts of interest between wives and husbands, and therefore women can be permitted to engage in combat because their interests are the same as their husbands'. Because marriages in most cases involve individuals from the same society, husbands and wives will have the same loyalties if the society has purely external war. And even if war occurs between communities and larger groups in the same society (i.e., "internal" war), there will be no conflict of interest between husband and wife if they both grew up in the same community. In contrast, internal war occurs at least occasionally in most societies, and wives usually marry in from other communities that might have been or will be at war with the husband's community. In this situation, there may be a conflict of interest between husband and wife; if women were to engage in combat, they might have to fight against their fathers, paternal uncles, and brothers. And wouldn't the wives try to warn kin in their home communities if the husbands planned to attack them? Indeed, the men's fear of their wives' disloyalty would explain why women in these societies are forbidden to make or handle weapons or go near meetings in which war plans are discussed.

Many countries today engage in purely external war between societies; so other things being equal, we would not expect conflicts of interest to impede women's participation in combat. Therefore, extrapolating from Adams's findings, we might expect that the barriers against female participation in combat will disappear completely. But other conditions may have to be present before women and men participate equally in combat. In Adams's study, not all societies with purely external war or intracommunity marriage had women warriors. So we may also have to consider the degree to which the society seeks to maximize reproduction (and therefore protect women from danger) and the degree to which the society depends on women for subsistence during wartime.

There are other related questions to explore: Does military participation by women increase women's participation in politics? Does the presence of war in a society decrease or increase women's political participation? Does women's participation in politics or in the military change the nature of war?

Sources: From David B. Adams, "Why There Are So Few Women Warriors," in *Behavior Science Research,* 18 (1983): 196–212; Joshua S. Goldstein, "War and Gender," in Carol R. Ember and Melvin Ember, eds., *Encyclopedia of Sex and Gender: Men and Women in the World's Cultures,* vol. 1 (New York: Kluwer Academic/Plenum Publishers, 2004), pp. 107–16.

Women as well as men serve on political councils in many Coast Salish communities. Here we see a swearing-in ceremony for the Special Chief's Council in Sardis, British Columbia.

potential fertility is more important to a population's reproduction and survival than their potential usefulness as warriors.[43] So the strength theory, the compatibility theory, and the expendability theory might all explain the predominance of men in warfare.

Two other factors may be involved in male predominance in politics. One is the generally greater height of men. Why height should be a factor in leadership is unclear, but studies suggest that taller persons are more likely to be leaders.[44] Finally, there is the possibility that men dominate politics because they get around more in the outside world than do women. Men's activities typically take them farther from home; women tend to work more around the home. If societies choose leaders at least in part because of what they know about the larger world, then men will generally have some advantage. In support of this reasoning, Patricia Draper found that in !Kung bands that had settled down, women no longer engaged in long-distance gathering, and they lost much of their former influence in decision making.[45] Involvement in child care may also detract from such influence. In a study of village leadership among the Kayapo of Brazil, Dennis Werner found that women with heavy child-care burdens were less influential than women not as involved in child care; perhaps they had fewer friends and missed many details of what was going on in the village.[46]

These various explanations suggest why men generally dominate politics, but we still need to explain why women participate in politics more in some societies than in others. Political scientist Marc Ross investigated this question in a cross-cultural survey of 90 societies.[47] In that sample, the degree of female participation in politics varied considerably. For example, among the Mende of Sierra Leone, women regularly held high office, but among the Azande of Zaire, women took no part in public life. One factor that appeared to predict the exclusion of women from politics was the organization of communities around male kin. As we will see later, when they marry, women usually have to leave their communities and move to their husband's place. If women are "strangers" in a community with many related males, then the males will have political advantages because of their knowledge of community members and past events.

The Relative Status of Women

There are probably as many definitions of status as there are researchers interested in the topic. To some, the relative status of the sexes means how much importance society confers on females versus males. To others, it means how much power and authority men and women have relative to each other. And to still others, it means what kinds of rights women and men possess to do what they want to do. In any case, many social scientists are asking why the status of women appears to vary from one society to another. Why do women have few rights and little influence in some societies and more of each in other societies? In other words, why is there variation in degree of **gender stratification**?

In the small Iraqi town of Daghara, women and men live very separate lives.[48] In many respects, women appear to have very little status. Like women in much of the Islamic world, women in Daghara live their lives mostly in seclusion, staying in their houses and interior courtyards. If women must go out, which they can do only with male approval, they must shroud their faces and bodies in long black cloaks. These cloaks must be worn in mixed company, even at home. Women are essentially excluded from political activities. Legally, they are considered to be under the authority of their fathers and husbands. Even the sexuality of women is controlled. There is strict emphasis on virginity before marriage. Because women are not permitted even casual conversations with strange men, the possibilities for extramarital or even premarital relationships are very slight. In contrast, hardly any sexual restrictions are imposed on men.

But some societies such as the Mbuti seem to approach equal status for males and females. Like most food collectors, the Mbuti have no formal political organization to make decisions or to settle disputes. Public disputes occur, and both women and men take part in the uproar that is part of such disputes. Not only do women make their positions known, but their opinions are often heeded. Even in domestic quarrels involving physical violence between husband and wife, others usually intervene to stop them, regardless of who hit whom first.[49] Women control the use of dwellings; they usually have equal say over the disposal of resources they or the men collect, over the upbringing of their children, and about whom their children should marry. One of the few signs of inequality is that women are somewhat more restricted than men with respect to extramarital sex.[50]

There are many theories about why women have relatively high or low status. One of the most common is that women's status will be high when they contribute substantially to primary subsistence activities. According to this theory, then, women should have very little status when food-getting depends

In some cultures, wives defer to their husbands in many contexts.

largely on hunting, herding, or intensive agriculture. A second theory suggests that where warfare is especially important, men will be more valued and esteemed than women. A third theory suggests that where there are centralized political hierarchies, men will have higher status. The reasoning in this theory is essentially the same as the reasoning in the warfare theory: Men usually play the dominant role in political behavior, so men's status should be higher wherever political behavior is more important or frequent. Finally, there is the theory that women will have higher status where kin groups and couples' place of residence after marriage are organized around women.

One of the problems in evaluating these theories is that decisions have to be made about the meaning of *status*. Does it mean value? Rights? Influence? And do all these aspects of status vary together? Cross-cultural research by sociologist Martin Whyte suggests that they do not. For each sample society in his study, Whyte rated 52 items that might be used to define the relative status of the sexes. These items included such things as which sex can inherit property, who has final authority over disciplining unmarried children, and whether the gods in the society are male, female, or both. The results of the study indicate that very few of these items are related. Therefore, Whyte concluded, we cannot talk about status as a single concept. Rather, it seems more appropriate to talk about the relative status of women in different spheres of life.[51]

Even though Whyte found no necessary connection between one aspect of status and another, he decided to ask whether some of the theories correctly predict why some societies have many, as opposed to few, areas in which the status of women is high. Let us turn first to the ideas that are not supported by the available cross-cultural evidence. The idea that generally high status derives from a greater caloric contribution to primary subsistence activities is not supported at all.[52] Women in intensive agricultural societies (who contribute less than men to primary subsistence) do tend to have lower status in many areas of life, just as in the Iraqi case described earlier. But in societies that depend mostly on hunting (where women also do little of the primary subsistence work), women seem to have higher status, which contradicts the theoretical expectation. Similarly, there is no consistent evidence that a high frequency of warfare generally lowers women's status in different spheres of life.[53]

What does predict higher status for women in many areas of life? Although the results are not strong, there is some support in Whyte's study for the theory that where kin groups and marital residence are organized around women, women have somewhat higher status. (We discuss these features of society more fully in the chapter on marriage, family, and kinship.) The Iroquois are a good example. Even though Iroquois women could not hold political office, they had considerable authority within and beyond the household. Related women lived together in longhouses with husbands who belonged to other kin groups. In the longhouse, the women's authority was clear, and they could ask objectionable men to leave. The women controlled the allocation of the food they produced. Allocation could influence the timing of war parties, since men could not undertake a raid without provisions. Women were involved in the selection of religious leaders, half of whom were women. Even in politics, although women could not speak or serve on the council, they largely controlled the selection of councilmen and could institute impeachment proceedings against those to whom they objected.[54]

If we look at nonindustrial or preindustrial societies, a generally lower status for women is more likely in societies with political hierarchies.[55] Lower status for women appears to be associated with other indicators of cultural complexity—social stratification, plow and irrigation agriculture, large settlements, private property, and craft specialization. One type of influence for women increases with cultural complexity—informal influence. But, as Whyte pointed out, informal influence may simply reflect a lack of *real* influence.[56] Why cultural complexity is associated with women having less authority in the home, less control over property, and more restricted sexual lives is not yet understood. However, the relationship between cultural complexity and gender equality appears to change when we include industrial and postindustrial societies. Judging by a comparative study of gender attitudes in 61 countries, it seems that developing countries relying on agriculture such as Nigeria and Peru have the least favorable attitudes toward gender equality, industrial societies such as Russia and Taiwan have moderately favorable attitudes, and postindustrial societies such as Sweden and the United States have the most favorable attitudes toward gender equality.[57]

Western colonialism appears to have been generally detrimental to women's status, perhaps because Westerners were accustomed to dealing with men. There are plenty of examples of Europeans restructuring landownership around men and teaching men modern farming techniques, even in places where women were usually the farmers. In addition, men more often than women could earn cash through wage labor or through sales of goods (such as furs) to Europeans.[58] Although the relative status of men and women may not have been equal before the Europeans arrived, colonial influences seem generally to have undermined the position of women.

Personality Differences

Much of the research on gender differences in personality has taken place in the United States and other Western countries where psychology is a major field of study. While such studies are informative, they do not tell us whether the observed differences hold true in cultures very different from our own. Fortunately, we now have systematic observational studies for various non-Western societies. These studies recorded the minute details of behavior of substantial numbers of males and females. Any conclusions about female-male differences in aggressiveness, for example, are based on actual counts of the number of times a particular individual tried to hurt or injure another person during a given amount of observation time. Almost all of these differences are subtle and a matter of degree, not a matter of a behavior being present or absent in females or males.

Which differences in personality are suggested by these systematic studies? Most of them have observed children in different cultural settings. The most consistent difference is in the area of aggression; boys try to hurt others more frequently than girls do. In an extensive comparative study of children's behavior, the Six Cultures project, this difference showed up as early as three to six years of age.[59] In the Six Cultures project, six different research teams observed children's behavior in Kenya (among the Gusii), Mexico, India, the Philippines, Okinawa, and the United States. A more recent cross-cultural comparison of four other cultures (the Logoli of Kenya, Nepal, Belize, and American Samoa) supports the sex difference in aggression.[60] Studies in the United States are consistent with the cross-cultural findings: In a large number of observation and experimental studies, boys exhibited more aggression than girls.[61]

Other female-male differences have turned up with considerable consistency, but we have to be cautious in accepting them, either because they have not been documented as well or because there are more exceptions. There seems to be a tendency for girls to exhibit more responsible behavior, including nurturance (trying to help others). Girls seem more likely to conform to adult wishes and commands. Boys try more often to exert dominance over others in order to get their own way. In play, boys and girls show a preference for their own gender. Boys seem to play in large groups, girls in small ones. And boys seem to maintain more distance between each other than girls do.[62]

If we assume that these differences are consistent across cultures, how can we explain them? Many writers and researchers believe that because certain female-male differences are so consistent, they are probably rooted in the biological differences between the two sexes. Aggression is one of the traits talked about most often in this connection, particularly because this male-female difference appears so early in life.[63] But an alternative argument is that societies bring up boys and girls differently because they almost

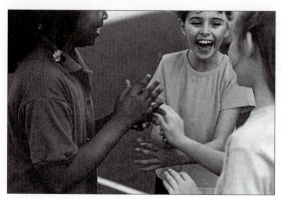

Cross-culturally, girls more often play in small, intimate groups, boys in larger groups.

universally require adult males and females to perform different types of roles. If most societies expect adult males to be warriors or to be prepared to be warriors, shouldn't we expect most societies to encourage or idealize aggression in males? And if females are almost always the caretakers of infants, shouldn't we also expect societies generally to encourage nurturant behaviors in females?

Researchers tend to adopt either the biological or the socialization view, but it is possible that both kinds of causes are important in the development of gender differences. For example, parents might turn a slight genetic difference into a large gender difference by maximizing that difference in the way they socialize boys versus girls.

It is difficult for researchers to distinguish the influence of genes and other biological conditions from the influence of socialization. We have research indicating that as early as birth, parents treat boy and girl infants differently.[64] In spite of the fact that objective observers can see no major "personality" differences between girl and boy infants, parents often claim to.[65] But parents may unconsciously want to see differences and may therefore produce them in socialization. So even early differences could be learned rather than genetic. Remember, too, that researchers cannot do experiments with people; for example, parents' behavior cannot be manipulated to find out what would happen if boys and girls were treated in exactly the same ways.

However, there is considerable experimental research on aggression in nonhuman animals. These experiments suggest that the hormone androgen is partly responsible for higher levels of aggression. For example, in some experiments, females injected with androgen at about the time the sexual organs develop (before or shortly after birth) behave more aggressively when they are older than do females without the hormone. These results may or may not apply to humans of course, but some researchers have investigated human females who were "androgenized" in the womb because of drugs given to their mothers to prevent miscarriage. By and large the results of these studies are similar to the experimental studies—androgenized human females show similar patterns of higher aggression.[66] Some scholars take these results to indicate that biological differences between males and females are responsible for the male-female difference in aggression;[67] others suggest that even these results are not conclusive, because females who get more androgen show generally disturbed metabolic systems, and general metabolic disturbance may itself increase aggressiveness. Furthermore, androgen-injected females may look more like males because they develop male-like genitals; therefore, they may be treated like males.[68]

Is there any evidence that socialization differences may account for differences in aggression? Although a cross-cultural survey of ethnographers' reports on 101 societies does show that more societies encourage aggression in boys than in girls, most societies show no difference in aggression training.[69] The few

societies that do show differences in aggression training can hardly account for the widespread sex differences in actual aggressiveness. But the survey does not necessarily mean that there are no consistent
differences in aggression training for boys and girls. All it shows is that there are no *obvious* differences.
For all we know, the learning of aggression and other "masculine" traits by boys could be produced by
subtle types of socialization.

One possible type of subtle socialization that could create gender differences in behavior is the chores
children are assigned. It is possible that little boys and girls learn to behave differently because their parents ask them to do different kinds of work. Beatrice and John Whiting reported from the Six Cultures
project that in societies where children were asked to do a great deal of work, they generally showed more
responsible and nurturant behavior. Because girls are almost always asked to do more work than boys,
they may be more responsible and nurturant for this reason alone.[70] If this reasoning is correct, we should
find that if boys are asked to do girls' work, they will learn to behave more like girls.

A study of Luo children in Kenya supports this view.[71] Girls were usually asked to babysit, cook, clean
house, and fetch water and firewood. Boys were usually asked to do very little because boys' traditional
work was herding cattle, and most families in the community studied had few cattle. But more boys
than girls had been born during that period, and many mothers without girls at home asked their sons
to do girls' chores. Systematic behavior observations showed that much of the behavior of the boys who
did girls' work was intermediary between the behavior of other boys and the behavior of girls. The boys
who did girls' work were more like girls in that they were less aggressive, less domineering, and more responsible than other boys, even when they weren't working. So it is possible that task assignment has an
important influence on how boys and girls learn to behave. These and other subtle forms of socialization
need to be investigated more thoroughly.

Misconceptions about Differences in Behavior

Before we leave the subject of behavior differences, we should note some widespread beliefs about them
that are not supported by research. Some of these mistaken beliefs are that girls are more dependent than
boys, that girls are more sociable, and that girls are more passive. The results obtained by the Six Cultures project cast doubt on all these notions.[72] First, if we think of dependency as seeking help and emotional support from others, girls are generally no more likely to behave this way than boys. To be sure,
the results do indicate that boys and girls have somewhat different styles of dependency. Girls more often
seek help and contact; boys more often seek attention and approval. As for sociability, which means seeking and offering friendship, the Six Cultures results showed no reliable differences between the sexes. Of
course, boys and girls may be sociable in different ways because boys generally play in larger groups than
girls. As for the supposed passivity of girls, the evidence is also not particularly convincing. Girls in the
Six Cultures project did not consistently withdraw from aggressive attacks or comply with unreasonable
demands. The only thing that emerged as a female-male difference was that older girls were less likely than
boys to respond to aggression with aggression. But this finding may not reflect passivity as much as the
fact that girls are less aggressive than boys, which we already knew.

So some of our common ideas about female-male differences are unfounded. Others, such as those
dealing with aggression and responsibility, cannot be readily dismissed and should be investigated further.

As we noted, an observed difference in aggression does not mean that males are aggressive and females are not. Perhaps because males are generally more aggressive, aggression in females has been studied less often. For that reason, Victoria Burbank focused on female aggression in an Australian aborigine
community she calls Mangrove. During the 18 months that she was there, Burbank observed some act
of aggression almost every other day. Consistent with the cross-cultural evidence, men initiated aggression more often than women, but women were initiators about 43 percent of the time. The women of

Mangrove engaged in almost all the same kinds of aggression as men did, including fighting, except that it tended not to be as lethal as male violence. Lethal weapons were most often used by men; when women fought with weapons, they mostly used sticks, not spears, guns, or knives. Burbank points out that, in contrast to Western cultures, female aggression is not viewed as unnatural or deviant but rather as a natural expression of anger.[73]

Sexuality

In view of the way the human species reproduces, it is not surprising that sexuality is part of our nature. But no society we know of leaves sexuality to nature; all have at least some rules governing "proper" conduct. There is much variation from one society to another in the degree of sexual activity permitted or encouraged before marriage, outside marriage, and even within marriage. And societies vary markedly in their tolerance of nonheterosexual sexuality.

Cultural Regulations of Sexuality: Permissiveness versus Restrictiveness

All societies seek to regulate sexual activity to some degree, and there is a lot of variation cross-culturally. Some societies allow premarital sex; others forbid it. The same is true for extramarital sex. In addition, a society's degree of restrictiveness is not always consistent throughout the life span or for all aspects of sex. For example, a number of societies ease sexual restrictions somewhat for adolescents, and many become more restrictive for adults.[74] Then, too, societies change over time. The United States has traditionally been restrictive, but until recently—before the emergence of the AIDS epidemic—more permissive attitudes were gaining acceptance.

Premarital Sex   The degree to which sex before marriage is approved or disapproved of varies greatly from society to society. The Trobriand Islanders, for example, approved of and encouraged premarital sex, seeing it as an important preparation for later marriage roles. Both girls and boys were given complete instruction in all forms of sexual expression at the onset of puberty and were allowed plenty of opportunity for intimacy. Some societies not only allow premarital sex on a casual basis but specifically encourage trial marriages between adolescents. Among the Ila-speaking peoples of central Africa, at harvest time girls were given houses of their own where they could play at being wife with the boys of their choice.[75]

Some cultures are more relaxed about sexuality than others. Does public sculpture reflect that? A park in Oslo, Norway, is dedicated to sculptures by Gustav Vigeland.

On the other hand, in many societies premarital sex was discouraged. For example, among the Tepoztlan Indians of Mexico, a girl's life became "crabbed, cribbed, confined" from the time of her first menstruation. She was not to speak to or encourage boys in the least way. To do so would be to court disgrace, to show herself to be crazy. The responsibility of guarding the chastity and reputation of one or more daughters of marriageable age was often a burden for the mother. One mother said she wished her 15-year-old daughter would marry soon because it was inconvenient to "spy" on her all the time.[76] In many Muslim societies, a girl's premarital chastity was tested after her marriage. After the wedding night, blood-stained sheets were displayed as proof of the bride's virginity.

Attitudes and practices can change markedly over time, as in the United States. Sex was generally delayed in the past until after marriage; in the 1990s, most Americans accepted or approved of premarital sex.[77]

Sex in Marriage   In most societies some form of face-to-face sexual intercourse or coitus is the usual pattern, most preferring the woman on her back and the man on top. Couples in most cultures prefer privacy. This is easier in societies with single family dwellings or separate rooms, but in societies with unpartitioned dwellings and multiple families living there, privacy is difficult to attain in the house. For example, the Siriono of Bolivia had as many as 50 hammocks 10 feet apart in their houses. Not surprisingly, couples in such societies prefer to have sex outdoors in a secluded location.[78]

Night is often preferred for sex, but some cultures specifically opted for day. For example, the Chenchu of India believed that a child conceived at night might be born blind. In some societies couples engage in sex quickly with little or no foreplay; in others foreplay may take hours.[79] Attitudes toward marital sex and the frequency of it vary widely from culture to culture. In one cross-cultural survey, 70 percent of the surveyed societies believe that frequent marital sex is viewed as a good thing, but in 9 percent frequent sex by married couples is viewed as undesirable, causing weakness, illness, and sometimes death.[80] People in most societies abstain from intercourse during menstruation, during at least part of pregnancy, and for a period after childbirth. Some societies prohibit sexual relations before various activities, such as hunting, fighting, planting, brewing, and iron smelting. Our own society is among the most lenient regarding restrictions on intercourse within marriage, imposing only rather loose restraints during mourning, menstruation, and pregnancy.[81]

Extramarital Sex   Extramarital sex is not uncommon in many societies. In about 69 percent of the world's societies men have extramarital sex more than occasionally, and in about 57 percent so do women. The frequency of such sexual activity is higher than we might expect, given that only a slight majority of societies (54 percent) say they allow extramarital sex for men, and only a small number (11 percent) say they allow it for women.[82]

In quite a few societies, then, there is quite a difference between the restrictive rule and actual practice. The Navajo of the 1940s were said to forbid adultery, but young married men under the age of 30 had 27 percent of their heterosexual contacts with women other than their wives.[83] And although people in the United States in the 1970s almost overwhelmingly rejected extramarital sex, 41 percent of married men and about 18 percent of married women had had extramarital sex. In the 1990s, proportionately more men and women reported that they had been faithful to their spouses.[84] Cross-culturally, most societies have a double standard with regard to men and women, with restrictions considerably greater for women.[85] A substantial number of societies openly accept extramarital relationships. The Chukchee of Siberia, who often traveled long distances, allowed a married man to engage in sex with his host's wife, with the understanding that he would offer the same hospitality when the host visited him.[86]

Although a society may allow extramarital sex, a recent cross-cultural study of individual reactions to extramarital sex finds that men and women try a variety of strategies to curtail such sex. Men are much more likely than women to resort to physical violence against their wives; women are more likely to distance themselves from their husbands. Gossip may be employed to shame the relationship and in more complex societies a higher authority may be asked to intervene. The researchers conclude that married women and men universally consider extramarital sex inappropriate, even in societies that permit it sometimes.[87]

Homosexuality   When most anthropologists discuss homosexuality they usually refer to sex between males or sex between females. But while the biological male/female dichotomy corresponds to the gender male/female dichotomy in the West, other societies do not have the same gender concepts, so that the meaning of homosexuality may be different in different societies. For example, the Navajo of the American Southwest traditionally recognized four genders. Only relationships between people of the same gender would be considered homosexual and they considered such relationships inappropriate.[88] Biologically speaking, some of the cross-gender relationships would be considered homosexual in the Western view. Most of the research to date has adopted the biological view that homosexuality is between people of the same biological sex.

The range in permissiveness or restrictiveness toward homosexual relations is as great as that for any other kind of sexual activity. Among the Lepcha of the Himalayas, a man was believed to become homosexual if he ate the flesh of an uncastrated pig. But the Lepcha said that homosexual behavior was practically unheard of, and they viewed it with disgust.[89] Perhaps because many societies deny that homosexuality exists, little is known about homosexual practices in the restrictive societies. Among the permissive ones, there is variation in the type and pervasiveness of homosexuality. In some societies homosexuality is accepted but limited to certain times and certain individuals. For example, among the Papago of the southwestern United States there were "nights of saturnalia" in which homosexual tendencies could be expressed. The Papago also had many male transvestites, who wore women's clothing, did women's chores, and, if not married, could be visited by men.[90] A woman did not have the same freedom of expression. She could participate in the saturnalia feasts but only with her husband's permission, and female transvestites were nonexistent.

Homosexuality occurs even more widely in other societies. The Berber-speaking Siwans of North Africa expected all males to engage in homosexual relations. In fact, fathers made arrangements for their unmarried sons to be given to an older man in a homosexual arrangement. Siwan custom limited a man to one boy. Fear of the Egyptian government made this a secret matter, but before 1909 such arrangements were made openly. Almost all men were reported to have engaged in a homosexual relationship as boys; later, when they were between 16 and 20, they married girls.[91] Such prescribed homosexual relationships between persons of different ages are a common form of homosexuality.[92] Among the most extremely prohomosexual societies, the Etoro of New Guinea preferred homosexuality to heterosexuality. Heterosexuality was prohibited as many as 260 days a year and was forbidden in or near the house and gardens. Male homosexuality, on the other hand, was not prohibited at any time and was believed to make crops flourish and boys become strong.[93] Even among the Etoro, however, men were expected to marry women after a certain age.[94]

It is only recently that researchers have paid much attention to erotic relationships between females. Although early studies found relatively few societies with female-female sexual relationships, Evelyn Blackwood located reports of ninety-five societies with such practices, suggesting that it is more common than previously thought.[95] As with male homosexuality, some societies institutionalize same-sex sexual relationships—the Kaguru of Tanzania have female homosexual relationships between older and younger women as part of their initiation ceremonies, reminiscent of the male-male "mentor" relationships in ancient Greece.

Reasons for Restrictiveness

The research to date suggests that societies that are restrictive with regard to one aspect of heterosexual sex tend to be restrictive with regard to other aspects. Thus, societies that frown on sexual expression by young children also punish premarital and extramarital sex.[96] Furthermore, such societies tend to insist on modesty in clothing and are constrained in their talk about sex.[97] But societies that are generally restrictive about heterosexuality are not necessarily restrictive about homosexuality. Societies restrictive about premarital sex are neither more nor less likely to restrict homosexuality. In the case of extramarital sex, the situation is somewhat different. Societies that have a considerable amount of male homosexuality tend to disapprove of males having extramarital heterosexual relationships.[98] If we are going to explain restrictiveness, then, it appears we have to consider heterosexual and homosexual restrictiveness separately.

Let us consider homosexual restrictiveness first. Research so far has not yielded any clear-cut predictions, although several cross-cultural predictors about male homosexuality are intriguing. One such finding is that societies that forbid abortion and infanticide for married women (most societies permit these practices for illegitimate births) are likely to be intolerant of male homosexuality.[99] This and other findings are consistent with the point of view that homosexuality is less tolerated in societies that would like to increase population. Such societies may be intolerant of all kinds of behaviors that minimize population growth. Homosexuality would have this effect, if we assume that a higher frequency of homosexual relations is associated with a lower frequency of heterosexual relations. The less frequently heterosexual relations occur, the lower the number of conceptions there might be. Another indication that intolerance may be related to a desire for population growth is that societies with famines and severe food shortages are more likely to allow homosexuality. Famines and food shortages suggest population pressure on resources; under these conditions, homosexuality and other practices that minimize population growth may be tolerated or even encouraged.[100] Population pressure may also explain why our own society has become somewhat more tolerant of homosexuality recently. Of course, population pressure does not explain why certain individuals become homosexual or why most individuals in some societies engage in such behavior, but it might explain why some societies view such behavior more or less permissively.

Let us now turn to heterosexual behavior. Greater restrictiveness toward premarital sex tends to occur in more complex societies—societies that have hierarchies of political officials, part-time or full-time craft specialists, cities and towns, and class stratification.[101] It may be that as social inequality increases and various groups come to have differential wealth, parents become more concerned with preventing their children from marrying "beneath them." Permissiveness toward premarital sexual relationships might lead a person to become attached to someone not considered a desirable marriage partner. Even worse, from the family's point of view, such "unsuitable" sexual liaisons might result in a pregnancy that could make it impossible for a girl to marry "well." Controlling mating, then, may be a way of trying to control property. Consistent with this view is the finding that virginity is more likely to be emphasized in rank and stratified societies, in which families are likely to exchange goods and money in the course of arranging marriages.[102]

The biological fact that humans depend on sexual reproduction does not by itself help explain why females and males differ in so many ways across cultures, or why societies vary in the way they handle male and female roles. We are only beginning to investigate these questions. When we eventually understand more about how and why females and males are different or the same in roles, personality, and sexuality, we may be better able to decide how much we want the biology of sex to shape our lives.

Summary

1. That humans reproduce sexually does not explain why males and females tend to differ in appearance and behavior, and to be treated differently, in all societies.

2. All or nearly all societies assign certain activities to females and other activities to males. These worldwide gender patterns of division of labor may be explained by male-female differences in strength,

by differences in compatibility of tasks with child care, or by economy-of-effort considerations and/or the expendability of men.

3.   Perhaps because women almost always have infant-and-child-care responsibilities, men in most societies contribute more to primary subsistence activities, in terms of calories. But women contribute substantially to primary subsistence activities in societies that depend heavily on gathering and horticulture and in which warfare occurs while primary subsistence work has to be done. When primary and secondary subsistence work are counted, women typically work more hours than men. In most societies men are the leaders in the political arena, and warfare is almost exclusively a male activity.

4.   The relative status of women compared with that of men seems to vary from one area of life to another. Whether women have relatively high status in one area does not necessarily indicate that they will have high status in another. Less complex societies, however, seem to approach more equal status for males and females in a variety of areas of life.

5.   Recent field studies have suggested some consistent female-male differences in personality: Boys tend to be more aggressive than girls, and girls seem to be more responsible and helpful than boys.

6.   Societies that are restrictive toward one aspect of heterosexual sex tend to be restrictive with regard to other aspects. And more complex societies tend to be more restrictive toward premarital heterosexual sex than less complex societies.

7.   Societal attitudes toward homosexuality are not completely consistent with attitudes toward sexual relationships between the sexes. Societal tolerance of homosexuality is associated with tolerance of abortion and infanticide and with famines and food shortages.

Glossary Terms

compatibility-with child-care theory (p. 118)   primary subsistence activities (p. 121)
economy-of-effort theory (p. 120)   secondary subsistence activities (p. 121)
expendability theory (p. 120)   sex differences (p. 116)
gender differences (p. 116)   sexually dimorphic (p. 117)
gender roles (p. 118)   strength theory (p. 118)
gender stratification (p. 127)

Critical Questions

1.   Would you expect female-male differences in personality to disappear in a society with complete gender equality in the workplace?

2.   Under what circumstances would you expect male-female differences in athletic performance to disappear?

3.   What conditions make the election of a female head of state most likely?

CHAPTER 7

MARRIAGE, FAMILY, AND KINSHIP

Chapter Outline

- Marriage
- The Family

- Marital Residence and Kinship

Why marriage is customary in nearly every society we know of is a classic and perplexing question, and one we attempt to deal with in this chapter. The universality of marriage does not mean that everyone in every society gets married, nor that marriage and family customs are the same in all societies. On the contrary, there is much variation from society to society in how one marries, whom one marries, and even how many persons a person can be married to simultaneously.

Families also are universal. All societies have parent-child social groups, although the form and size of families may vary. Some societies have large extended families with two or more related parent-child groups; others have smaller independent families. One-parent families are becoming increasingly common in our own and other societies. Marriage has not disappeared in these places—it is still customary to marry—but more individuals are choosing now to have children without being married.

As we will see, kin groups that include several or many families and hundreds or even thousands of people are found in many societies and structure many areas of social life. Kin groups may have important economic, social, political, and religious functions.

Marriage

When anthropologists speak of marriage, they do not mean to imply that couples everywhere must get marriage certificates or have wedding ceremonies, as in our own society. **Marriage** merely means a socially approved sexual and economic union, usually between a woman and a man. It is presumed, by both the couple and others, to be more or less permanent, and it subsumes reciprocal rights and obligations between the two spouses and between spouses and their future children.[1]

It is a socially approved sexual union in that a married couple does not have to hide the sexual nature of their relationship. A woman might say, "I want you to meet my husband," but she could not say, "I want you to meet my lover" without causing some embarrassment in most societies. Although the union may ultimately be dissolved by divorce, couples in all societies begin marriage with some idea of permanence in mind. Implicit too in marriage are reciprocal rights and obligations. These may be more or less

Weddings in some societies are very elaborate. Here a Minangkabau bride dressed in elaborate clothes sits in the windowsill of a home in Padang, West Sumatra, Indonesia.

specific and formalized regarding matters of property, finances, and child rearing. Marriage entails both a sexual and an economic relationship, as George Peter Murdock noted: "Sexual relations can occur without economic cooperation, and there can be a division of labor between men and women without sex. But marriage unites the economic and the sexual."[2]

Why Is Marriage Universal?

Because virtually all societies practice female-male marriage as we have defined it, we can assume that the custom is adaptive. Several interpretations have traditionally been offered to explain why all human societies have the custom of marriage. Each suggests that marriage solves problems found in all societies—how to share the products of a gender division of labor; how to care for infants, who are dependent for a long time; and how to minimize sexual competition. To evaluate the plausibility of these interpretations, we must ask whether marriage provides the best or the only reasonable solution to each problem. After all, we are trying to explain a custom that is presumably a universal solution. The comparative study of other animals, some of which have something like marriage, may help us to evaluate these explanations.

Gender Division of Labor   We noted in the chapter on sex and gender that males and females in every society perform different economic activities. This gender division of labor has often been cited as a reason for marriage because society has to have some mechanism by which women and men share the products of their labor.[3] But it seems unlikely that marriage is the only possible solution. All the products brought in by both women and men could be shared in the group. Or a small group of men and women, such as brothers and sisters, might be pledged to cooperate economically. Thus, although marriage may solve the problem of sharing the fruits of a division of labor, it clearly is not the only possible solution.

Prolonged Infant Dependency   Humans exhibit the longest period of infant dependency of any primate. The child's prolonged dependence places the greatest burden on the mother, who is the main child caregiver in most societies. Prolonged child care may limit the kinds of work mothers can do. Also, they may need the help of a man to do certain types of work, such as hunting, that are incompatible with child care. Because of this prolonged dependency, it has been suggested, marriage is necessary.[4] But here the argument becomes essentially the same as the division-of-labor argument, and it has the same logical weakness. It is not clear why a group of women and men, such as a hunter-gatherer band, could not cooperate in providing for dependent children without marriage.

Sexual Competition   Unlike most other female primates, the human female may engage in intercourse at any time throughout the year. Some scholars have suggested that more or less continuous female sexuality created a serious problem—considerable sexual competition between males for females. It is argued that society had to prevent such competition in order to survive, that it had to develop marriage to minimize the rivalry among males for females in order to reduce the chance of lethal and destructive conflict.[5]

There are several problems with this argument. First, why should continuous female sexuality make for more sexual competition in the first place? One might argue the other way around. There might be more if females were less frequently interested in sex. Second, males of many animal species, even some that have relatively frequent female sexuality (as do many of our close primate relatives), do not show much aggression over females. Third, why couldn't sexual competition, even if it existed, be regulated by cultural rules other than marriage? For instance, society might have adopted a rule whereby men and women circulated among all the opposite-sex members of the group, each person staying a specified length of time with each partner. Such a system presumably would solve the problem of sexual competition. On the other hand, such a system might not work particularly well if individuals came to prefer certain other individuals. Jealousies attending those attachments might give rise to even more competition.

Other Mammals and Birds: Postpartum Requirements   None of the theories we have discussed explains convincingly why marriage is the only or the best solution to a particular problem. Also, we now have some comparative evidence on mammals and birds that casts doubt on those theories.[6] How can evidence from other animals help us evaluate theories about human marriage? If we look at the animals that, like humans, have some sort of stable female-male mating, as compared with those that are completely promiscuous, we can perhaps see what sorts of factors may predict male-female bonding in the warm-blooded animal species. Most species of birds, and some mammals such as wolves and beavers, have "marriage." In a random sample of 40 mammal and bird species, none of the 3 factors previously discussed —division of labor, prolonged infant dependency, and greater female sexuality—predicts or is correlated strongly with male-female bonding. With respect to division of labor by sex, most other animals have nothing comparable to a humanlike division of labor, but many have stable female-male matings anyway. The two other supposed factors—prolonged infant dependency and female sexuality—predict just the opposite of what we might expect. Mammal and bird species that have longer dependency periods or more female sexuality are less likely to have stable matings.

Does anything predict male-female bonding? One factor does among mammals and birds, and it may also help explain human marriage. Animal species in which females can simultaneously feed themselves and their babies after birth (*postpartum*) tend not to have stable matings; species in which postpartum mothers cannot feed themselves and their babies at the same time tend to have stable matings. Among the typical bird species, a mother would have difficulty feeding herself and her babies simultaneously. Because the young cannot fly for a while and must be protected in a nest, the mother risks losing them to other animals if she goes off to obtain food. But if she has a male bonded to her (as most bird species do), he can bring back food or take a turn watching the nest. Among animal species that have no postpartum feeding problem, babies almost immediately after birth are able to travel with the mother as she moves about to eat (as do grazers such as horses), or the mother can transport the babies as she moves about to eat (as do baboons and kangaroos). We think the human female has a postpartum feeding problem. When humans lost most of their body hair, babies could not readily travel with the mother by clinging to her fur. And when humans began to depend on certain kinds of food-getting that could be dangerous (such as hunting), mothers could not engage in such work with their infants along.[7]

"I do love you. But, to be perfectly honest, I would have loved any other lovebird who happened to turn up."
(Rothco Cartoons)

Recent research on the Hadza foragers of Tanzania appears to support this view. Frank Marlowe found that the caloric contribution of mothers and fathers depends on whether or not they have a nursing infant. Women may generally contribute more calories than men to the diet, but married women who are nursing contribute substantially less than other married women. The lower contribution of nursing mothers appears to be made up by the father. Fathers with nursing children contribute significantly more food to the household than fathers with older children.[8]

Even if we assume that human mothers have a postpartum feeding problem, we still have to ask if marriage is the most likely solution to the problem. We think so, because other conceivable solutions probably would not work as well. For example, if a mother took turns babysitting with another mother, neither might be able to collect enough food for both mothers and the two sets of children dependent on them. But a mother and father share the same set of children, and therefore it would be easier for them to feed themselves and their children adequately. Another possible solution is no pair bonding at all, just a promiscuous group of males and females. But in that kind of arrangement, we think, a particular mother probably would not always be able to count on some male to watch her baby when she had to go out for food or to bring her food when she had to watch her baby. Thus, it seems to us that the problem of postpartum feeding by itself helps to explain why some animals, including humans, have relatively stable male-female bonds.[9] Of course, there is still the question of whether research on other animals can be applied to human beings. We think it can, but not everybody will agree.

How Does One Marry?

When we say that marriage is a socially approved sexual and economic union, we mean that all societies have some way of marking the onset of a marriage, but the ways of doing so vary considerably. For reasons that we don't fully understand, some cultures mark marriages by elaborate rites and celebrations; others mark marriages in much more informal ways. And most societies have economic transactions before, during, or even after the onset of the marriages.

Economic Aspects of Marriage   "It's not man that marries maid, but field marries field, vineyard marries vineyard, cattle marry cattle." In its down-to-earth way, this German peasant saying indicates that in many societies marriage involves economic considerations. In about 75 percent of the societies known to anthropology,[10] one or more explicit economic transactions take place before or after the marriage.

Bride Price   **Bride price or bride wealth** is a gift of money or goods from the groom or his kin to the bride's kin. The gift usually grants the groom the right to marry the bride and the right to her children. Bride price is the most common form of economic transaction. In one cross-cultural sample, 44 percent of the societies with economic transactions at marriage practiced bride price; in almost all of those societies the bride price was substantial.[11] Bride price occurs all over the world but is especially common in Africa and Oceania. Payment can be made in different currencies; livestock and food are two of the more common. With the increased importance of commercial exchange, money has increasingly become part of the bride price payments.

What kinds of societies are likely to have the custom of bride price? Cross-culturally, societies with bride price are likely to practice horticulture and lack social stratification. Bride price is also likely where women contribute a great deal to primary subsistence activities[12] and where they contribute more than men to all kinds of economic activities.[13] Although these findings might suggest that women are highly valued in such societies, recall that the status of women relative to men is not higher in societies in which women contribute a lot to primary subsistence activities. Indeed, bride price is likely to occur in societies

A priest in India prays for young women to get good husbands and to have many sons. Marriages are often still arranged.

and eastern and southern Europe. Implicit in the arranged marriage is the conviction that the joining together of two kin groups to form new social and economic ties is too important to be left to free choice.

In many places arranged marriages are beginning to disappear, and couples are beginning to have more say about their marriage partners. As recently as 1960, marriages were still arranged on the Pacific island of Rotuma, and sometimes the bride and groom did not meet until the wedding day. Today weddings are much the same, but couples are allowed to "go out" and have a say about whom they wish to marry.[24]

Exogamy and Endogamy   Marriage partners often must be chosen from outside one's own kin group or community; this is known as a rule of **exogamy**. Exogamy may mean marrying outside a particular group of kin or outside a particular village or group of villages. When there are rules of exogamy, violations are often believed to cause harm. On the islands of Yap in Micronesia, people who are related through women are referred to as "people of one belly." The elders say that if two people from the same kinship group married, they would not have any female children and the group would die out.[25]

A study of foragers and horticulturalists found a clear relationship between population density and the distance between the communities of the husband and wife—the lower the density, the greater the marriage distance. Because foragers generally have lower densities than horticulturalists, they generally have further to go to find mates. Among the !Kung, for instance, the average husband and wife had lived 65 kilometers (40 miles) from each other before they were married.[26]

A rule of **endogamy** obliges a person to marry within some group. The caste groups of India traditionally have been endogamous. The higher castes believed that marriage with lower castes would "pollute" them, and such unions were forbidden. Caste endogamy is also found in some parts of Africa.

Cousin Marriages   Kinship terminology for most people in the United States does not differentiate between types of cousins. In some other societies such distinctions may be important, particularly with regard to first cousins; the terms for the different kinds of first cousins may indicate which cousins are suitable marriage partners (sometimes even preferred mates) and which are not. Although most societies prohibit marriage with all types of first cousins,[27] some societies allow and even prefer particular kinds of cousin marriage.

Cross-cousins are children of **siblings** of the opposite sex; that is, a person's cross-cousins are father's sisters' children and mother's brothers' children. **Parallel cousins** are children of siblings of the same sex; a person's parallel cousins, then, are father's brothers' children and mother's sisters' children. The Chippewa Indians used to practice cross-cousin marriage, as well as cross-cousin joking. With his female cross-cousins, a Chippewa man was expected to exchange broad, risqué jokes, but he would not do so with his parallel cousins, with whom severe propriety was the rule. In general, in any society in which cross-cousin marriage is allowed but parallel-cousin is not, there is a joking relationship between a man and his female cross-cousins. This attitude contrasts with the formal and very respectful relationship the man maintains with female parallel cousins. Apparently, the joking relationship signifies the possibility of marriage, whereas the respectful relationship signifies the extension of the incest taboo to parallel cousins.

Parallel-cousin marriage is fairly rare, but Muslim societies usually prefer such marriages, allowing other cousin marriages as well. The Kurds, who are mostly Sunni Muslims, prefer a young man to marry his father's brother's daughter (for the young woman this would be her father's brother's son). The father and his brother usually live near each other, so the woman will stay close to home in such a marriage. The bride and groom are also in the same kin group, so marriage in this case also entails kin group endogamy.[28]

There is evidence from cross-cultural research that cousin marriages are most apt to be permitted in relatively large and densely populated societies. Perhaps this is because the likelihood of such marriages, and therefore the risks of harmful inbreeding effects, are minimal in those societies.[29]

How Many Does One Marry?

We are accustomed to thinking of marriage as involving just one man and one woman at a time—**monogamy**—but most societies known to anthropology have allowed a man to be married to more than one woman at the same time—**polygyny**. At any given time, however, the majority of men in societies permitting polygyny are married monogamously; few or no societies have enough women to permit most men to have at least two wives. Polygyny's mirror image—one woman being married to more than one man at the same time, called **polyandry**—is practiced in very few societies. Polygyny and polyandry are the two types of **polygamy**, or plural spouse marriage. **Group marriage**, in which more than one man is married to more than one woman at the same time, sometimes occurs but is not customary in any known society.

Polygyny   The Old Testament has many references to men with more than one wife simultaneously: King David and King Solomon are just two examples of men polygynously married. Polygyny in many societies is a mark of a man's great wealth or high status. In such societies only the very wealthy can, and are expected to, support more than one wife. But a man does not always have to be wealthy to be polygynous; indeed, in some societies in which women are important contributors to the economy, it seems that men try to have more than one wife in order to become wealthier. For example, among the Siwai, a society in the South Pacific, status is achieved through feast giving. Pork is the main dish at these feasts, so the Siwai associate pig raising with prestige. This interest in pigs sparks an interest in wives, because in Siwai society women raise the food needed to raise pigs. Thus, although having many wives does not in itself confer status among the Siwai, the increase in pig herds that may result from polygyny is a source of prestige for the owner.[30]

Polygynously married Siwai men do seem to have greater prestige, but they complain that a household with multiple wives is difficult. Sinu, a Siwai, described his plight:

> There is never peace for a long time in a polygynous family. If the husband sleeps in the house of one wife, the other one sulks all the next day. If the man is so stupid as to sleep two consecutive nights in the house of one wife, the other one will refuse to cook for him, saying, "So-and-so is your wife; go to her for food. Since I am not good enough for you to sleep with, then my food is not good enough for you to eat."[31]

Why might there be little or no jealousy between co-wives in a society? One possible reason is that a man is married to two or more sisters—**sororal polygyny**; it seems that sisters, having grown up together, are more likely to get along and cooperate as co-wives than are co-wives who are not also sisters—**nonsororal polygyny**. Other customs may also lessen jealousy between co-wives:

1. Co-wives who are not sisters tend to have separate living quarters; sororal co-wives almost always live together.
2. Co-wives have clearly defined equal rights in matters of sex, economics, and personal possessions.
3. Senior wives often have special prestige, which may compensate the first wife for her loss of physical attractiveness.[32]

We must remember that, although jealousy is commonly mentioned in polygynous marriages, people who practice polygyny think it has considerable advantages. In a study conducted by Philip and Janet Kilbride in Kenya, female as well as male married people agreed that polygyny had economic and political advantages. Because they tend to be large, polygynous families provide plenty of farm labor and extra food that can be marketed. They also tend to be influential in their communities and are likely to produce individuals who become government officials.[33] And in South Africa, Connie Anderson found that women choose to be married to a man with other wives because the other wives could help with child care and household work, provide companionship, and allow more freedom to come and go. Some women said they chose polygynous marriages because there was a shortage of marriageable males.[34]

How can we account for the fact that polygyny is allowed and often preferred in most of the societies known to anthropology? One theory is that polygyny will be permitted in societies that have a long **postpartum sex taboo**.[35] Recall that John Whiting suggested that couples, particularly in societies where

Polygyny is practiced by some in this country, even though it is prohibited by law.

staple foods have little protein, abstain from sexual intercourse for a long time after their child is born to protect their child from *kwashiorkor*. If a child gets protein from mother's milk during its first few years, the likelihood of contracting kwashiorkor may be greatly reduced. Societies with long postpartum sex taboos also tend to be polygynous. Perhaps, Whiting suggests, a man's having more than one wife is a cultural adjustment to the taboo since men may seek other sexual relationships during the period of a long postpartum sex taboo. However, it is not clear why polygyny is the only possible solution to the problem. After all, it is conceivable that all of a man's wives might be subject to the postpartum sex taboo at the same time. Furthermore, there may be sexual outlets outside marriage.

Another explanation of polygyny is that it is a response to an excess of women over men due largely to the prevalence of warfare in a society. Because men and not women are generally the warriors, warfare almost always takes a greater toll of men's lives. Given that almost all adults in noncommercial societies are married, polygyny may be a way of providing spouses for surplus women. Indeed, there is evidence that societies with imbalanced sex ratios in favor of women tend to have both polygyny and high male mortality in warfare. Conversely, societies with balanced sex ratios tend to have both monogamy and low male mortality in warfare.[36]

A third explanation is that a society will allow polygyny when men marry at an older age than women. The argument is similar to the sex ratio interpretation. Delaying the age of marriage for men would produce an artificial, though not an actual, excess of marriageable women. Why marriage for men is delayed is not clear, but the delay does predict polygyny.[37]

Is one of these explanations better than the others, or are all three factors—long postpartum sex taboo, an imbalanced sex ratio in favor of women, and delayed age of marriage for men—important in explaining polygyny? One way of trying to decide among alternative explanations is to do what is called a *statistical-control analysis,* which allows us to see if a particular factor still predicts when the effects of other possible factors are removed. In this case, when the possible effect of sex ratio is removed, a long postpartum sex taboo no longer predicts polygyny and hence is probably not a cause of polygyny.[38] But both an actual excess of women and a late age of marriage for men seem to be strong predictors of polygyny. Added together, these two factors predict even more strongly.[39]

Behavioral ecologists have also suggested ecological reasons why both men and women might prefer polygynous marriages. If there are enough resources, men might prefer polygyny because they can have more children if they have more than one wife. If resources are highly variable and men control resources, women might find it advantageous to marry a man with many resources even if she is a second wife. A recent study of foragers suggests that foraging societies in which men control more hunting or fishing territory are more likely to be polygynous.[40] The main problem with the theory of variable resources and their marital consequences is that many societies, particularly in the "modern" world, have great variability in wealth, but little polygyny. So behavioral ecologists have had to argue that polygyny is lacking because of socially imposed constraints. Degree of disease in the environment may also be a factor. Bobbi Low has suggested that a high incidence of disease may reduce the prevalence of "healthy" men. In such cases it may be to a woman's advantage to marry a "healthy" man even if he is already married, and it may be to a man's advantage to marry several unrelated women to maximize genetic variation (and disease resistance) among his children. Indeed, societies with many pathogens are more likely to have polygyny.[41] Further research is needed to compare the degree of disease explanation of polygyny with the imbalanced sex-ratio explanation.

Polyandry George Peter Murdock's "World Ethnographic Sample" included only four societies (less than 1 percent of the total) in which polyandry, or the marriage of several men to one woman, was practiced.[42] When the husbands are brothers we call it *fraternal polyandry*; if they are not brothers, it is *nonfraternal polyandry*. Some Tibetans, the Toda of India, and the Sinhalese of Sri Lanka have practiced fraternal polyandry. Among the Tibetans who practice fraternal polyandry, biological paternity seems to be of no particular concern; there is no attempt to link children biologically to a particular brother, and all children are treated the same.[43]

One possible explanation for the practice of polyandry is a shortage of women. The Toda practiced female infanticide;[44] the Sinhalese had a shortage of women but denied the practice of female infanticide.[45] A correlation between shortage of women and polyandry would account for why polyandry is so rare in the ethnographic record; an excess of men is rare cross-culturally.

Another possible explanation is that polyandry is an adaptive response to severely limited resources. Melvyn Goldstein studied Tibetans who live in the northwestern corner of Nepal, above 12,000 feet in elevation. Cultivable land is extremely scarce there, with most families having less than an acre. The people say they practice fraternal polyandry in order to prevent the division of a family's farm and animals. Instead of dividing up their land among them and each taking a wife, brothers preserve the family farm by sharing a wife. Although not recognized by the Tibetans, their practice of polyandry minimizes population growth. There are as many women as men of marriageable age. But about 30 percent of the women do not marry, and, although these women do have some children, they have far fewer than married women. Thus, the practice of polyandry minimizes the number of mouths to feed and therefore maximizes the standard of living of the polyandrous family.[46]

The Family

All societies have families. A **family** is a social and economic unit consisting minimally of one or more parents and their children. Members of a family always have certain reciprocal rights and obligations, particularly economic ones. Family members usually live in one household, but common residence is not a defining feature of families. In simpler societies, the family and the household tend to be indistinguishable; it is only in more complex societies, and in societies becoming dependent on commercial exchange, that some members of a family may live elsewhere.[47]

Variation in Family Form

Most societies have families that are larger than the single-parent family (the parent in such families is usually the mother, in which case the unit is called the **matrifocal family**), the monogamous (single-couple) family (called the **nuclear family**), or the polygamous family. The **extended family** is the prevailing form of family in more than half the societies known to anthropology.[48] It may consist of two or more single-parent, monogamous, polygynous, or polyandrous families linked by a blood tie. Most commonly, the extended family consists of a married couple and one or more of the married children, all living in the same house or household. An extended family, however, is sometimes composed solely of families linked through a sibling tie. Such a family might consist of two married brothers, their wives, and their children. Extended families may be very large, containing many relatives and including three or four generations.

Extended-Family Households

In a society composed of extended-family households, marriage does not bring as pronounced a change in lifestyle as it does in our culture, where the couple typically moves to a new residence and forms a new, and basically independent, family unit. In extended families, the newlyweds are assimilated into an existing family unit. Margaret Mead described such a situation in Samoa:

. . . the young couple live in the main household, simply receiving a bamboo pillow, a mosquito net and a pile of mats for their bed. . . . The wife works with all the women of the household and waits on all the men. The husband shares the enterprises of the other men and boys. Neither in personal service given or received are the two marked off as a unit.[49]

A young couple in Samoa, as in other societies with extended families, generally has little decision-making power over the governing of the household. Often the responsibility of running the household rests with the senior male. Nor can the new family accumulate its own property and become independent; it is a part of the larger corporate structure. Eventually the young people will have authority when the parents die.

Possible Reasons for Extended-Family Households

Why do most societies known to anthropology commonly have extended-family households? Extended-family households are found most frequently in societies with sedentary agricultural economies. M. F. Nimkoff and Russell Middleton suggested that the extended family may be a social mechanism that prevents the economically ruinous division of family property in societies in which property such as cultivated land is important.[50]

But agriculture is only a weak predictor of extended-family households. Many agriculturalists lack them, and many nonagricultural societies have them. A different theory is that extended-family households come to prevail in societies that have incompatible activity requirements—that is, requirements that cannot be met by a mother or a father in a one-family household. In other words, extended-family households are generally favored when the work a mother has to do outside the home (cultivating fields or gathering foods far away) makes it difficult for her to also care for her children and do other household tasks. Similarly, extended families may be favored when the required outside activities of a father (warfare, trading trips, or wage labor far away) make it difficult for him to do the subsistence work required of males. There is cross-cultural evidence that societies with such incompatible activity requirements are more

Kazaks usually live in extended families and collectively herd their livestock. The youngest son will inherit the father's house, and the older sons will build their own houses nearby when they get married.

ONE-PARENT FAMILIES: WHY THE RECENT INCREASE?

Not only is the custom of marriage almost universal, but in most societies known to anthropology most people marry. And they usually remarry if they divorce. This means that, except for the death of a spouse or temporarily during times of divorce or separation, one-parent families are relatively uncommon in most societies.

In many Western countries, however, there has been a dramatic increase recently in the percentage of one-parent families, most of which (about 90 percent) are female-headed families. For example, in the 1960s about 9 percent of families in the United States were one-parent families, but by 2003 the figure jumped to about 30 percent. Whereas Sweden once led the Western countries in percentage of one-parent families—about 13 percent in the 1970s—the United States now has the higher percentage.

Before we examine the reasons for the increase, we need to consider that there are a variety of ways to become a one-parent family. First, many one-parent families result from the divorce or separation of two-parent families. Second, many one-parent families result from births out of wedlock. In addition, some result from the death of a spouse and others from the decision by a single person to have a child.

Many researchers suggest that the ease of divorce is largely responsible for the increase in one-parent families. On the face of it, this explanation seems plausible. But it is flawed. In many countries during the late 1960s and early 1970s, changes in the law made getting a divorce much easier, and the percentage of one-parent families did rise after that. But why did so many countries ease divorce restrictions at the same time? A high divorce rate by itself will make for a higher percentage of one-parent households only if individuals do not remarry quickly. In the United States, for example, remarriage rates did decline sharply in the mid-1960s, particularly among younger, better educated women, and so the percentage of one-parent households may have risen for that reason. In many other countries, divorce rates stabilized in the 1980s, but the percentage of one-parent families still increased. Thus, easier divorce does not fully explain the increase in number of one-parent families.

Although some parents are clearly choosing to stay single, many might prefer to marry if they could find an appropriate spouse. In some countries, and among some ethnic groups within some countries, there are many fewer males than females, and sometimes a high proportion of the males have poor economic prospects. In the former Soviet Union, there are many more women than men because males are more likely to have died from war, alcoholism, and accidents. The United States does not have such a skewed sex ratio, but in some neighborhoods, particularly poor neighborhoods, there are very high mortality rates for young males. And many males in such neighborhoods do not have work. One study by Daniel Lichter and his colleagues estimated that for every 100 African-American women between the ages of 21 and 28, there were fewer than 80 available African-American men. If we count only men who are employed full or part time, the number of available men per 100 women drops below 50. And a comparison of 85 countries finds that single parenthood is much more likely when there is higher male unemployment as well as when there are fewer men than women of a comparable age. So there may be considerable merit to the argument that one-parent families (usually headed by women) will be likely when a spouse (particularly an employed one) is hard to find.

Another popular explanation for the rise in number of one-parent families is that, in contrast to the past, women can manage without husbands because of support from the state. This scenario seems to fit Sweden, where unmarried and divorced mothers receive many social supports and allowances for maternity and educational leave. But Iceland has few social supports from the government and yet has the highest rate of out-of-wedlock births of all the Scandinavian countries. In the United States, the welfare argument fails to predict changes over time. The program called Aid to Families with Dependent Children provided aid largely to single mothers. If the theory about government help was correct, increases in such aid would generally predict increases in the percentage of mother-headed households. But, in fact, during the 1970s the percentage of families receiving aid and the value of aid decreased, while the percentage of mother-headed households increased. In the 1980s it was more difficult to go "on welfare," but the percentage of mother-headed households increased anyway.

Women might be more able to manage alone if they have high-paying employment, and therefore we might expect more one-parent families by choice, as more women enter the job market. But, although this may explain the choices of some women, recent research finds that employed women generally are *more* rather than less likely to marry.

In any case, there seems to be a general association between commercial economies and the possibility of one-parent families. Is there something about subsistence economies that promotes marriage and something about commercial economies that detracts from it? Although marriage is not universally based on love or companionship, it entails a great deal of economic and other kinds of interdependence, particularly in not-so-commercial economies. Market economies allow other possibilities; goods and services can be bought and sold, and governments may take over functions normally handled by kin and family. So the one-parent family is likely to remain an option—either a choice or a necessity—for some people.

Sources: Alisa Burns and Cath Scott, *Mother-Headed Families and Why They Have Increased* (Hillsdale, NJ: Lawrence Erlbaum Associates, 1994); David Popenoe, *Disturbing the Nest: Family Change and Decline in Modern Societies* (New York: Aldine, 1988); Daniel T. Lichter, Diane K. McLaughlin, George Kephart, and David J. Landry, "Race and the Retreat from Marriage: A Shortage of Marriageable Men?" *American Sociological Review,* 57 (1992): 781–99; Nigel Barber, "Paternal Investment Prospects and Cross-National Differences in Single Parenthood," *Cross-Cultural Research,* 37 (2003): 163–77; Jason Fields, *America's Families and Living Arrangements: 2003* (Washington, D.C.: Current Population Reports, P20-553, U.S. Census Bureau, 2003).

likely to have extended-family households than societies with compatible activity requirements, regardless of whether or not the society is agricultural. Even in commercial societies, a family may be able to obtain the necessary help by "buying" the required services so the need for extended families may be lessened.[51] Of course, even in societies with money economies, not everyone can buy required services. Those who are poor may need to live in extended families, and extended-family living may become more common even in the middle class when the economy is depressed.

In many societies there are kin groups even larger than extended families. The rest of this chapter discusses the varieties of such groupings.

Marital Residence and Kinship

In the United States and Canada, as well as in many other industrial societies, a young man and woman usually establish a place of residence apart from their parents or other relatives when they marry, if they have not already moved away before that. Our society is so oriented toward this pattern of marital residence—*neolocal (new-place) residence*—that it seems to be the obvious and natural one to follow. Young adults of all income levels learn to live away from home most of the year if they join the army or attend an out-of-town college. In any case, when a young person marries, he or she generally lives apart from family.

So familiar is neolocal residence to us that we tend to assume that all societies must practice the same pattern. On the contrary, of the 565 societies in George Peter Murdock's "World Ethnographic Sample," only about 5 percent followed this practice.[52] About 95 percent of the world's societies have had some other pattern of residence whereby a new couple settles within, or very close to, the household of the parents or some other close relative of either the groom or the bride. As we shall see, marital residence largely predicts the types of kin groups found in a society.

Patterns of Marital Residence

In societies in which newly married couples customarily live with or close to their kin, the pattern of residence varies. Children in all societies are required to marry outside the nuclear family, because of the incest taboo, and, with few exceptions, couples in almost all societies live together after they are married. Therefore some children have to leave home when they marry. But which married children remain at home and which reside elsewhere? Societies vary in the way they deal with this question, but there are not many different patterns. The prevailing one could be one of the following (the percentages of each in the ethnographic record do not sum to 100 because of rounding):

1. **Patrilocal residence.**   The son stays and the daughter leaves, so that the married couple lives with or near the husband's parents (67 percent of all societies in the ethnographic record).
2. **Matrilocal residence.**   The daughter stays and the son leaves, so that the married couple lives with or near the wife's parents (15 percent of all societies).
3. **Bilocal residence.**   Either the son or the daughter leaves, so that the married couple lives with or near either the wife's or the husband's parents (7 percent of all societies).

In many societies known to anthropology, the bride goes to live with or near the husband's family. In the town of Itako, Japan, a bride is transported to the bridegroom's place.

4. **Avunculocal residence.** Both son and daughter normally leave, but the son and his wife settle with or near his mother's brother (4 percent of all societies).[53]

In these definitions, we use the phrase "the married couple lives *with or near*" a particular set of in-laws. When couples live with or near the kin of a spouse, the couple may live in the same household with those kin, creating an *extended-family* household, or they may live separately in an *independent-family* household, but nearby. (Because matrilocal, patrilocal, and avunculocal residence specify just one pattern, they are often called nonoptional or **unilocal residence** patterns.) A fifth pattern of residence is neolocal, in which the newly married couple does not live with or near kin.

5. **Neolocal residence.** Both son and daughter leave; married couples live apart from the relatives of both spouses (5 percent of all societies). This is in the ethnographic record; in the modern world neolocal residence is customary more often.

How does place of residence affect the social life of the couple? Because the pattern of residence governs with whom or near whom individuals live, it largely determines which people those individuals interact with and have to depend on. If a married couple is surrounded by the kin of the husband, for example, chances are that those relatives will figure importantly in the couple's future. Whether the couple lives with or near the husband's or the wife's kin can also have important consequences for the status of the husband or wife. If married couples live patrilocally, as occurs in most societies, the wife may be far from her own kin. In any case, she will be an outsider among a group of male relatives who have grown up together. The feeling of being an outsider is particularly strong when the wife has moved into a patrilocal extended-family household.

Among the Tiv of central Nigeria,[54] the patrilocal extended family consists of the "great father," who is the head of the household, and his younger brothers, his sons, and his younger brothers' sons. Also included are the in-marrying wives and all unmarried children. (The sisters and daughters of the household head who have married would have gone to live where their husbands lived.) Authority is strongly vested in the male line, particularly the oldest of the household, who has authority over bride price, disputes, punishment, and plans for new buildings.

A somewhat different situation exists if the husband comes to live with or near his wife's parents. In this case, the wife and her kin take on somewhat greater importance, and the husband is the outsider. As we shall see, however, the matrilocal situation is not quite the mirror image of the patrilocal, because in matrilocal societies the husband's kin often are not far away. Moreover, even though residence is matrilocal, women often do not have as much to say in decision making as their brothers do.

If the married couple does not live with or near the parents or close kin of either spouse, the situation is again quite different. It should not be surprising that relatives and kinship connections do not figure very largely in everyday life in neolocal residence situations. Toward the end of this chapter we consider the factors that may explain residential variation; these same factors may also help explain the types of kinship groups that develop.

The Structure of Kinship

In noncommercial societies, kinship connections structure many areas of social life—from the kind of access an individual has to productive resources to the kind of political alliances formed between communities and larger territorial groups. In some societies, in fact, kinship connections have an important bearing on matters of life and death.

If kinship is important, which set of kin does a person affiliate with and depend on? After all, if every single relative were counted as equally important, there would be an unmanageably large number of people in each person's kinship network. Consequently, in most societies in which kinship connections are important, rules allocate each person to a particular and definable set of kin.

Types of Affiliation with Kin   We distinguish three main types of affiliation with kin: *unilineal descent*, *ambilineal descent*, and *bilateral kinship*. The first two types (unilineal descent and ambilineal descent) are based on **rules of descent**, rules that connect individuals with particular sets of kin because of known or presumed common ancestry.

Unilineal descent refers to the fact that a person is affiliated with a group of kin through descent links of one sex only—either males only or females only. Thus unilineal descent can be either patrilineal or matrilineal.

1. **Patrilineal descent** affiliates an individual with kin of both sexes related to him or her *through men only*. As Figure 7.1 indicates, in patrilineal systems the children in each generation belong to the kin group of their father; their father, in turn, belongs to the group of his father; and so on. Although a man's sons and daughters are all members of the same descent group, affiliation with that group is transmitted only by the sons to their children. Just as patrilocal residence is much more common than matrilocal residence, patrilineal descent is more common than matrilineal descent.

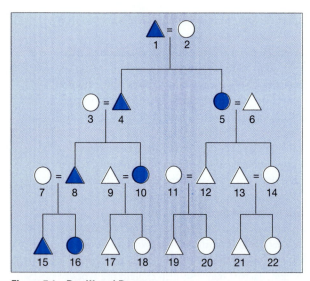

Note: A triangle represents a male; a circle represents a female; an equal sign (=) represents a marriage; vertical lines show descent; horizontal lines indicate siblings.

Figure 7.1   Patrilineal Descent

Individuals 4 and 5, who are the children of 1 and 2, affiliate with their father's patrilineal kin group, represented by the color blue. In the next generation, the children of 3 and 4 also belong to the blue kin group, since they take their descent from their father, who is a member of that group. However, the children of 5 and 6 do not belong to this patrilineal group, since they take their descent from their father, who is a member of a different group. That is, although the mother of 12 and 14 belongs to the blue patrilineal group, she cannot pass on her descent affiliation to her children, and since her husband (6) does not belong to her patrilineage, her children (12 and 14) belong to their father's group. In the fourth generation, only 15 and 16 belong to the blue patrilineal group, since their father is the only male member of the preceding generation who belongs to the blue patrilineal group. In this diagram, then, 1, 4, 5, 8, 10, 15, and 16 are affiliated by the patrilineal descent; all the other individuals belong to other patrilineal groups.

2. **Matrilineal descent** affiliates an individual with kin of both sexes related to him or her *through women only.* In each generation, then, children belong to the kin group of their mother (see Figure 7.2). Although a woman's sons and daughters are all members of the same descent group, only her daughters can pass on their descent affiliation to their children.

Unilineal rules of descent affiliate an individual with a line of kin extending back in time and into the future. By virtue of this line of descent, whether it extends through males or females, some very close relatives are excluded. For example, in a patrilineal system, your mother and your mother's parents do not belong to your patrilineal group, but your father and his father (and their sisters) do. In your own generation in a matrilineal or patrilineal system, some cousins are excluded, and in your children's generation, some of your nieces and nephews are excluded.

Unilineal rules of descent can form clear-cut, nonoverlapping and hence unambiguous, groups of kin, which can act as separate units even after the death of individual members. Referring again to Figures 7.1 and 7.2, we can see that the individuals in the highlight color belong to the same patrilineal or matrilineal descent group without ambiguity; individuals in the fourth generation belong to the group just as much as those in the first generation. In contrast to unilineal descent, **ambilineal descent** affiliates an individual with kin related to him or her through men *or* women. In other words, some people in the society affiliate with a group of kin through their fathers; others, through their mothers. Consequently, the descent groups show both female and male genealogical links and they often if not usually overlap in membership

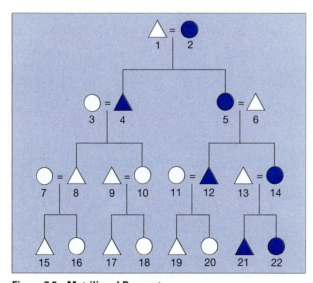

Figure 7.2 Matrilineal Descent

Individuals 4 and 5, who are the children of 1 and 2, affiliate with their mother's kin group, represented by the color blue. In the next generation, the children of 5 and 6 also belong to the blue kin group, since they take their descent from their mother, who is a member of that group. However, the children of 3 and 4 do not belong to this matrilineal group, since they take their descent from their mother, who is a member of a different group; their father, although a member of the blue matrilineal group, cannot pass his affiliation on to them under the rule of matrilineal descent. In the fourth generation, only 21 and 22 belong to the blue matrilineal group, since their mother is the only female member of the preceding generation who belongs. Thus, individuals 2, 4, 5, 12, 14, 21, and 22 belong to the same matrilineal group.

These three rules of descent (patrilineal, matrilineal, and ambilineal) are usually, but not always, mutually exclusive. Most societies can be characterized as having only one rule of descent, but sometimes two principles are used to affiliate individuals with different sets of kin for different purposes. Some societies have, then, what is called **double descent or double unilineal descent**, whereby an individual affiliates for some purposes with a group of matrilineal kin and for other purposes with a group of patrilineal kin.

Many societies, including our own, do not have lineal (matrilineal, patrilineal, or ambilineal) descent groups—sets of kin who believe they descend from a common ancestor. These are societies with **bilateral kinship**. *Bilateral* means "two-sided," and in this case it refers to the fact that one's relatives on both the mother's and father's sides are equal in importance or, more usually, in unimportance. Kinship reckoning in bilateral societies does not refer to common descent but rather is horizontal, moving outward from close to more distant relatives rather than upward to common ancestors (see Figure 7.3).

The term **kindred** describes a person's bilateral set of relatives who may be called upon for some purpose. Most bilateral societies have kindreds that overlap in membership. In North America, we think of the kindred as including the people we might invite to weddings, funerals, or some other ceremonial occasion; a kindred, however, is not usually a definite group. As anyone who has been involved in creating a wedding invitation list knows, a great deal of time may be spent deciding which relatives ought to be invited and which ones can legitimately be excluded. Societies with bilateral kinship differ in precisely how distant relatives have to be before they are lost track of or before they are not included in ceremonial activities.

The distinctive feature of bilateral kinship is that, aside from brothers and sisters, no two persons belong to exactly the same kin group. Your kindred contains close relatives spreading out on both your mother's and father's sides, but the members of your kindred are affiliated only by way of their connection to you (**ego**, or the focus). Thus, the kindred is an *ego-centered* group of kin. Because different people (except for brothers and sisters) have different mothers and fathers, your first cousins will have different kindreds, and even your own children will have a different kindred from yours. It is the ego-centered nature

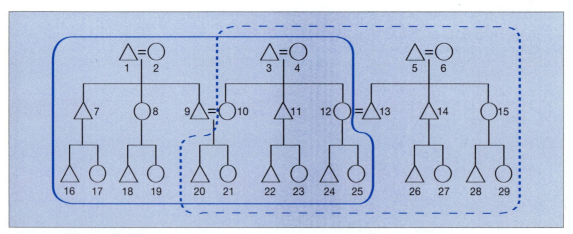

Figure 7.3   Bilateral Kinship

In a bilateral system the kindred is ego-centered; hence, it varies with different points of reference (except for brothers and sisters). In any bilateral society, the kindred minimally includes parents, grandparents, aunts, uncles, and first cousins. So, if we look at the close kindred of the brother and sister 20 and 21 (enclosed by the solid line), it would include their parents (9 and 10), their aunts and uncles (7, 8, 11, 12), their grandparents (1, 2, 3, 4), and their first cousins (16–19, 22–25). But the kindred of the brother and sister 24 and 25 (shown by the dashed line) includes only some of the same people (3, 4, 10–12, 20–23); in addition, the kindred of 24 and 25 includes people not in the kindred of 20 and 21 (5, 6, 13–15, 26–29).

of the kindred that makes it difficult for it to serve as a permanent or persistent group. The only thing the people in a kindred have in common is the ego who brings them together. A kindred usually has no name, no common purpose, and only temporary meetings centered around the ego.[55] Because everyone belongs to several different and overlapping kindreds, the society is not divided into clear-cut groups.

Groups in Unilineal Descent Systems

In a society with unilineal descent, people usually refer to themselves as belonging to a particular unilineal group or set of groups because they believe they share common descent in either the male (patrilineal) or female (matrilineal) line. Several types of unilineal descent groups are distinguished by anthropologists: lineages, clans, phratries, and moieties.

Lineages   A **lineage** is a set of kin whose members trace descent from a common ancestor through known links. There may be *patrilineages* or *matrilineages*, depending on whether the links are traced through males only or through females only. Lineages are often designated by the name of the common male or female ancestor. In some societies, people belong to a hierarchy of lineages. That is, they first trace their descent back to the ancestor of a minor lineage, then to the ancestor of a larger and more inclusive major lineage, and so on.

Clans   A **clan** (also sometimes called a **sib**) is a set of kin whose members believe themselves to be descended from a common ancestor, but the links back to that ancestor are not specified. In fact, the common ancestor may not even be known. Clans with patrilineal descent are called *patriclans;* clans with matrilineal descent are called *matriclans.* Clans often are designated by an animal name (Bear, Wolf), called a **totem**, which may have some special significance for the group and, at the very least, is a means of group identification. The word *totem* comes from the Ojibwa Indian word *ototeman,* "a relative of mine."

Totem poles often symbolize the history of a descent group. A totem pole in Ketchikan, Alaska.

Phratries   A **phratry** is a unilineal descent group composed of supposedly related clans or sibs. As with clans, the descent links in phratries are unspecified.

Moieties   When a whole society is divided into two unilineal descent groups, we call each group a **moiety**. (The word *moiety* comes from a French word meaning "half.") The people in each moiety believe themselves to be descended from a common ancestor, although they cannot specify how. Societies with moiety systems usually have relatively small populations (fewer than 9,000 people). Societies with phratries and clans tend to be larger.[56]

Combinations   Many societies have two or more types in various combinations. For example, some societies have lineages and clans; others may have clans and phratries but no lineages; and still others may have clans and moieties but neither phratries nor lineages. Even if societies have more than one type of unilineal kin group—for example, lineages and clans—there is no ambiguity about membership. Small groups are simply subsets of larger units; the larger units include people who say they are unilineally related further back in time.

Patrilineal Organization   Patrilineal organization is the most frequent type of descent system. The Kapauku Papuans, a people living in the central highlands of western New Guinea, are an example of a patrilineal society with various types of descent groups.[57] The male members of a patrilineage—all the living males who can trace their actual relationship through males to a common ancestor—constitute the male population of a single village or, more likely, a series of adjoining villages. The male members of the lineage live together by virtue of a patrilocal rule of residence and a fairly stable settlement pattern. A son stays near his parents and brings his wife to live in or near his father's house; the daughters leave home and go to live with their husbands. If the group lives in one place over a long period, the male descendants of one man will live in the same territory.

The members of the same patrilineage address each other affectionately, and within this group law and order are maintained by a headman. Killing within the lineage is considered a serious offense, and any fighting that takes place is done with sticks rather than lethal weapons such as spears.

The Kapauku also belong to larger and more inclusive patrilineal descent groups—clans and phratries. If a member of the patriclan eats the clan's plant or animal totem, it is believed that the person will become deaf. A Kapauku is also forbidden to marry anyone from his or her clan. In other words, the clan is exogamous. Unlike the members of the patrilineage, the male members of the patriclan do not all live together. The lineage is also the largest group of kinsmen that acts together politically. Among clan members there is no mechanism for resolving disputes, and members of the same patriclan (who belong to different lineages) may even go to war with one another.

The most inclusive patrilineal descent group among the Kapauku is the phratry, each of which is composed of two or more clans. The members of a phratry observe all the totemic taboos of the clans that belong to that phratry. Intermarriage of members of the same clan is forbidden, but members of the same phratry, if they belong to different clans, may marry.

Matrilineal Organization   Although societies with matrilineal descent seem in many respects like mirror images of their patrilineal counterparts, they differ in one important way. That difference has to do with who exercises authority. In patrilineal systems, descent affiliation is transmitted through males, and it is also the males who exercise authority. Consequently, in the patrilineal system, lines of descent and of authority converge. In a matrilineal system, however, although the line of descent passes through females, females rarely exercise authority in their kin groups. Usually males do. Thus, the lines of authority and descent do not converge.[58] Since males exercise authority in the kin group, an individual's mother's brother becomes an important authority figure, because he is the individual's closest male matrilineal relative in the parental generation. The individual's father does not belong to the individual's matrilineal kin group and thus has no say in that kin group.

The divergence of authority and descent in a matrilineal system has some effect on community organization and marriage. Most matrilineal societies practice matrilocal residence. Daughters stay at home after marriage and bring their husbands to live with them; sons leave home to join their wives. But the sons who are required to leave will be the ones who eventually exercise authority in their kin groups. This situation presents a problem. The solution that seems to have been arrived at in most matrilineal societies is that, although the males move away to live with their wives, they usually do not move too far away; indeed, they often marry women who live in the same village. Thus, matrilineal societies tend not to be locally exogamous—that is, members often marry people from inside the village—whereas patrilineal societies are often locally exogamous.[59]

The matrilineal organization on Chuuk, a group of small islands in the Pacific, illustrates the general pattern of authority in matrilineal systems.[60] The Chuukese have both matrilineages and matriclans. The matrilineage is a property-owning group whose members trace descent from a known common ancestor in the female line. The female lineage members and their husbands occupy a cluster of houses on the matrilineage's land. The property of the lineage group is administered by the oldest brother of the group, who allocates the productive property of his matrilineage and directs the work of the members. He also represents the group in dealings with the district chief and all outsiders, and he must be consulted on any matter that affects the group. There is also a senior woman of the lineage who exercises some authority, but only insofar as the activities of the women are concerned. She may supervise the women's cooperative work (they usually work separately from the men) and manage the household.

Within the nuclear family, the father and mother have the primary responsibility for raising and disciplining their children. When a child reaches puberty, however, the father's right to discipline or exercise authority over the child ceases. The mother continues to exercise her right of discipline, but her brother may interfere, especially after puberty. On Chuuk, men rarely move far from their birthplace. As Ward Goodenough pointed out, "Since matrilocal residence takes the men away from their home lineages, most of them marry women whose lineage houses are within a few minutes' walk of their own."[61]

Functions of Unilineal Descent Groups

Unilineal descent groups exist in societies at all levels of cultural complexity.[62] Apparently, however, they are most common in noncommercial food-producing, as opposed to food-collecting, societies.[63] Unilineal descent groups often have important functions in the social, economic, political, and religious realms of life:

1. **Regulating marriage.**   In unilineal societies, individuals are not usually permitted to marry within their own unilineal descent groups. In general, the incest taboo in unilineal societies is extended to some, if not all, presumed unilineal relatives.

2. **Economic functions.**   Members of a person's lineage or clan are often required to side with that person in any quarrel or lawsuit, to help him or her get established economically, to contribute to a bride price or fine, and to support the person in life crises. Mutual aid often extends to economic cooperation on a regular basis. The unilineal descent group may act as a corporate unit in landownership.

3. **Political functions.**   Headmen or elders may also have the right to settle disputes between two members within a lineage, although they generally lack power to force a settlement. And they may act as intermediaries in disputes between a member of their own clan and a member of an

opposing kin group. One of the most important political functions of unilineal descent groups is their role in warfare—the attempt to resolve disputes within and without the society by violent action. In societies without towns or cities, the organization of such fighting is often in the hands of descent groups.

4. **Religious Functions.**   A clan or lineage may have its own religious beliefs and practices, worshiping its own gods or goddesses and ancestral spirits.

Ambilineal Systems

Societies with ambilineal descent groups are far less numerous than unilineal or even bilateral societies. Ambilineal societies, however, resemble unilineal ones in many ways. For instance, the members of an ambilineal descent group believe that they are descended from a common ancestor, although frequently they cannot specify all the genealogical links. The descent group is commonly named and may have an identifying emblem or even a totem; land and other productive resources may be owned by the descent group; and myths and religious practices are often associated with the group. Marriage is often regulated by group membership, just as in unilineal systems, although kin group exogamy is not nearly as common as in unilineal systems. Moreover, ambilineal societies resemble unilineal ones in having various levels or types of descent groups. They may have lineages and higher orders of descent groups, distinguished (as in unilineal systems) by whether or not all the genealogical links to the supposed common ancestors are specified.[64]

Explaining Variation in Residence

If in most societies married couples live with or near kin, then why in some societies, such as our own, do couples typically live apart from kin? And, among the societies in which couples live with or near kin, why do most choose the husband's side (patrilocal residence), but some the wife's side (matrilocal residence)? Why do some non-neolocal societies allow a married couple to go to either the wife's or the husband's kin (bilocal residence), whereas most others do not allow a choice?

Neolocal Residence   Many anthropologists have suggested that neolocal residence is related to the presence of a money or commercial economy. They argue that when people can sell their labor or their products for money, they can buy what they need to live, without having to depend on kin. Indeed, neolocal residence tends to occur in societies with monetary or commercial exchange, whereas societies without money tend to have patterns of residence that locate a couple near or with kin.[65] The presence of money, then, partially accounts for neolocal residence: Money seems to allow couples to live on their own. Still, this fact does not quite explain why they choose to do so. One reason may be that in commercial societies, couples better on their own because the jobs available require physical or social mobility. Or perhaps couples prefer to live apart from kin because they want to avoid some of the interpersonal tensions and demands that may be generated by living with or near kin.

Matrilocal versus Patrilocal Residence   It was traditionally assumed that in societies in which married children live near or with kin, the pattern of residence will tend to be patrilocal if males contribute more to the economy and matrilocal if women contribute more. However plausible that assumption may seem, the cross-cultural evidence does not support it. Where men do most of the primary subsistence work, residence is patrilocal no more often than would be expected by chance. Conversely, where women do an equal amount or more of the subsistence work, residence is no more likely to be matrilocal than patrilocal.[66] And if we counted all work inside and outside the home, most societies should be matrilocal because women usually do more. But that is not true either; most societies are not matrilocal.

We can predict whether residence will be matrilocal or patrilocal from the type of warfare practiced in the society. In most societies known to anthropology, neighboring communities or districts are enemies. The type of warfare that breaks out periodically between such groups is called *internal,* because the fighting occurs between groups that speak the same language. In other societies, the warfare is never within the same society but only with other language groups. This pattern of warfare is referred to as purely *external.* Cross-cultural evidence suggests that in societies where warfare is at least sometimes internal, residence is almost always patrilocal rather than matrilocal. In contrast, residence is usually matrilocal when warfare is purely external.[67]

How can we explain this relationship between type of warfare and matrilocal versus patrilocal residence? One theory is that patrilocal residence tends to occur with internal warfare because there may be concern over keeping sons close to home to help with defense. Because women do not usually constitute the fighting force in any society, having sons reside at home after marriage might be favored as a means of maintaining a loyal and quickly mobilized fighting force in case of surprise attack from nearby. If warfare is purely external, however, people may not be so concerned about keeping their sons at home because families need not fear attack from neighboring communities or districts.

With purely external warfare, then, the pattern of residence may be determined by other considerations, especially economic ones. If in societies with purely external warfare the women do most of the primary subsistence work, families might want their daughters to remain at home after marriage, so the pattern of residence might become matrilocal. If warfare is purely external but men still do more of the primary subsistence work, residence should still be patrilocal. Thus, the need to keep sons at home after marriage when there is internal warfare may take precedence over any considerations based on division of labor. It is perhaps only when internal warfare is nonexistent that a female-dominant division of labor may give rise to matrilocal residence.[68]

The frequent absence of men because of long-distance trade or wage labor in distant places may also provide an impetus for matrilocal residence even after warfare ceases. For example, among the Miskito of eastern Central America, matrilocality allowed domestic and village life to continue without interruption when men were away from home for long periods of time, working as lumberers, miners, and river transporters. Even though some men would always be away from home, the Miskito continued to get food in their traditional ways, from farming (done mostly by the women) and from hunting and fishing (which was mostly men's work).[69]

Bilocal Residence In societies that practice bilocal residence, a married couple goes to live with or near either the husband's or the wife's parents. Although this pattern seems to involve a choice for the married couple, theory and research suggest that bilocal residence may occur out of necessity instead. Elman Service suggested that bilocal residence is likely to occur in societies that have recently suffered a severe and drastic loss of population because of the introduction of new infectious diseases.[70] Over the past 500 years, contact with Europeans in many parts of the world has resulted in severe population losses among non-European societies that lacked resistance to the Europeans' diseases. If couples need to live with some set of kin in order to make a living in noncommercial societies, it seems likely that couples in depopulated, noncommercial societies might have to live with whichever spouse's parents and other relatives are still alive. This interpretation is supported by the cross-cultural evidence. Recently depopulated societies tend to have bilocal residence or frequent departures from unilocality, whereas societies that are not recently depopulated tend to have one pattern or another of unilocal residence.[71]

In hunter-gatherer societies, a few other circumstances may also favor bilocal residence. Bilocality tends to be found among those hunter-gatherers who have very small bands or unpredictable and low rainfall. Residential "choice" in these cases may be a question of adjusting marital residence to where the couple will have the best chance to survive or to find close relatives with whom to live and work.[72]

Avunculocal Residence   Now that we have learned about matrilineal systems, the avunculocal pattern of residence, whereby married couples live with or near the husband's mother's brother, may become clearer. Although avunculocal residence is relatively rare, just about all avunculocal societies are matrilineal. As we have seen, the mother's brother plays an important role in decision making in most matrilineal societies. Aside from his brothers, who is a boy's closest male matrilineal relative? His mother's brother. Going to live with the mother's brother, then, provides a way of localizing male *matrilineal* relatives. But why should some matrilineal societies practice that form of residence? The answer may involve a recent change in the prevailing type of warfare.

Avunculocal societies, in contrast with matrilocal societies, fight internally. Just as patrilocality may be a response to keep patrilineally related men home after marriage, so avunculocality may be a way of keeping related—in this case, matrilineally related—men together after marriage to provide for quick mobilization in case of surprise attack from nearby. Societies that already have strong, functioning matrilineal descent groups may choose initially, when faced with the emergence of fighting close to home, to switch to avunculocality rather than patrilocality. Avunculocal residence would keep a higher number of related men together after marriage, compared with patrilocality, because there would be more possible links through women than through men if many men were dying relatively young in the warfare.[73]

The Emergence of Unilineal Systems

Unilineal kin groups play very important roles in the organization of many societies. But not all societies have such groups. In societies that have complex systems of political organization, officials and agencies take over many of the functions that might be performed by kin groups, such as the organization of work and warfare and the allocation of land. But not all societies that lack complex political organization have unilineal descent systems. Why, then, do some societies have unilineal descent systems, but others do not?

Trobriand Islanders have avunculocal residence and matrilineal descent groups.

It is generally assumed that unilocal residence, patrilocal or matrilocal, is necessary for the development of unilineal descent. Patrilocal residence, if practiced for some time in a society, will generate a set of patrilineally related males who live in the same territory. Matrilocal residence over time will similarly generate a localized set of matrilineally related females. It is no wonder, then, that matrilocal and patrilocal residence are cross-culturally associated with matrilineal and patrilineal descent, respectively.[74]

But, although unilocal residence might be necessary for the formation of unilineal descent groups, it is apparently not the only condition required. For one thing, many societies with unilocal residence lack unilineal descent groups. For another, merely because related males or related females live together by virtue of a patrilocal or matrilocal rule of residence, it does not necessarily follow that the related people will actually view themselves as a descent group and function as such. Thus, it appears that other conditions are needed to supply the impetus for the formation of unilineal descent groups.

There is evidence that unilocal societies that engage in warfare are more apt to have unilineal descent groups than unilocal societies without warfare.[75] It may be, then, that the presence of fighting in societies lacking complex systems of political organization provides an impetus to the formation of unilineal descent groups. Unilineal descent groups provide individuals with unambiguous groups of persons who can fight or form alliances as discrete units.[76] There is no ambiguity about an individual's membership. It is perfectly clear whether someone belongs to a particular clan, phratry, or moiety. It is this feature of unilineal descent groups that enables them to act as separate and distinct units—mostly, perhaps, in warfare.

Summary

1. All societies known today have the custom of marriage. Marriage is a socially approved sexual and economic union usually between a man and a woman that is presumed to be more or less permanent and that subsumes reciprocal rights and obligations between the two spouses and between the spouses and their children.

2. Marriage arrangements often include an economic element including bride-price (the most common form of economic transaction), bride-service, female exchange, dowry, and indirect dowry.

3. Every society tells people whom they cannot marry, whom they can marry, and sometimes even whom they should marry. No society in recent times has allowed sex or marriage between brothers and sisters, mothers and sons, or fathers and daughters.

4. Most societies allow a man to be married to more than one woman at a time (polygyny). Monogamy is less common and polyandry, the marriage of one woman to several husbands, is rare.

5. The prevailing form of family in most societies is the extended family. It consists of two or more single-parent, monogamous (nuclear), polygynous, or polyandrous families linked by blood ties.

6. In our society, and in many other industrial societies, a newly married couple usually establishes a place of residence apart from parents or relatives (neolocal residence). But about 95 percent of the world's societies have some pattern of residence whereby the new couple settles within or very close to the household of the parents or some other close relative of the groom or bride. The four major patterns in which married couples live with or near kinsmen are these: patrilocal residence (the most common), matrilocal residence, bilocal residence, and avunculocal residence.

7. In most societies where kinship is important, rules of affiliation allocate each person to a particular and definable set of kin. The three main types of affiliation with kin are unilineal descent, ambilineal descent, and bilateral kinship.

8. With unilineal descent people usually refer to themselves as belonging to a particular unilineal group or set of groups because they believe they share common descent in either the male or the female line. These people form what is called a unilineal descent group. There are several types, and a society may have more than one type: lineages, clans, phratries, and moieties.

Glossary Terms

ambilineal descent (p. 155)
avunculocal residence (p. 153)
bilateral kinship (p. 156)
bilocal residence (p. 152)
bride price or bride wealth (p. 141)
bride service (p. 142)
clan or sib (p. 157)
cross-cousins (p. 145)
double descent or double unilineal
   descent (p. 156)
dowry (p. 142)
ego (p. 156)
endogamy (p. 144)
exogamy (p. 144)
extended family (p. 148)
family (p. 148)
group marriage (p. 145)
incest taboo (p. 143)
indirect dowry (p. 143)
kindred (p. 156)
lineage (p. 157)
marriage (p. 138)

matrifocal family (p. 148)
matrilineal descent (p. 155)
matrilocal residence (p. 152)
moiety (p. 158)
monogamy (p. 145)
neolocal residence (p. 153)
nonsororal polygyny (p. 146)
nuclear family (p. 148)
parallel cousins (p. 145)
patrilineal descent (p. 154)
patrilocal residence (p. 152)
phratry (p. 158)
polyandry (p. 145)
polygamy (p. 145)
polygyny (p. 145)
postpartum sex taboo (p. 146)
rules of descent (p. 154)
siblings (p. 145)
sororal polygyny (p. 146)
totem (p. 157)
unilineal descent (p. 154)
unilocal residence (p. 153)

Critical Questions

1. Do you think extended-family households will become more common in our society? Explain your answer.

2. Why is polyandry so much less common than polygyny?

3. Why might it be important for unilineal descent groups to be nonoverlapping in membership?

CHAPTER 8

POLITICAL LIFE

Chapter Outline

- Types of Political Organization
- The Spread of State Societies
- Variation in Political Process
- Resolution of Conflict

For people in the United States, the phrase *political life* has many connotations. It may call to mind the various branches of government: the executive branch, from the president on the national level to governors on the state level to mayors on the local level; legislative institutions, from Congress to state legislatures to city councils; and administrative bureaus, from federal government departments to local agencies.

Political life may also evoke thoughts of political parties, interest groups, lobbying, campaigning, and voting. In other words, when people living in the United States think of political life, they may think first of "politics," the activities (not always apparent or public) that influence who is elected or appointed to political office, what public policies are established, how they get established, and who benefits from those policies.

But in the United States and in many other countries, *political life* involves even more than government and politics. Political life also involves ways of preventing or resolving troubles and disputes both within and outside the society. Internally, a complex society such as ours may employ mediation or arbitration to resolve industrial disputes, a police force to prevent crimes or track down criminals, and courts and a penal system to deal with lawbreakers as well as with social conflict in general. Externally, such a society may establish embassies in other nations and develop and utilize its armed forces both to maintain security and to support domestic and foreign interests.

Formal governments have become more widespread around the world over the last 100 years, as powerful colonizing countries have imposed political systems upon others or as people less formally organized realized that they needed governmental mechanisms to deal with the larger world. But many societies known to anthropology did not have political officials or political parties or courts or armies. Indeed, the band or village was the largest autonomous political unit in 50 percent of the societies in the ethnographic record, as of the times they were first described. And those units were only informally organized; that is, they did not have individuals or agencies formally authorized to make and implement policy or resolve disputes. Does this mean they did not have political life? If we mean political life as we know it in our own society, then the answer has to be that they did not. But if we look beyond our formal institutions and mechanisms—if we ask what functions these institutions and mechanisms perform—we find that all societies have had political activities and beliefs to create and maintain social order and cope with social disorder.

Many kinds of groups including descent groups have political functions. But when anthropologists talk about *political organization* or *political life,* they are particularly focusing on activities and beliefs pertaining to *territorial groups.* Territorial groups, in whose behalf political activities may be organized, range from small communities, such as bands and villages, to large communities, such as towns and cities, to multilocal groups, such as districts or regions, entire nations, or even groups of nations.

As we shall see, the different types of political organization, as well as how people participate in politics and how they cope with conflict, are often strongly linked to variation in food-getting, economy, and social stratification.

Types of Political Organization

Societies in the ethnographic record vary in *level of political integration*—that is, the largest territorial group on whose behalf political activities are organized—and in the degree to which political authority is centralized or concentrated in the integrated group. When we describe the political integration of particular societies, we focus on their traditional political systems.

Elman Service suggested that most societies can be classified into four principal types of political organization: bands, tribes, chiefdoms, and states.[1] Although Service's classification does not fit all societies, it is a useful way to show how societies vary in trying to create and maintain social order. We often use the present tense in our discussion, because that is the convention in ethnographic writing, but the reader should remember that most societies that used to be organized at the band, tribe, or chiefdom level are now incorporated into larger political entities. With a handful of exceptions, there are no politically autonomous bands or tribes or chiefdoms in the world anymore.

Band Organization

Some societies were composed of fairly small and usually nomadic groups of people. Each of these groups is conventionally called a **band** and is politically autonomous. That is, in **band organization** the local group or community is the largest group that acts as a political unit. Because most recent food collectors had band organization, some anthropologists contend that this type of political organization characterized nearly all societies before the development of agriculture, or until about 10,000 years ago. But we have to remember that almost all of the described food-collecting societies are or were located in marginal environments; and almost all were affected by more dominant societies nearby.[2] So it is possible that what we call "band organization" may not have been typical of food collectors in the distant or prehistoric past.

Bands are typically small, with less than 100 people usually, often considerably less. Each small band occupies a large territory, so population density is low. Band size often varies by season, with the band breaking up or recombining according to the food resources available at a given time and place. Inuit bands, for example, are smaller in the winter, when food is hard to find, and larger in the summer, when there is sufficient food to feed a larger group.

Political decision making within the band is generally informal. The "modest informal authority"[3] that does exist can be seen in the way decisions affecting the group are made. Because the formal, permanent office of leader typically does not exist, decisions such as when camp has to be moved or how a hunt is to be arranged are either agreed upon by the community as a whole or made by the best-qualified member. Leadership, when it is exercised by an individual, is not the consequence of bossing or throwing one's weight about. Each band may have its informal **headman**, or its most proficient hunter, or a person most accomplished in rituals. There may be one person with all these qualities, or several persons, but such a person or persons will have gained status through the community's recognition of skill, good sense, and humility. Leadership, in other words, stems not from power but from influence, not from office but from admired personal qualities. For example, among the Iglulik Inuit:

> Within each settlement . . . there is as a rule an older man who enjoys the respect of the others and who decides when a move is to be made to another hunting center, when a hunt is to be started, how the spoils are to be divided, when the dogs are to be fed . . . . He is called *isumaitoq*, "he who thinks." It is not always the oldest man, but as a rule an elderly man who is a clever hunter or, as head of a large family, exercises great authority. He cannot be called a chief; there is no obligation to follow his counsel; but they do so in most cases, partly because they rely on his experience, partly because it pays to be on good terms with this man.[4]

A summary of the general features of band organization can be found in Table 8.1 on page 168. Note, however, that there are exceptions to these generalizations. For example, not all known food collectors are organized at the band level or have all the features of a band type of society. Classic exceptions are the Native American societies of the Northwest Pacific coast, who had enormous resources of salmon and other fish, relatively large and permanent villages, and political organization beyond the level of the typical band societies in the ethnographic record.

Type of Organization	Highest Level of Political Integration	Specialization of Political Officials	Predominant Mode of Subsistence	Community Size and Population Density	Social Differentiation	Major Form of Distribution
Table 8.1 Suggested Trends in Political Organization and Other Social Characteristics						
Band	Local group or band	Little or none: informal leadership	Food collecting	Very small communities, very low density	Egalitarian	Mostly reciprocity
Tribe	Sometimes multilocal group	Little or none: informal leadership	Extensive (shifting) agriculture and/or herding	Small communities, low density	Egalitarian	Mostly reciprocity
Chiefdom	Multilocal group	Some	Extensive or intensive agriculture and/or herding	Large communities, medium density	Rank	Reciprocity and redistribution
State	Multilocal group, often entire language group	Much	Intensive agriculture and herding	Cities and towns, high density	Class and caste	Mostly market exchange

Tribal Organization

When local communities mostly act autonomously but there are kinship groups (such as clans or lineages) or associations (such as age-sets—see page 169) that can potentially integrate several local groups into a larger unit (**tribe**), we say that the society has **tribal organization**. The term *tribe* is sometimes used to refer to an entire society; that is, an entire language group may be called a tribe. But a tribal type of political system does not usually permit the entire society to act as a unit; all the communities in a tribal society may be linked only occasionally for some political (usually military) purpose. Thus, what distinguishes tribal from band political organization is the presence in the former of some multilocal, but not usually society-wide, integration. The multilocal integration, however, is *not permanent*, and it is *informal* in the sense that it is not headed by political officials. Frequently, the integration is called into play only when an outside threat arises; when the threat disappears, the local groups revert to self-sufficiency.[5] Tribal organization may seem fragile—and, of course, it usually is—but the fact that there are social ways to integrate local groups into larger political entities means that societies with tribal organization are militarily a good deal more formidable than societies with band organization.

Societies with tribal political organization are similar to band societies in their tendency to be egalitarian (see Table 8.1). At the local level, informal leadership is also characteristic. In those tribal societies where kinship provides the basic framework of social organization, the elders of the local kin groups tend to have considerable influence; where age-sets are important, a particular age-set is looked to for leadership. But, in contrast to band societies, societies with tribal organization generally are food producers.

And because cultivation and animal husbandry are generally more productive than hunting and gathering, the population density of tribal societies is generally higher, local groups are larger, and the way of life is more sedentary than in hunter-gatherer bands.

Kinship Bonds   Frequently communities are linked to each other by virtue of belonging to the same kin group, usually a unilineal group such as a lineage or clan. A **segmentary lineage system** is one type of tribal integration based on kinship. A society with such a system is composed of segments, or parts, each similar to the others in structure and function. Every local segment belongs to a hierarchy of lineages stretching farther and farther back genealogically. The hierarchy of lineages, then, unites the segments into larger and larger genealogical groups. The closer two groups are genealogically, the greater their general closeness. In the event of a dispute between members of different segments, people related more closely to one contestant than to another take the side of their nearest kinsman.

The Tiv of northern Nigeria offer a classic example of a segmentary lineage system, one that happens to link all the Tiv into a single genealogical structure or tribe. The Tiv are a large society, numbering more than 800,000. There are four levels of lineages. Each of the smallest lineages is in turn embedded in more inclusive lineages. Territorial organization follows lineage hierarchy. The most closely related lineages have territories near each other. All of Tivland is said to descend from one ancestor.[6]

Tiv lineage organization is the foundation of Tiv political organization. A dispute between the smallest neighboring lineages (and territories) remains minor, since no more than "brother" segments are involved. But a dispute between two small lineages from different larger lineages involves those larger lineages as well, with the requirement that smaller lineages within the larger support each other. This process of mutual support, called **complementary opposition**, means that segments will unite only in a confrontation with some other group. Groups that will fight with each other in a minor dispute might coalesce at some later time against a larger group.

The segmentary lineage system was presumably very effective in allowing the Tiv to intrude into new territory and take land from other tribal societies with smaller descent groups. Individual Tiv lineage segments could call on support from related lineages when faced with border troubles. Conflicts within the society—that is, between segments—especially in border areas, were often turned outward, "releasing internal pressure in an explosive blast against other peoples."[7]

A segmentary lineage system may generate a formidable military force, but the combinations of manpower it produces are temporary, forming and dissolving as the occasion demands.[8] Tribal political organization does not make for a political system that more or less permanently integrates a number of communities.

Age-Set Systems   Age-sets (groups of males of a certain age-range) can function as the basis of a tribal type of political organization, as among the Karimojong of northeastern Uganda.[9] As herders, Karimojong adults are often separated from their usual settlements. Herders will meet, mingle for a while, then go their separate ways, but each may call upon other members of his age-set wherever he goes. The age-set system is important among the Karimojong because it immediately allocates a place to each individual in the system and thereby establishes for him an appropriate pattern of response. A quarrel in camp will be settled by the representatives of the senior age-set who are present, regardless of which section of the tribe they may belong to.

Among the Karimojong, political leaders are not elected from among the elders of a particular age-set, nor are they appointed; they acquire their positions informally. Usually a man's background, and the ability he has demonstrated in public debates over a period of time, will result in his being considered by the men of his neighborhood to be their spokesman. His function is to announce what course of action seems required in a particular situation, to initiate that action, and then to coordinate it after it has begun.

Chiefdom Organization

Whereas a tribe has some informal mechanism that can integrate more than one community, a **chiefdom** has some *formal* structure that integrates more than one community into a political unit. The formal structure could consist of a council with or without a chief, but most commonly there is a person—the **chief**—who has higher rank or authority than others. Most societies at the chiefdom level of organization contain more than one multicommunity political unit or chiefdom, each headed by a district chief or a council. There may also be more than one level of chief beyond the community, such as district chiefs and higher-level chiefs. Compared with tribal societies, societies with chiefdoms are more densely populated and their communities more permanent, partly as a consequence of their generally greater economic productivity (see Table 8.1 on page 168).

The position of chief, which is sometimes hereditary and generally permanent, bestows high status on its holder. Most chiefdoms have social ranking and accord the chief and his family greater access to prestige. The chief may redistribute goods, plan and direct the use of public labor, supervise religious ceremonies, and direct military activities on behalf of the chiefdom. In South Pacific chiefdoms, the chiefs carried out most of these duties. In Fijian chiefdoms, for example, the chief was responsible for the redistribution of goods and the coordination of labor:

> [The chief] could summon the community's labor on his own behalf, or on behalf of someone else who requested it, or for general purposes . . . . Besides his right to summon labor he accumulated the greater proportion of the first fruits of the yam crop . . . and he benefited from other forms of food presentation, or by the acquisition of special shares in ordinary village distribution . . . . Thus, the paramount [chief] would collect a significant part of the surplus production of the community and redistribute it in the general welfare.[10]

In contrast to leaders in tribal societies, who generally have to earn their privileges by their personal qualities, hereditary chiefs are said to have those qualities in their "blood." A high-ranking chief in Polynesia, a huge triangular area of islands in the South Pacific, inherited special religious power called *mana.* Mana sanctified his rule and protected him.[11] Chiefs in Polynesia had so much religious power that missionaries could convert people to Christianity only after their chiefs had been converted.[12]

Men present *kava,* a special drink, to a chief in Fiji. The chief wears a tie.

In most chiefdoms, the chiefs did not have the power to compel people to obey them; people would act in accordance with the chief's wishes because the chief was respected and often had religious authority. But in the most complex paramount chiefdoms, such as those of Hawaii and Tahiti, the chiefs seemed to have more compelling sanctions than the "power" of respect or mana. Substantial amounts of goods and services collected by the chiefs were used to support subordinates, including specialists such as high priests, political envoys, and warriors who could be sent to quell rebellious factions.[13] When redistributions do not go to everybody—when chiefs are allowed to keep items for their own purposes—and when a chief begins to use armed force, the political system is on the way to becoming what we call a state.

State Organization

A **state**, according to one more or less standard definition, is "an autonomous political unit, encompassing many communities within its territory and having a centralized government with the power to collect taxes, draft men for work or war, and decree and enforce laws."[14] States, then, have a complex, centralized political structure that includes a wide range of permanent institutions with legislative, executive, and judicial functions and a large bureaucracy. Central to this definition is the concept of legitimate force used to implement policies both internally and externally. In states, the government tries to maintain a monopoly on the use of physical force.[15] This monopoly can be seen in the development of formal and specialized instruments of social control: a police force, a militia, or a standing army.

Just as a particular society may contain more than one band, tribe, or chiefdom, so may it contain more than one state. The contiguously distributed population speaking a single language may or may not be politically unified in a single state. Ancient Greece was composed of many city-states; so, too, was Italy until the 1870s. German speakers are also not politically unified; Austria and Germany are separate states, and Germany itself was not politically unified until the 1870s. We say that a society has **state organization** when it is composed of one or more political units that are states.

A state may include more than one society. Multisociety states often are the result of conquest or colonial control when the dominant political authority, itself a state, imposes a centralized government over a territory with many different societies and cultures, as the British did in Nigeria and Kenya. Colonialism is a common feature of state societies.

Nearly all of the multisociety states that emerged after World War II were the results of successful independence movements against colonial powers.[16] Most have retained their political unity despite the fact that they still contain many different societies. Multisociety or multiethnic states may also form voluntarily, in reaction to external threat. Switzerland comprises cantons, each of which speaks mainly French, German, Italian, or Romansch; the various cantons confederated originally to shake off control by the Holy Roman Empire. But some states have lost their unity recently, including the former Union of Soviet Socialist Republics (USSR) and much of Yugoslavia.

In addition to their strictly political features, state-organized societies are generally supported by intensive agriculture. The high productivity of the agriculture allows for the emergence of cities, a high degree of economic and other kinds of specialization, and market or commercial exchange. In addition, state societies usually have class stratification (see Table 8.1 on page 168). Cities have grown tremendously in the past 100 years, largely as a result of migration and immigration.

When states come into existence, people's access to scarce resources is radically altered. So, too, is their ability not to listen to leaders: You cannot refuse to pay taxes and go unpunished. Of course, the rulers of a state do not maintain the social order by force alone. The people must believe, at least to some extent, that those in power have a legitimate right to govern. If the people think otherwise, history suggests that those in power may eventually lose their ability to control. Witness the recent downfall of Communist parties throughout most of eastern Europe and the former Soviet Union.

Humans are a social bunch. They generally live in groups or communities. These groups range in size from bands to villages to town and cities. Each may function as a political entity; activities are organized in their behalf by headmen, mayors, councils, and other political "officials" and groups. Nearly half of the world's human population now live in cities, which are usually defined as communities in which few are directly involved in food getting. An even larger proportion of humanity will be urban dwellers 30 years from now.

The growth of cities over the past century or so is not due to more births than deaths in the cities. Rather, cities have grown mostly because of migration from rural areas within and outside of the country. Recall the exodus of the Irish to Britain and the United States because of the "potato famine," the massive migrations from the villages of Germany, Italy, and Greece in the nineteenth and twentieth centuries, and the huge migrations, particularly in the past 50 years, from rural Mexico and China. It is probably safe to say that millions of people in many parts of the world would move to the United States, Canada, and Western Europe tomorrow, if they could. Poverty is one "push" factor. Fleeing from persecution is another. Many parts of the world are not safe, particularly for poor people. Or other places look more promising. Think of the state of California in the United States. The vast majority of its inhabitants were born elsewhere. True, in the modern world it is possible for some people to go "home" for a visit, even halfway around the world. But for many migrants, now and in the recent past, the move was one way. Because you may have run away from poverty, persecution, and war, you couldn't (or wouldn't) go home again.

An increasing number of anthropologists call themselves "urban anthropologists." They study why people move, and how they adjust to new places. They do so because so many people are moving now. There are villages in rural Spain and France that are mostly empty during the week. The owners live and work in Barcelona or Paris, and they hardly ever go "home." Indeed, their village houses may not even be available to them much, because they are usually rented to tourists! From across the Atlantic, no less.

Cities everywhere have problems, even in the most developed countries. It is difficult and expensive to provide water, power, sanitation, and other services to perhaps millions of city-dwellers. Yet in every country people are leaving rural areas and going to cities for a variety of reasons. Some are political refugees, like the Hmong from Laos. Then there are the people from Congo, Sudan, Kosovo, and Northern Ireland who have fled civil wars. There are other reasons to leave, too. Technological improvements may have reduced the need for rural labor, as happened in the U.S. South after the 1930s. Or the rural opportunities cannot support the increased number of mouths to be fed. Then people go to cities where there are jobs available. In the more urbanized countries the cities have acquired "suburbs," where many of the people in a metropolitan area may actually live, but hardly anyone is left on the farm—just a few percent of the population in the more developed countries.

With the building of suburbs in many countries in the last half of the twentieth century, cities lost population as people moved to the suburbs to have more living space or "better" schools for their children, or to escape the threat of violence. But recently the flow has started to reverse in North America and elsewhere. People are coming back to the cities, perhaps because they are tired of commuting long distances to jobs and recreation. This is particularly so with wealthier people whose children have grown up and moved away; with more people living longer, many want to move closer to the places where they mostly spend their time. Despite the social inequality and violence, cities have always been the places to go for jobs and other activities. Theaters, restaurants, museums, hospitals, and professional sports stadiums have always been located in or near cities.

The "push" out of the rural areas, the "pull" of the cities, is hard to resist, despite the enormous political problems of urban living. As the old song laments, "How ya gonna keep 'em down on the farm after they've seen Paree?"

Source: Melvin Ember and Carol R. Ember, eds., *Encyclopedia of Urban Cultures: Cities and Cultures around the World,* 4 vols. (Danbury, CT: Grolier/Scholastic, 2002).

Popular will can change governments. Massive protest in Ukraine led a newly elected president to resign.

A state society can retain its legitimacy, or at least its power, for a long time. For example, the Roman Empire was a complex state society that dominated the Mediterranean and Near East for hundreds of years. It began as a city-state that waged war to acquire additional territory. At its height, the Roman Empire embraced more than 55 million people;[17] the capital city of Rome had a population of well over a million.[18] The empire included parts of what are now Great Britain, France, Spain, Portugal, Germany, Rumania, Turkey, Greece, Armenia, Egypt, Israel, and Syria.

Factors Associated with Variation in Political Organization

The kinds of political organization we call band, tribal, chiefdom, and state are points on a continuum of levels of political integration or unification, from small-scale local autonomy to large-scale regional unification. There also is variation in political authority, from a few temporary and informal political leaders to large numbers of permanent, specialized political officials, from the absence of coercive political power to the monopoly of public force by a central authority. These aspects of variation in political organization are generally associated with shifts from food collection to more intensive food production, from small to large communities, from low to high population densities, from an emphasis on reciprocity to redistribution to market exchange, and from egalitarian to rank to fully stratified class societies.

The associations just outlined, which seem to be confirmed by the available cross-cultural evidence, are summarized in Table 8.1 on page 168. With regard to the relationship between level of subsistence technology and political complexity, it was found that the greater the importance of agriculture in a society, the larger the population that is politically unified and the greater the number and types of political officials.[19] Another cross-cultural survey reported a similar trend: The more intensive the agriculture, the greater the likelihood of state organization; conversely, societies with no more than local political institutions are likely to depend on hunting, gathering, and fishing.[20]

With regard to community size, the first of these studies also suggested that the larger the leading community, the wider the range of political officials in the society.[21] Robert Textor presented a similar finding: Societies with state organization tend to have cities and towns, whereas those with only local political organization are more likely to have communities with an average population of fewer than 200 persons.[22] Cross-cultural research also tends to confirm that societies with higher levels of political integration are more likely to exhibit social differentiation, especially in the form of class distinctions.[23]

Does this evidence provide us with an explanation for why political organization varies? Clearly, the data indicate that several factors are associated with political development, but exactly why changes in organization occur is not yet understood. Although economic development may be a necessary condition for political development,[24] that relation does not fully explain why political organization should become more complex just because the economy can support it. Some theorists have suggested that competition between groups may be a more important reason for political consolidation. For example, Elman Service suggested competition as a reason why a society might change from a band level of political organization to a tribal level. Band societies are generally hunter-gatherers. With a changeover to agriculture, population density and competition between groups may increase. Service believed that such competition would foster the development of some informal organization beyond the community—namely, tribal organization—for offense and defense.[25] Indeed, both unilineal kinship groups and age-set systems seem to be associated with warfare.

Among agriculturalists, defensive needs might also be the main reason for switching from informal multivillage political organization to more formal chiefdom organization. Formally organized districts are probably more likely to defeat autonomous villages or even segmentary lineage systems.[26] In addition, there may be economic reasons for political development. With regard to chiefdoms, Service suggested that chiefdoms will emerge when redistribution between communities becomes important or when large-scale coordinated work groups are required. The more important these activities are, the more important—and hence more "chiefly"—the organizer and his family presumably become.[27] But redistribution is far from a universal activity of chiefs.[28]

Theory and research on the anthropology of political development have focused mostly on the high end of the scale of political complexity, and particularly on the origins of the first state societies. Those earliest states apparently rose independently of one another, after about 3500 B.C., in what are now southern Iraq, Egypt, northwestern India, northern China, and central Mexico. Several theories have been proposed to explain the rise of the earliest states, but no one theory seems to fit all the known archaeological sequences culminating in early state formation. The reason may be that different conditions in different places favored the emergence of centralized government. The state, by definition, implies the power to organize large populations for collective purposes. In some areas, the impetus may have been the need to organize necessary local or long-distance trade or both. In other areas, the state may have emerged as a way to control defeated populations that could not flee. In still other instances, other factors or a combination of factors may have fostered the development of states. It is still not clear what the specific conditions were that led to the emergence of the state in each of the early centers.[29]

The Spread of State Societies

The state level of political development has come to dominate the world. Societies with states have larger communities and higher population densities than do band, tribal, and chiefdom societies. They also have armies that are ready to fight at almost any time. State systems that have waged war against chiefdoms and tribes have almost always won, and the result has usually been the political incorporation of the losers. For example, the British and, later, the U.S. colonization of much of North America led to the defeat and incorporation of many Native American societies.

The defeat and incorporation of the Native Americans was at least partly due to the catastrophic depopulations they suffered because of epidemic diseases, such as smallpox and measles, that European colonists introduced. Catastrophic depopulation was commonly the outcome of the first contacts between European Americans and the natives of North and South America, as well as the natives of the far islands in the Pacific. People in the New World and the Pacific had not been exposed, and therefore were not

In the governance structure of the European Union (EU), the executive branch (the European Commission) consists of one representative from each EU country.

resistant, to the diseases the European Americans carried with them when they began to colonize the world. Before the expansion of Europeans, the people of the New World and the Pacific had been separated for a long time from the people and diseases on the geographically continuous landmass we separate into Europe, Africa, and Asia. Smallpox, measles, and the other former scourges of Europe had largely become childhood diseases that most individuals of European ancestry survived.[30]

Whether by depopulation, conquest, or intimidation, the number of independent political units in the world has decreased strikingly in the last 3,000 years, and especially in the last 200 years. Robert Carneiro estimated that in 1000 B.C., there may have been between 100,000 and 1 million separate political units in the world; today there are fewer than 200.[31] In the ethnographic record, about 50 percent of the 2,000 or so societies described within the last 150 years had only local political integration. That is, the highest level of political integration in one out of two recent societies was the local community.[32] Thus, most of the decrease in the number of independent political units has occurred fairly recently.

But the recent secessions from the former Soviet Union and Yugoslavia and other separatist movements around the world suggest that ethnic rivalries may make for departures from the trend toward larger and larger political units. Ethnic groups that have been dominated by others in multinational states may opt for political autonomy, at least for a while. On the other hand, the separate nations of Western Europe are becoming more unified every day, both politically and economically. So the trend toward larger and larger political units may be continuing, even if there are departures from it now and then.

Extrapolating from past history, a number of investigators have suggested that the entire world will eventually come to be politically integrated, perhaps as soon as the twenty-third century and no later than A.D. 4850.[33] Only the future will tell if this prediction will come true. And only the future will tell if further political integration in the world will occur peacefully—with all parties agreeing—or by force or the threat of force, as has happened so often in the past.

Variation in Political Process

Anthropologists are increasingly interested in the politics, or political processes, of the societies they study: who acquires influence or power, how they acquire it, and how political decisions are made. But even though we have descriptive accounts of politics in many societies, there is still relatively little comparative or cross-cultural research on what may explain variation in politics.

Getting to Be a Leader

In those societies that have hereditary leadership, which is common in rank societies and in state societies with monarchies, rules of succession usually establish how leadership is inherited. But for societies whose leaders are *chosen,* either as informal leaders or as elected political officials, we need a lot more research to understand why some kinds of people are chosen over others.

A few studies have investigated the personal qualities of leaders in tribal societies. One study, conducted among the Mekranoti-Kayapo of central Brazil, found that leaders, in contrast to followers, tend to be rated by their peers as higher in intelligence, generosity, knowledgeability, ambitiousness, and aggressiveness. Leaders also tend to be older and taller. And despite the egalitarian nature of Mekranoti society (at least with respect to sharing resources), sons of leaders are more likely than others to become leaders.[34]

Research in another Brazilian society, the Kagwahiv of the Amazon region, suggests another personal quality of leaders: They seem to have positive feelings about their fathers and mothers.[35] In many respects, studies of leaders in the United States show them to be not that different from their counterparts in Brazil. But there is one major difference: Mekranoti and Kagwahiv leaders are not wealthier than others; in fact, they give their wealth away. U.S. leaders are generally wealthier than others.[36]

"Big Men"   In some egalitarian tribal societies, the quest for leadership seems quite competitive. In parts of New Guinea and South America, "big men" compete with other ambitious men to attract followers. Men who want to compete must show that they have magical powers, success in gardening, and bravery in war. But, most important, they have to collect enough goods to throw big parties at which the goods are given away. Big men have to work very hard to attract and keep their followings, for dissatisfied followers can always join other aspiring men.[37] The wives of big men are often leaders too. Among the Kagwahiv, for example, a headman's wife is usually the leader of the women in the community; she is responsible for much of the planning for feasts and often distributes the meat at them.[38]

How does a man get to be a big man? Among the Kumdi-Engamoi, a central Highlands group, a man who wants to be considered a *wua nium* (literally, a "great-important-wealthy man") needs to have many wives and daughters, because the amount of land controlled by a man and how much can be produced on that land depend on the number of women in his family. The more wives he has, the more land he is given to cultivate. He must also be a good speaker. Everyone has the right to speak and give speeches, but to get to be known as a big man requires speaking well and forcefully and knowing when to sum up a consensus. It usually takes a man until his thirties or forties to acquire more than one wife and to make his name through exchanges. When a man wants to inaugurate an exchange, he needs to get shells and pigs from his family and relatives. Once he has achieved a reputation as a *wua nium,* he can keep it only if he continues to perform well—that is, if he continues to distribute fairly, make wise decisions, speak well, and conduct exchanges.[39]

"Big Women"   In contrast to most of mainland New Guinea, the islands off the southeastern coast are characterized by matrilineal descent. But, like mainland New Guinea, the islands also have a shifting system of leadership in which people compete for "big" status. Here, though, the people competing are women as well as men, and so there are "big women" as well as "big men." On the island of Vanatinai, for example, women and men compete with each other to exchange valuables. Women lead canoe expeditions to distant islands to visit male as well as female exchange partners, women mobilize relatives and exchange partners to mount large feasts, and the women get to keep the ceremonial valuables exchanged, at least for a while.[40]

The prominence of women on Vanatinai may be linked to the disappearance of warfare—the colonial powers imposed peace; we call this "pacification." Inter-island exchanges became frequent when war

In many egalitarian societies, leadership shifts informally from one person to another. In much of New Guinea, there is more competition for achieving "big" status. On Vanatinai, the women compete as well as the men, so there are "big women" as well as "big men." Here a "big woman" paints the face of her cousin's widow for a feast honoring the dead man.

became less common in the early twentieth century, giving women and men more freedom to travel. For men, but not women, war provided a path to leadership; champion warriors would acquire great renown and influence. It is not that women did not participate in war; they did, which is unusual cross-culturally, but a woman could not become a war leader. Now, in the absence of war, women have an opportunity through exchanges to become leaders, or "big women."

Political Participation

Political scientist Marc Ross conducted cross-cultural research on variation in degree of political participation. Ross phrased the research question: "Why is it that in some polities there are relatively large numbers of persons involved in political life, while in others political action is the province of very few?"[41]

Political participation in preindustrial societies ranges from widespread to low or nonexistent. In 16 percent of the societies examined, there is widespread participation; decision-making forums are open to all adults. The forums may be formal (councils and other governing bodies) or informal. Next in degree of political participation are societies (37 percent) that have widespread participation by some but not all adults (men but not women, certain classes but not others). Next are societies (29 percent) that have some but not much input by the community. Finally, 18 percent of the societies have low or nonexistent participation, which means that leaders make most decisions, and involvement of the average person is very limited.

Degree of political participation seems to be high in small-scale societies, as well as in modern democratic nation-states, but not in between (feudal states and preindustrial empires). Why? In small-scale societies leaders do not have the power to force people to act; thus a high degree of political participation may be the only way to get people to go along with decisions. In modern democracies, which have many powerful groups outside the government—corporations, unions, and other interest groups are examples— the central authorities may only theoretically have the power to force people to go along; in reality, they rely mostly on voluntary compliance. For example, the U.S. government failed when it tried with force (Prohibition, 1920–1933) to stop the manufacture, transport, and sale of alcoholic beverages.

Negotiation and Mediation   In many conflicts, the parties to a dispute may come to a settlement themselves by **negotiation**. There aren't necessarily any rules for how they will do so, but any solution is "good" if it restores peace.[53] Sometimes an outside or third party is used to help bring about a settlement between the disputants. We call it **mediation** when the outside party tries to help bring about a settlement, but that third party does not have the formal authority to force a settlement. Both negotiation and mediation are likely when the society is relatively egalitarian and it is important for people to get along.[54]

Among the Nuer of East Africa, a pastoral and horticultural people, disputes within the community can be settled with the help of an informal mediator called the "leopard-skin chief." This man is not a political chief but a mediator. His position is hereditary, has religious overtones, and makes its holder responsible for the social well-being of the district. Matters such as cattle stealing rarely come to the attention of the leopard-skin chief; the parties involved usually prefer to settle in their own private way. But if, for example, a murder has been committed, the culprit will go at once to the house of the leopard-skin chief. Immediately the chief cuts the culprit's arm so that blood flows; until the cut has been made the murderer may not eat or drink. If the murderer is afraid of vengeance by the slain man's family, he will remain at the house of the leopard-skin chief, which is considered sanctuary. Then, within the next few months, the chief attempts to mediate between the parties to the crime.

The chief elicits from the slayer's kin that they are prepared to pay compensation to avoid a feud, and he persuades the dead man's kin that they ought to accept compensation, usually in the form of cattle. During this period neither party may eat or drink from the same vessels as the other, and they may not, therefore, eat in the house of the same third person. The chief then collects the cattle—some 40 to 50 beasts—and takes them to the dead man's home, where he performs various sacrifices of cleansing and atonement.[55]

Throughout the process, the chief acts as a go-between. He has no authority to force either party to negotiate, and he has no power to enforce a solution once it has been arrived at. However, he is able to take advantage of the fact that because both disputants belong to the same community and are anxious to avoid a blood feud, they usually are willing to come to terms.

Ritual Reconciliation—Apology   The desire to restore a harmonious relationship may also explain ceremonial apologies. An apology is based on deference—the guilty party shows obeisance and asks for forgiveness. Such ceremonies tend to occur in recent chiefdoms.[56] Among the Fijians of the South Pacific, there is a strong ethic of harmony and mutual assistance, particularly within a village. When a person offends someone of higher status, the offended person and other villagers begin to avoid, and gossip about, the offender. If offenders are sensitive to village opinion, they will perform a ceremony of apology called *i soro*. One of the meanings of *soro* is "surrender." In the ceremony the offender bows the head and remains silent while an intermediary speaks, presents a token gift, and asks the offended person for forgiveness. The apology is rarely rejected.[57]

Oaths and Ordeals   Still another way of peacefully resolving disputes is through oaths and ordeals, both of which involve appeals to supernatural power. An **oath** is the act of calling upon a deity to bear witness to the truth of what one says. An **ordeal** is a means used to determine guilt or innocence by submitting the accused to dangerous or painful tests believed to be under supernatural control.[58]

A common kind of ordeal, found in almost every part of the world, is scalding. Among the Tanala of Madagascar, the accused person, having first had his hand carefully examined for protective covering, has to reach his hand into a cauldron of boiling water and grasp, from underneath, a rock suspended there. He then plunges his hand into cold water, has it bandaged, and is led off to spend the night under guard. In the morning his hand is unbandaged and examined. If there are blisters, he is guilty.

Oaths and ordeals have also been practiced in Western societies. Both were common in medieval Europe. Even today, in our own society, vestiges of oaths can be found. Children can be heard to say, "Cross my heart and hope to die," and witnesses in courts of law are obliged to swear to tell the truth.

Why do some societies use oaths and ordeals? John Roberts suggested that their use tends to be found in fairly complex societies in which political officials lack sufficient power to make and enforce judicial decisions or would make themselves unnecessarily vulnerable were they to attempt to do so. So the officials may use oaths and ordeals to let the gods decide guilt or innocence. When political officials gain more power, oaths and ordeals seem to decline or disappear.[59] In contrast, smaller and less complex societies probably have no need for elaborate mechanisms such as courts and oaths and ordeals to ascertain guilt. In such societies, everyone is aware of what crimes have been committed and who the guilty parties probably are.

Adjudication, Courts, and Codified Law   We call it **adjudication** when a third party acting as judge makes a decision that the disputing parties have to accept. Judgment may be rendered by one person (a judge), a panel of judges, a jury, or a political agent or agency (a chief, a royal personage, a council). Courts are often open to an audience, but they need not be. Judges and courts may rely on codified law and stipulated punishments, but codified law is not necessary for decisions to be made. Our own society relies heavily on codified law and courts to resolve disputes peacefully, but courts often, if not usually, rely on precedent—that is, the outcomes of previous, similar cases. Codified laws and courts are not limited to Western societies. From the late seventeenth to the early twentieth centuries, for example, the Ashanti of West Africa had a complex political system with legal codes.[60] Ashanti punishments could be severe. Physical mutilation, such as slicing off the nose or an ear—even castration in sexual offenses— was often employed. Fines were more frequent, however, and death sentences could often be commuted to banishment and confiscation of goods.

Why do some societies have codified systems and others do not? One explanation, advanced by E. Adamson Hoebel, A. R. Radcliffe-Brown, and others, is that in small, closely knit communities there is little need for formal legal guidelines because competing interests are minimal. Hence, simple societies need little codified law. There are relatively few matters to quarrel about, and the general will of the group is sufficiently well known and demonstrated frequently enough to deter transgressors.

Many societies have adopted courts to resolve disputes, as here in Papua New Guinea.

This point of view is echoed in Richard Schwartz's study of two Israeli settlements. In one communal kibbutz, a young man aroused a good deal of community resentment because he had accepted an electric teakettle as a gift. It was the general opinion that he had overstepped the code about not having personal possessions, and he was so informed. Accordingly, he gave the kettle to the communal infirmary. Schwartz observed that "no organized enforcement of the decision was threatened, but had he disregarded the expressed will of the community, his life . . . would have been made intolerable by the antagonism of public opinion."[61]

In this community, where people worked and ate together, not only did everyone know about transgressions, but a wrongdoer could not escape public censure. Thus, public opinion was an effective sanction. In another Israeli community, however, where individuals lived in widely separated houses and worked and ate separately, public opinion did not work as well. Not only were community members less aware of problems, but they had no quick way of making their feelings known. As a result, they established a judicial body to handle trouble cases.

Larger, more heterogeneous and stratified societies are likely to have more frequent disputes, which at the same time are less visible to the public. Individuals in stratified societies are generally not so dependent on community members for their well-being and hence are less likely to know of, or care about, others' opinions. It is in such societies that codified laws and formal authorities for resolving disputes develop—in order, perhaps, that disputes may be settled impersonally enough so that the parties can accept the decision and social order can be restored.

A good example of how more formal systems of law develop is the experience of towns in the American West during the gold-rush period. These communities were literally swamped by total strangers. The townsfolk, having no control (authority) over these intruders because the strangers had no local ties, looked for ways to deal with the trouble cases that were continually flaring up. A first attempt at a solution was to hire gunslingers, who were also strangers, to act as peace officers or sheriffs, but this strategy usually failed. Eventually, towns succeeded in having federal authorities send in marshals backed by federal power.

Is there some evidence to support the theory that codified law is necessary only in larger, more complex societies? Data from a large, worldwide sample of societies suggest that codified law is associated with political integration beyond the local level. Murder cases, for example, are dealt with informally in societies that have only local political organization. In societies with multilocal political units, murder cases tend to be judged or adjudicated by specialized political authorities.[62] There is also some cross-cultural evidence that violence within a society tends to be less frequent when there are formal authorities (chiefs, courts) who have the power to punish murderers.[63] In general, adjudication or enforced decisions by outside authorities tend to occur in hierarchical societies with social classes and centralized power.[64]

Violent Resolution of Conflict

People are likely to resort to violence when regular, effective alternative means of resolving a conflict are not available. Some societies consider violence between individuals to be appropriate under certain circumstances; when it is not, we call it **crime**. When violence occurs between political entities such as communities, districts, or nations, we call it **warfare**. The type of warfare, of course, varies in scope and complexity from society to society. Sometimes a distinction is made among feuding, raiding, and large-scale confrontations.

Some scholars talk about a cultural pattern of violence. But are some cultures more violent than others? The answer seems to be yes. More often than not, societies with one type of violence have others. Societies with more war tend to have warlike sports, malevolent magic, severe punishment for crimes, high murder rates, feuding, and family violence. What might explain this tendency? One suggestion is that if war is frequent, the society may have to encourage boys to be aggressive, so that they can grow up to be effective warriors. But this socializing for aggression can spill over into other areas of life; high rates of crime and other violence may be inadvertent or unintended consequences of the encouragement of aggressiveness.[65]

Individual Violence   Although at first it may seem paradoxical, violent behavior itself is often used to try to control behavior. In some societies it is considered necessary for parents to beat children who misbehave. They don't consider this criminal behavior or child abuse; they consider it punishment (see the discussion of family violence in the chapter on global issues). Similar views may attach to interpersonal behavior between adults. If a person trespasses on your property or hurts someone in your family, some societies consider it appropriate or justified to kill or maim the trespasser. Is this social control, or is it just lack of control? Most societies have norms about when such "punishment" is or is not appropriate, so the behavior of anyone who contemplates doing something wrong, as well as the behavior of the person wronged, is likely to be influenced by the "laws" of their society. For example, systems of individual self-help are characteristic of egalitarian societies.[66] How is this different from "community action," which earlier we classified under peaceful resolution of conflict? Because community action is explicitly based on obtaining a consensus, it is likely to lead to the ending of a particular dispute. Individual action, or self-help, particularly if it involves violence, is not.

Feuding   Feuding is an example of how individual self-help may not lead to a peaceful resolution of conflict. **Feuding** is a state of recurring hostilities between families or groups of kin, usually motivated by a desire to avenge an offense—whether insult, injury, deprivation, or death—against a member of the group. The most common characteristic of the feud is that responsibility to avenge is carried by all members of the kin group. The killing of any member of the offender's group is considered appropriate revenge, because the kin group as a whole is regarded as responsible. Feuds are by no means limited to small-scale societies; they occur as frequently in societies with high levels of political organization.[67]

Raiding   **Raiding** is a short-term use of force, planned and organized, to realize a limited objective. This objective is usually the acquisition of goods, animals, or other forms of wealth belonging to another, often neighboring community.

Raiding is especially prevalent in pastoral societies, in which cattle, horses, camels, or other animals are prized and an individual's own herd can be augmented by theft. Raids are often organized by temporary leaders or coordinators whose authority may not last beyond the planning and execution of the venture. Raiding may also be organized for the purpose of capturing people. Sometimes people are taken to marry—the capture of women to be wives or concubines is fairly common[68]—or to be slaves. Slavery has been practiced in about 33 percent of the world's known societies, and war has been one way of obtaining slaves either to keep or to trade for other goods.[69] Raiding, like feuding, is often self-perpetuating: the victim of a raid today becomes the raider tomorrow.[70]

Large-Scale Confrontations   Individual episodes of feuds and raids usually involve relatively small numbers of persons and almost always an element of surprise. Because they are generally attacked without warning, the victims are often unable to muster an immediate defense. Large-scale confrontations, in contrast, involve a large number of persons and planning by both sides of strategies of attack and defense. Large-scale warfare is usually practiced among societies with intensive agriculture or industrialization. Only these societies possess a technology sufficiently advanced to support specialized armies, military leaders, strategists, and so on. But large-scale confrontations are not limited to state societies; they occur, for example, among the horticultural Dugum Dani of central New Guinea.

The military history of the Dani, with its shifting alliances and confederations, is reminiscent of that of Europe, although Dani battles involve far fewer fighters and less sophisticated weaponry. Among the Dani, long periods of ritual warfare are characterized by formal battles announced through a challenge sent by one side to the opposing side. If the challenge is accepted, the protagonists meet at the agreed-upon battle site to set up their lines. Fighting with spears, sticks, and bows and arrows begins at midmorning and continues either until nightfall or until rain intervenes. There may also be a rest period during the midday heat during which the two sides shout insults at each other or talk and rest among themselves.

The front line of battle is composed of about a dozen active warriors and a few leaders. Behind them is a second line, still within arrow range, composed of those who have just left the forward line or are preparing to join it. The third line, outside arrow range, is composed of noncombatants—males too old or too young to participate and those recovering from wounds. This third line merely watches the battle taking place on the grassy plain. On the hillsides far back from the front line, some of the old men help to direct ancestral ghosts to the battle by gouging a line in the ground that points in the direction of the battlefield.[71]

Yet, as total as large-scale confrontations may be, even warfare has cultural rules. Among the Dani, for instance, no fighting occurs at night, and weapons are limited to simple spears and bows and arrows. Similarly, in state societies, governments will sign "self-denying" pacts restricting the use of poison gas, germ warfare, and so forth. Unofficially, private arrangements are common. One has only to glance through the memoirs of national leaders of the two world wars to become aware of locally arranged truces, visits to one another's front positions, exchanges of prisoners of war, and so on.

Explaining Warfare

Most societies anthropology knows about have had warfare between communities or larger territorial groups. The vast majority of the societies in a recent cross-cultural study had at least occasional wars when they were first described, unless they had been pacified or incorporated by more dominant societies.[72] Yet relatively little research has been done on the possible causes of war and why it varies in type and frequency. For instance, why have some people fought a great deal, and others only infrequently? Why in some societies does warfare occur internally, within the society or language group?

We have answers, based on cross-cultural studies, to some of those questions. There is evidence that people in preindustrial societies go to war mostly out of fear, particularly a fear of expectable but unpredictable natural disasters (e.g., droughts, floods, locust infestations) that will destroy food resources. People may think they can protect themselves against such disasters ahead of time by taking things from defeated enemies. In any case, preindustrial societies with higher frequencies of war are very likely to have had a history of expectable but unpredictable disasters. The fact that chronic (annually recurring and therefore predictable) food shortages do not predict higher frequencies of war suggests that people go to war in an attempt to cushion the impact of the disasters they expect to occur in the future but cannot predict. Consistent with this tentative conclusion is the fact that the victors in war almost always take land or other resources from the defeated. And this is true for simpler as well as more complex preindustrial societies.[73] Might similar motives affect decisions about war and peace in the modern world?

We know that complex or politically centralized societies are likely to have professional armies, hierarchies of military authority, and sophisticated weapons.[74] But surprisingly, the frequency of warfare seems to be not much greater in complex societies than in simple band or tribal societies.[75] We have some evidence that warfare is unlikely to occur internally (within a society) if it is small in population (21,000 or fewer people) or territory; in a larger society there is a high likelihood of warfare within the society, between communities or larger territorial divisions.[76] In fact, complex societies, even if they are politically unified, are not less likely than simpler societies to have internal warfare.[77]

What about the idea that men in band and tribal societies may mostly go to war over women?[78] If this were true, those band and tribal societies with the most frequent wars should have shortages of women, and those with little or no war—less often than once in 10 years—should have more equal numbers of women and men. But the cross-cultural evidence clearly contradicts this theory. Band and tribal societies with more wars do not have fewer women.[79]

What, if anything, do we know about recent warfare between nation-states? Although many people think that military alliances lessen the chance of war, it turns out that nations formally allied with other nations do not necessarily go to war less often than nations lacking formal alliances. Countries that are allies are, of course, less likely to go to war with each other; however, alliances can drag dependent allies into wars they don't want. Countries that are economically interdependent, that trade with each other for necessities, are less likely to go to war with each other.[80] Finally, military equality between nations, particularly when preceded by a rapid military buildup, seems to increase rather than lessen the chance of war between those nations.[81]

Clearly, these findings contradict some traditional beliefs about how to prevent war. Military buildups do not make war less likely, but trade does. What else may? We have already noted that participatory ("democratic") political systems are less likely to go to war with each other than are authoritarian political systems. Later, in the chapter on global issues, we discuss how the results of cross-cultural and cross-national studies may translate into policies that could minimize the risk of war in the world.

Summary

1. All societies have customs or procedures that, organized on behalf of territorial groups, result in decision making and the resolution of disputes. These ways of creating and maintaining social order and coping with social disorder vary from society to society.

2. Societies with a band type of political organization are composed of fairly small, usually nomadic groups. Each of these bands is politically autonomous, the band being the largest group that acts as a political unit. Authority within the band is usually informal. Societies with band organization generally are egalitarian hunter-gatherers. But band organization may not have been typical of food collectors in the distant past.

3. Societies with tribal organization are generally egalitarian. But in contrast with band societies, they generally are food producers, have a higher population density, and are more sedentary. Tribal organization is defined by the presence of groupings, such as clans and age-sets, that can integrate more than one local group into a larger whole.

4. The personal qualities of leaders in tribal societies seem to be similar to the qualities of leaders in the United States, with one major difference: U.S. leaders are generally wealthier than others in their society.

5. Chiefdom organization differs from tribal organization in having formal authority structures that integrate multicommunity political units. Compared with societies with tribal organization, societies with chiefdoms are more densely populated, their communities are more permanent, and there is some form of social ranking. Chiefs generally hold their positions permanently.

6. A state has been defined as a political unit composed of many communities and having a centralized government with the authority to make and enforce laws, collect taxes, and draft men for military service. In state societies, the government tries to maintain a monopoly on the use of physical force. In addition, states are generally characterized by class stratification, intensive agriculture, commercial exchange, a high degree of economic and other specialization, and extensive foreign trade.

7. Degree of political participation seems to be high in small-scale societies, as well as in modern democratic nation-states, but not in those in between, such as feudal states and preindustrial empires.

8. Many societies lack specialized offices and institutions for dealing with conflict. Yet all societies have peaceful, regularized ways of handling at least certain disputes. Avoidance, community action, and negotiation and mediation are more common in simpler societies. Ritual apology occurs frequently in chiefdoms. Oaths and ordeals tend to occur in complex societies in which political officials lack power to enforce judicial decisions. Adjudication is more likely in stratified, more complex societies. Capital punishment seems to exist in nearly all societies, from the simplest to the most complex.

9. People are likely to resort to violence when regular, effective alternative means of resolving a conflict are not available. Violence that occurs between political entities such as communities, districts, or nations is generally referred to as warfare. Preindustrial societies with higher warfare frequencies are likely to have had a history of unpredictable disasters that destroyed food supplies. More often than not, societies with one type of violence have others.

Glossary Terms

adjudication (p. 181)

band (p. 167)

band organization (p. 167)

chief (p. 170)

chiefdom (p. 170)

codified laws (p. 178)

complementary opposition (p. 169)

crime (p. 182)

feuding (p. 183)

headman (p. 167)

mediation (p. 180)

negotiation (p. 180)

oath (p. 180)

ordeal (p. 180)

raiding (p. 183)

segmentary lineage system (p. 169)

state (p. 171)

state organization (p. 171)

tribal organization (p. 168)

tribe (p. 168)

warfare (p. 182)

Critical Questions

1. When, if ever, do you think the world will be politically unified? Why do you think so?

2. Why don't informal methods of social control work well in societies like our own? Why don't formal methods work better than they do?

3. What does research on war and violence suggest about how to minimize them?

CHAPTER 9

RELIGION AND MAGIC

Chapter Outline

- Variation in Religious Beliefs
- Variation in Religious Practices
- Religion and Adaptation

As far as we know, all societies have possessed beliefs that can be grouped under the term *religion.* These beliefs vary from culture to culture and from time to time. Yet, despite their variety, we shall define **religion** as any set of attitudes, beliefs, and practices pertaining to *supernatural power,* whether that power be forces, gods, spirits, ghosts, or demons.

In our society, we divide phenomena into the natural and the supernatural, but not all languages or cultures make such a neat distinction. Moreover, what is considered **supernatural**—powers believed to be not human or not subject to the laws of nature—varies from society to society. Some of the variation is determined by what a society regards as natural. For example, some illnesses commonly found in our society are believed to result from the natural action of bacteria and viruses. In other societies, and even among some people in our own society, illness is thought to result from supernatural forces, and thus it forms a part of religious belief.

Beliefs about what is, or is not, a supernatural occurrence also vary within a society at a given time or over time. In Judeo-Christian traditions, for example, floods, earthquakes, volcanic eruptions, comets, and epidemics were once considered evidence of supernatural powers intervening in human affairs. It is now generally agreed that they are simply natural occurrences—even though many still believe that supernatural forces may be involved. Thus, the line between the natural and the supernatural varies in a society according to what people believe about the causes of things and events in the observable world. Similarly, what is considered sacred in one society may not be so considered in another.

In many cultures, what we would consider religious is embedded in other aspects of everyday life. That is, it is often difficult to separate the religious, economic, or political from other aspects of the culture. Such cultures have little or no specialization of any kind; there are no full-time priests, no purely religious activities. So the various aspects of culture we distinguish (e.g., in the chapter titles of this book) are not separate and easily recognized in many societies, as they are in complex societies such as our own. However, it is sometimes difficult for us to agree whether or not a particular custom of ours is religious. After all, the categorizing of beliefs as religious, political, or social is a relatively new custom. The ancient Greeks, for instance, did not have a word for religion, but they did have many concepts concerning the behavior of their gods and their own expected duties to the gods.

Variation in Religious Beliefs

There is no general agreement among scholars as to why people need religion, or how spirits, gods, and other supernatural beings and forces come into existence. Yet there is general recognition of the enormous variation in the details of religious beliefs and practices. Societies differ in the kinds of supernatural beings or forces they believe in and the character of those beings. They also differ in the structure or hierarchy of those beings, in what the beings actually do, and in what happens to people after death. Variation exists also in the ways in which the supernatural is believed to interact with humans.

Types of Supernatural Forces and Beings

Supernatural Forces   Some supernatural forces have no personlike character. For example, a supernatural, impersonal force called **mana**, after its Malayo-Polynesian name, is thought to inhabit some objects but not others, some people but not others. A farmer in Polynesia places stones around a field; the crops are bountiful; the stones have mana. During a subsequent year the stones may lose their mana and the

Beneath the gods
be guardian spirits f
moted to the rank o
them are of the hob;
small mishaps; still
Many Native Am
hood. For example, :
sent out on overnig
they could also be u
ways successful. Wh
human form. Conve

Ghosts are super
tives. The belief that
universality of the l
experience that are :
feeling that the dead
cologne in a room n
loved ones live on i
ghosts is generated b
close relatives and fr
Although the bel
the life of the living
ple are likely to belie
The descent group i

A Guatemalan Maya
lieved that the spirit

THE USEFULNESS OF RELIGION:
TABOOS AMONG NEW ENGLAND FISHERMEN

People who engage in risky activities may try to ensure their safety by carrying or wearing lucky charms. They believe the charms protect them by invoking the help of supernatural beings or forces. We might also believe we can protect ourselves by not doing some things. For example, baseball players on a hitting streak may choose not to change their socks or sweatshirt for the next game (to continue their luck). Or we obey a prohibition because we think that by doing so we can avoid supernatural punishment. For example, we may fast or give up certain foods for a period of time. Why? God knows!

Whether or not religious beliefs and practices can affect our success or reduce our risk, we may consider them useful or adaptive if they reduce our anxieties. And reducing anxiety might indirectly maximize our success. Doesn't an actor try to reduce his or her "stage fright" before a performance? Prohibitions (taboos) are perhaps particularly likely to be adaptive in this way. Consider some research on New England fishermen that suggests how their taboos, or "rituals of avoidance," may reduce anxiety.

John Poggie and Richard Pollnac interviewed a random sample of 108 commercial fishermen from three New England ports. They were trying to explain the number of taboos among the fishermen, as measured by asking them to describe all the superstitions related to fishing they could remember. The fishermen were often embarrassed when they talked about their ritual beliefs and practices. They would say they did not really believe in their taboos, but they admitted that they would not break them while fishing. The taboos prohibited saying or doing a certain thing, or something bad would happen. Most frequently mentioned were "Don't turn a hatch cover upside down," "Don't whistle on a boat," and "Don't mention the word *pig* on board." When the fishermen were asked what these taboos meant, they talked about personal safety and preventing bad luck.

The results of the study suggest that anxiety about personal danger while fishing is the main stimulus for the taboo behavior observed among the fishermen. For example, there are more taboos reported when the duration of exposure to danger is longer. Fishermen who go out just for the day report significantly fewer taboos than fishermen who go out for longer periods of time. And longer trips are clearly more dangerous because they are farther from shore. If there is a storm, the farther out you are, the more risk of disaster because you are exposed longer to rough seas. And it is more difficult to deal with illness, injury, breakdowns, and damage to the boat far from shore. Also consistent with the conclusion that the fishermen's taboos reduce anxiety is the fact that inshore fishermen (those who are after shellfish close to shore) report a significantly smaller number of taboos than offshore fishermen (who go out farther in trawlers).

On shore, the fishermen express some disbelief in the effectiveness of their taboos. (They are called "superstitions," you know!) But at sea it seems that the omnipresence of danger raises anxiety levels and discourages the fishermen from testing their disbelief. It won't hurt to practice the taboo at sea, they say, but it might hurt not to!

Sources: John J. Poggie, Jr., and Richard B. Pollnac, "Danger and Rituals of Avoidance among New England Fishermen," *MAST: Maritime Anthropological Studies,* 1 (1988): 66–78; John J. Poggie, Jr., Richard B. Pollnac, and Carl Gersuny, "Risk as a Basis for Taboos among Fishermen in Southern New England," *Journal for the Scientific Study of Religion,* 15 (1976): 257–62.

crops will be poor. People may also possess mana, as, for example, the chiefs in Polynesia were said to do. However, such power is not necessarily possessed permanently; chiefs who were unsuccessful in war or other activities were said to have lost their mana.

There's room in the world f(
in rocks, those who believ
clouds . . . .

(© 1984 by Sidney Harris)

The word *ma*
We can compare
clubs. A ballplaye
that more runs or
does not.

Objects, perso
by pointing out
touched, for thei
Taboos surround
be touched sexua
mally kill and eat
during menstrua

Supernatural Be

such as gods and
the beings of non
conceived in the
of celestial bodies
but some of them
all peoples includ

After their effe
interested in its c
human beings, es
ty has a creator go
for example, reco
ture. They call up
universe runs. Th
were three gods o

storing grain, one

despite the deaths of individual members.[6] The dead feel concern for the fortunes, the prestige, and the continuity of their descent group as strongly as the living. As a Lugbara elder (in northern Uganda in Africa) put it, "Are our ancestors not people of our lineage? They are our fathers and we are their children whom they have begotten. Those that have died stay near us in our homes and we feed and respect them. Does not a man help his father when he is old?"[7]

The Character of Supernatural Beings

Whatever type they may be, the gods or spirits venerated in a given culture tend to have certain personality or character traits. They may be unpredictable or predictable, aloof from or interested in human affairs, helpful or punishing. Why do the gods and spirits in a particular culture exhibit certain character traits rather than others?

We have some evidence from cross-cultural studies that the character of supernatural beings may be related to the nature of child training. Melford Spiro and Roy D'Andrade suggested that the god-human relationship is a projection of the parent-child relationship, in which case child-training practices might well be relived in dealings with the supernatural.[8] For example, if a child was nurtured immediately by her parents when she cried or waved her arms about or kicked, she might grow up expecting to be nurtured by the gods when she attracted their attention by performing a ritual. On the other hand, if her parents often punished her, she would grow up expecting the gods to punish her if she disobeyed them. William Lambert, Leigh Minturn Triandis, and Margery Wolf, in another cross-cultural study, found that societies with hurtful or punitive child-training practices are likely to believe that their gods are aggressive and malevolent; societies with less punitive child training are more likely to believe that the gods are benevolent.[9] These results are consistent with the Freudian notion that the supernatural world should parallel the natural. It is worth noting in this context that some peoples refer to the god as their father and to themselves as his children.

Structure or Hierarchy of Supernatural Beings

The range of social structures in human societies from egalitarian to highly stratified has its counterpart in the supernatural world. Some societies have gods or spirits that are not ranked; one god has about as much power as another. Other societies have gods or spirits that are ranked in prestige and power. For example, on the Pacific islands of Palau, which was a rank society, gods were ranked as people were. Each clan worshiped a god and a goddess that had names or titles similar to clan titles. Although a clan god was generally important only to the members of that clan, the gods of the various clans in a village were believed to be ranked in the same order that the clans were. Thus, the god of the highest-ranking clan was respected by all the clans of the village. Its shrine was given the place of honor in the center of the village and was larger and more elaborately decorated than other shrines.[10]

Although the Palauans did not believe in a high god or supreme being who outranked all the other gods, some societies do. Consider Judaism, Christianity, and Islam, which we call **monotheistic** religions. Although *monotheism* means "one god," most monotheistic religions actually include more than one supernatural being (e.g., demons, angels, the Devil). But the supreme being or high god, as the creator of the universe or the director of events (or both), is believed to be ultimately responsible for all events.[11] A **polytheistic** religion recognizes many important gods, no one of which is supreme.

Why do some societies have a belief in a high god and others do not? Recall Swanson's suggestion that people invent gods who personify the important decision-making groups in their society. He therefore hypothesized that societies with hierarchical political systems should be more likely to believe in a high god. In his cross-cultural study of 50 societies (none of which practiced any of the major world religions), he found that belief in a high god is strongly associated with three or more levels of "sovereign" (decision-making) groups. Of the 20 sample societies that had a hierarchy of three or more sovereign groups—for instance, family, clan, and chiefdom—17 possessed the idea of a high god. Of the 19 societies that had fewer than 3 levels of decision-making groups, only 2 had a high god.[12] Consistent with Swanson's findings, societies dependent on food production are more likely to have a belief in a high god than are food-collecting societies.[13] These results strongly suggest, then, that the realm of the gods parallels and may reflect the everyday social and political worlds. In the past, many state societies had state religions in which the political officials were also the officials of the temples (e.g., the pharaohs in Egypt). In recent times most state societies have separated church and state, as in the United States and Canada.

Intervention of the Gods in Human Affairs

According to Clifford Geertz, it is when faced with ignorance, pain, and the unjustness of life that a person explains events by the intervention of the gods.[14] Thus, in Greek religion the direct intervention of Poseidon as ruler of the seas prevented Odysseus from getting home for ten years. In the Old Testament, the direct intervention of Yahweh caused the great flood that killed most of the people in the time of Noah. In other societies, people may search their memories for a violated taboo that has brought punishment through supernatural intervention.

In addition to unasked-for divine interference, there are numerous examples of requests for divine intervention, either for good for oneself and friends or for evil for others. Gods are asked to intervene in the weather and make the crops grow, to send fish to the fisherman and game to the hunter, to find lost things, and to accompany travelers and prevent accidents. They are asked to stop the flow of lava down the side of a volcano, to stop a war, or to cure an illness.

The gods do not intervene in all societies. In some, they intervene in human affairs; in others, they are not the slightest bit interested; and in still others, they interfere only occasionally. We have little research on why gods are believed to interfere in some societies and not in others. We do, however, have some evidence suggesting when the gods will take an interest in the morality or immorality of human behavior. Swanson's study suggests that the gods are likely to punish people for immoral behavior when there are considerable differences in wealth in the society.[15] His interpretation is that supernatural support of moral behavior is particularly useful where inequalities tax the ability of the political system to maintain social order and minimize social disorder. Envy of others' privileges may motivate some people to behave immorally; the belief that the gods will punish such behavior might deter it.

Variation in Religious Practices

Beliefs are not the only elements of religion that vary from society to society. There is also variation in how people interact with the supernatural. The manner of approach to the supernatural varies from supplication—requests, prayers, and so on—to manipulation. And societies vary in the kinds of religious practitioners they have.

Ways to Interact with the Supernatural

How to get in touch with the supernatural is a universal problem. Wallace identified a number of ways used by people the world over, though not necessarily all together, including, but not limited to, prayer (asking for supernatural help), physiological experience (doing things to the body and mind), simulation

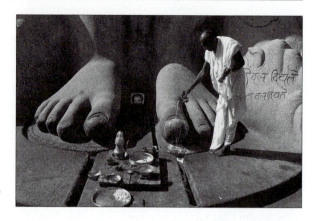

A worshipper makes offerings at the feet of a statue in an Indian temple.

(manipulating imitations of things), feasts, and sacrifices.[16] Prayer can be spontaneous or memorized, private or public, silent or spoken. The Lugbara do not say the words of a prayer aloud, for doing so would be too powerful; they simply think about the things that are bothering them. The gods know all languages.[17]

Doing things to the body or mind may involve drugs (hallucinogenics such as peyote or opiates) or alcohol; social isolation or sensory deprivation; dancing or running until exhausted; being deprived of food, water, and sleep; and listening to repetitive sounds such as drumming. Such behaviors may induce trances or altered states of consciousness.[18] Erika Bourguignon found that achieving these altered states, which she generally referred to as *trances,* is part of religious practice in 90 percent of the world's societies.[19] In some societies, trances are thought to involve the presence of a spirit or power inside a person that changes or displaces that person's personality or soul. These types are referred to as possession trances. Other types of trances may involve the journey of a person's soul, experiencing visions, or transmitting messages from spirits. Possession trances are especially likely in societies that depend on agriculture and have social stratification, slavery, and more complex political hierarchies. Nonpossession trances are most likely to occur in food-collecting societies. Societies with moderate levels of social complexity have both possession and nonpossession trances.[20]

One puzzle is why there is a preponderance of women thought to be possessed. Alice Kehoe and Dody Giletti suggested that women are more likely than men to suffer from nutritional deficiencies because of pregnancy, lactation, and men's priority in gaining access to food. Calcium deficiency in particular can cause muscular spasms, convulsive seizures, and disorientation, all of which may foster the belief that an individual is possessed.[21] Douglas Raybeck and his colleagues suggest that women's physiology makes them more susceptible to calcium deficiency even with an equivalent diet. In addition, women are subject to more stress because they are usually less able to control their lives. Higher levels of stress, they suggest, lowers the body's reserves of calcium.[22] Erika Bourguignon suggests a more psychological explanation of women's preponderance in possession trances. In many societies, women are brought up to be submissive. But when possessed, women are taken over by spirits and they are not responsible for what they do or say—therefore they can unconsciously do what they are not able to do consciously.[23]

Voodoo employs simulation, or the imitation of things. Dolls are made in the likeness of an enemy and then are maltreated in hopes that the original enemy will experience pain and even death.

Divination seeks practical answers from the supernatural about anything that is troublesome: decisions to be made, interpersonal problems, or illness. Diviners use a variety of methods, including altered states of consciousness and simulation through the use of objects such as Ouija boards or tarot cards.[24]

Omar Moore suggested that among the Naskapi hunters of Labrador, divination is an adaptive strategy for successful hunting. The Naskapi consult the diviner every three or four days when they have no luck in hunting. The diviner holds a caribou bone over the fire, as if the bone were a map, and the burns and cracks that appear in it indicate where the group should hunt. Moore, unlike the Naskapi, did not believe that the diviner really can find out where the animals will be; the cracks in the bones merely provide a way of randomly choosing where to hunt. Because humans are likely to develop customary patterns of action, they might be likely to look for game according to some plan. But game might learn to avoid hunters who operate according to a plan. Thus, any method of ensuring against patterning or predictable plans—any random strategy—may be advantageous. Divination by "reading" the bones would seem to be a random strategy. It also relieves any individual of the responsibility of deciding where to hunt, a decision that might arouse anger if the hunt failed.[25]

The eating of a sacred meal is found in many religions. For instance, Holy Communion is a simulation of the Last Supper. Australian aborigines, normally forbidden to eat their totem animal, have one totem feast a year at which they eat the totem. Feasts are often part of marriage and funeral ceremonies, as well as a fringe benefit of the sacrifice of food to the gods.

Some societies make sacrifices to a god in order to influence the god's action, either to divert anger or to attract goodwill. Characteristic of all sacrifices is that something of value is given up to the gods, whether it be food, drink, sex, household goods, or the life of an animal or person. Some societies feel that the god is obligated to act on their behalf if they make the appropriate sacrifice. Others use the sacrifice in an attempt to persuade the god, realizing there is no guarantee that the attempt will be successful.

Of all types of sacrifice, we probably think that the taking of human life is the ultimate. Nevertheless, human sacrifice is not rare in the ethnographic and historical records. Why have some societies practiced it? One cross-cultural study found that among preindustrial societies, those with full-time craft specialists, slavery, and the corvée are most likely to practice human sacrifice. The suggested explanation is that the sacrifice mirrors what is socially important: Societies that depend mainly on human labor for energy (rather than animals or machines) may think of a human life as an appropriate offering to the gods when people want something very important.[26]

Magic

All these modes of interacting with the supernatural can be categorized in various ways. One dimension of variation is how much people in society rely on pleading or asking or trying to persuade the supernatural to act on their behalf, as opposed to whether they believe they can compel the supernatural to help by performing certain acts. For example, prayer is asking; performing voodoo is presumably compelling. When people believe their action can compel the supernatural to act in some particular and intended way, anthropologists often refer to the belief and related practice as **magic**.

Magic may involve manipulation of the supernatural for good or for evil. Many societies have magical rituals designed to ensure good crops, the replenishment of game, the fertility of domestic animals, and the avoidance and cure of illness in humans. We tend to associate the belief in magic with societies simpler than our own. But as many as 80,000 people in the United States take magic seriously.[27] Many claim to be witches. An understanding of why magic appeals to some individuals but not others in our own society may help us explain why magic is an important part of religious behavior in many societies.

As we will see, the witch doctor and the shaman often employ magic to effect a cure. But the use of magic to bring about harm has evoked perhaps the most interest.

Sorcery and Witchcraft   Sorcery and witchcraft are attempts to invoke the spirits to work harm against people. Although the words *sorcery* and *witchcraft* are often used interchangeably, they are also often distinguished. **Sorcery** may include the use of materials, objects, and medicines to invoke supernatural malevolence. **Witchcraft** may be said to accomplish the same ills by means of thought and emotion alone. Evidence of witchcraft can never be found. This lack of visible evidence makes an accusation of witchcraft both harder to prove and harder to disprove.

To the Azande of Zaire, in central Africa, witchcraft was part of everyday living. It was not used to explain events for which the cause was known, such as carelessness or violation of a taboo, but to explain the otherwise unexplainable. A man is gored by an elephant. He must have been bewitched, because he had not been gored on other elephant hunts. A man goes to his beer hut at night, lights some straw, and holds it aloft to look at his beer. The thatch catches fire and the hut burns down. The man has been bewitched, for huts did not catch fire on hundreds of other nights when he and others did the same thing. Some of the pots of a skilled potter break; some of the bowls of a skilled carver crack. Witchcraft. Other pots, other bowls treated exactly the same have not broken.[28]

The witch craze in Europe during the sixteenth and seventeenth centuries and the witch trials in 1692 in Salem, Massachusetts, remind us that the fear of others, which the belief in witchcraft presumably represents, can increase and decrease in a society within a relatively short period of time. Many scholars have tried to explain these witch hunts. One factor often suggested is political turmoil, which may give rise to widespread distrust and a search for scapegoats. In the case of Europe during the sixteenth and seventeenth centuries, small regional political units were being incorporated into national states, and political allegiances were in flux. In addition, as Swanson noted, the commercial revolution and related changes were producing a new social class, the middle class, and "were promoting the growth of Protestantism and other heresies from Roman Catholicism."[29] In the case of Salem, the government of Massachusetts colony was unstable and there was much internal dissension. In 1692, the year of the witchcraft hysteria, Massachusetts was left without an English governor, and judicial practices broke down. These extraordinary conditions saw the accusation of a single person for witchcraft become the accusation of hundreds and the execution of 20 people. Swanson suggested that the undermining of legitimate political procedures may have generated the widespread fear of witches.[30]

It is also possible that epidemics of witchcraft accusation, as in Salem as well as other New England and European communities, may be the result of real epidemics—epidemics of disease. The disease implicated in Salem and elsewhere is the fungus disease called ergot, which can grow on rye plants. (The rye flour that went into the bread that the Salem people ate may have been contaminated by ergot.) It is now known that people who eat grain products contaminated by ergot suffer from convulsions, hallucinations, and other symptoms, such as crawling sensations in the skin. We also now know that ergot contains LSD, the drug that produces hallucinations and other delusions that resemble those occurring in severe mental disorders.

The presumed victims of bewitchment in Salem and other places had symptoms similar to victims of ergot poisoning today. They suffered from convulsions and the sensations of being pricked, pinched, or bitten. They had visions and felt as if they were flying through the air. We cannot know for sure that ergot poisoning occurred during those times when witchcraft accusations flourished. There is no direct evidence, of course, since the "bewitched" were not medically tested. But we do have some evidence that seems to be consistent with the ergot theory. Ergot is known to flourish on rye plants under certain climatic conditions, particularly a very cold winter followed by a cool, moist spring and summer. Tree-ring growth indicates that the early 1690s were particularly cold in eastern New England; and the outbreaks of witchcraft accusation in Europe seem to have peaked with colder winter temperatures.[31] Interestingly, too, when witchcraft hysteria was greatest in Europe, Europeans were using an ointment containing a skin-penetrating substance that we now know produces hallucinations and a vivid sensation of flying.[32] It may not be cause for wonder, then, that our popular image of witches is of people flying through the air on broomsticks.

But whether or not epidemics of witchcraft hysteria are due to epidemics of ergot poisoning or episodes of political turmoil or both, we still have to understand why so many societies in the ethnographic record believe in witchcraft and sorcery in the first place. Why do so many societies believe that there are ways to invoke the spirits to work harm against people? One possible explanation, suggested by Beatrice Whiting, is that sorcery or witchcraft will be found in societies that lack procedures or judicial authorities to deal with crime and other offenses. Her theory is that all societies need some form of social control—some way of deterring most would-be offenders and of dealing with actual offenders. In the absence of judicial officials who, if present, might deter and deal with antisocial behavior, sorcery may be a very effective social-control mechanism. If you misbehave, the person you mistreated might cause you to become ill or even die. The cross-cultural evidence seems to support this theory. Sorcery is more important in societies that lack judicial authorities than in those that have them.[33]

Types of Practitioners

Individuals may believe that they can directly contact the supernatural, but almost all societies also have part-time or full-time religious or magical practitioners. Research suggests there are four major types of practitioners: shamans, sorcerers or witches, mediums, and priests. As we shall see, the number of types of practitioners in a society seems to vary with degree of cultural complexity.[34]

The Shaman   The word *shaman* may come from a language that was spoken in eastern Siberia. The **shaman** is usually a part-time male specialist who has fairly high status in his community and is often involved in healing.[35] We discuss the role of the shaman as healer in the chapter on applied and practicing anthropology, where we discuss medical anthropology. More generally the shaman deals with the spirit world to try to get their help or to keep them from causing harm.[36] Here we focus on the methods used by shamans to help others.

The shaman enters into a trance, or some other altered state of consciousness, and then journeys to other worlds in order to get help from guardians or other spirits. Dreams may be used to provide insight or as a way for shamans to commune with spirits. People may seek help for practical matters, such as where to get food resources or whether to relocate, but solving a health problem is most often the goal of the shaman.[37] Shamans may also bring news from spirits, such as a warning about an impending disaster.[38]

Shamans are usually male, but here we see female shamans in Korea perform a healing ritual.

Someone may receive a "call" to the role of shaman in recovering from an illness, through a vision quest, or in a dream. Shamans-in-training may enhance the vividness of their imagery by using hallucinogens, sleep or food deprivation, or engaging in extensive physical activity such as dancing. An important part of the process of being a shaman is learning to control the imagery and the spirit powers. Shamanistic training can take several years under the guidance of a master shaman.[39]

Westerners often call shamans "witch doctors" because they don't believe that shamans can effectively cure people. Do shamans effectively cure people? Actually, Westerners are not the only skeptics. A Native American named Quesalid from the Kwakiutl of the Pacific Northwest didn't believe that shamanism was effective either. So he began to associate with the shamans in order to spy on them and was taken into their group. In his first lessons, he learned

> a curious mixture of pantomime, prestidigitation, and empirical knowledge, including the art of simulating fainting and nervous fits, . . . sacred song, the technique for inducing vomiting, rather precise notions of auscultation or listening to sounds within the body to detect disorders and obstetrics, and the use of "dreamers," that is, spies who listen to private conversations and secretly convey to the shaman bits of information concerning the origins and symptoms of the ills suffered by different people. Above all, he learned the *ars magna*. . . . The shaman hides a little tuft of down in the corner of his mouth, and he throws it up, covered with blood at the proper moment—after having bitten his tongue or made his gums bleed—and solemnly presents it to his patient and the onlookers as the pathological foreign body extracted as a result of his sucking and manipulations.[40]

His suspicions were confirmed, but his first curing was a success. The patient had heard that Quesalid had joined the shamans and believed that only he could heal him. Quesalid remained with the shamans for the four-year apprenticeship, during which he could take no fee, and he became increasingly aware that his methods worked. He visited other villages, competed with other shamans in curing hopeless cases and won, and finally seemed convinced that his curing system was more valid than those of other shamans. Instead of denouncing the trickery of shamans, he continued to practice as a renowned shaman.[41]

Sorcerers and Witches   In contrast with shamans, who have fairly high status, sorcerers and witches of both sexes tend to have very low social and economic status in their societies.[42] Suspected sorcerers and witches are usually feared because they are thought to know how to invoke the supernatural to cause illness, injury, and death. Because sorcerers use materials for their magic, evidence of sorcery can be found, and suspected sorcerers are often killed for their malevolent activities. Because witchcraft supposedly is accomplished by thought and emotion alone, it may be harder to prove that someone is a witch, but the difficulty of proving witchcraft has not prevented people from accusing and killing others for being witches.

Mediums   **Mediums** tend to be females. These part-time practitioners are asked to heal and divine while in possession trances—that is, when they are thought to be possessed by spirits. Mediums are described as having tremors, convulsions, seizures, and temporary amnesia.

Priests   **Priests** are generally full-time male specialists who officiate at public events. They have very high status and are thought to be able to relate to superior or high gods who are beyond the ordinary person's control. In most societies with priests, the people who get to be priests obtain their offices through inheritance or political appointment.[43] Priests are sometimes distinguished from other people by special clothing or a different hairstyle. The training of a priest can be vigorous and long, including fasting, praying, and physical labor, as well as learning the dogma and the ritual of his religion. Priests in the United States complete four years of theological school and sometimes serve first as apprentices under established priests. The priest does not receive a fee for his services but is supported by donations from parishioners or followers. Priests often have some political power as a result of their office—the chief priest is sometimes also the head of state or is a close adviser to the chief of state—and their material well-being is a direct reflection of their position in the priestly hierarchy.

It is the dependence on memorized ritual that both marks and protects the priest. If a shaman repeatedly fails to effect a cure, he will probably lose his following, for he has obviously lost the support of the spirits. But if a priest performs his ritual perfectly and the gods choose not to respond, the priest will usually retain his position and the ritual will preserve its assumed effectiveness. The nonresponse of the gods will be explained in terms of the people's unworthiness of supernatural favor.

Practitioners and Social Complexity   More complex societies tend to have more types of religious or magical practitioners. If a society has only one type of practitioner, it is almost always a shaman; such societies tend to be nomadic or seminomadic food collectors. Societies with two types of practitioners (usually shaman-healers and priests) have agriculture. Those with three types of practitioners are agriculturalists or pastoralists with political integration beyond the community (the additional practitioner type tends to be either a sorcerer-witch or a medium). Finally, societies with all four types of practitioners have agriculture, political integration beyond the community, and social classes.[44]

Religion and Adaptation

Many anthropologists take the view that religions are adaptive because they reduce the anxieties and uncertainties that afflict all peoples. We do not really know that religion is the only means of reducing anxiety and uncertainty, or even that individuals or societies *have* to reduce their anxiety and uncertainty. Still, it seems likely that certain religious beliefs and practices have directly adaptive consequences. For example, the Hindu belief in the sacred cow has seemed to many to be the very opposite of a useful or adaptive custom. Their religion does not permit Hindus to slaughter cows. Why do the Hindus retain such a belief? Why do they allow all those cows to wander around freely, defecating all over the place, and not slaughter any of them? The contrast with our own use of cows could hardly be greater.

Marvin Harris suggested that the Hindu use of cows may have beneficial consequences that some other use of cows would not have. Harris pointed out that there may be a sound economic reason for not slaughtering cattle in India. The cows, and the males they produce, provide resources that could not easily be gotten otherwise. At the same time, their wandering around to forage is no strain on the food-producing economy.

The resources provided by the cows are varied. First, a team of oxen and a plow are essential for the many small farms in India. The Indians could produce oxen with fewer cows, but to do so they would have to devote some of their food production to the feeding of those cows. In the traditional system, they do not feed the cows, and even though poor nutrition makes the cows relatively infertile, males, which are castrated to make oxen, are still produced at no cost to the economy. Second, cow dung is essential as a cooking fuel and fertilizer. The National Council of Applied Economic Research estimated that an amount of dung equivalent to 45 million tons of coal is burned annually. Moreover, it is delivered practically to the door each day at no cost. Alternative sources of fuel, such as wood, are scarce or costly. In addition, about 340 million tons of dung are used as manure—essential in a country obliged to derive three harvests a year from its intensively cultivated land. Third, although Hindus do not eat beef, cattle that die naturally or are butchered by non-Hindus are eaten by the lower castes, who, without the upper-caste taboo against eating beef, might not get this needed protein. Fourth, the hides and horns of the cattle that die are used in India's enormous leather industry. Therefore, because the cows do not themselves consume resources needed by people and it would be impossible to provide traction, fuel, and fertilizer as cheaply by other means, the taboo against slaughtering cattle may be very adaptive.[45]

Religious Change

The long history of religion includes periods of strong resistance to change as well as periods of radical change. Anthropologists have been especially interested in the founding of new religions or sects. The appearance of new religions is one of the things that may happen when cultures are disrupted by contact with dominant societies. Various terms have been suggested for these religious movements—cargo cults, nativistic movements, messianic movements, millenarian cults. Wallace suggested that they are all examples of **revitalization movements**, efforts to save a culture by infusing it with a new purpose and new life.[46] Change may come about more directly by the presence of missionaries who try to convert people to their religion.

Revitalization Movements: The Seneca and the Religion of Handsome Lake   The Seneca reservation of the Iroquois on the Allegheny River in New York State was a place of "poverty and humiliation" by 1799.[47] Demoralized by whiskey and dispossessed from their traditional lands, unable to compete with the new technology because of illiteracy and lack of training, the Seneca were at an impasse. In this setting, Handsome Lake, the 50-year-old brother of a chief, had the first of a number of visions. In them, he met with emissaries of the Creator who showed him heaven and hell and commissioned him to revitalize Seneca religion and society. This he set out to do for the next decade and a half. He used as his principal text the *Gaiwiio,* or "Good Word," a gospel that contains statements about the nature of religion and eternity and a code of conduct for the righteous. The *Gaiwiio* is interesting both for the influence of Quaker Christianity it clearly reveals[48] and for the way the new material was merged with traditional Iroquois religious concepts.

Handsome Lake's teaching seems to have led to a renaissance among the Seneca. Temperance was widely accepted, as were schooling and new farming methods. By 1801, corn yields had been increased tenfold, new crops (oats, potatoes, flax) had been introduced, and public health and hygiene had improved considerably. Handsome Lake himself acquired great power among his people. He spent the remainder of his life fulfilling administrative duties, acting as a representative of the Iroquois in Washington, and preaching his gospel to neighboring tribes. By the time of Handsome Lake's death in 1815, the Seneca clearly had undergone a dramatic rebirth, attributable at least in part to the new religion. Later in the century, some of Handsome Lake's disciples founded a church in his name that, despite occasional setbacks and political disputes, survives to this day.

Although many scholars believe cultural stress gives rise to these new religious movements, it is still important to understand exactly what the stresses are and how strong they have to become before a new movement emerges. Do different kinds of stresses produce different kinds of movements? And does the nature of the movement depend on the cultural elements already present?

Religious Conversion

Religious change usually does not occur in a vacuum, but is often associated with economic and political changes. Missionaries are some of the earliest settlers in interior regions and out-of-the-way places. Of course, the presence of missionaries does not always mean that people convert to the new religion.

A revitalization movement that became known as the Ghost Dance spread eastward from the Northwest from the 1870s to the 1890s. It was generally believed that if people did the dance correctly, ghosts would come to life with sufficient resources to allow the people to return to their old ways, and, as a result of some cataclysm, the whites would disappear.

Source: Ogallala Sioux performing the Ghost Dance at the Pine Ridge Indian Agency, South Dakota. Illustration by Frederic Remington, 1890. The Granger Collection.

Missionaries have not met with equal success in all parts of the world. In some places, large portions of the native population have converted to the new religion with great zeal. In others, missionaries have been ignored, forced to flee, or even killed. We do not fully understand why missionaries have been successful in some societies and not in others. Yet, in many parts of the world, Western missionary activity has been a potent force for all kinds of cultural change. One possible reason is that missionaries offer resources that enable natives to minimize economic and other risks in the new, Western-dominated social environment.[49]

Christianity on Tikopia Tikopia was one of the few Polynesian societies to retain its traditional religious system into the first decades of the twentieth century. An Anglican mission was first established on the island in 1911. With it came a deacon and the founding of 2 schools for about 200 pupils. By 1929, approximately half the population had converted, and in the early 1960s almost all Tikopia gave at least nominal allegiance to Christianity.[50]

Traditional Tikopian belief embraced a great number of gods and spirits of various ranks who inhabited the sky, the water, and the land. One god in particular—the original creator and shaper of the culture—was given a place of special importance, but he was in no way comparable to the all-powerful God of Christianity. Unlike Christianity, Tikopian religion made no claim to universality. The Tikopian gods did not rule over all creation, only over Tikopia. It was thought that if one left Tikopia, one left the gods behind.

The people of Tikopia interacted with their gods and spirits primarily through religious leaders who were also the heads of descent groups. Clan chiefs presided over rituals associated with the everyday aspects of island life, such as house construction, fishing, planting, and harvesting. The chief was expected to intercede with the gods on the people's behalf, to persuade them to bring happiness and prosperity to the group. Indeed, when conditions were good it was assumed that the chief was doing his job well. When disaster struck, the prestige of the chief often fell in proportion. Why did the Tikopia convert to Christianity? Firth suggested several contributing factors.

First, the mission offered the people the prospect of acquiring new tools and consumer goods. Although conversion alone did not provide such benefits, attachment to the mission made them more attainable. Later, it became apparent that education, particularly in reading and writing English, was helpful in getting ahead in the outside world. Mission schooling became valued and provided a further incentive for adopting Christianity.

Second, conversion may have been facilitated by the ability of chiefs, as religious and political leaders, to bring over entire descent groups to Christianity. Should a chief decide to transfer his allegiance to Christianity, the members of his kin group usually followed him. In 1923, when Tafua, chief of the Faea district of Tikopia, converted to the new religion, he brought with him his entire group—nearly half the population of the island. The ability of the chiefs to influence their kin groups, however, was both an asset and a hindrance to missionary efforts, since some chiefs steadfastly resisted conversion.

A final blow to traditional Tikopian religion came in 1955, when a severe epidemic killed at least 200 people in a population of about 1,700. According to Firth, "the epidemic was largely interpreted as a sign of divine discrimination," because three of the outstanding non-Christian religious leaders died.[51] Subsequently, the remaining non-Christian chiefs voluntarily converted to Christianity, and so did their followers. By 1966, all Tikopia, with the exception of one old woman, had converted to the new faith.

Although many Tikopians feel their conversion to Christianity has been a unifying, revitalizing force, the changeover from one religion to another has not been without problems. Christian missionaries on Tikopia have succeeded in eliminating the traditional Tikopian population-control devices of abortion, infanticide, and male celibacy. It is very possible that the absence of these controls will continue to intensify population pressure. The island, with its limited capacity to support life, can ill afford this outcome. Firth summed up the situation Tikopian society faced:

> In the history of Tikopia complete conversion of the people to Christianity was formerly regarded as a solution to their problems; it is now coming to be realized that the adoption and practice of Christianity itself represents another set of problems. As the Tikopia themselves are beginning to see, to be Christian Polynesians in the modern technologically and industrially dominated world, even in the Solomon Islands, poses as many questions as it supplies answers.[52]

Fundamentalism

For some scholars one of the main attributes of fundamentalism is the literal interpretation of a sacred scripture. But recent scholars have suggested that fundamentalist movements need to be understood more broadly as religious/political movements that appear in response to the rapidly changing environment of the modern world. In this broader view, fundamentalism occurs in many religions, including Christian, Jewish, Islam, Sikh, Buddhist, and Hindu. Although each movement is different in content, Richard Antoun suggests that fundamentalist movements have the following elements in common: the selective use of scripture to inspire and assert proof of particular certainties; the quest for purity and traditional values in what is viewed as an impure world; active opposition to what is viewed as a permissive secular society and a nation-state that separates religion from the state; and an incorporation of selected modern elements such as television to promote the movements' aims.[53]

Fundamentalist religious movements do appear to be linked to the anxieties and uncertainties associated with culture change in general and globalization in particular. Many people in many countries are repelled by new behaviors and attitudes, and react in a way that celebrates the old. As Judith Nagata puts it, fundamentalism is a "quest for certainty in an uncertain world."[54] Protestant fundamentalism flourished at the end of the nineteenth century in the United States as immigrant groups came into the country in great numbers and the country became industrialized and increasingly urbanized. The fundamentalists denounced foreign influences, the decline of the Bible as a guide to moral behavior, and the teaching of evolution; and they succeeded in getting the country to prohibit the sale of alcoholic beverages. Recent Islamic fundamentalist movements seem to be responses to a different kind of challenge to the social order—increasing Westernization. Westernization may have first arrived in conjunction with colonial rule. Later it may have been promoted by Western-educated native elites.[55] Antoun suggests that fundamentalist movements deliberately push certain practices because the leaders know they will outrage the secular opposition. Examples in recent Islamic fundamentalist movements are the extreme punishment of cutting off a hand for theft and requiring women to be covered by veils or head-to-toe covering in public.[56] Unfortunately, in present-day discourse, fundamentalism tends to be equated by Westerners with Islam itself. But, in historical perspective, all major religions have had fundamentalist movements in times of rapid culture change.

The Appeal of Religion

There are many religions in the United States today, and new sects, often derisively called cults, emerge regularly. Few of us realize that nearly all of the major churches or religions in the world began as minority sects or cults. Indeed, some of the most established and prestigious Protestant churches were considered radical social movements at first. For example, what we now know as the United Church of Christ, which includes the Congregational Church, was founded by radicals in England who wanted church governance to be in the hands of the local congregation. Many of these radicals became the people we call Pilgrims, who had to flee to the New World. But they were very fundamentalist in their beliefs; for example, as late as the 1820s, Congregationalist-dominated towns in Connecticut prohibited celebrations of Christmas outside of church because such celebrations were not mentioned in the Bible. Nowadays, Congregationalists are among the most liberal Protestants.

We should not be surprised to learn that most of the various Protestant churches today, including some considered very conservative, began as militant sects that set out to achieve a better world. After all, that's why we call them "Protestant." At first, the rebellion was against Rome and the Catholic Church. Later, sects developed in opposition to church and government hierarchies. And remember that Christianity itself began as a radical group in the hinterland of the Roman Empire. So new sects or cults were probably always political and social, as well as religious, movements. Recall that the word *millennium,* as used in discussions of religious movements, refers to a wished-for or expected future time when human life and society will be perfect and free of troubles; the world will then be prosperous, happy, and peaceful.[57] Nowadays, the wish for a better world may or may not be religiously inspired. Some people who seek a more perfect world believe that humans alone must achieve it.

How should we categorize this wish for a better world? Should we call it "conservative" because the imagined world may have existed in the past? If the imagined world does not yet exist, is it "radical" to believe it can be achieved? Maybe the wish for a more perfect world is neither conservative nor radical. Maybe it is just that people who are not satisfied with the world as it is think that something can be done to improve things, with or without divine assistance. However it will come, the "millennium" will be different from now, and better.

Ideas about the millennium, and the origins of new cults and religions, might best be viewed then as human hopes: Which ones do people have? Do they vary from culture to culture, and why? Are some hopes universal? And how might they be achieved?

Summary

1. Religion is any set of attitudes, beliefs, and practices pertaining to supernatural power. Such beliefs may vary within a culture as well as among societies, and they may change over time.

2. There are wide variations in religious beliefs. Societies vary in the number and kinds of supernatural entities in which they believe. There may be impersonal supernatural forces (e.g., mana and taboo), supernatural beings of nonhuman origin (gods and spirits), and supernatural beings of human origin (ghosts and ancestor spirits). The religious belief system of a society may include any or all such entities.

3. Gods and spirits may be unpredictable or predictable, aloof from or interested in human affairs, helpful or punishing. In some societies, all gods are equal in rank; in others, there is a hierarchy of prestige and power among gods and spirits, just as among the humans in those societies.

4. A monotheistic religion is one in which there is one high god, as the creator of the universe or the director of events (or both); all other supernatural beings are either subordinate to, or function as alternative manifestations of, this god. A high god is generally found in societies with a high level of political development.

5. Faced with ignorance, pain, and injustice, people frequently explain events by claiming intervention by the gods. Such intervention has also been sought by people who hope it will help them achieve their own ends. The gods are likely to punish the immoral behavior of people in societies that have considerable differences in wealth.

6. Various methods have been used to attempt communication with the supernatural. Among them are prayer, taking drugs or otherwise affecting the body and mind, simulation, feasts, and sacrifices.

7. When people believe that their actions can compel the supernatural to act in a particular and intended way, anthropologists refer to the belief and related practice as magic. Sorcery and witchcraft are attempts to make the spirits work harm against people.

8. Almost all societies have part-time or full-time religious or magical practitioners. Recent cross-cultural research suggests that there are four major types of practitioners: shamans, sorcerers or witches, mediums, and priests. The number of types of practitioners seems to vary with degree of cultural complexity: the more complex the society, the more types of practitioners.

9. The history of religion includes periods of strong resistance to change and periods of radical change. One explanation for this cycle is that religious practices always originate during periods of stress. Religious movements have been called revitalization movements—efforts to save a culture by infusing it with a new purpose and new life. Religious change is often promoted by the efforts of missionaries, but it is not clearly understood why some societies are more likely to convert than others. Finally, fundamentalist movements appear in response to the rapidly changing environment of the modern world.

10. One appeal of religion may be the wish for a better world.

Glossary Terms

ancestor spirits (p. 191)
divination (p. 194)
ghosts (p. 191)
gods (p. 190)
magic (p. 195)
mana (p. 188)
mediums (p. 198)
monotheistic (p. 192)
polytheistic (p. 192)

priests (p. 198)
religion (p. 188)
revitalization movements (p. 200)
shaman (p. 197)
sorcery (p. 196)
spirits (p. 191)
supernatural (p. 188)
taboo (p. 190)
witchcraft (p. 196)

Critical Questions

1. How does your conception of God compare with beliefs about supernatural beings in other religious systems?

2. What do you think is the future of religion? Explain your answer.

3. Could any of the religious practices you know about be classified as magic? Are they associated with anxiety-arousing situations?

CHAPTER 10

CULTURE CHANGE AND GLOBALIZATION

Chapter Outline

- How and Why Cultures Change
- Culture Change and Adaptation
- Types of Culture Change in the Modern World
- Ethnogenesis: The Emergence of New Cultures
- Globalization: Problems and Opportunities
- Cultural Diversity in the Future

Most of us are aware that "times have changed," especially when we compare our lives with those of our parents. Witness the recent changes in attitudes about sex and marriage, as well as the changes in women's roles. But such culture change is not unusual. Throughout history humans have replaced or altered customary behaviors and attitudes as their needs have changed. Just as no individual is immortal, no particular cultural pattern is impervious to change. Anthropologists, therefore, want to understand how and why culture change occurs.

Three general questions can be asked about culture change: What is the source of a new trait? Why are people motivated, unconsciously as well as consciously, to adopt it? And is the new trait adaptive? The source of the change may be inside or outside the society. That is, a new idea or behavior may originate within the society, or it may come from another society. With regard to motivation, people may adopt the new idea or behavior voluntarily, even if unconsciously, or they may be forced to adopt it. Finally, the outcome of culture change may or may not be beneficial. In this chapter, we first discuss the various processes of culture change in terms of the three dimensions of source, motivation, and outcome. Then we discuss some of the major types of culture change in the modern world. As we will see, these changes are associated largely with the expansion of Western societies over the last 500 years. New cultures and new identities may arise, in a process called *ethnogenesis*. Finally, we discuss *globalization*—the ongoing spread of cultural features around the world—and what it portends for the future of cultural diversity.

How and Why Cultures Change

Discoveries and inventions, which may originate inside or outside a society, are ultimately the sources of all culture change. But they do not necessarily lead to change. If an invention or discovery is ignored, no change in culture results. It is only when society accepts an invention or discovery and uses it regularly that we can begin to speak of culture change.

Discovery and Invention

The new thing discovered or invented, the innovation, may be an object—the wheel, the plow, the computer—or it may involve behavior and ideas—buying and selling, democracy, monogamy. According to Ralph Linton, a discovery is any addition to knowledge and an invention is a new application of knowledge.[1] Thus, a person might discover that children can be persuaded to eat nourishing food if the food is associated with an imaginary character that appeals to them. And then someone might exploit that discovery by inventing a character named Popeye who appears in a series of animated cartoons, acquiring miraculous strength by devouring cans of spinach.

Unconscious Invention   In discussing the process of invention, we should differentiate between various types of inventions. One type is the consequence of a society's setting itself a specific goal, such as eliminating tuberculosis or placing a person on the moon. Another type emerges less intentionally. This second process of invention is often referred to as *accidental juxtaposition* or *unconscious invention*. Linton suggested that some inventions, especially those of prehistoric days, were probably the consequences of literally dozens of tiny initiatives by "unconscious" inventors. These inventors made their small contributions, perhaps over many hundreds of years, without being aware of the part they were playing in bringing one invention, such as the wheel or a better form of hand ax, to completion.[2] In reconstructing the process of invention in prehistoric times, however, we should be careful not to look back on our ancestors with a smugness generated by our more highly developed technology. We have become accustomed to turning to the science sections of our magazines and newspapers and finding, almost daily, reports of miraculous new discoveries and inventions. From our point of view, it is difficult to imagine such a simple invention as the wheel taking so many centuries to come into being. We are tempted to surmise that early humans were less intelligent than we are. But the capacity of the human brain has been the same for perhaps 100,000 years; there is no evidence that the inventors of the wheel were any less intelligent than we are.

Intentional Innovation   Some discoveries and inventions arise out of deliberate attempts to produce a new idea or object. It may seem that such innovations are obvious responses to perceived needs. For example, during the Industrial Revolution there was a great demand for inventions that would increase productivity. James Hargreaves, in eighteenth-century England, is an example of an inventor who responded to an existing demand. Textile manufacturers were clamoring for such large quantities of spun yarn that cottage laborers, working with foot-operated spinning wheels, could not meet the demand. Hargreaves, realizing that prestige and financial rewards would come to the person who invented a method of spinning large quantities of yarn in a short time, set about the task and developed the spinning jenny.

A study of innovation among Ashanti artist-carvers in Ghana suggests that creativity is more likely in some socioeconomic groups than in others.[3] Some carvers produced only traditional designs; others departed from tradition and produced "new" styles of carving. Two groups were found to innovate the most—the wealthiest and the poorest carvers. These two groups of carvers may tolerate risk more than the middle socioeconomic group. Innovative carving entails some risk because it may take more time and it may not sell. Wealthy carvers can afford the risk, and they may gain some prestige as well as income if their innovation is appreciated. The poor are not doing well anyway, and they have little to lose by trying something new.

Some societies encourage innovativeness more than others and this can vary substantially over time. Patricia Greenfield and her colleagues describe the changes in weaving in a Mayan community in the Zinacantán region of Chiapas, Mexico.[4] In 1969 and 1970, innovation was not valued. Rather, tradition was; there was the old "true way" to do everything, including how one dressed. There were only four simple weaving patterns, and virtually all males wore ponchos with the same pattern. By 1991, virtually no poncho was the same and the villagers had developed elaborate brocaded and embroidered designs. In a period of 20 years, innovation had increased dramatically.

Who Adopts Innovations?   Once someone discovers or invents something, there is still the question of whether the innovation will be adopted by others. Many researchers have studied the characteristics of "early adopters." Such individuals tend to be educated, high in social status, upwardly mobile, and, if they are property owners, to have large farms and businesses. The individuals who most need technological improvements—those who are less well off—are generally the last to adopt innovations. The theory is that only the wealthy can afford to take the substantial risks associated with new ways of doing things. In periods of rapid technological change, therefore, the gap between rich and poor is likely to widen because the rich adopt innovations sooner, and benefit more from them, than the poor.[5]

Costs and Benefits   An innovation that is technologically superior is not necessarily going to be adopted. There are costs as well as benefits for both individuals and large-scale industries. Take the computer keyboard. The keyboard used most often on computers today is called the QWERTY keyboard (named after the letters on the left side of the line of keys below the row of number keys). This keyboard was actually invented to slow typing speed down! Early typewriters had mechanical keys that jammed if the typist went too fast.[6] Computer keyboards don't have that problem, so an arrangement of keys that allowed faster typing would probably be better. Different keyboard configurations have been invented, but they haven't caught on. Most people probably would find it too hard or too time-consuming to learn a new style of typing, so the original style of keyboard persists.

Diffusion

The source of new cultural elements in a society may also be another society. The process by which cultural elements are borrowed from another society and incorporated into the culture of the recipient group is called **diffusion**. Borrowing sometimes enables a group to bypass stages or mistakes in the development of a process or institution. For example, Germany was able to accelerate its program of industrialization in the nineteenth century because it was able to avoid some of the errors made by its English and Belgian competitors by taking advantage of technological borrowing. Japan did the same somewhat later. Indeed, in recent years some of the earliest industrialized countries have fallen behind their imitators in certain areas of production, such as automobiles, televisions, cameras, and computers.

In a known-well passage, Linton conveyed the far-reaching effects of diffusion by considering the first few hours in the day of an American man in the 1930s. This man

> . . . awakens in a bed built on a pattern which originated in the Near East but which was modified in northern Europe before it was transmitted to America. He throws back covers made from cotton, domesticated in India, or linen, domesticated in the Near East, or silk, the use of which was discovered in China. All of these materials have been spun and woven by processes invented in the Near East . . . . He takes off his pajamas, a garment invented in India, and washes with soap invented by the ancient Gauls. He then shaves, a masochistic rite which seems to have derived from either Sumer or ancient Egypt.

Americans have not adopted most features of Japanese culture, but the interest in sushi is spreading.

Before going out for breakfast he glances through the window, made of glass invented in Egypt, and if it is raining puts on overshoes made of rubber discovered by the Central American Indians and takes an umbrella, invented in southeastern Asia . . . .

On his way to breakfast he stops to buy a paper paying for it with coins, an ancient Lydian invention . . . . His plate is made of a form of pottery invented in China. His knife is of steel, an alloy first made in southern India, his fork a medieval Italian invention, and his spoon a derivative of a Roman original . . . . After his fruit (African watermelon) and first coffee (an Abyssinian plant) . . . he may have the egg of a species of bird domesticated in Indo-China, or thin strips of the flesh of an animal domesticated in Eastern Asia which have been salted and smoked by a process developed in northern Europe . . . .

While smoking (an American Indian habit) he reads the news of the day, imprinted in characters invented by the ancient Semites upon a material invented in China by a process invented in Germany. As he absorbs the accounts of foreign troubles he will, if he is a good conservative citizen, thank a Hebrew deity in an Indo-European language that he is 100 percent American.[7]

The Selective Nature of Diffusion   Although there is a temptation to view the dynamics of diffusion as similar to a stone sending concentric ripples over still water, this would be an oversimplification of the way diffusion actually occurs. Not all cultural traits are borrowed as readily as the ones we have mentioned, nor do they usually expand in neat, ever-widening circles. Rather, diffusion is a selective process. The Japanese, for instance, accepted much from Chinese culture, but they also rejected many traits. Rhymed tonal poetry, civil service examinations, and foot binding, which were favored by the Chinese, were never adopted in Japan. The poetry form was unsuited to the structure of the Japanese language; the examinations were unnecessary in view of the entrenched power of the Japanese aristocracy; and foot binding was repugnant to a people who abhorred body mutilation of any sort.

Not only would we expect societies to reject items from other societies that are repugnant, we would also expect them to reject ideas and technology that do not satisfy some psychological, social, or cultural need. After all, people are not sponges; they don't automatically soak up the things around them. If they did, the amount of cultural variation in the world would be extremely small, which is clearly not the case.

Finally, diffusion is selective because the overt form of a particular trait, rather than its function or meaning, frequently seems to determine how the trait will be received. For example, the enthusiasm in women for bobbed hair (short haircuts) that swept through much of North America in the 1920s never caught on among the Native Americans of northwestern California. To many women of European ancestry, short hair was a symbolic statement of their freedom. To Native American women, who traditionally cut their hair short when in mourning, it was a reminder of death.[8]

Acculturation

On the surface, the process of change called **acculturation** seems to include much of what we have discussed under the label of diffusion, since acculturation refers to the changes that occur when different cultural groups come into intensive contact. As in diffusion, the source of new cultural items is the other society. But more often than not, the term *acculturation* is used by anthropologists to describe a situation in which one of the societies in contact is much more powerful than the other. Thus, acculturation can be seen as a process of extensive cultural borrowing in the context of superordinate-subordinate relations between societies.[9] The borrowing may sometimes be a two-way process, but generally it is the subordinate or less powerful society that borrows the most. The concept of diffusion can then be reserved for the voluntary borrowing of cultural elements, in contrast with borrowing under external pressure, which characterizes acculturation.

A subordinate society may acculturate to a dominant society even in the absence of direct or indirect force. The dominated people may elect to adopt cultural elements from the dominant society in order to survive in their changed world. Or, perceiving that members of the dominant society enjoy more secure living conditions, the dominated people may identify with the dominant culture in the hope that by doing so they will be able to share some of its benefits. For example, in Arctic areas many Inuit and Lapp groups seemed eager to replace dog sleds with snowmobiles without any coercion.[10]

But many millions of people never had a chance to acculturate after contact with Europeans. They simply died, sometimes directly at the hands of the conquerors, but probably more often as a result of the new diseases the Europeans inadvertently brought with them. Depopulation because of measles, smallpox, and tuberculosis was particularly common in North and South America and on the islands of the Pacific. Those areas had previously been isolated from contact with Europeans and from the diseases of that continuous landmass we call the Old World—Europe, Asia, and Africa.[11]

Nowadays, many powerful nations—and not just Western ones—may seem to be acting in more humanitarian ways to improve the life of previously subjugated as well as other "developing" peoples. For better or worse, these programs, however, are still forms of external pressure. The tactic used may be persuasion rather than force, but most of the programs are nonetheless designed to bring about acculturation in the direction of the dominant societies' cultures. For example, the introduction of formal schooling cannot help but instill new values that may contradict traditional cultural patterns. And even health-care programs may alter traditional ways of life by undermining the authority of shamans and other leaders and by increasing population beyond the number that can be supported in traditional ways. Confinement to "reservations" or other kinds of direct force are not the only ways a dominant society can bring about acculturation.

The process of acculturation also applies to immigrants, most of whom, at least nowadays, choose to leave one country for another. Immigrants are almost always a minority in the new country and therefore are in a subordinate position. If the immigrant's culture changes, it is almost always in the direction of the dominant culture. Immigrant groups vary considerably in the degree and speed with which they

Students and teachers stand outside of the Lincoln Institution, an Indian girls' school in Delaware County, Pennsylvania. This picture was taken in October 1884.

adopt the new culture and the social roles of the new society in which they live. An important area of research is explaining the variation in acculturation and assimilation. (*Assimilation* is a concept very similar to acculturation, but assimilation is a term more often used by sociologists to describe the process by which individuals acquire the social roles and culture of the dominant group.) Why do some immigrant groups acculturate or assimilate faster than others? Recall the comparative study by Robert Schrauf that assessed the degree to which immigrant groups coming to North America retained their native language over time. He looked at whether they lived in tightly knit communities, retained religious rituals, had separate schools and special festivals, visited their homeland, did not intermarry, or worked with others of their ethnic group. All of these factors might be expected to lead to retention of the native language (and presumably other cultural patterns), but only living in tightly knit communities and retaining religious rituals strongly predicted retaining the native language over a long period of time.[12]

Revolution

Certainly the most drastic and rapid way a culture can change is as a result of **revolution**—replacement, usually violent, of a country's rulers. Historical records, as well as our daily newspapers, indicate that people frequently rebel against established authority. Rebellions, if they occur, almost always occur in state societies, where there is a distinct ruling elite. They take the form of struggles between rulers and ruled, between conquerors and conquered, or between representatives of an external colonial power and segments of the native society. Rebels do not always succeed in overthrowing their rulers, so rebellions do not always result in revolutions. And even successful rebellions do not always result in culture change; the individual rulers may change, but customs or institutions may not. The sources of revolution may be mostly internal, as in the French Revolution, or partly external, as in the Russian-supported 1948 revolution in Czechoslovakia and the U.S.-supported 1973 revolution against President Allende in Chile.

The American War of Independence toward the end of the eighteenth century is a good example of a colonial rebellion, the success of which was at least partly a result of foreign intervention. The American rebellion was a war of neighboring colonies against the greatest imperial power of the time, Great Britain. In the nineteenth century and continuing into the middle and later years of the twentieth century, there would be many other wars of independence, in Latin America, Europe, Asia, and Africa. We don't always remember that the American rebellion was the first of these anti-imperialist wars in modern times, and the model for many that followed. And just like many of the most recent liberation movements, the American rebellion was also part of a larger worldwide war, involving people from many rival nations. Thirty thousand German-speaking soldiers fought, for pay, on the British side; an army and navy from France fought on the American side. There were volunteers from other European countries, including Denmark, Holland, Poland, and Russia.

One of these volunteers was a man named Kosciusko from Poland, which at the time was being divided between Prussia and Russia. Kosciusko helped win a major victory for the Americans, and subsequently directed the fortification of what later became the American training school for army officers, West Point. After the war he returned to Poland and led a rebellion against the Russians, which was only briefly successful. In 1808 he published the *Manual on the Maneuvers of Horse Artillery,* which was used for many years by the American army. When he died he left money to buy freedom and education for American slaves. The executor of Kosciusko's will was Thomas Jefferson.

As in many revolutions, those who were urging revolution were considered "radicals." At a now famous debate in Virginia in 1775, delegates from each colony met at a Continental Congress. Patrick Henry put forward a resolution to prepare for defense against the British armed forces. The motion barely passed, by a vote of 65 to 60. Henry's speech is now a part of American folklore. He rose to declare

Revolutionary leaders are often from high-status backgrounds. Here we see a depiction of Patrick Henry giving his famous speech to the aristocratic landowners in the Virginia Assembly on March 23, 1775. Urging the Virginians to fight the British, Henry said that the choice was "liberty or death."

Source: Currier & Ives, "Give Me Liberty or Give Me Death!" 1775. Lithograph, 1876. © The Granger Collection, New York.

that it was insane not to oppose the British and that he was not afraid to test the strength of the colonies against Great Britain. Others might hesitate, he said, but he would have "liberty or death." The "radicals" who supported Henry's resolution included many aristocratic landowners, two of whom, George Washington and Thomas Jefferson, became the first and third occupants of the highest political office in what became the United States of America.[13]

Not all peoples who are suppressed, conquered, or colonialized eventually rebel against established authority. Why this is so, and why rebellions and revolts are not always successful in bringing about culture change, are still open questions. The classic revolutions of the past occurred in countries that were industrialized only incipiently at best. For the most part, the same is true of the rebellions and revolutions in recent years; they have occurred mostly in countries we call "developing." The evidence from a worldwide survey of developing countries suggests that rebellions have tended to occur where the ruling classes depended mostly on the produce or income from land, and therefore were resistant to demands for reform from the rural classes that worked the land. In such agricultural economies, the rulers are not likely to yield political power or give greater economic returns to the workers, because to do so would eliminate the basis (landownership) of the rulers' wealth and power.[14]

The idea of revolution has been one of the central myths and inspirations of many groups both in the past and in the present. The colonial empire building of countries such as England and France created a worldwide situation in which rebellion became nearly inevitable. In numerous technologically underdeveloped lands, which have been exploited by more powerful countries for their natural resources and cheap labor, a deep resentment has often developed against the foreign ruling classes or their local clients. Where the ruling classes, native or foreign, refuse to be responsive to those feelings, rebellion becomes the only alternative. In many areas, it has become a way of life.

Culture Change and Adaptation

The chapter on the study of culture discussed the general assumption that most of the customary behaviors of a culture are probably adaptive, or at least not maladaptive, in that environment. A custom is adaptive if it increases the likelihood that the people practicing it will survive and reproduce. Even though customs are learned and not genetically inherited, cultural adaptation may be like biological adaptation or evolution in another respect. The frequency of certain genetic alternatives is likely to increase over time if those genetic traits increase their carriers' chances of survival and reproduction. Similarly, the frequency of a new learned behavior will increase over time and become customary in a population if the people with that behavior are most likely to survive and reproduce. Thus, if a culture is adapted to its environment, culture change should also be adaptive—not always, to be sure, but commonly.

One of the most important differences between cultural evolution and genetic evolution is that individuals can often decide whether or not to accept and follow the way their parents behave or think, whereas they cannot decide whether or not to inherit certain genes. When enough individuals change their behavior and beliefs, we say that the culture has changed. Therefore, it is possible for culture change to occur much more rapidly than genetic change.

Robert Boyd and Peter Richerson have shown mathematically that when the environment is relatively stable and individual mistakes are costly, staying with customary modes of behavior (usually transmitted by parents) is probably more adaptive than changing.[15] But what happens when the environment, particularly the social environment, is changing? There are plenty of examples in the modern world: People have to migrate to new places for work; medical care leads to increased population so that land is scarcer; people have had land taken away from them and are forced to make do with less land; and so on.

It is particularly when circumstances change that individuals are likely to try ideas or behaviors that are different from those of their parents. Most people would want to adopt behaviors that are more suited to their present circumstances, but how do they know which behaviors are better? There are various ways to find out. One way is by experimenting, trying out various new behaviors. Another way is to evaluate the experiments of others. If a person who tries a new technique seems successful, we would expect that person to be imitated, just as we would expect people to stick with new behaviors they have personally tried and found successful. Finally, one might choose to do what most people in the new situation decide to do.[16]

We can expect, then, that the choices individuals make may often be adaptive ones. But it is important to note that adopting an innovation from someone in one's own society or borrowing an innovation from another society is not always or necessarily beneficial, either in the short or the long run. First, people may make mistakes in judgment, especially when some new behavior seems to satisfy a physical need. Why, for example, have smoking and drug use diffused so widely even though they are likely to reduce a person's chances of survival? Second, even if people are correct in their short-term judgment of benefit, they may be wrong in their judgment about long-run benefit. A new crop may yield more than the old crop for five consecutive years, but the new crop may fail miserably in the sixth year because of lower than normal rainfall or because the new crop depleted soil nutrients. Third, people may be forced by the more powerful to change, with few if any benefits for themselves.

Whatever the motives for humans to change their behavior, the theory of natural selection suggests that new behavior is not likely to become cultural or remain cultural over generations if it has harmful reproductive consequences, just as a genetic mutation with harmful consequences is not likely to become frequent in a population.[17] Still, we know of many examples of culture change that seem maladaptive—the switch to bottle-feeding rather than nursing infants, which may spread infection because contaminated water is used, or the adoption of alcoholic beverages, which may lead to alcoholism and early death. In the last few hundred years, the major stimulus to culture change, adaptive and maladaptive, has been the new social environment produced by the arrival of people from Western societies and the growth of a global economy.

Types of Culture Change in the Modern World

Many of the cultural changes in the world from A.D. 1500 to the present have been caused, directly or indirectly, by the dominance and expansion of Western societies.[18] Thus, much of the culture change in the modern world has been externally induced, if not forced. This is not to say that cultures are changing now only because of external pressures; but externally induced changes have been the changes most frequently studied by anthropologists and other social scientists. Most of the external pressures have come from Western societies, but not all. Far Eastern societies, such as Japan and China, have also stimulated culture change. And the expansion of Islamic societies after the eighth century A.D. made for an enormous amount of culture change in the Near East, Africa, Europe, and Asia.

Commercialization

One of the most important changes resulting from the expansion of Western societies is the increasingly worldwide dependence on commercial exchange. The borrowed customs of buying and selling may at first be supplementary to traditional means of distributing goods in a society. But as the new commercial customs take hold, the economic base of the receiving society alters. Inevitably, this alteration is accompanied by other changes, which have broad social, political, and even biological and psychological ramifications.

In examining contemporary patterns of change, however, we should bear in mind that commercialization has occurred in many parts of the world in the ancient past. The Chinese, Persians, Greeks, Romans, Arabs, Phoenicians, and Hindus were some of the early state societies that pushed commercial enterprises in other areas. We may cast some light on how and why some earlier cultures changed when we consider several questions: How, and why, does a contemporary society change from a subsistence to a commercial economic base? What are the resultant cultural changes? Why do they occur?

In general, the evidence available suggests that a previously noncommercial people may begin to sell and buy things simply in order to live, not just because they may be attracted by goods they can obtain only by commercial exchange. If the resources available to a group have been significantly reduced per person—because the group has been forced to resettle on a small "reservation" or because population has increased—the group may be likely to take advantage of any commercial opportunities that become available, even if such opportunities require considerably more work, time, and effort.[19]

Migratory Labor   One way commercialization can occur is for some members of a community to move to a place that offers the possibility of working for wages. This happened in Tikopia, an island near the Solomon Islands in the South Pacific. In 1929, when Raymond Firth first studied the island, its economy was still essentially noncommercial—simple, self-sufficient, and largely self-contained.[20] Some Western goods were available but, with the exception of iron and steel in limited quantities, not sought after. Their possession and use were associated solely with Europeans. This situation changed dramatically with World War II. During the war, military forces occupied neighboring islands, and people from Tikopia migrated to those islands to find employment. In the period following the war, several large commercial interests extended their activities in the Solomons, thus creating a continued demand for labor. As a result, when Firth revisited Tikopia in 1952, he found the economic situation significantly altered.

urban societies perhaps needs some qualification. The contemporary, highly industrialized urban society has little need of peasants. Their scale of production is small and their use of land "uneconomic." A highly industrialized society with a large population of nonfood producers requires mechanized agriculture. As a result, the peasant has passed, or is passing, out of all but the most peripheral existence in industrial countries. It is the preindustrial city, and the social organization it represents, that generates and maintains peasants. They cultivate land; they furnish the required quantity of food, rent, and profit on which the remainder of society, particularly the people in the cities, depends.

What changes does the development of a peasantry entail? In some respects there is little disturbance of the cultivator's (now peasant's) former way of life. The peasant still has to produce enough food to meet family needs, to replace what has been consumed, to cover a few ceremonial obligations (e.g., the marriage of a child, village festivals, and funerals). But in other respects the peasant's situation is radically altered. For in addition to the traditional obligations—indeed, often in conflict with them—the peasant now has to produce extra crops to meet the requirements of a group of outsiders—landlords or officials of the state. These outsiders expect to be paid rent or taxes in produce or currency, and they are able to enforce their expectations because they control the military and the police.

Introduction of Commercial and Industrial Agriculture   Commercialization can come about through the introduction of commercial agriculture, cultivation for sale rather than personal consumption. The system of agriculture may come to be industrialized. In other words, some of the production processes, such as plowing, weeding, irrigation, and harvesting, can be done by machine. Commercial agriculture is, in fact, often as mechanized as any manufacturing industry. Land is worked for the maximum return it will yield, and labor is hired and fired just as impersonally as in other industries.

The introduction of commercial agriculture brings several important social consequences. Gradually, a class polarization develops. Farmers and landlords become increasingly separated from laborers and tenants, just as in the town the employer becomes socially separated from the employees. Gradually, too, manufactured items of all sorts are introduced into rural areas. Laborers migrate to urban centers in search of employment, often meeting even less sympathetic conditions there than exist in the country.

The changeover to commercial agriculture may result in an improved standard of living in the short and long run. But sometimes the switch is followed by a decline in the standard of living if the market price for the commercial crop declines. For example, the changeover of the farmer-herders of the arid *sertão* region of northeastern Brazil after 1940 to the production of sisal (a plant whose fibers can be made into twine and rope) seemed to be a move that could provide a more secure living in their arid environment. But when the world price for sisal dropped (because of the availability of nylon and Dacron rope) and the wages of sisal workers declined, many workers were forced to curtail the caloric intake of their children. The poorer people were obliged to save their now more limited food supplies for the money earners, at the expense of the children.[24]

Commercialization can start in various ways: People can begin to sell and buy because they begin to work near home or away for wages, or because they begin to sell nonagricultural products, surplus food, or cash crops (crops grown deliberately for sale). One type of commercialization does not exclude another; all types can occur in any society. However commercialization begins, it seems to have predictable effects on traditional economics. The ethic of generalized reciprocity declines, particularly with respect to giving money away. (Perhaps because it is nonperishable and hideable, money seems more likely than other goods to be kept for one's immediate family rather than shared with others.) Property rights become individualized rather than collective when people begin to buy and sell. And even in societies that were previously egalitarian, commercialization usually results in more unequal access to resources and hence a greater degree of social stratification.

Contact with the West first brought medical devastation to many populations previously unexposed to European illnesses. However, with the acceptance of modern medical care throughout much of the developing world, infant mortality has declined and life expectancies have gone up. These achievements have largely come about because of the control of major epidemic diseases, such as smallpox (now eradicated), cholera, yellow fever, syphilis, and tuberculosis, as well as the inoculation of children against childhood diseases. Improvements in medical health are by no means uniform. The AIDS epidemic, which we discuss in the chapter on applied and practicing anthropology, is spreading throughout much of the world. Overall deaths from infectious diseases may have declined, but other health problems have increased. As more people survive into older ages, problems of hypertension, heart disease, cancer, and diabetes increase. Some of the increase in these chronic diseases is due to the aging of populations, but much of it appears to be due to changes in lifestyle that accompany modernization.

A lot of research has focused on the Samoans of the South Pacific. The Samoans traditionally depended on root and tree crop horticulture. As did many other people in the modern world, Samoans increasingly moved to urban areas, worked for wages, and started buying most of their food. Researchers reported substantial increases, within a relatively short time, in rates of hypertension, diabetes, and obesity across a wide range of age groups. For example, in 1990 about two-thirds of American Samoans were severely overweight, up substantially from the situation in the 1970s. And Samoans from more rural areas show less hypertension and physiological signs of stress. Among the lifestyle changes thought to be responsible are less physical activity and changes in diet to low-fiber, high-calorie foods. Stress may also increase as more individuals buy material things and status goods without having the economic resources to support them.

When food is not plentiful, the "thrifty gene" helps people survive on less. But when the food supply becomes plentiful and reliable, people may become overweight, as in the Marquesas.

What about genetic factors? Could some genetic predisposition be interacting with modernization to create obesity in the Samoan population? One possibility is referred to as the "thrifty" gene. The geneticist James Neel suggested that individuals who have very efficient metabolisms and can store calories in fatty tissue are most apt to survive and reproduce in environments with frequent famines or chronic food shortages. In time, populations in such environments would have a high prevalence of individuals with "thrifty" genes. What happens, though, when such individuals no longer need to exercise much or have access to high-calorie foods? Neel suggested that adult-onset diabetes might result, a scenario that is consistent with the increase in diabetes in Samoa and other parts of Polynesia. It is also consistent with the increase in obesity and hypertension.

The "thrifty" gene theory does not just pertain to Samoans and other Polynesian populations. Probably most human populations have had to cope with food uncertainty. If the food supply increases with modernization, accompanied by a reduction in physical activity and a switch to high-calorie diets, then increases in obesity, diabetes, and hypertension may often accompany modernization. Understanding both biological and cultural factors is essential in helping populations adapt to conditions of urban life.

Sources: John S. Allen and Susan M. Cheer, "The Non-Thrifty Genotype," *Current Anthropology,* 37 (1996): 831–42; James R. Bindon and Douglas E. Crews, "Changes in Some Health Status Characteristics of American Samoan Men," *American Journal of Human Biology,* 5 (1993): 31–37; James R. Bindon, Amy Knight, William W. Dressler, and Douglas E. Crews, "Social Context and Psychosocial Influences on Blood Pressure among American Samoans," *American Journal of Physical Anthropology,* 103 (1997): 7–18; Stephen T. McGarvey, "The Thrifty Gene Concept and Adiposity Studies in Biological Anthropology," *Journal of the Polynesian Society,* 103 (1994): 29–42; J. D. Pearson, Gary D. James, and Daniel E. Brown, "Stress and Changing Lifestyles in the Pacific," *American Journal of Human Biology,* 5 (1993): 49–60; World Bank, *World Development Report 1995: Workers in an Integrating World* (Oxford: Oxford University Press, 1995).

Political and Social Change

In addition to commercialization and religious change brought about by the expansion of Western and other countries, political changes have often occurred when a foreign system of government has been imposed. But, as recent events in the former Soviet Union and South Africa indicate, dramatic changes in a political system can also occur more or less voluntarily. Perhaps the most striking type of political change in recent years is the spread of participatory forms of government—"democracy."

To political scientists, democracy is usually defined in terms of voting by a substantial proportion of the citizenry, governments brought to power by periodic contested elections, a chief executive either popularly elected or responsible to an elected legislature, and often also civil liberties such as free speech. Depending on which criteria are used, only 12 to 15 countries qualified as democracies as of the beginning of the twentieth century. The number decreased after World War I, as emerging democratic institutions were replaced by dictatorships in Russia, Italy, Germany, central Europe, Japan, and elsewhere. After World War II, despite all the rhetoric associated with the founding of the United Nations, the picture was not much different. Some members of the new North Atlantic Treaty Organization (NATO) were not democracies, and neither were many members of the wider Western alliance system, in Latin America, the Middle East, and Asia.

It was not until the 1970s and 1980s that people, not just political scientists, started noticing that democracy was becoming more common in the world. By the early 1990s, President George H. W. Bush and then-candidate Bill Clinton were talking about the spread of the "democratic peace." As of 1992, about half of the countries in the world had more or less democratic governments, and others were in transition to democracy.[25] Social scientists do not yet understand why this change is happening. But it is possible that the global communication of ideas has a lot to do with it. Authoritarian governments can censor their own newspapers and prevent group meetings, but they really cannot stop the movement of ideas via telephone lines and the Internet. The movement of ideas, of course, does not explain the acceptance of those ideas. Why democracy has recently diffused to more countries than ever before still requires explanation.

Another frequent type of culture change in the modern world is increasing social stratification. Because of economic change, some groups become more privileged and powerful than others. For example, it has been suggested that the introduction of new technology may generally make for an increase in degree of social stratification.[26] When the snowmobile began to be used for herding by the Lapps or Saami, those who for various reasons could participate in the "snowmobile revolution" gained economic, social, and political advantages. But those who could not acquire the new machines tended to become an economically and generally deprived class—without machines *or* reindeer.[27]

Ethnogenesis: The Emergence of New Cultures

Many of the processes that we have discussed—the expansion and domination by the West and other powerful nations, the deprivation of the ability of peoples to earn their livelihoods by traditional means, the imposition of schools or other methods to force acculturation, the attempts to convert people to other religions, and globalization—have led to profound changes in culture. But if culture change in the modern world has made cultures more alike in some ways, it has not eliminated cultural differences. Indeed, people are still quite variable culturally from one place to the next. New differences have also emerged. Often, in the aftermath of violent events such as depopulation, relocation, enslavement, and genocide by dominant powers, deprived peoples have created new cultures in a process called **ethnogenesis**.[28]

Bobby Henry, a Seminole medicine man, sings a song in 2003 during ceremonies honoring a Seminole chief who died 165 years before.

The emergence of the Seminole in Florida is an example of ethnogenesis. The early settlers who moved to what is now Florida and later became known as Seminole largely derived from the Lower Creek Kawita chiefdom. The Kawita chiefdom, like other southeastern Muskogean chiefdoms, was a large, complex, multiethnic paramount chiefdom. Its ruler, Kawita, relied on allegiance and tribute from outlying districts; ritual and linguistic hegemony was imposed by the ruler.[29]

A combination of internal divisions among the Lower Creek, vacant land in northern Florida, and weak Spanish control over northern Florida apparently prompted dissidents to move away and settle in three different areas in Florida. Three new chiefdoms were established, essentially similar to those the settlers left and still under the supposed control of Kawita.[30] But the three chiefdoms began to act together under the leadership of Tonapi, the Talahassi chief. After 1780, over a period of 40 or so years, the three Seminole chiefdoms formally broke with Kawita. Not only was geographic separation a factor, but the political and economic interests of the Creek Confederacy and of the Seminole had diverged. For example, the Creek supported neutrality in the American Revolution, but the Seminole took the side of the British. It was during this time that the British encouraged slaves to escape by promising freedom in Florida. These Maroon communities allied themselves with the emerging Seminole. The composition of the Seminole population again changed dramatically after the War of 1812 and the Creek War of 1814.[31] First, a large number of Creek refugees, mostly Upper Creek Talapusa (who spoke a different Muskogean language), became Seminole. Second, the Seminole ranks were also expanded by a large number of escaped slaves and Maroons who fled when the Americans destroyed a British fort in 1816. Larger-scale political events continued to influence Seminole history. When the Americans conquered Florida, they insisted on dealing with one unified Seminole council, they removed the Seminole to a reserve in Florida, and later, after the second Seminole war, removed most of them to Oklahoma.[32]

Globalization: Problems and Opportunities

Investment capital, people, and ideas are moving around the world at an ever faster rate.[33] Transportation now allows people and goods to circle the globe in days; telecommunications and the Internet make it possible to send a message around the world in seconds and minutes. Economic exchange is enormously more global and transnational. The word **globalization** is often used nowadays to refer to "the massive flow of goods, people, information, and capital across huge areas of the earth's surface."[34] The process of globalization has resulted in the worldwide spread of cultural features, particularly in the domain of economics and international trade. We buy from the same companies (that have factories all over the world), we sell our products and services for prices that are set by world market forces. We can eat pizza, hamburgers, curry, or sushi in most urban centers. In some ways, cultures are changing in similar directions. They have become more commercial, more urban, and more international. The job has become more important, and kinship less important, as people travel to and work in other countries, and return just periodically to their original homes. Ideas about democracy, the rights of the individual, alternative medical practices and religions, have become more widespread; people in many countries of the world watch the same TV shows, wear similar fashions, listen to the same or similar music. In short, people are increasingly sharing behaviors and beliefs with people in other cultures, and the cultures of the world are less and less things "with edges," as Paul Durrenberger says.[35]

But diffusion of a culture trait does not mean that it is incorporated in exactly the same way, and the spread of certain products and activities through globalization does not mean that change happens in the same way everywhere. For example, the spread of multinational fast-food restaurants like McDonald's or Kentucky Fried Chicken has come to symbolize globalization. But the behavior of the Japanese in such restaurants is quite different from behavior in the United States. Perhaps the most surprising difference is that the Japanese in McDonald's actually have more familial intimacy and sharing than in more traditional restaurants. We imagine that establishments like McDonald's promote fast eating. But Japan has long had fast food—noodle shops at train stations, street vendors, and boxed lunches. Sushi, which is usually ordered in the United States at a sit-down restaurant, is usually served in Japan at a bar with a conveyor belt—individuals only need to pluck off the wanted dish as it goes by. Observations at McDonald's in Japan suggest that mothers typically order food for the family while the father spends time with the children at a table, a rare event since fathers often work long hours and cannot get home for dinner often. Food, such as French fries, is typically shared by the family. Even burgers and drinks are passed around with many people taking a bite or a sip. Such patterns typify long-standing family practices.

Democracy—contested elections with widespread voting—is spreading around the world. In this rural area of South Africa, people line up to vote.

Japan has historically borrowed food, such as the Chinese noodle soup, now called ramen. Indeed, in a survey, ramen was listed as the most representative Japanese food. The burger was the second most-often listed. McDonald's has become Japanese—the younger generation does not even know that McDonald's is a foreign company—they think it is Japanese.[36]

Globalization is not new. The world has been global and interdependent since the sixteenth century.[37] What we currently call "globalization" is a more widespread version of what we used to call by various other names—diffusion, acculturation, colonialism, imperialism, or commercialization. But globalization is now on a much grander scale; enormous amounts of international investment fuel world trade. Shifts in the world marketplace may drastically affect a country's well-being more than ever before. For example, 60 percent of Pakistan's industrial employment is in textile and apparel manufacturing, but serious unemployment resulted when that manufacturing was crippled by restrictive American import policies and fears about war between India and Afghanistan.[38]

As we have seen in this chapter, there are many negative effects of colonialism, imperialism, and globalization. Many native peoples in many places lost their land and have been forced to work for inadequate wages in mines and plantations and factories that are owned by foreign capitalists. Frequently, there is undernutrition if not starvation. But are there any positive consequences? As we discussed in the social stratification chapter, the "human development indicators" collected by the United Nations suggest an improvement in many respects, including increases in most countries in life expectancy and literacy. Much of the improvement in life expectancy is undoubtedly due to the spread of medicines developed in the advanced economies of the West. There is generally less warfare as colonial powers enforced pacification within the colonies that later became independent states. Most important, perhaps, has been the growth of middle classes all over the world, whose livelihoods depend on globalizing commerce. The middle classes in many countries have become strong and numerous enough to pressure governments for democratic reforms and the reduction of injustice.

World trade is the primary engine of economic development. Per capita income is increasing. Forty years ago, the countries of Asia were among the poorest countries in the world in terms of per capita income. Since then, because of their involvement in world trade, their incomes have risen enormously. In 1960, South Korea was as poor as India. Now its per capita income is 20 times higher than India's. Singapore is an even more dramatic example. In the late 1960s, its economy was a disaster. Today its per capita income is higher than Britain's.[39] Mexico used to be a place where North Americans built factories to produce garments for the North American market. Now its labor is no longer so cheap. But because it has easy access to the North American market and because its plentiful labor is acquiring the necessary skills, Mexico is now seeing the development of high-tech manufacturing with decent salaries.[40]

There is world trade also in people. Many countries of the world now export people to other countries. Mexico has done so for a long time. Virtually every family in a Bangladesh village depends on someone who works overseas and sends money home. Without those remittances, many would face starvation. The government encourages people to go abroad to work. Millions of people from Bangladesh are now overseas on government-sponsored work contracts.[41]

But does a higher per capita income mean that life has improved generally in a country? Not necessarily. As we saw in the chapter on social stratification, inequality within countries can increase with technological improvements because the rich often benefit the most. In addition, economic wealth is increasingly concentrated in a relatively small number of countries. Obviously, then, not everyone is better off even if on average most countries are doing better. Poverty has become more common as countries have become more unequal.

While many of the changes associated with globalization seem to be driven by the economic and political power of the richer countries, the movement of ideas, art, music, and food is more of a two-way process. A large part of that process involves the migration of people who bring their culture with them. As we have seen from the boxes on migrants and immigrants in previous chapters, movements of people have played a large role in the entry of food such as tortilla chips and salsa, sushi, and curries into the United States, music like reggae and many types of dance music from Latin America, and African carvings and jewelry such as beaded necklaces. Recently there has even been increased interest in acquiring indigenous knowledge of plants, the knowledge of indigenous healers, and learning about shamanistic trances. As indigenous knowledge comes to be viewed as potentially valuable, shamans have been able to speak out on national and international issues. In Brazil, shamans have organized to speak out against "biopiracy"—what is perceived as the unethical appropriation of biological knowledge for commercial purposes. In a more globalized world, shamans and other indigenous activists can be heard by more people than ever before. Despite the fact that indigenous people constitute less than one percent of the Brazilian population, some activist groups have been able to keep in touch with international environmentalists, using tape recorders and video cameras to convey information about their local situation.[42]

It is probably not possible to go back to a time when societies were not so dependent on each other, not so interconnected through world trade, not so dependent on commercial exchange. Even those who are most upset with globalization find it difficult to imagine that it is possible to return to a less connected world. For better or worse, the world is interconnected and will remain so. The question now is whether the average economic improvements in countries will eventually translate into economic improvements for most individuals.

Cultural Diversity in the Future

Measured in terms of travel time, the world today is much smaller than it has ever been. It is possible now to fly halfway around the globe in the time it took people less than a century ago to travel to the next state. In the realm of communication, the world is even smaller. We can talk to someone on the other side of the globe in a matter of minutes, we can send that person a message (by fax or Internet) in seconds, and through television we can see live coverage of events in that person's country. More and more people are drawn into the world market economy, buying and selling similar things and, as a consequence, altering the patterns of their lives in sometimes similar ways. Still, although modern transportation and communication facilitate the rapid spread of some cultural characteristics to all parts of the globe, it is highly unlikely that all parts of the world will end up the same culturally. Cultures are bound to retain some of their original characteristics or develop distinctive new adaptations. Even though television has diffused around the world, local people continue to prefer local programs when they are available. And even when people all over the world watch the same program, they may interpret it in very different ways. People are not just absorbing the messages they get; they often resist or revise them.[43]

Until recently, researchers studying culture change generally assumed that the differences between people of different cultures would become minimal. But in the last 30 years or so, it has become increasingly apparent that, although many differences disappear, many people are affirming ethnic identities in a process that often involves deliberately introducing cultural difference.[44] Eugeen Roosens describes the situation of the Huron of Quebec, who in the late 1960s seemed to have disappeared as a distinct culture. The Huron language had disappeared and the lives of the Huron were not obviously distinguishable from those of the French Canadians around them. The Huron then developed a new identity as they actively worked to promote the rights of indigenous peoples like themselves. That their new defining cultural symbols bore no resemblance to the past Huron culture is beside the point.

One fascinating possibility is that ethnic diversity and ethnogenesis may be a result of broader processes. Elizabeth Cashdan found that ethnic diversity appears to be related to environmental unpredictability, which is associated with greater distance from the equator.[45] There appear to be many more cultural groups nearer to the equator than in very northern and southern latitudes. Perhaps, Cashdan suggests, environmental unpredictability in the north and south necessitates wider ties between social groups to allow cooperation in case local resources fail. This may minimize the likelihood of cultural divergence, that is, ethnogenesis. Hence there will be fewer cultures farther from the equator.

Future research on culture change should increase our understanding of how and why various types of change are occurring. If we can increase our understanding of culture change in the present, we should be better able to understand similar processes in the past. We may be guided in our efforts to understand culture change by the large number of cross-cultural correlations that have been discovered between a particular cultural variation and its presumed causes.[46] All cultures have changed over time; variation is the product of differential change. Thus, the variations we see are the products of change processes, and the discovered predictors of those variations may suggest how and why the changes occurred.

Summary

1. Culture is always changing. Because culture consists of learned patterns of behavior and belief, cultural traits can be unlearned and learned anew as human needs change.

2. Discoveries and inventions, though ultimately the sources of all culture change, do not necessarily lead to change. Only when society accepts an invention or discovery and uses it regularly can culture change be said to have occurred.

3. The process by which cultural elements are borrowed from another society and incorporated into the culture of the recipient group is called diffusion. Cultural traits do not necessarily diffuse; that is, diffusion is a selective, not automatic, process. A society accepting a foreign cultural trait is likely to adapt it in a way that effectively harmonizes it with the society's own traditions.

4. When a group or society is in contact with a more powerful society, the weaker group is often obliged to acquire cultural elements from the dominant group. This process of extensive borrowing in the context of superordinate-subordinate relations between societies is called acculturation. In contrast with diffusion, acculturation comes about as a result of some sort of external pressure.

5. Perhaps the most drastic and rapid way a culture can change is by revolution—a usually violent replacement of the society's rulers. Rebellions occur primarily in state societies, where there is a distinct ruling elite. However, not all peoples who are suppressed, conquered, or colonized eventually rebel or successfully revolt against established authority.

6. Even though customs are not genetically inherited, cultural adaptation may be somewhat similar to biological adaptation. Traits (cultural or genetic) that are more likely to be reproduced (learned or inherited) are likely to become more frequent in a population over time. And if culture is generally adapted to its environment, then culture change should also be generally adaptive.

7. Many of the cultural changes observed in the modern world have been generated, directly or indirectly, by the dominance and expansion of Western societies. One of the principal changes resulting from the expansion of Western culture is the increasing dependence of much of the world on commercial exchange. The borrowed custom of buying and selling may at first be supplementary to

The news on television and in the newspapers makes us aware every day that terrible social problems threaten people around the world. War, crime, family violence, natural disasters, poverty, famine—all these and more are the lot of millions of people in many places. And now there is an increasing threat of terrorism. Can anthropological and other research help us solve these global social problems? Many anthropologists and other social scientists think so.

High-tech communications have increased our awareness of problems all over the world, and we seem to be increasingly aware of, and bothered by, problems in our own society. For these two reasons, and perhaps also because we know much more than we used to about human behavior, we may be more motivated now to try to solve those problems. We call them "social problems" not just because a lot of people worry about them but also because they have social causes and consequences, and treating or solving them requires changes in social behavior. Even AIDS, which we discuss in the next chapter, is partly a social problem. It may be caused by a virus, but it is mostly transmitted by social (sexual) contact with another person. And the main ways to avoid it—abstinence and "safe" sex—require changes in social behavior.

The idea that we can solve social problems, even the enormous ones such as war and family violence, is based on two assumptions. First, we have to assume that it is possible to discover the causes of a problem. And two, we have to assume that we may be able to do something about the causes, once they are discovered, and thereby eliminate or reduce the problem. Not everyone would agree with these assumptions. Some would say that our understanding of a social problem cannot ever be sufficient to suggest a solution guaranteed to work. To be sure, no understanding in science is perfect or certain; there is always some probability that even a well-supported explanation is wrong or incomplete. But the uncertainty of knowledge does not rule out the possibility of application. With regard to social problems, the possible payoff from even incomplete understanding could be a better and safer world. This possibility is what motivates many researchers who investigate social problems. After all, the history of the various sciences strongly supports the belief that scientific understanding can often allow humans to control nature, not just predict and explain it. Why should human behavior be any different?

So what do we know about some of the global social problems, and what policies or solutions are suggested by what we know?

Natural Disasters and Famine

Natural events such as floods, droughts, earthquakes, and insect infestations are usually but not always beyond human control, but their effects are not.[1] We call such events accidents or emergencies when only a few people are affected, but we call them disasters when large numbers of people or large areas are affected. The harm caused is not just a function of the magnitude of the natural event. Between 1960 and 1980, 43 natural disasters in Japan killed an average of 63 people per disaster. During the same period, 17 natural disasters in Nicaragua killed an average of 6,235 people per disaster. In the United States, between 1960 and 1976, the average flood or other environmental disturbance killed just one person, injured a dozen, and destroyed fewer than five buildings. These comparative figures demonstrate that climatic and other events in the physical environment become disasters because of events or conditions in the social environment.

If people live in houses that are designed to withstand earthquakes—if governing bodies require such construction and the economy is developed enough so that people can afford such construction—the effects of an earthquake will be minimized. If poor people are forced to live in deforested floodplains in order to be able to find land to farm (as in coastal Bangladesh), if the poor are forced to live in shanties built on precarious hillsides (like those of Rio de Janeiro), the floods and landslides that follow severe hurricanes and rainstorms can kill thousands and even hundreds of thousands.

Thus, natural disasters can have greater or lesser effects on human life, depending on social conditions. And therefore disasters are also social problems, problems that have social causes and possible social solutions. Legislating safe construction of a house is a social solution. The 1976 earthquake in Tangsham, China, killed 250,000 people, mostly because they lived in top-heavy adobe houses that could not withstand severe shaking, whereas the 1989 Loma Prieta earthquake in California, which was of comparable intensity, killed 65 people.

One might think that floods, of all disasters, are the least influenced by social factors. After all, without a huge runoff from heavy rains or snow melt, there cannot be a flood. But consider why so many people have died from Hwang River floods in China. (One such flood, in 1931, killed nearly 4 million people, making it the deadliest single disaster in history.) The floods in the Hwang River basin have occurred mostly because the clearing of nearby forests for fuel and farmland has allowed enormous quantities of silt to wash into the river, raising the riverbed and increasing the risk of floods that burst the dams that normally would contain them. The risk of disastrous flooding would be greatly reduced if different social conditions prevailed—if people were not so dependent on firewood for fuel, or if they did not have to farm close to the river, or if the dams were higher and more numerous.

Famines, episodes of severe starvation and death, often appear to be triggered by physical events such as a severe drought or a hurricane that kills or knocks down food trees and plants. But famines do not inevitably follow such an event. Social conditions can prevent a famine or increase the likelihood of one. Consider what is likely to happen in Samoa after a hurricane.[2] Whole villages that have lost their coconut and breadfruit trees, as well as their taro patches, pick up and move for a period of time to other villages where there are relatives and friends. The visitors stay and are fed until some of their cultivated trees and plants start to bear food again, at which point they return home. This kind of intervillage reciprocity probably could occur only in a society that has relatively little inequality in wealth. Nowadays, the central government or international agencies may also help out by providing food and other supplies.

The average flood in the United States does not kill that many people, but the storm surges from Hurricane Katrina and inadequate levees caused major flooding, massive homelessness, and hundreds of deaths in New Orleans (pictured here) and surrounding areas of the Gulf Coast in 2005.

Researchers point out that famine rarely results from just one bad food production season. During one bad season, people can usually cope by getting help from relatives, friends, and neighbors or by switching to less desirable foods. The famine in the African Sahel in 1974 occurred after eight years of bad weather; a combination of drought, floods, and a civil war in 1983 to 1984 contributed to the subsequent famine in the Sahel, Ethiopia, and Sudan.[3] Famine almost always has some social causes. Who has rights to the available food, and do those who have more food distribute it to those who have less? Cross-cultural research suggests that societies with individual property rights rather than shared rights are more likely to suffer famine.[4] Nonetheless, government assistance can lessen the risk of famine in societies with individual property.

Relief provided by government may not always get to those who need it the most. In India, for example, the central government provides help in time of drought to minimize the risk of famine. But the food and other supplies provided to a village may end up being unequally distributed, following the rules of social and gender stratification. Members of the local elite arrange to function as distributors and find ways to manipulate the relief efforts to their advantage. Lower-class and lower-caste families still suffer the most. Within the family, biases against females, particularly young girls and elderly women, translate into their getting less food. It is no wonder, then, that in times of food shortage and famine, the poor and other socially disadvantaged persons are especially likely to die.[5]

Thus, the people of a society may not all be equally at risk in case of disaster. In socially stratified societies, the poor particularly suffer. It is they who are likely to be forced to overcultivate, overgraze, and deforest their land, making it more susceptible to degradation. A society most helps those it values the most.

People in the past, and even recently in some places, viewed disasters as divine retribution for human immorality. For example, the great Flood described in the Old Testament was understood to be God's doing. But scientific research increasingly allows us to understand the natural causes of disasters, and particularly the social conditions that magnify or minimize their effects. To reduce the impact of disasters, then, we need to reduce the social conditions that magnify the effects of disasters. If humans are responsible for those social conditions, humans can change them. If earthquakes destroy houses that are too flimsy, we can build stronger houses. If floods caused by overcultivation and overgrazing kill people directly (or indirectly by stripping their soils), we can grow new forest cover and provide new job opportunities to floodplain farmers. If prolonged natural disasters or wars threaten famine, social distribution systems can lessen the risk. In short, we may not be able to do much about the weather or other physical causes of disasters, but we can do a lot—if we want to—about the social factors that make disasters disastrous.

Inadequate Housing and Homelessness

In most nations, the poor typically live in inadequate housing, in areas we call *slums*. In many of the developing nations, where cities are growing very rapidly, squatter settlements emerge as people build dwellings (often makeshift) that are typically declared illegal, either because the land is illegally occupied or because the dwellings violate building codes. Squatter settlements are often located in degraded environments that are subject to flooding and mudslides or have inadequate or polluted water. The magnitude of the problem is made clear in some statistics. As of the 1980s, 40 percent of the population in Nairobi, Kenya, lived in unauthorized housing, and 67 percent of the people in five of El Salvador's major cities lived in illegal dwellings.[6]

But contrary to what some people have assumed, not all dwellers in illegal settlements are poor; all but the upper-income elite may be found in such settlements.[7] Moreover, although squatter settlements have problems, they are not chaotic and unorganized places that are full of crime. Most of the dwellers

Shown here is a homeless boy in Calcutta, India with his belongings.

are employed, aspire to get ahead, live in intact nuclear families, and help each other.[8] People live in such settlements because they cannot find affordable housing and they house themselves as best they can. Many researchers think that such self-help tendencies should be assisted to improve housing, because governments in developing countries can seldom afford costly public housing projects. But they could invest somewhat in infrastructure—sewers, water supplies, roads—and provide construction materials to those who are willing to do the work required to improve their dwellings.[9]

Housing in slum areas or shantytowns does provide shelter, minimal though it may be. But many people in many areas of the world have no homes at all. Even in countries such as the United States, which are affluent by world standards, large numbers of people are homeless. They sleep in parks, over steam vents, in doorways, subways, and cardboard boxes. In 1987 it was estimated that there were more than 1 million homeless people in the United States.[10] Now there are about three quarters of a million homeless.[11]

Who are the homeless, and how did they get to be homeless? We have relatively little research on these questions, but what we do have suggests differences in the causes of homelessness in different parts of the world. In the United States, unemployment and the shortage of decent low-cost housing appear to be at least partly responsible for the large number of homeless persons.[12] But there is also another factor: the deliberate policy to reduce the number of people hospitalized for mental illness and other disabilities. For example, from the mid-1960s to the mid-1990s, New York State released thousands of patients from mental hospitals. Many of these ex-patients had to live in cheap hotels or poorly monitored facilities with virtually no support network. With very little income, they found it especially hard to cope with their circumstances. Ellen Baxter and Kim Hopper, who studied the homeless in New York City, suggest that one event is rarely sufficient to render a person homeless. Rather, poverty and disability (mental or physical) seem to lead to one calamity after another and, finally, homelessness.[13]

Many people cannot understand why homeless individuals do not want to go to municipal shelters. But observations and interviews with the homeless suggest that violence pervades the municipal shelters, particularly the men's shelters. Many feel safer on the streets. Some private charities provide safe shelters and a caring environment. These shelters are filled, but the number of homeless they can accommodate is small.[14] Even single-room-occupancy hotels are hardly better. Many of them are infested with vermin, the common bathrooms are filthy, and they, like the shelters, are often dangerous.[15]

Scientists are increasingly sure that the world is heating up. And they are worried about the consequences. The more the temperature rises, the more the Greenland and Arctic ice will melt. The resulting higher sea level will flood many low-lying coastal areas, including many world cities. The weather in many places will also probably change, and not always for the better. For example, areas that now get enough rainfall to grow crops may turn into deserts.

The world is warming probably for several reasons. One of them is our increasing use of fossil fuels, particularly oil. We burn those fuels to make electricity, to power our cars (with the gasoline made from oil), to heat our homes, and to cook food. The emissions from all that burning may contribute to a "greenhouse effect": The atmosphere reflects the warmth produced on earth, and temperatures rise. And the air gets dirtier, resulting in other harmful consequences such as a higher incidence of breathing disorders.

Can people do anything about global warming and air pollution? Surely the answer is yes. If at least some of the problem is of human making, we could change our behavior and at least partly solve the problem. One way would be to reduce our use of oil as fuel. But how could we do that?

In the year 2000 the first hybrid cars were sold in the United States. These cars are powered by an electric motor and a small gasoline engine. The combination reduces the amount of fuel needed, because the electric motor moves the car much of the time. The battery that powers the electric motor is recharged by braking and by the gasoline engine when it is on, which is not much of the time. (For example, at a stop light, the gasoline engine turns off.) So a hybrid car allows a gallon of gasoline to go a lot farther. If most cars were hybrid cars, we would need much less oil to make the gasoline needed.

It is estimated that hybrid cars could cut greenhouse emissions by up to half, which would help alleviate or even reverse global warming and air pollution. So, given this rosy scenario, what is discouraging the world from switching to hybrid cars?

The answer is probably economics and politics. There is money to be made from the dependence on oil, particularly when supplies are short. The shorter the supplies, the more the oil producers abroad and the refiners at home can charge their customers. And the more the oil comes from abroad, the more the United States and other governments may feel that they have to keep the foreign producers happy. But this obligation runs counter to a foreign policy that would encourage democracy in the world; many of the countries that produce our oil are dictatorships. So the oil companies are dependent on those regimes to keep their refineries going, and they lobby governments (ours included) to maintain friendly relations with many of those regimes. Can we expect the oil companies to want to escape their dependence on foreign suppliers, if they are making a lot of money from that dependence? Hardly.

Our market economy does offer a way out of this dilemma. If hybrid cars and other ways to reduce the need for fossil fuels become more economical, the marketplace will turn the tide. Ironically, it will be the capitalist laws of supply and demand that may reduce the influence of oil companies on politics and help us solve the problems of global warming and air pollution. Even if the automobile manufacturers wanted to continue doing business as usual, they will not be able to resist making more fuel-efficient cars. Consumers will want to buy them to reduce their gasoline expenses. No car company will be able to ignore that kind of pressure from the marketplace. There seems to be more interest now in making and buying hybrid vehicles, and there is the possibility of transforming organic garbage into oil.

Sources: J. Oerlemans, "Extracting a Climate Signal from 169 Glacial Records," *Science* (April 28, 2005): 675–77; Matthew L. Wald, "Hybrid Cars Show Up in M.I.T.'s Crystal Ball," *The New York Times,* November 3, 2000, p. F1; and the special advertisement produced by energy companies, "Energy: Investing for a New Century," *The New York Times,* October 30, 2000, pp. EN1–8; Daniel Duane, "Turning Garbage into Oil," *New York Times Magazine,* December 14, 2003, p. 100.

Some poor individuals may be socially isolated, with few or no friends and relatives and little or no social contact. But a society with many such individuals does not necessarily have much homelessness. Socially isolated individuals, even mentally ill individuals, could still have housing, or so the experience of Melbourne, Australia, suggests. Universal health insurance there pays for health care as well as medical practitioners' visits to isolated and ill individuals, wherever they live. Disabled individuals receive a pension or sickness benefits sufficient to allow them to live in a room or apartment. And there is still a considerable supply of cheap housing in Melbourne. Research in Melbourne suggests that a severe mental disorder often precedes living in marginal accommodations—city shelters, commercial shelters, and cheap single rooms. About 50 percent of the people living in such places were diagnosed as previously having some form of mental illness; this percentage is similar to what seems to be the case for homeless people and people living in marginal accommodations in the United States.

The contrast between the United States and Australia makes it clear that homelessness is caused by social and political policies. Individuals with similar characteristics live in both Australia and the United States, but in the United States a larger percentage of them are homeless.[16]

Because homelessness cannot occur if everybody can afford housing, some people would say that homelessness can happen only in a society with great extremes in income. Statistics on income distribution in the United States clearly show that since the 1970s the rich have gotten much richer and the poor have gotten much poorer. The United States now has more income inequality than most other industrialized countries, such as Japan and Italy. In fact, the profile of inequality in the United States more closely resembles that of developing countries, such as China.[17]

In the United States, and many other countries, most homeless persons are adults. Whereas adults are "allowed" to be homeless, public sensibilities in the United States appear to be outraged by the sight of children living in the streets; when authorities discover homeless children, they try to find shelters or foster homes for them. But many countries have "street children." It has been estimated that 80 million of the world's children live in the streets. Forty million of them live in Latin America, 20 million in Asia, 10 million in Africa and the Middle East, and 10 million elsewhere.[18]

Lewis Aptekar, who studied street children in Cali, Colombia, reported some surprises.[19] Whereas many of the homeless in the United States and Australia are mentally disabled, the street children in Cali, ranging in age from 7 to 16, are mostly free of mental problems; by and large they also test normally on intelligence tests. In addition, even though many street children come from abusive homes or never had homes, they usually seem happy and enjoy the support and friendship of other street children. They cleverly and creatively look for ways to get money, frequently through entertaining passersby.

Although the observer might think that the street children must have been abandoned by their families, in actuality most of them have at least one parent they keep in touch with. Street life begins slowly, not abruptly; children usually do not stay on the streets full time until they are about 13 years old. Though street children in Cali seem to be in better physical and mental shape than their siblings who stay at home, they often are viewed as a "plague." The street children come from poor families and cope with their lives as best they can, so why are they not viewed with pity and compassion? Aptekar suggests that well-off families see the street children as a threat because a life independent of family may appeal to children, even those from well-off families, who wish to be free of parental constraint and authority.

Whether people become homeless, whether there are shantytowns, seems to depend on a society's willingness to share wealth and help those in need. The street children of Cali may remind us that children as well as adults need companionship and care. Addressing physical needs without responding to emotional needs may get people off the streets, but it won't get them a "home."

Family Violence and Abuse

In U.S. society we hear regularly about the abuse of spouses and children, which makes us think that such abuse is increasing—but is it? This seems to be a simple question, but it is not so simple to answer. We have to decide what we mean by *abuse*.

Is physical punishment of a child who does something wrong child abuse? Not so long ago, teachers in public schools in the United States were allowed to discipline children by hitting them with rulers or paddles, and many parents used switches or belts. Many would consider these practices to be child abuse, but were they abusive when they were generally accepted? Some would argue that abuse is going beyond what a culture considers appropriate behavior. Others would disagree and would focus on the violence and severity of parents' or teachers' behavior, not the cultural judgment of appropriateness. And abuse need not involve physical violence. It could be argued that verbal aggression and neglect may be just as harmful as physical aggression. Neglect presents its own problems of definition. People from other cultures might argue that we act abusively when we put an infant or child alone in a room to sleep.[20] Few would disagree about severe injuries that kill a child or spouse or require medical treatment, but other disciplinary behaviors are more difficult to judge.

To avoid having to decide what is or is not abuse, many researchers focus their studies on variation in the frequencies of specific behaviors. For example, one can ask which societies have physical punishment of children without calling physical punishment abusive.

According to three national interview surveys of married or cohabiting couples in the United States conducted in 1975, 1985, and 1992, physical violence against children appears to have decreased in frequency over time, as did serious assaults by husbands against wives. But serious assaults by wives on husbands did not decrease.[21] The decreasing rates of abuse may be mostly due to reporting differences: Wife and child beating is less acceptable now. For example, men report dramatically fewer assaults on their wives, but wives report only slight declines.[22] However, the United States remains a society with a lot of physical violence in families. In 1992 alone, one out of ten couples had a violent assault episode and one out of ten children was severely assaulted by a parent.[23] A survey conducted in the mid-1990s found that about 75 percent of the violence against women comes from a male intimate partner, such as a husband. In contrast, most of the violence men experience comes from strangers and acquaintances. Just as women face more risk from those close to them, so do children. When a child is the target of violence, it usually comes from the birth mother.[24]

Cross-culturally, if one form of family violence occurs, others are also likely. So, for example, wife beating, husband beating, child punishment, and fighting among siblings are all significantly associated with each other. But the relationships between these types of family violence are not that strong, which means that they cannot be considered as different facets of the same phenomenon. Indeed, somewhat different factors seem to explain different forms of family violence.[25] We focus here on two forms of violence that are most prevalent cross-culturally: violence against children and violence against wives.

Violence against Children

Cross-culturally, many societies practice and allow infanticide. Frequent reasons for infanticide include illegitimacy, deformity of the infant, twins, too many children, or that the infant is unwanted. Infanticide is usually performed by the mother, but this does not mean that she is uncaring; it may mean that she cannot adequately feed or care for the infant or that it has a poor chance of surviving. The reasons for infanticide are similar to those given for abortion. Therefore, it seems that infanticide may be performed when abortion does not work or when unexpected qualities of the infant (e.g., deformity) force the mother to reevaluate her ability to raise the child.[26]

Physical punishment of children occurs at least sometimes in over 70 percent of the world's societies.[27] And physical punishment is frequent or typical in 40 percent of the world's societies. Why? A recent cross-cultural study suggests that the major reason parents physically punish children is to prepare them for a life of power inequality, which will require them to fear those more powerful. Societies with class stratification and political hierarchy, either native or introduced (colonialism), are very likely to practice corporal punishment of children.[28] Research in the United States is consistent with the cross-cultural finding: Those at the bottom of the socioeconomic hierarchy are more likely than those at the top to practice corporal punishment of children.[29]

Violence against Wives

Cross-culturally, wife beating is the most common form of family violence; it occurs at least occasionally in about 85 percent of the world's societies. In about half the societies, wife beating is sometimes serious enough to cause permanent injury or death.[30] It is often assumed that wife beating is common in societies in which males control economic and political resources. In a cross-cultural test of this assumption, David Levinson found that not all indicators of male dominance predict wife beating, but many do. Specifically, wife beating is most common when men control the products of family labor, when men have the final say in decision making in the home, when divorce is difficult for women, when remarriage for a widow is controlled by the husband's kin, and when women do not have any female work groups.[31] Similarly, in the United States, the more one spouse in the family makes the decisions and has the power, the more physical violence occurs in the family. Wife beating is even more likely when the husband controls the household and is out of work.[32]

Wife beating appears to be related to broader patterns of violence. Societies that have violent methods of conflict resolution within communities, physical punishment of criminals, high frequency of warfare, and cruelty toward enemies generally have more wife beating.[33] Corporal punishment of children may be related to wife beating. In the United States, many parents think that corporal punishment is necessary to teach children right and wrong. Corporal punishment of children may also teach that it is appropriate to hit people if you think they are misbehaving. As of 1995, one out of four parents hit children with objects.[34] Research in the United States supports the idea that individuals (males and females) who were punished corporally as adolescents are more likely to approve of marital violence and are more likely to commit it.[35]

Reducing the Risk

What can be done to minimize family violence? First, we have to recognize that probably nothing can be done as long as people in a society do not acknowledge that there is a problem. If severe child punishment and wife beating are perfectly acceptable by almost everyone in a society, they are unlikely to be considered social problems that need solutions. In our own society many programs are designed to take abused children or wives out of the family situation or to punish the abuser. (Of course, in these situations the violence has already occurred and was serious enough to have been noticed.) Cross-culturally, at least with respect to wife beating, intervention by others seems to be successful only if the intervention occurs before violence gets serious. As one would expect, however, those societies most prone to a high rate of wife beating are the least likely to practice immediate intervention. More helpful perhaps, but admittedly harder to arrange, is the promotion of conditions of life that are associated with low family violence. Research so far suggests that promoting the equality of men and women and the sharing of child rearing responsibilities may go a long way toward lessening incidents of family violence.[36] And reducing the risk of corporal punishment of children may reduce the risk of violence when they have families.

Crime

What is a crime in one society is not necessarily a crime in another. Just as it is difficult to decide what constitutes abuse, it is difficult to define *crime*. In one society, it may be a crime to walk over someone's land without permission; in another, there might not be any concept of personal ownership, and therefore no concept of trespassing. In seeking to understand variation in crime, it is not surprising that many researchers have preferred to compare those behaviors that are more or less universally considered crimes and that are reliably reported. For example, in a large-scale comparison of crime in 110 nations over a span of 70 years, Dane Archer and Rosemary Gartner concentrated on homicide rates. They argued that homicide is harder for the public to hide and for officials to ignore than are other crimes. A comparison of interviews about crime with police records suggests that homicide is the most reliably reported crime in official records.[37]

One of the clearest findings to emerge from comparative studies of crime is that war is associated with higher rates of homicide. Archer and Gartner compared changes in homicide rates of nations before and after major wars. Whether a nation is defeated or victorious, homicide rates tend to increase after a war. This result is consistent with the idea that a society or nation legitimizes violence during wartime. That is, during wartime, societies approve of killing the enemy; afterward, homicide rates may go up because inhibitions against killing have been relaxed.[38] Ted Gurr suggested that the long-term downtrend in crime in Western societies seems to be consistent with an increasing emphasis on humanistic values and nonviolent achievement of goals. But such goals may be temporarily suspended during wartime. In the United States, for example, surges in violent crime rates occurred during the 1860s and 1870s (during and after the Civil War), after World War I, after World War II, and during the Vietnam War.[39]

In the types of societies that anthropologists have typically studied, homicide statistics were not usually available; so cross-cultural studies of homicide usually measure homicide rates by comparing and rank-ordering ethnographers' statements about the frequency of homicide. For example, the statement that murder is "practically unheard of" is taken to mean that the murder rate is lower than where it is reported that "homicide is not uncommon." Despite the fact that the data on cultural homicide rates are not quantitative, the cross-cultural results are consistent with the cross-national results; more war is usually associated with more homicide and assault, as well as with socially approved aggressive behaviors (as in aggressive games) and severe physical punishment for wrongdoing.[40] A cross-cultural study suggests that the more war a society has, the more socialization or training of aggression in boys it will have, and such socialization strongly predicts higher rates of homicide and assault.[41]

Capital punishment—execution of criminals—is severe physical punishment for wrongdoing. It is commonly thought that would-be murderers are deterred by the prospect of capital punishment. Yet cross-national research suggests otherwise. More countries show murder rates going down rather than up after capital punishment was abolished.[42] Capital punishment may legitimize violence rather than deter it.

Research conducted in the United States suggests that juvenile delinquents (usually boys) are likely to come from broken homes, with the father absent for much of the time the boy is growing up. The conclusion often drawn is that father absence somehow increases the likelihood of delinquency and adult forms of physical violence. But other conditions that may cause delinquency are also associated with broken homes, conditions such as the stigma of not having a "regular" family and the generally low standard of living of such families. It is therefore important to conduct research in other societies, in which father absence does not occur in concert with these other factors, to see if father absence by itself is related to physical violence.

For example, in many polygynous societies, children grow up in a mother-child household; the father lives separately and is seldom around the child. Does the father-absence explanation of delinquency and violence fit such societies? The answer is apparently yes: Societies in which children are reared in mother-child households or the father spends little time caring for the child tend to have more physical violence by males than do societies in which fathers spend time with children.[43] The rate of violent crime is also more frequent in nations that have more women than men, which is consistent with the theory that father absence increases violence.[44]

More research is needed to discover exactly what accounts for these relationships. It is possible, as some suggest, that boys growing up without fathers are apt to act "supermasculine," to show how "male" they are. But it is also possible that mothers who rear children alone have more frustration and more anger, and therefore are likely to provide an aggressive role model for the child. In addition, high male mortality in war predicts polygyny, as we saw in the chapter on marriage, family, and kinship; therefore, boys in polygynous societies are likely to be exposed to a warrior tradition.[45]

Trying to act supermasculine, however, may be likely to involve violence only if aggression is an important component of the male gender role in society. If men were expected by society to be sensitive, caring, and nonviolent, boys who grew up without fathers might try to be supersensitive and supercaring. So society's expectations for males probably shape how growing up in a mother-child household affects behavior in adolescence and later.[46] The expectations for males may also be influenced by the media. Numerous studies in the United States show that even controlling for other factors like parental neglect, family income, and mental illness, more television watching in childhood and adolescence predicts more overt aggression later. Estimates show that an hour of prime-time television depicts 3 to 5 violent acts, and an hour of children's television depicts 20 to 25 violent acts.[47]

One widely held idea is that poor economic conditions increase the likelihood of crime, but the relationship does not appear to be strong. Also, the findings are somewhat different for different types of crime. For example, hundreds of studies in this and other countries do not show a clear relationship between changes in economic well-being as measured by unemployment rates and changes in violent crime as measured by homicide. The rate of homicide does not appear to increase in bad times. Property crimes, however, do increase with increases in unemployment. Violent crime does appear to be associated with one economic characteristic: Homicide is usually highest in nations with high income inequality. Why income inequality predicts homicide but downturns in the economy do not is something of a puzzle.[48]

Evidence indicates that violence on television encourages violence in real life.

The fact that property crime is linked to unemployment is consistent with the cross-cultural finding that theft (but not violent crime) tends to occur less often in egalitarian societies than in stratified ones. Societies with equal access to resources usually have distribution mechanisms that offset any differences in wealth. Hence theft should be less of a temptation and therefore less likely in an egalitarian society. Theft rates are higher in socially stratified societies despite the fact that they are more likely than egalitarian societies to have police and courts to punish crime. Societies may try to deter property and other crimes when the rates of such are high, but we do not know that these efforts actually reduce the rates.

So what does the available research suggest about how we might be able to reduce crime? The results so far indicate that homicide rates are highest in societies that socialize their boys for aggression. Such socialization is linked to war and other forms of socially approved violence—capital punishment, television and movie violence by heroes, violence in sports. The statistical evidence suggests that war encourages socialization for aggression, which in turn results unintentionally in high rates of violence. The policy implication of these results is that if we can reduce socialization for aggression, by reducing the risk of war and therefore the necessity to produce effective warriors, and if we can reduce other forms of socially approved violence, we may thereby reduce the rates of violent crime. The reduction of inequalities in wealth may also help to reduce crime, particularly theft. And although it is not yet clear why, it appears that raising boys with a male role model around may reduce the likelihood of male violence in adulthood.

War

War is an unfortunate fact of life in most societies known to anthropology, judging by the cross-cultural research we referred to in the chapter on political life. Almost every society had at least occasional wars when it was first described, unless it had been pacified (usually by Western colonial powers).[49] Since the Civil War, the United States has not had any wars on its territory, but it is unusual in that respect. Before pacification, most societies had frequent armed combat between communities or larger units that spoke the same language. That is, most warfare was internal to the society or language group. Even some wars in modern times involved speakers of the same language; recall the wars between Italian states before the unification of Italy and many of the "civil" wars of the past two centuries. Although people in some societies might

A society might encourage boys to play soldier, perhaps to prepare them to be courageous in combat later on. Cross-culturally, socialization for aggression strongly predicts homicide and assault.

fight against people in other societies, such "external" wars were usually not organized on behalf of the entire society or even a major section of it.[50] That is, warfare in the ethnographic record did not usually involve politically unified societies. Finally, the absolute numbers of people killed may have been small, but this does not mean that warfare in nonindustrial societies was a trivial matter. Indeed, it appears that nonindustrial warfare may have been even more lethal *proportionately* than modern warfare, judging by the fact that wars killed 25 to 30 percent of the males in some nonindustrial societies.[51]

In the chapter on political life, we discussed the possibility that people in nonindustrial societies go to war mostly out of fear, particularly a fear of expectable but unpredictable natural disasters (droughts, floods, hurricanes, among others) that destroy food supplies.[52] People with more history of such disasters have more war. It seems as if people go to war to protect themselves ahead of time from disasters, inasmuch as the victors in war almost always take resources (land, animals, other things) from the defeated, even when the victors have no current resource problems. Another factor apparently making for more war is teaching children to mistrust others. People who grow up to be mistrustful of others may be more likely to go to war than to negotiate or seek conciliation with "enemies." Mistrust or fear of others seems to be partly caused by threat or fear of disasters.[53]

Is warfare in and between modern state societies explainable in much the same way that nonindustrial warfare seems to be explainable? If the answer to that question turns out to be yes, it will certainly be a modified yes, because the realities of industrialized societies require an expanded conception of disasters. In the modern world, with its complex economic and political dependencies among nations, we may not be worried only about weather or pest disasters that could curtail food supplies. Possible curtailments of other resources, particularly oil, may also scare us into going to war. According to some commentators, the decision to go to war against Iraq after it invaded Kuwait in 1991 fits this theory of war.

But even if the "threat-to-resources" theory is true, we may be coming to realize (since the end of the Cold War) that war is not the only way to ensure access to resources. There may be a better way in the modern world, a way that is more cost-effective as well as more preserving of human life. If it is true that war is most likely when people fear unpredictable disasters of any kind, the risk of war should lessen when people realize that the harmful effects of disasters could be reduced or prevented by international cooperation. Just as we have the assurance of disaster relief within our country, we could have the assurance of disaster relief worldwide. That is, the fear of unpredictable disasters and the fear of others, and the consequent risk of war, could be reduced by the assurance ahead of time that the world would help those in need in case of disaster. Instead of going to war out of fear, we could go to peace by agreeing to share. The certainty of international cooperation could compensate for the uncertainty of resources.

Consider how Germany and Japan have fared in the years since their "unconditional surrender" in World War II. They were forbidden to participate in the international arms race and could rely on others, particularly the United States, to protect them. Without a huge burden of armaments, Germany and Japan thrived. But countries that competed militarily, particularly the United States and the Soviet Union at the height of the Cold War, experienced economic difficulties. Doesn't that scenario at least suggest the wisdom of international cooperation, particularly the need for international agreements to ensure worldwide disaster relief? Compared with going to war and its enormous costs, going to peace would be a bargain!

Recent research in political science and anthropology suggests an additional way to reduce the risk of war. Among the societies known to anthropology, studies indicate that people in more participatory— that is, more "democratic"—political systems rarely go to war with each other.[54] Thus, if authoritarian governments were to disappear from the world, because the powerful nations of the world stopped supporting them militarily and otherwise, the world could be more peaceful for this reason too.

Although democratically governed states rarely go to war with each other, it used to be thought that they are not necessarily more peaceful in general, that they are as likely to go to war as are other kinds of

Ethnic conflicts appear to be on the rise. In recent years, violent conflicts have erupted between ethnic groups in the former Yugoslavia, Russia, and Spain (in Europe), in Rwanda and Sierra Leone (in Africa), and in Sri Lanka and Indonesia (in Asia)—to name just a few of the many instances. Such conflicts are often thought to be intractable and inevitable because they are supposedly based on ancient hatreds. But is that true?

Social scientists are a long way from understanding the conditions that predict ethnic conflicts, but they do know that ethnic conflicts are not necessarily ancient or inevitable. For example, anthropologists who did fieldwork in the former Yugoslavia in the 1980s described villages where different ethnic groups had lived side by side for a long time without apparent difficulty. The differences between them were hardly emphasized. Mary Kay Gilliland worked in a midsize town (Slavonski Brod) in the Slavonian region of Croatia, which was part of Yugoslavia. The people in the town identified themselves as from Slavonia, rather than as Croats, Serbs, Hungarians, Czechs, Muslims (from Bosnia or from Albania), or Roma (Gypsies). Mixed marriages were not uncommon and people discussed differences in background without anger. But in 1991, when Gilliland returned to Croatia, people complained about Serb domination of the Yugoslav government and there was talk of Croatia seceding. Symbols of Croat nationalism had appeared—new place names, a new flag—and Croats were now said to speak Croatian, rather than the language they shared with the Serbs (Serbo-Croatian or Croato-Serbian). Later in 1991, violence broke out between Serbs and Croats, and atrocities were committed on both sides. Ethnicity became a matter of life or death and Croatia seceded from Yugoslavia. At the same time, Tone Bringa, a Norwegian anthropologist who worked in Bosnia (which was then still a region of Yugoslavia), reported that the people there also paid little attention to ethnicity. A few years later, however, ethnic violence erupted among Bosnian Serbs, Muslims, and Croats, and only the intervention of the United Nations established a precarious peace.

Ethnic conflict is often associated with secessionist movements; secession often occurs after the eruption of ethnic conflict. In the American Revolution, the region that became the United States seceded from Great Britain and declared independence. The ethnic differences between the Americans and the British were not great—not many years had passed since the first British colonizers had come to America—but there still was a secessionist movement, and there was violence. Ethnic differences do not always lead to violence. Sometimes, probably even most of the time, people of different ethnic backgrounds live in peace with one another. So why do some places with ethnic differences erupt in violence, but not all? Why do different ethnic groups get along in some places?

We need research to answer this question. With all of the forced and voluntary immigration in the world, many countries are becoming more multiethnic or multicultural. The possibility of ethnic violence has become a global social problem. Gilliland suggests, among other things, that discontent over economic and political power (inequitable access to resources and opportunities) drove the Croatians to violence and secession. Other scholars have suggested other possible answers to the question of why ethnic relations do not always become ethnic conflict and violence. Violence may erupt in the absence of strong unifying interests (cross-cutting ties) between the parties. Another suggested factor is the absence of constitutional ways to resolve conflict. What we need now are cross-cultural, cross-national, and cross-historical studies to measure each of the possible explaining factors, so that we can compare how well (or poorly) they predict ethnic conflict throughout the world, controlling for the effects of the other factors. If we knew which factors generally give rise to ethnic violence, we might be able to think of ways to reduce or eliminate the causal conditions.

Sources: Mary Kay Gilliland, "Nationalism and Ethnogenesis in the Former Yugoslavia," in Lola Romanucci-Ross and George A. De Vos, eds., *Ethnic Identity*, 3rd ed. (Walnut Creek, CA: AltaMira Press, 1995), pp. 197–221; Tone Bringa, *Being Muslim the Bosnian Way* (Princeton, NJ: Princeton University Press, 1995), as examined in eHRAF World Cultures on the Web; Marc Howard Ross, "Ethnocentrism and Ethnic Conflict," in *Research Frontiers*, in Carol R. Ember, Melvin Ember, and Peter N. Peregrine, eds., *New Directions in Anthropology* (Upper Saddle River, NJ: Prentice Hall, CD-ROM, 2004).

At a public planning meeting in Salina, New York, a town resident raises questions. Societies with participatory democracies are less likely to fight with other democracies.

political systems, but not so much with each other. For example, the United States has gone to war with Grenada, Panama, and Iraq—all authoritarian states—but not with democratic Canada, with which the United States has also had disputes. But now a consensus is emerging among political scientists that democracies are not only unlikely to go to war with each other, they are also less warlike in general.[55] The theory suggested by the cross-national and cross-cultural results is that democratic conflict resolution within a political system generalizes to democratic conflict resolution between political systems, particularly if the systems are both democratic. If our participatory institutions and perceptions allow us to resolve our disputes peacefully, internally and externally, we may think that similarly governed people would also be disposed to settle things peacefully. Therefore, disputes between participatory political systems should be unlikely to result in war.

The understanding that participatory systems rarely fight each other, and knowing why they do not, would have important consequences for policy in the contemporary world. The kinds of military preparations believed necessary and the costs people would be willing to pay for them might be affected. On the one hand, understanding the relationship between democracy and peace might encourage war making against authoritarian regimes to overturn them—with enormous costs in human life and otherwise. On the other hand, understanding the consequences of democracy might encourage us to assist the emergence and consolidation of more participatory systems of government in the countries of eastern Europe, the former Soviet Union, and elsewhere. In any case, the relationship between democracy and peace strongly suggests that it is counterproductive to support any undemocratic regimes, even if they happen to be enemies of our enemies, if we want to minimize the risk of war in the world. The latest cross-national evidence suggests that extending democracy around the world would minimize the risk of war. Encouraging nations to be more interdependent economically, and encouraging the spread of international nongovernmental organizations (like professional societies and trade associations) to provide informal ways to resolve conflicts, would also minimize the risk of war, judging by results of recent research by political scientists.[56]

Terrorism

Ever since September 11, 2001, when terrorists crashed airliners into the World Trade Center towers in New York City and into the Pentagon in Arlington, Virginia, people all over the world realize that terrorism has become a social problem globally. It is now painfully clear that organized groups of terrorists can train their people to kill themselves and thousands of others half a world away, not only by hijacking airliners and flying them into skyscrapers, but also by using easily transported explosives and biological weapons. Social scientists are now actively trying to understand terrorism, in the hope that research may lead to ways to minimize the likelihood of future attacks. But there are lots of questions to answer. What is terrorism and how shall it be defined? How long has terrorist activity been around? What are the causes of terrorism? What kind of people are likely to become terrorists? And what are the consequences of terrorism?

Answering these questions is not so simple. Most people can point to instances that hardly anyone would have trouble calling terrorism—spraying nerve gas in a Japanese subway, Palestinian suicide bombers targeting Israeli civilians, Ku Klux Klan members lynching African Americans.[57] It is harder to identify the boundaries between terrorism, crime, political repression, and warfare.[58] Most researchers agree that terrorism involves the threat or use of violence against civilians. Terrorism is usually also politically or socially organized, in contrast to most crimes, which are usually perpetrated by individuals acting on their own. (To be sure, crime can be socially organized too, as, for example, in what we call "organized crime.") One marker of the difference between most crime and terrorism is that criminals rarely take public credit for their activities, because they want to avoid being caught. In terrorism, the perpetrators usually proclaim their responsibility. In terrorism also, the violence is directed mostly at unarmed people, including women and children. It is intended to frighten the "enemy," to *terrorize* them, to scare them into doing something that the terrorists want to see happen. Generally, then, **terrorism** may be defined as the use or threat of violence to create terror in others, usually for political purposes.[59] Some define terrorism as perpetrated by groups that are not formal political entities. However, this criterion presents some difficulty. What are we to call it when governments support death squads and genocide against their own civilians? Some scholars call this "state terror."[60] And what are we to call the activities of some governments that support secret operations against other countries (often referred to as "state-sponsored terrorism")? Finally, while some nations conducting war explicitly try to avoid civilian casualties and focus primarily on combatants (armed soldiers), their weapons, and resources or "assets" such as factories, air strips, and fuel depots, many attacks in wartime throughout history have purposefully targeted civilians (e.g., the United States dropped atomic bombs on Hiroshima and Nagasaki to persuade the Japanese to end World War II).

One thing is certain about terrorism: It is not a new development. Some of the words we use for terrorists (e.g., "zealots" and "assassins") derive from terrorist movements in the past. The Zealots, Jewish nationalists who revolted against the Romans occupying Judea in the first century, would hide in crowds

People light candles in memory of those killed by terrorist attacks on trains in Madrid, Spain in 2004.

and stab officials and priests as well as soldiers. In the eleventh and twelfth centuries in southwest Asia, the Fedayeen (a group of Muslim Isma'ili Shi'ites) undertook to assassinate Sunni rulers despite the near certainty of their own capture or death. The rulers said that the Fedayeen were under the influence of hashish and called them "Hashshashin," which is the root of the later term "assassin."[61] In the late eighteenth and early nineteenth centuries, the "reign of terror" occurred during and after the French Revolution. In the early and middle twentieth century, the dictator Joseph Stalin ordered the execution of many millions of people who were considered enemies of the Soviet state. Six million Jews and millions of other innocents were exterminated by the German Third Reich in the 1930s and 1940s.[62] And many Latin American regimes, such as that in Argentina, terrorized and killed dissidents in the 1970s and 1980s.[63] Now there is a heightened fear of terrorists who may have access to weapons of mass destruction. In a world made smaller by global transportation, cell phones, and the Internet, terrorism is a greater threat than ever before.

We still lack systematic research that explains why terrorism occurs and why people are motivated to become terrorists. But there is a good deal of research about state terrorism. Political scientist R. J. Rummel estimates that nearly 170 million people have been killed by governments in the twentieth century (he calls this kind of terrorism "democide"). State terrorism has been responsible for four times more deaths than all the wars, civil and international, that occurred in the twentieth century. Regimes in the Soviet Union (1917–1987), China (1923–1987), and Germany (1933–1945) were responsible for killing more than a total of 100 million civilians. Proportionately the Khmer Rouge regime in Cambodia topped them all, killing over 30 percent of its population from 1975 to 1978.[64] What predicts state terrorism against one's own people? Rummel finds one clear predictor—totalitarian governments. By far they have the highest frequencies of domestic state terrorism, controlling for factors such as economic wealth, type of religion, and population size. As Rummel puts it, "power kills; absolute power kills absolutely."[65] Democratic countries are less likely to practice state terrorism, but when they do it occurs during or after a rebellion or a war.[66]

We know relatively little so far about what predicts who will become a terrorist. We do know that terrorists often come from higher social statuses and generally have more education than the average person.[67] If state terrorism is more likely to occur in totalitarian regimes, terrorists and terrorist groups may be more likely to occur in such societies. If so, the spread of democracy may be our best hope of minimizing the risk of terrorism in the world, just as the spread of democracy seems to minimize the likelihood of war between countries.

Making the World Better

Many social problems afflict our world, not just the ones discussed in this chapter.[68] We don't have the space to discuss the international trade in drugs and how it plays out in violence, death, and corruption. We haven't talked about the negative effects of environmental degradations such as water pollution, ozone depletion, and destruction of forests and wetlands. We haven't said much about overpopulation, refugees, the energy crisis, global warming, and a host of other problems that we should care about and do something about if we hope to make this a safer world. But we have tried in this chapter to encourage positive thinking about global issues; we have suggested how the results of past and future scientific research could be applied to solving some of those problems.

We may know enough now that we can do something about some of our problems, and we will discover more through future research. Social problems are mostly of human making and are therefore susceptible to human unmaking.

Summary

1. We may be more motivated now to try to solve social problems because worldwide communication has increased our awareness of them elsewhere, because we seem to be increasingly bothered by problems in our own society, and because we know more than we used to about various social problems that afflict our world.

2. The idea that we can solve global social problems is based on two assumptions. We have to assume that it is possible to discover the causes of a problem, and we have to assume that we will be able to do something about the causes once they are discovered and thereby eliminate or reduce the problem.

3. Disasters such as earthquakes, floods, and droughts can have greater or lesser effects on human life, depending on social conditions. Therefore disasters are partly social problems, with partly social causes and solutions.

4. Whether people become homeless, and whether there are shantytowns, seems to depend on a society's willingness to share wealth and to help those in need.

5. Promoting the equality of men and women and the sharing of child-rearing responsibilities may reduce family violence.

6. We may be able to reduce rates of violent crime if we can reduce socialization and training for aggression. To do that we would have to reduce the likelihood of war, the high likelihood of which predicts more socialization for aggression and other forms of socially approved aggression. The reduction of inequalities in wealth may also help to reduce crime, particularly theft. And raising boys with a male role model around may reduce the likelihood of male violence in adulthood.

7. People seem to be most likely to go to war when they fear unpredictable disasters that destroy food supplies or curtail the supplies of other necessities. Disputes between more participatory (more "democratic") political systems are unlikely to result in war. Therefore, the more democracy spreads in the world, and the more people all over the world are assured of internationally organized disaster relief, the more they might go to peace rather than to war to solve their problems.

8. Terrorism has occurred throughout history. State terrorism has killed more than all wars in the twentieth century and seems to be predicted mostly by totalitarianism.

Glossary Term

terrorism (p. 242)

Critical Questions

1. What particular advantages do anthropologists have in trying to solve practical problems?

2. Select one of the social problems discussed in this chapter and suggest what you think could be done to reduce or eliminate it.

3. Do global problems require solutions by global agencies? If so, which?

CHAPTER 12

APPLIED AND PRACTICING ANTHROPOLOGY

Chapter Outline

- Motives for Applying and Practicing Anthropology
- Ethics of Applied Anthropology
- Evaluating the Effects of Planned Change
- Difficulties in Instituting Planned Change
- Cultural Resource Management
- Forensic Anthropology
- Medical Anthropology

Anthropology is no longer a merely academic subject. One out of two anthropologists in the United States is employed outside of colleges and universities. This situation reflects an increasing realization that anthropology, what it has discovered and can discover about humans, is useful. Anthropologists who call themselves applied or practicing anthropologists are usually employed in nonacademic settings, working for government agencies, international development agencies, private consulting firms, public health organizations, medical schools, public interest law firms, community development agencies, charitable foundations, and even profit-seeking corporations. Why are so many anthropologists hired to help solve practical problems? In this chapter, we describe how anthropology has been, or could be, used to solve practical problems.

Applied or practicing anthropology as a profession is explicitly concerned with making anthropological knowledge useful. Many applied anthropologists participate in or evaluate programs intended to improve people's lives. Applied or practicing anthropologists may be involved in one or more phases of a program: assembling relevant knowledge, developing plans, assessing the likely social and environmental impact of particular plans, implementing the program, and monitoring the program and its effects.[1] And there are still other ways to use anthropology. One frequent type of applied work is **cultural resource management**, the "social impact" studies required by many government and private programs. For example, archaeologists are hired to study, record, and preserve "cultural resources" that will be disturbed or destroyed by construction projects. Another frequent and popular type of applied work is **forensic anthropology**—the use of anthropology to help solve crimes. And then there is **medical anthropology**, the application of anthropological knowledge to the study of health and illness. We devote the second half of this chapter to this fast-growing specialty.

Motives for Applying and Practicing Anthropology

Anthropologists have always cared and worried about the people they study, just as they care and worry about family and friends back home. It is upsetting if most of the families in your place of fieldwork have lost many of their babies to diseases that could be eliminated by medical care. It is upsetting when outside political and economic interests threaten to deprive your fieldwork friends of their resources and pride. Anthropologists have usually studied people who are disadvantaged—by imperialism, colonialism, and other forms of exploitation—and so it is no wonder that we feel protective about the people we have lived and shared with in the field.

A member of the Argentine Forensic Anthropology Team exhumes remains of one of the many "disappeared" Argentine civilians.

But caring is not enough to improve others' lives. We may need basic research that allows us to understand how a condition might be successfully treated. A particular proposed "improvement" might actually not be an improvement; well-meaning efforts have sometimes produced harmful consequences. And even if we know that a change would be an improvement, there is still the problem of how to make that change happen. The people to be affected may not want to change. Is it ethical to try to persuade them? And, conversely, is it ethical *not* to try? Applied anthropologists must take all of these matters into consideration in determining whether and how to act in response to a perceived need.

Applied anthropology in the United States developed out of anthropologists' personal experiences with disadvantaged people in other cultures.[2] Today anthropologists are also interested in studying and solving problems in our own society. Indeed, as noted earlier, there are as many anthropologists now working in nonacademic settings as in academic settings.[3] These practicing anthropologists often work on specific projects that aim to improve people's lives, usually by trying to change behavior or the environment; or the anthropologists monitor or evaluate efforts by others to bring about change.[4] Usually the problems and projects are defined by the employers or clients (the client is sometimes the "target" population), not by the anthropologists.[5] But anthropologists are increasingly called upon to participate in deciding exactly what improvements might be possible, as well as how to achieve them.

Ethics of Applied Anthropology

An anthropologist's first responsibility is to those who are being studied; everything should be done to ensure that their welfare and dignity will be protected. Anthropologists also have a responsibility to those who will read about their research; research findings should be reported openly and truthfully.[6] But because applied anthropology often deals with planning and implementing changes in some target population, ethical responsibilities can become complicated. Perhaps the most important ethical question is: Will the change truly benefit the target population?

In May 1946, the Society for Applied Anthropology established a committee to draw up a specific code of ethics for professional applied anthropologists. After many meetings and revisions, a statement on ethical responsibilities was finally adopted in 1948, and in 1983 the statement was revised.[7] According to the code, the target community should be included as much as possible in the formulation of policy, so that people in the community may know in advance how the program will affect them. Perhaps the most important aspect of the code is the pledge not to recommend or take any action that is harmful to the interests of the community. The National Association of Practicing Anthropologists goes further: If the work the employer expects of the employee violates the ethical principles of the profession, the practicing anthropologist has the obligation to try to change those practices or, if change cannot be brought about, to withdraw from the work.[8]

Thayer Scudder described the situation of Gwembe Tonga villagers who were relocated after a large dam was built in the Zambezi Valley of central Africa. Economic conditions improved during the 1960s and early 1970s, as the people increasingly produced goods and services for sale. But then conditions deteriorated. By 1980, the villagers were in a miserable state; rates of mortality, alcoholism, theft, assault, and murder were up. Why? One reason was that they had cut back on producing their own food in favor of producing for the world market. Such a strategy works well when world market prices are high; however, when prices fall, so does the standard of living.[9] The situation described by Scudder illustrates the ethical dilemma for many applied anthropologists. As he said: "So how is it that I can still justify working for the agencies that fund such projects?" He points out that large-scale projects are almost impossible to stop. The anthropologist can choose to stand on the sidelines and complain or try to influence the project to benefit the target population as much as possible.[10]

The problem described by Scudder comes about in part because the anthropologist is not often involved until after a decision is made to go ahead with a change program. This situation has begun to change as applied anthropologists are increasingly asked to participate in earlier stages of the planning process. Anthropologists are also increasingly asked to help in projects initiated by the affected party. Such requests may range from help in solving problems in corporate organizations to helping Native Americans with land claims. If the project is consistent with the wishes of the affected population, the results are not likely to put the anthropologist into an ethical dilemma.

Evaluating the Effects of Planned Change

The decision as to whether a proposed change would benefit the target population is not always easy to make. In certain cases, as when improved medical care is involved, the benefits offered to the target group would seem to be unquestionable—we all feel sure that health is better than illness. However, this may not always be true. Consider a public health innovation such as inoculation against disease. Although it would undoubtedly have a beneficial effect on the survival rate of a population, a reduction in the mortality rate might have unforeseen consequences that would in turn produce new problems. Once the inoculation program was begun, the number of children surviving would probably increase. But it might not be possible to increase the rate of food production, given the level of technology, capital, and land resources possessed by the target population. Thus, the death rate, because of starvation, might rise to its previous level and perhaps even exceed it. The inoculation program would not affect the death rate; it might merely change the causes of death. This example shows that even if a program of planned change has beneficial consequences in the short run, a great deal of thought and investigation have to be given to its longterm effects.

Debra Picchi raised questions about the long-term effects on the Bakairí Indians of a program by the National Brazilian Indian Foundation (FUNAI) to produce rice with machine technology.[11] The Bakairí of the Mato Grosso region largely practice slash-and-burn horticulture in gallery forests along rivers, with supplementary cattle raising, fishing, and hunting. In the early part of the twentieth century their population had declined to 150 people and they were given a relatively small reserve. Some of it was gallery forest, but a larger part was parched and infertile (*cerrado*). When the Bakairí population began to increase, FUNAI introduced a scheme to plant rice on formerly unused *cerrado* land, using machinery, insecticides, and fertilizer. FUNAI paid the costs for the first year and expected that by the third year the scheme would be self-supporting. The project did not go so well because FUNAI did not deliver all the equipment needed and did not provide adequate advice. So only half the expected rice was produced. Still, it was more food than the Bakairí had previously, so the program should have been beneficial to them.

But there were unanticipated negative side effects. Nutritionally, to be sure, the Bakairí are growing an additional starchy food. But use of the *cerrado* for agriculture reduces the area on which cattle can be grazed; cattle are an important source of high-quality protein. So the now-mechanized agriculture has reduced the availability of animal protein. The mechanization also makes the Bakairí more dependent on cash for fuel, insecticides, fertilizer, and repairs. But cash is hard to come by. Only some individuals can be hired—usually men with outside experience who have the required knowledge of machinery. So the cash earned in the now-mechanized agriculture goes mainly to a relatively small number of people. It is debatable whether the new inequalities of income provide long-term effects that are beneficial to most Bakairí.

These failures were not the fault of anthropologists—indeed, most instances of planned change by governments and other agencies usually have begun without the input of anthropologists at all. Applied anthropologists have played an important role in pointing out the problems with programs like these that fail to evaluate long-term consequences. Such evaluations are an important part of convincing governments and other agencies to ask for anthropological help in the first place.

Difficulties in Instituting Planned Change

Whether a program of planned change can be successfully implemented depends largely on whether the targeted population wants the proposed change and likes the proposed program. Before an attempt can be made at cultural innovation, the innovators must determine whether the target population is aware of the benefits of the proposed change. Lack of awareness can be a barrier to solving the problem at hand. For example, health workers have often had difficulty convincing people that they were becoming ill because something was wrong with their water supply. Many people do not believe that disease can be transmitted by water. At other times, the target population is perfectly aware of the problem. A case in point involved Taiwanese women who were introduced to family-planning methods beginning in the 1960s. The women knew they were having more children than they wanted or could easily afford, and they wanted to control their birth rate. They offered no resistance—they merely had to be given the proper devices and instructions, and the birth rate quickly fell to a more desirable, and more manageable, level.[12]

Resistance by the Target Population

Not all proposed change programs are beneficial to the target population. Sometimes resistance is rational. Applied anthropologists have pointed to cases where the judgment of the affected population has been better than that of the agents of change. One such example occurred during a Venezuelan government-sponsored program to give infants powdered milk. The mothers rejected the milk, even though it was free, on the grounds that it implied that the mothers' milk was no good.[13] But who is to say that the resistance was not in fact intuitively smart, reflecting an awareness that such a milk program would not benefit the children? Medical research now indicates quite clearly that mothers' milk is far superior to powdered milk or formula. First, human milk best supplies the nutrients needed for human development. Second, it is now known that the mother, through her milk, is able to transmit antibodies (disease resistances) to the baby. And third, nursing delays ovulation and usually increases the spacing between births.[14]

The switchover to powdered milk and formula in many underdeveloped areas has been nothing short of a disaster, resulting in increased malnutrition and misery. For one thing, powdered milk must be mixed with water, but if the water and the bottles are not sterilized, more sickness is introduced. Then, too, if powdered milk has to be purchased, mothers without cash are forced to dilute the milk to stretch it. And if a mother feeds her baby formula or powder for even a short time, the process is tragically irreversible, for her own milk dries up and she cannot return to breast-feeding even if she wants to.

As the Venezuelan example suggests, individuals may be able to resist proposed medical or health projects because acceptance is ultimately a personal matter. Large development projects planned by powerful governments or agencies rarely are stoppable, but even they can be resisted successfully. The Kayapo of the Xingu River region of Brazil were able to cancel a plan by the Brazilian government to build dams along the river for hydroelectric power. The Kayapo gained international attention when some of their leaders appeared on North American and European television and then successfully organized a protest in 1989 by members of several tribal groups. Their success seemed to come in part from their ability to present themselves to the international community as guardians of the rain forest—an image that resonated with international environmental organizations that supported their cause. Although to outsiders it might seem that the Kayapo want their way of life to remain as it was, the Kayapo are not opposed to all change. In fact, they want greater access to medical care, other government services, and manufactured goods from outside.[15]

Indians protest construction of a dam in their area.

But even if a project is beneficial to a population, it may still meet with resistance. Factors that may hinder acceptance can be divided roughly into three, sometimes overlapping, categories: *cultural, social,* and *psychological* barriers.

Cultural barriers are shared behaviors, attitudes, and beliefs that tend to impede the acceptance of an innovation. For example, members of different societies may view gift giving in different ways. Particularly in commercialized societies, things received for nothing are often believed to be worthless. When the government of Colombia instituted a program of giving seedling orchard trees to farmers in order to increase fruit production, the farmers showed virtually no interest in the seedlings, many of which proceeded to die of neglect. When the government realized that the experiment had apparently failed, it began to charge each farmer a nominal fee for the seedlings. Soon the seedlings became immensely popular and fruit production increased.[16] The farmers' demand for the seedlings may have increased because they were charged a fee and therefore came to value the trees. The market demand for fruit may also have increased.

It is very important for agents of change to understand what the shared beliefs and attitudes are. First, indigenous cultural concepts or knowledge can sometimes be used effectively to enhance educational programs. For instance, in a program in Haiti to prevent child mortality from diarrhea, change agents used the terminology for traditional native herbal tea remedies (*rafrechi,* or cool refreshment) to identify the new oral rehydration therapy, which is a very successful medical treatment. In native belief, diarrhea is a "hot" illness and appropriate remedies have to have cooling properties.[17] Second, even if indigenous beliefs are not helpful to the campaign, not paying attention to contrary beliefs can undermine the campaign. But uncovering contrary beliefs is not easy, particularly when they do not emerge in ordinary conversation. (Later in this chapter, concerning medical anthropology, we discuss cultural theories about illness more extensively.) The acceptance of planned change may also depend on social factors. Research suggests that acceptance is more likely if the change agent and the target or potential adopter are similar socially. But change agents may have higher social status and more education than the people they are trying to influence. So change agents may work more with higher-status individuals because they are more likely to accept new ideas. If lower-status individuals also have to be reached, change agents of lower status may have to be employed.[18]

Finally, acceptance may depend on psychological factors—that is, how the individuals perceive both the innovation and the agents of change. In the course of trying to encourage women in the southeastern

United States to breast-feed rather than bottle-feed their infants, researchers discovered a number of reasons why women were reluctant to breast-feed their infants, even though they heard it was healthier. Many women did not have confidence that they would produce enough milk for their babies; they were embarrassed about breast-feeding in public; and their family and friends had negative attitudes.[19] In designing an educational program, change agents may have to address such psychological concerns directly.

Discovering and Utilizing Local Channels of Influence

In planning a project involving cultural change, the administrator of the project should find out what the normal channels of influence are in the population. In most communities, there are preestablished networks for communication, as well as persons of high prestige or influence who are looked to for guidance and direction. An understanding of such channels of influence is extremely valuable when deciding how to introduce a program of change. In addition, it is useful to know at what times, and in what sorts of situations, one channel is likely to be more effective in spreading information and approval than another.

An example of the effective use of local channels of influence occurred when an epidemic of smallpox broke out in the Kalahandi district of the state of Orissa in India. The efforts of health workers to vaccinate villagers against the disease were consistently resisted. The villagers, naturally suspicious and fearful of these strange men with their equally strange medical equipment, were unwilling to offer themselves, and particularly their babies, to the peculiar experiments the strangers wished to perform. Afraid of the epidemic, the villagers appealed for help to their local priest, whose opinions on such matters they trusted. The priest went into a trance, explaining that the illness was the result of the goddess Thalerani's anger with the people. She could be appeased, he continued, only by massive feasts, offerings, and other demonstrations of the villagers' worship of her. Realizing that the priest was the village's major opinion leader, at least in medical matters, the frustrated health workers tried to get the priest to convince his people to undergo vaccination. At first, the priest refused to cooperate with the strange men, but when his favorite nephew fell ill, he decided to try any means available to cure the boy. He thereupon went into another trance, telling the villagers that the goddess wished all her worshippers to be vaccinated. Fortunately, the people agreed, and the epidemic was largely controlled.[20]

If channels of influence are not stable, using influential persons in a campaign can sometimes backfire. In the educational campaign in Haiti to promote the use of oral rehydration therapy to treat diarrhea in children, Mme. Duvalier, the first lady of Haiti at the time, lent her name to the project. Because there were no serious social or cultural barriers to the treatment and mothers reported that children took to the solutions well, success was expected. But in the middle of the campaign, Haiti became embroiled in political turmoil and the first lady's husband was overthrown. Some of the public thought that the oral rehydration project was a plot by the Duvaliers to sterilize children, and this suspicion fueled resistance.[21] Even after the Duvalier regime was toppled, people in Haiti were suspicious of any government-sponsored program.

Cultural Resource Management

Large-scale programs of planned change have an impact not only on living people. They can also have an impact on the archaeological record left by the ancestors of living people. Recovering and preserving the archaeological record before programs of planned change disturb or destroy it is called *cultural resource management (CRM)*. CRM work is carried out by archaeologists who are often called "contract archaeologists" because they typically work under contract to a government agency, a private developer, or a native group.

Commuters look at fourth century ruins uncovered as part of a large-scale CRM project associated with construction of the Athens metro system.

What kinds of impact can programs of planned change have on the archaeological record? In the 1960s a large number of hydroelectric dam projects were initiated to provide flood control and to bring a stable source of electrical power to developing nations. In Egypt a dam was built on the Nile River at a site called Aswan. Archaeologists realized that once the dam was in place a huge lake would form behind it, submerging thousands of archaeological sites, including the massive temple of Rameses II. Something needed to be done; the archaeological record had to be salvaged or protected. In the language of CRM, there needed to be a *mitigation plan* put into action. And there was. As the Aswan dam was being built, archaeologists went to work excavating sites that would be flooded. Archaeologists and engineers designed a way to take apart the temple of Rameses II and rebuild it, piece by piece, on higher ground where it would not be flooded. By the time the dam was completed in 1965, hundreds of sites had been investigated and two entire temple complexes moved.

Large-scale development projects are not the only projects that involve CRM archaeologists. In many nations, including the United States and Canada, historic preservation laws require any project receiving federal funds to ensure that archaeological resources are protected or their damage mitigated. Highway construction projects in the United States are common places to find CRM archaeologists at work. Virtually all highway projects rely on federal funding, and before a highway can be built a complete archaeological survey of the proposed right-of-way has to be made. If archaeological sites are found, potential damage to them must be mitigated. A CRM archaeologist will work with the construction company, the state archaeologist, and perhaps a federal archaeologist to decide on the best course of action. In some cases the archaeological site will be excavated. In others, the right-of-way may be moved. In still others, the decision is to allow the archaeological site to be destroyed, because it would be too costly to excavate or the site may not be significant enough to warrant excavation. Regardless of the decision, the CRM archaeologist plays a crucial role in assessing and protecting the archaeological record.

CRM archaeologists do not work only for state or federal agencies. In many nations today CRM archaeologists are also working with native peoples to protect, preserve, and manage archaeological materials for them. Indeed, archaeologist John Ravesloot recently stated that "the future of American archaeology is with Indian communities functioning as active, not passive, participants in the interpretation, management, and preservation of their rich cultural heritage."[22] One example of such a working relationship is the Zuni Heritage and Historic Preservation Office. During the 1970s the Pueblo of Zuni decided it needed to train tribal members in archaeology in order to ensure that Zuni cultural resources and properties were managed properly. It hired three professional archaeologists and, with additional assistance from the National Park Service and the Arizona State Museum, initiated a program to train and employ tribal members in cultural resource management. Working with these non-Zuni archaeologists, the Pueblo of Zuni was able to establish its own historic preservation office that today manages and coordinates all historic preservation on the Zuni reservation, a task that was managed by the federal government until 1992. The Pueblo also established the Zuni Cultural Resource Enterprise, a Zuni-owned CRM business that employs both Zuni and non-Zuni archaeologists and carries out contract archaeology projects both on and off the Zuni reservation.[23]

Cultural resource management is a growing field. Indeed, a 1994 survey conducted by the Society for American Archaeology showed that more than 25 percent of archaeologists in the United States were employed in private CRM firms working on federally funded contracts, and another 25 percent worked directly for state and federal agencies. Thus 50 percent of all employed archaeologists in the United States had jobs directly related to CRM.[24] As development and construction projects continue to affect the archaeological record, the need for well-trained CRM archaeologists is not likely to decline.

Forensic Anthropology

Many of us are fascinated by detective stories. We are interested in crimes and why they occur, and we like to read about them, fictional or not. Forensic anthropology is the specialty in anthropology that is devoted to solving crimes. It is attracting increasing attention by the public, and an increasing number of practitioners. One forensic anthropologist says she is called "the bone lady" by law enforcement personnel.[25] Like others in her line of work, she is asked to dig up or examine human bones to help solve crimes. Often the task is simple: Are these the bones of a man or woman? How old was the person? Forensic anthropologists can answer such questions fairly easily, particularly if the remains include most bones of the skeleton. Other times the question may be more difficult to answer. For example, can the forensic anthropologist say that a skull is probably from an Asian male? (The police suspect that the skeletal remains they found are from an Asian man who disappeared under mysterious circumstances five years before.) But it is difficult enough to assign an unambiguous "racial" classification to living persons. Bones alone are even more ambiguous because different features in the skeleton do not all vary in correlated ways, as we noted in our earlier discussion of "race" in the chapter on social stratification. Still, the forensic anthropologist can suggest whether the skeletal remains show a constellation of features typically associated with a particular region of the world. Sometimes the forensic anthropologist can suggest the cause of death when the law enforcement people are stumped.

Some cultural anthropologists have also done forensic work, often in connection with legal cases involving Native Americans. For example, Barbara Joans was asked in 1978 to advise the defense in a trial of six older Bannock-Shoshoni women from the Fort Hall reservation who were accused of fraud. They had received "supplemental security income (SSI)," which the social service agency claimed they had no right to receive because they had not reported receiving rent money on land that they owned. Joans presented evidence that the women, although they spoke some English, did not have enough proficiency to understand the nuances of what the SSI people told them. The judge agreed with the defense and ruled that in the future the SSI would have to use a Bannock-Shoshoni interpreter when they went to the reservation to describe the requirements of the program.[26]

In recent years, Clyde Snow and other forensic anthropologists have been called on to confirm horrendous abuses of human rights. Governments have been responsible for the systematic killing of their citizens, and forensic anthropologists have helped to bring the perpetrators to justice. For example, Snow and other forensic anthropologists helped to confirm that the military dictatorship in Argentina in the 1980s was responsible for the deaths of many Argentine civilians who had "disappeared." The forensic anthropologists were also able to determine the location of mass graves and the identity of victims of state-organized brutality in Guatemala. In addition to bringing the perpetrators to justice, confirming the massacres and identifying the victims help the families of the "disappeared" put their anguish behind them.

Medical Anthropology

Illness and death are significant events for people everywhere. No one is spared. So it should not be surprising that how people understand the causes of illness and death, how they behave, and what resources they marshal to cope with these events are extremely important. Some argue that we will never completely understand how to treat illness effectively until we understand the cultural behaviors, attitudes, values, and the larger social and political milieux in which people live. Others argue that society and culture have little to do with the outcome of illness—the reason that people die needlessly is that they do not get the appropriate medical treatment.

But anthropologists, particularly medical anthropologists, who are actively engaged in studying health and illness, are increasingly realizing that biological *and* social factors need to be considered if we are to reduce human suffering. For instance, some populations have an appalling incidence of infant deaths due to diarrhea. The origin of this situation is mostly biological, in the sense that the deaths are caused by bacterial infection. But why are so many infants exposed to those bacteria? Usually, the main reason is social. The affected infants are likely to be poor. Because they are poor, they are likely to live with infected drinking water. Similarly, malnutrition may be the biological result of a diet poor in protein, but such a diet is usually also a cultural phenomenon, reflecting a society with classes of people with very unequal access to the necessities of life. In many ways, therefore, medical anthropology, and anthropology in general, are developing in the direction of a "biocultural synthesis."[27]

Cultural Understandings of Health and Illness

Medical researchers and medical practitioners in the United States and other Western societies do not exist in a social vacuum. Many of their ideas and practices are influenced by the culture in which they live. We may think of medicine as purely based on "fact," but on reflection it is clear that many ideas stem from the culture in which the researchers reside. Consider the recent shift in attitudes toward birth. It was not so long ago in the United States that fathers were excluded from the birth, hospitals whisked the baby away from the mother and only brought the baby to her infrequently, and visitors (but not attending nurses and doctors) had to wear masks when holding the baby. Rationalizations were given for those practices, but looking back at them, they do not appear to be based on scientific evidence. Many medical anthropologists now argue that the *biomedical paradigm* (the system in which physicians are trained) itself needs to be understood as part of the culture.

Discovering the health-related beliefs, knowledge, and practices of a cultural group—its **ethnomedicine**—is one of the goals of medical anthropology. How do cultures view health and illness? What are their theories about the causes of illness? Do those theories impact on how illnesses are treated? What is the therapeutic process? Are there specialized medical practitioners, and how do they heal? Are there special medicines, and how are they administered? These are just some of the questions asked by the anthropological study of ethnomedicine.

Concepts of Balance or Equilibrium   In many cultures it is thought that the body should be kept in equilibrium or balance. The balance may be between hot and cold, or wet and dry, as in many cultures of Latin America and the Caribbean.[28] The notion of balance is not limited to opposites. For example, the ancient Greek system of medicine, stemming from Hippocrates, assumed that there were four "humors"—blood, phlegm, yellow bile, and black bile—that must be kept in balance. These humors have hot and cold and wet and dry properties. The Greek medical system was widely diffused in Europe and spread to parts of the Islamic world. In Europe, the humoral medical system was dominant until it was replaced by the germ theory in the 1900s.[29] In the Ayurvedic system, whose practice dates back 4,000 years in North India, Pakistan, Bangladesh, Sri Lanka, and in the Arab world, there are three humors (phlegm, bile, and flatulence), and a balance between hot and cold is also important.[30] The Chinese medical system, which dates back about 3,500 years, initially stressed the balance between the contrasting forces of *yin* and *yang* and later added the concept of humors, which were six in number in Chinese medicine.[31]

The concepts of hot and cold and *yin* and *yang* are illustrated in Emily Ahern's ethnographic description of the medical system of the Taiwanese Hokkien.[32] Both hot and cold substances are required by the body; when the body is out of balance, a lack of one substance can be restored by eating or drinking the missing substance. So, for example, when Ahern was faint with heat, she was told to drink some bamboo-shoot soup because it was "cold." In the winter, you need more hot substances; in the summer, you want fewer. Some people can tolerate more imbalance than others; the old, for instance, can tolerate less imbalance than the young. A loss of blood means a loss of heat. So, for a month after childbirth, women eat mostly a soup made of chicken, wine, and sesame oil—all "hot" ingredients. Hot things to eat are generally oily, sticky, or come from animals; cold things tend to be soupy, watery, or made from plants.

Supernatural Forces   The Taiwanese Hokkien believe that most illnesses have natural or physiological causes, but around the world it is more common to believe that illnesses are caused by supernatural forces. In fact, in a cross-cultural study of 139 societies, George P. Murdock found that only two societies did not have the belief that gods or spirits could cause illness, making such a belief a near-universal. And 56 percent of those sample societies thought that gods or spirits were the major causes of illness.[33] As we discussed in the chapter on religion and magic, sorcery and witchcraft are common in the world's societies. Although both sorcery and witchcraft are practiced by humans and may be used for good or evil, making people ill is one of their major uses. Illness can also be thought of as caused by the loss of one's soul,

In China and elsewhere, tai chi exercises are believed to bring harmony and balance.

fate, retribution for violation of a taboo, or contact with a polluting or tabooed substance or object. Sorcery is believed to be a cause of illness by most societies on all continents; retribution because of violation of a taboo is also very frequent in all but one region of the world. The belief that soul loss can cause illness is absent in the area around the Mediterranean, uncommon in Africa, infrequent in the New World and the Pacific, and has its highest frequency in Eurasia.[34]

On Chuuk (Truk), an atoll in the central Pacific, serious illnesses and death are mainly believed to be the work of spirits. Occasionally, the spirits of relatives are to blame, although they usually do not cause serious damage. More often, illness is caused by the spirit of a particular locality or a ghost on a path at night.[35] Nowadays, one of two therapeutic options or their combination is often chosen—hospital medicine or Chuuk medicine. Chuuk medical treatment requires a careful evaluation of symptoms by the patient and his or her relatives, because different spirits inflict different symptoms. If the symptom match is clear, the patient may choose an appropriate Chuuk medical formula to cure the illness. The patient may also ask whether he or she has done something wrong, and if so, what might point to the appropriate spirit and countervailing formula. For example, there is a taboo on having sexual relations before going to sea. If a person who violated this prohibition becomes ill, the reef spirits will be suspected. The Chuuk medical formula is supposed to cure illness quickly and dramatically. It is for this reason that Chuuk patients ask for a discharge from a hospital if their condition does not improve quickly. If treatment fails, the Chuukese believe that they need to reevaluate the diagnosis, sometimes with the aid of a diviner.[36] In contrasting their theories of illness to the American germ theory, the people of Chuuk point out that while they have seen ghosts, they have never seen the germs that Americans talk about. Using both methods, some people recover and some do not, so the ultimate cause is a matter of faith.[37]

The Biomedical Paradigm   In most societies, people simply think that their ideas about health and illness are true. Often it is not until they confront another medical system that people develop any awareness that there may be another way of viewing things. Western medical practice has spread widely. People with other medical systems have had to recognize that their ideas about health and illness may be considered deficient by Western practitioners, so it is often necessary to decide which course (Western or non-Western) to follow in dealing with illness. Change, however, is not entirely one-way. For example, for a long time the Chinese practice of acupuncture was disparaged by the Western medical profession, but now more medical practitioners are recognizing that acupuncture may provide effective treatment of certain conditions.

People treat themselves with herbal medicines bought from an herbalist in Ghana.

Most medical anthropologists use the term **biomedicine** to refer to the dominant medical paradigm in Western cultures today, with the *bio* part of the word emphasizing the biological emphasis of this medical system. As Robert Hahn points out, biomedicine appears to focus on specific diseases and cures for those diseases. Health is not the focus, as it is thought to be the *absence* of disease. Diseases are considered to be purely natural, and there is relatively little interest in the person or the larger social and cultural systems. Doctors generally do not treat the whole body but tend to specialize, with the human body partitioned into zones that belong to different specialties. Death is seen as a failure, and biomedical practitioners do everything they can to prolong life, regardless of the circumstances under which the patient would live his or her life.[38]

Treatment of Illness

Anthropologists who study diseases in this and other cultures can be roughly classified into two camps. First, there are those (the more relativistic) who think that the culture so influences disease symptoms, incidence, and treatment that there are few if any cultural universals about any illness. If each culture is unique, we should expect its conception and treatment of an illness to be unique too, not like beliefs and practices in other cultures. Second, there are those (the more universalistic) who see cross-cultural similarities in the conception and treatment of illness, despite the unique qualities (particularly in the belief system) of each culture. For example, native remedies may contain chemicals that are the same as, or similar in effect to, chemicals used in remedies by Western biomedicine.[39] The reader should note that our classification here of medical anthropologists is a crude one; many medical anthropologists do not fall unambiguously into one or the other group. And the reality might be that a given culture is very much like other cultures in some respects but unique in other respects.

In their extensive research on Maya ethnomedicine, Elois Ann Berlin and Brent Berlin make a strong case that although studies of the Maya have emphasized beliefs about illness that are based on supernatural causes, a good deal of Maya ethnomedicine is about natural conditions, their signs and symptoms, and the remedies used to deal with those conditions. In regard to gastrointestinal diseases, the Berlins found that the Maya have a wide-ranging and accurate understanding of anatomy, physiology, and symptoms. Furthermore, the remedies they use, including recommendations for food, drink, and herbal medicines, have properties that are not that different from those of the biomedical profession.[40]

Carole Browner also suggests that the emphasis on "hot-cold" theories of illness in Latin America has been overemphasized, to the neglect of other factors that influence choices about reproductive health and female health problems. In a study of the medical system in a highland Oaxacan community, Browner finds that certain plants are used to expel substances from the uterus—to facilitate labor at full term, to produce an abortion, or to induce menstrual flow. Other plants are used to retain things in the uterus—to prevent excess blood loss during menstruation, to help healing after delivery, and to prevent miscarriage. Most of these plant remedies appear to work.[41]

The biomedical establishment has become increasingly aware of the value of studying the "traditional" medicinal remedies discovered or invented by people around the world. In studying the indigenous medicines of the Hausa of Nigeria, Nina Etkin and Paul Ross asked individuals to describe the physical attributes of more than 600 plants and their possible medicinal uses, more than 800 diseases and symptoms, and more than 5,000 prepared medicines. While many medicines were used for treating sorcery, spirit aggression, or witchcraft, most medicines were used for illnesses regarded by the Hausa as having natural causes. Malaria is a serious endemic medical problem in the Hausa region, as in many areas of Africa. The Hausa use approximately 72 plant remedies for conditions connected with malaria—among them anemia, intermittent fever, and jaundice. Experimental treatment of malaria in laboratory animals supports the efficacy of many of the Hausa remedies. But perhaps the most important part of the Etkin and Ross findings is the role of diet. While most medical research does not consider the possible medical efficacy of the *foods* that people eat in combating illness, food is, of course, consumed in much larger quantities and more often than medicine. It is noteworthy, therefore, that the Hausa eat many plants with antimalarial properties; in fact, dietary consumption of these plants appears to be greatest during the time of year when the risk of malarial infection is at its highest. Recent research has also discovered that foods and spices like garlic, onions, cinnamon, ginger, and pepper have antiviral or antibacterial properties.[42]

Medical Practitioners   In our society we may be so used to consulting a full-time medical specialist (if we do not feel better quickly) that we tend to assume that biomedical treatment is the only effective medical treatment. If we are given a medicine, we expect it to have the appropriate medical effect and make us feel better. So many in the biomedical system, practitioners and patients alike, are perplexed by the seeming effectiveness of other medical systems that involve symbolic or ritual healing.

Illness may be viewed as being due to something being out of order in one's social life. The cause could be retribution for one's own bad behavior or thoughts, or the work of an angry individual practicing sorcery or witchcraft. Or a bad social situation or a bad relationship may be thought of as provoking physical symptoms because of anxiety or stress. In societies with occupational specialization, priests, who are formally trained full-time religious practitioners, may be asked to convey messages or requests for healing to higher powers.[43] Societies with beliefs in sorcery and witchcraft as causes of illness typically have practitioners who are believed to be able to use magic in reverse—that is, to undo the harm invoked by sorcerers and witches. Sometimes sorcerers or witches themselves may be asked to reverse illnesses caused by others. However, they may not be sought out because they are often feared and have relatively low status.[44] Shamans are perhaps the most important medical practitioners in societies lacking full-time occupational specialization.

After working with shamans in Africa, E. Fuller Torrey, a psychiatrist and anthropologist, concluded that they use the same mechanisms and techniques to cure patients as psychiatrists and achieve about the same results. He isolated four categories used by healers the world over:

1. **The naming process.**   If a disease has a name—"neurasthenia" or "phobia" or "possession by an ancestral spirit" will do—then it is curable; the patient realizes that the doctor understands his case.

2. **The personality of the doctor.**   Those who demonstrate some empathy, nonpossessive warmth, and genuine interest in the patient get results.

3. **The patient's expectations.**   One way of raising the patient's expectations of being cured is the trip to the doctor; the longer the trip, the easier the cure. An impressive setting (the medical center) and impressive paraphernalia (the stethoscope, the couch, attendants in uniform, the rattle, the whistle, the drum, the mask) also raise the patient's expectations. The healer's training is important: High fees also help to raise a patient's expectations. (The Paiute doctors always collect their fees before starting a cure; if they don't, it is believed that they will fall ill.)

4. **Curing techniques.**   Drugs, shock treatment, conditioning techniques, and so on have long been used in many different parts of the world.[45]

Biomedical research is not unaware of the effect of the mind on healing. In fact, considerable evidence has accumulated that psychological factors can be very important in illness. Patients who believe that medicine will help them often recover quickly even if the medicine is only a sugar pill or a medicine not particularly relevant to their condition. Such effects are called *placebo* effects.[46] Placebos do not just have psychological effects. Although the mechanisms are not well understood, they may also alter body chemistry and bolster the immune system.[47]

Shamans may coexist with medical doctors. Don Antonio, a respected Otomi Indian shaman in central Mexico, has many patients, perhaps not as many as before modern medicine, but still plenty. In his view, when he was born God gave him his powers to cure, but his powers are reserved for removing "evil" illnesses (those caused by sorcerers). "Good" illnesses can be cured by herbs and medicine, and he refers patients with those illnesses to medical doctors; he believes that doctors are more effective than he could be in those cases. The doctors, however, do not seem to refer any patients to Don Antonio or other shamans![48]

The most important full-time medical practitioner in the biomedical system is the physician, and the patient-physician relationship is central. In the ideal scheme of things, the physician is viewed as having the ability, with some limits, of being able to treat illness, alleviate suffering, and prolong the life of the patient, as well as offering promises of patient confidentiality and privacy. The patient relies on the physician's knowledge, skill, and ethics. Consistent with the biomedical paradigm, doctors tend to treat patients as having "conditions" rather than as complete persons. Physicians presumably rely on science for authoritative knowledge, but they place a good deal of importance on the value of their own clinical experience. Often physicians consider their own observations of the patient to be more valuable than the reports by the patient. Since patients commonly go to physicians to solve a particular condition or sickness, physicians tend to try to do something about it even in the face of uncertainty. Physicians tend to rely on technology for diagnoses and treatment and place relatively low value on talking with patients. In fact, physicians tend to give patients relatively little information, and they may not listen very well.[49]

Despite the importance of physicians in biomedicine, patients do not always seek physician care. In fact, one-third of the population of the United States regularly consults with alternative practitioners, such as acupuncturists or chiropractors, often unbeknown to the physician. Somewhat surprisingly, individuals with more education are more likely to seek alternative care.[50]

A Navajo medicine man performs a healing ceremony involving a snake painted on the ground.

Political and Economic Influences on Health

People with more social, economic, and political power in a society are generally healthier.[51] Inequality in health in socially stratified societies is not surprising. The poor usually have more exposure to disease because they live in more crowded conditions. And the poor are more likely to lack the resources to get quality care. For many diseases, health problems, and death rates, incidence or relative frequency varies directly with social class. In the United Kingdom, for example, people in the higher social classes are less likely to have headaches, bronchitis, pneumonia, heart disease, arthritis, injuries, and mental disorders, to name just a few of the differences.[52] Ethnic differences also predict health inequities. In South Africa under apartheid, the 14 percent minority population, referred to as "white," controlled most of the income of the country and most of the high-quality land. "Blacks" were restricted to areas with shortages of housing, inadequate housing, and little employment. To get a job, families often had to be disrupted; usually the husband would have to migrate to find work. "Blacks" lived, on average, about nine years less than "whites" in 1985 and "black" infants died at about seven times the rate of "white" infants. In the United States recently, the differences between African Americans and European Americans in health are not as stark as in South Africa, but those favoring European Americans are still substantial. As of 2004, the difference in life expectancy was approximately five years, and African-American infant mortality was about twice the rate for European American infants. Robert Hahn has estimated that poverty accounts for about 19 percent of the overall mortality in the United States.[53]

Inequities, because of class and ethnicity, are not limited to within-society differences. Power and economic differentials *between* societies also have profound health consequences. Over the course of European exploration and expansion, indigenous peoples died in enormous numbers from introduced diseases, wars, and conquests; they had their lands expropriated and diminished in size and quality. When incorporated into colonial territories or into countries, indigenous people usually become minorities and they are almost always very poor. These conditions of life not only affect the incidence of disease, they also tend to lead to greater substance abuse, violence, depression, and other mental pathologies.[54] Medical anthropologists have studied an enormous variety of health conditions and diseases. We focus here on AIDS and undernutrition.

AIDS

We may think that epidemics are a thing of the past. But the sudden emergence of the disease we call **AIDS (acquired immune deficiency syndrome)** reminds us that new diseases, or new varieties of old diseases, can appear at any time. Like all other organisms, disease-causing organisms also evolve. The human immunodeficiency virus (HIV) that causes AIDS emerged only a couple of decades ago. Viruses and bacteria are always mutating, and new strains emerge that are initially a plague on our genetic resistance and on medical efforts to contain them.

AIDS is a leading cause of death of people between the ages of 25 and 44 in the United States and Western Europe. It is the leading cause of adult death in many countries as well.[55] AIDS is a frightening epidemic not only because of its death toll. It is also frightening because it takes a long time (on average, four years) after exposure for symptoms to appear. This means that many people who have been infected by HIV but do not know they are infected may continue, unknowingly, to transmit the virus to others.[56]

Transmission occurs mostly via sexual encounters, through semen and blood. Drug users may also transmit HIV by way of contaminated needles. Transmission by blood transfusion has been virtually eliminated in this and other societies by medical screening of blood supplies. In many countries, however, there is still no routine screening of blood prior to transfusions. HIV may be passed from a pregnant woman to her offspring through the placenta and after birth through her breast milk. The rate of transmission between a mother and her baby is 20 to 40 percent. Children are also at great risk because they are likely to be orphaned by a parent's death from AIDS. At the turn of the twenty-first century approximately 14 million children were parentless because of AIDS.[57]

Many people think of AIDS as only a medical problem that requires only a medical solution, without realizing that there are behavioral, cultural, and political issues that need to be addressed as well. It is true that developing a vaccine or a drug to prevent people from getting AIDS and finding a permanent cure for those who have it will finally solve the problem. But, for a variety of reasons, we can expect that the medical solution alone will not be sufficient, at least not for a while. First, to be effective worldwide, or even within a country, a vaccine has to be inexpensive and relatively easy to produce in large quantities; the same is true of any medical treatment. Second, governments around the world have to be willing and able to spend the money and hire the personnel necessary to manage an effective program.[58] Third, future vaccination and treatment will require the people at risk to be willing to get vaccinated and treated, which is not always the case. Witness the fact that the incidence of measles is on the rise in the United States because many people are not having their children vaccinated.

There are now expensive drug treatments that significantly reduce the degree of HIV infection, but we do not know if an effective and inexpensive vaccine or treatment will be developed soon. In the meantime, the risk of HIV infection can be reduced only by changes in social, particularly sexual, behavior. But to persuade people to change their sexual behavior, it is necessary to find out exactly what they do sexually, and why they do what they do.

Research so far suggests that different sexual patterns are responsible for HIV transmission in different parts of the world. In the United States, England, northern Europe, Australia, and Latin America, the recipients of anal intercourse, particularly men, are the most likely individuals to acquire HIV infection; vaginal intercourse can also transmit the infection, usually from the man to the woman. Needle sharing can transmit the infection, too. In Africa, the most common mode of transmission is vaginal intercourse, and so women get infected more commonly in Africa than elsewhere.[59] In fact, in Africa there are slightly more cases of HIV in women as compared with men.[60]

A neighborhood self-help group in Tamil Nadu, India, collects rice for people with HIV and AIDS. Each member of the group puts aside one handful of rice every time she cooks a meal. The group members also contribute money to pay for drugs to treat neighbors with HIV and AIDs.

As of now, there are only two known ways to reduce the likelihood of sexual HIV transmission. One way is to abstain from sexual intercourse; the other is to use condoms. Educational programs that teach how AIDS spreads and what one can do about it may reduce the spread somewhat, but such programs may fail where people have incompatible beliefs and attitudes about sexuality. For example, people in some central African societies believe that deposits of semen after conception are necessary for a successful pregnancy and generally enhance a woman's health and ability to reproduce. It might be expected then that people who have these beliefs about semen would choose not to use condoms; after all, condoms in their view are a threat to public health.[61] Educational programs may also emphasize the wrong message. Promiscuity may increase the risk of HIV transmission, so hardly anyone would question the wisdom of advertising to reduce the number of sexual partners. And, at least in the homosexual community in the United States, individuals report fewer sexual partners than in the past. What was not anticipated, however, was that individuals in monogamous relationships, who may feel safe, are less likely to use condoms or to avoid the riskiest sexual practices. Needless to say, sex with a regular partner who is infected is not safe![62] In what may seem like something of a paradox, the United Nations observed that for most women in the world today, the major risk factor for being infected with HIV is being married.[63] It is not marriage, *per se,* that causes the risk of HIV infection; rather, the proximate cause may be the lower likelihood of condom use or abstinence between a husband and wife.

Undernutrition

What people eat is intrinsically connected to their survival and the ability of a population to reproduce itself, so we would expect that the ways people obtain, distribute, and consume food have been generally adaptive.[64] For example, the human body cannot synthesize eight amino acids. Meat can provide all of these amino acids, and combinations of particular plants can also provide them for a complete complement of protein. The combination of maize and beans in many traditional Native American diets, or *tortillas* and *frijoles* in Mexico, can provide all the needed amino acids. In places where wheat (often made into bread) is the staple, dairy products combined with wheat also provide complete protein.[65] Even the way that people have prepared for scarcity, such as breaking up into mobile bands, cultivating crops that can better withstand drought, and preserving food in case of famine, are probably adaptive practices in unpredictable environments. As we saw in the box on obesity, hypertension, and diabetes in the chapter on culture change and globalization, geneticists have proposed that populations in famine-prone areas may have had genetic selection for "thrifty genes"—genes that allow individuals to need a minimum of food and store the extra in fatty tissue to get them past serious scarcity.

Often the switch to commercial or cash crops has harmful effects on nutrition. As we noted in the chapter on culture change and globalization, when the farmer-herders of the arid region in northeastern Brazil started growing sisal, a drought-resistant plant used for making twine and rope, many of them abandoned subsistence agriculture. The small landholders used most of their land for sisal growing and when the price of sisal fell they had to work as laborers for others to try to make ends meet. Food then had to be mostly bought, but if a laborer or sisal grower didn't earn enough, there was not enough food for the whole family.

Analysis of allocation of food in some households by Daniel Gross and Barbara Underwood suggests that the laborer and his wife received adequate nutrition, but the children often received much less than required. Lack of adequate nutrition usually results in retarded weight and height in children. As is commonly the case when there is substantial social inequality, the children from lower-income

Cultures differ in what is considered beautiful. In many cultures, fat people are deemed more beautiful than thin people. Melvin Ember did fieldwork years ago on the islands of American Samoa. When he returned to the main island after three months on a distant island, he met with a Samoan chief. The chief said: "You look good. You gained weight." In reality, Ember had lost 30 pounds. The chief did not remember how heavy Ember had been, but clearly he thought that fat was better than thin. As another example, the Azawagh Arabs of Niger ensure that young girls become fat by sometimes forcing them to drink large quantities of milk-based porridge.

Worldwide, fatness is generally deemed more desirable than thinness, particularly for women. Fatness is valued in many cultures because it is seen as a marker of health, fertility, and higher status in societies with social stratification. This view is in strong contrast to the ideal in the United States and other Western societies, where fatness is thought to be unattractive and to reflect laziness, a lack of self-control, and poor health. Thinness, particularly in the upper classes, is considered beautiful. How can we explain these differences in what is considered beautiful?

People who have efficient metabolisms and can store calories in fatty tissue may be most apt to survive and reproduce in environments with famines or food shortages, so natural selection may favor "thrifty genes" in such environments. Would such societies also be likely to value fatness? Recent cross-cultural research suggests something more complicated. It appears that societies with unpredictable resources actually value thinness, particularly when they have no way of storing food. Shouldn't someone who stores calories on the body be better off than someone who is thin when facing starvation, particularly if there is no food storage? Perhaps, but ten thin people will generally consume less than ten heavier people, so there is a group advantage to being thin. Indeed, many societies with famine encourage fasting or eating light meals, as among the Gurage of Ethiopia. The strongest cross-cultural predictor of valuing fatness in women is "machismo" or "protest masculinity." Societies with a strong emphasis on male aggression, strength, and sexuality are the most likely to value fatness in women; those with little machismo value thinness. Why machismo is associated with valuing fatness in women is not clear. One suggestion is that machismo reflects male insecurity and fear of women. Macho men may not look for intimacy with their wives, but they may want to show how potent they are by having many children. If fatness suggests fertility, men may look for wives who are fatter. Along these lines, the ideal of thinness in women became common in North America with the rise of women's movements in the 1920s and late 1960s. Thin became more popular when women began to question early marriage and having many children.

Cultural beliefs about what is a beautiful body can impose pressures on females to achieve the ideal body type, whether it be fat or thin. In the United States and other Western countries, the effort to be thin can be carried to an extreme, resulting in the eating disorders anorexia and bulimia. Those who have these often fatal illnesses regularly eat little and regularly force themselves to throw up, thus depriving their bodies of nutrients in their quest to be thinner. The irony of "thinness" being idealized in the United States and other Western countries is that obesity is becoming more common in those societies. In 2001 the incidence of obesity increased in the United States to 31 percent and medical researchers worried about the increase in heart disease and diabetes. Whether or not obesity is a result of eating disorders is debatable. Researchers are finding biological causes of obesity, such as resistance to the hormone leptin, which regulates appetite, suggesting that much of the obesity "epidemic" has biological causes. Still, fast food, increasing sedentariness, and large portion sizes are probably contributing factors.

Sources: Peter J. Brown, "Culture and the Evolution of Obesity," in Aaron Podolefsky and Peter J. Brown, eds., *Applying Cultural Anthropology*, 4th ed. (Mountain View, CA: Mayfield, 1999), p. 100; Martha O. Loustaunau and Elisa J. Sobo, *The Cultural Context of Health, Illness, and Medicine* (Westport, CT: Bergin and Garvey, 1997), p. 85; Naomi Wolf, *The Beauty Myth* (New York: Morrow, 1991); Rebecca Popenoe, *Feeding Desire* (London: Routledge, 2004); Carol R. Ember, Melvin Ember, Andrey Korotayev, and Victor de Munck, "Valuing Thinness or Fatness in Women," *Evolution and Human Behavior*, 26 (2005): 257–70; J. L. Anderson, C. B. Crawford, J. Nadeau, and T. Lindberg, "Was the Dutchess of Windsor Right?" *Ethology and Sociobiology*, 13 (1992): 197–227; Jeffrey M. Friedman, "A War on Obesity, Not the Obese," *Science* (February 7, 2003), pp. 856–58.

Shown here is a sisal plant in Bahia, Brazil. The switch to sisal production led to undernutrition in children.

groups weigh substantially less than those from higher-income groups. But even though there were some economic differences before sisal production, the effects on nutrition appeared negligible before, judging from the fact that there was little or no difference in weight among adults from higher and lower socioeconomic positions who grew up prior to sisal production. But more recently, 45 percent of the children from lower economic groups were undernourished as compared with 23 percent of those children from the higher economic groups.[66]

This is not to say that commercialization is always deleterious to adequate nutrition. For example, in the Highlands of New Guinea there is evidence that the nutrition of children improved when families started growing coffee for sale. However, in this case the families still had land to grow some crops for consumption. The extra money earned from coffee enabled them to buy canned fish and rice, which provided children with higher amounts of protein than the usual staple of sweet potatoes.[67]

Nutritional imbalances for females have a far-reaching impact on reproduction and the health of the infants they bear. In some cultures, the lower status of women has a direct bearing on their access to food. While the custom of feeding males first is well known, it is less often realized that females end up with less nutrient-dense food such as meat. Deprivation of food sometimes starts in infancy where girl babies, as in India, are weaned earlier than boy babies.[68] Parents may be unaware that their differential weaning practice has the effect of reducing the amount of high-quality protein that girl infants receive. Indeed, in Ecuador, Lauris McKee found that parents thought that earlier weaning of girls was helpful to them. They believed that mothers' milk transmitted sexuality and aggression, both ideal male traits, to their infants and so it was important that girl babies be weaned early. Mothers weaned their girls at about 11 months and their boys about 20 months, a 9-month difference. McKee found that girl infants had a significantly higher mortality than boy infants in their second year of life, suggesting that the earlier weaning time for girls and their probable undernutrition may have been responsible.[69]

Applied and practicing anthropologists are not the only ones interested in solving problems. Many researchers in anthropology and the other social sciences do *basic research* on social problems. Such research may involve fieldwork to get a broad understanding of cultural ideas and practices about health, illness, or violence. Or basic research may involve testing theories about the possible causes of specific problems. The results of such tests could suggest solutions to the problems if the causes, once discovered, can be reduced or eliminated. It is often the case that basic research has unintended payoffs. Even if a study is not directed to a practical problem, it may end up suggesting a solution.

Summary

1. Applied, or practicing, anthropologists may be involved in one or more phases of programs that are designed to change peoples' lives: assembling relevant knowledge, constructing alternative plans, assessing the likely social and environmental impact of particular plans, implementing the programs, and monitoring the programs and their effects. Today many anthropologists are finding employment outside of anthropology departments—in medical schools, health centers, development agencies, urban-planning agencies, and other public and private organizations.

2. The code of ethics for those who work professionally as applied anthropologists specifies that the target population should be included as much as possible in the formulation of policy. The most important aspect of the code is the pledge not to be involved in any plan whose effect will not be beneficial. It is often difficult to evaluate the effects of planned changes. Long-term consequences may be detrimental even if the changes are beneficial in the short run.

3. Even if a planned change will prove beneficial to its target population, the people may not accept it. Target populations may reject or resist a proposed innovation for various reasons: because they are unaware of the need for the change; because they misinterpret the symbols used to explain the change or fail to understand its real purpose; because their customs and institutions conflict with the change; because they are afraid of it; or because they unconsciously or consciously know it is not good for them. To be effective, change agents may have to discover and use the traditional channels of influence in introducing their projects to the target population.

4. Cultural resource management (CRM) usually takes the form of "contract archaeology" to record and/or conserve the archaeology of a building site.

5. Forensic anthropology is the use of anthropology to help solve crimes.

6. Medical anthropologists suggest that biological and social factors need to be considered if we are to understand how to treat illness effectively and reduce the suffering in human life.

7. Researchers are finding evidence that many of the plant remedies used by indigenous peoples contain chemicals that are the same as, or similar in effect to, chemicals used in remedies by Western biomedicine.

8. People with more social, economic, and political power in a society are generally healthier.

9. Many people think of AIDS as only a medical problem that requires only a medical solution, without realizing that there are behavioral, cultural, and political issues that need to be addressed as well. It is true that developing a vaccine or a drug to prevent people from getting AIDS and finding a permanent cure for those who have it will finally solve the problem.

10. The ways that people obtain, distribute, and consume food have been generally adaptive. Geneticists have proposed that populations in famine-prone areas may have had genetic selection for "thrifty genes." Many of the serious nutritional problems of today are due to rapid culture change, particularly those making for an increasing degree of social inequality.

Glossary Terms

AIDS (acquired immune deficiency
     syndrome) (p. 260)
biomedicine (p. 257)
cultural resource management (CRM) (p. 246)

ethnomedicine (p. 254)
forensic anthropology (p. 246)
medical anthropology (p. 246)

Critical Questions

1.   What particular advantages do anthropologists have in trying to solve practical problems?

2.   Is it ethical to try to influence people's lives when they have not asked for help? Explain your answer.

3.   If you were interested in solving a practical problem, would you do basic or applied research on the problem? Why?

4.   Do people get sick just because they are exposed to germs?

5.   Why do native remedies often contain chemicals that are the same as, or similar in effect to, chemicals used in remedies by Western biomedicine?

GLOSSARY

Accent   Differences in pronunciation characteristic of a group.

Acculturation   The process of extensive borrowing of aspects of culture in the context of superordinate-subordinate relations between societies; usually occurs as the result of external pressure.

Adaptive customs   Customs that enhance survival and reproductive success in a particular environment. Usually applied to biological evolution, the term is also often used by cultural anthropologists to refer to cultural traits that enhance reproductive success.

Adjudication   The process by which a third party acting as judge makes a decision that the parties to a dispute have to accept.

AIDS (acquired immune deficiency syndrome)   A disease caused by the HIV virus.

Ambilineal descent   The rule of descent that affiliates individuals with groups of kin related to them through men or women.

Ancestor spirits   Supernatural beings who are the ghosts of dead relatives.

Anthropological linguistics   The anthropological study of languages.

Anthropology   A discipline that studies humans, focusing on the study of differences and similarities, both biological and cultural, in human populations. Anthropology is concerned with typical biological and cultural characteristics of human populations in all periods and in all parts of the world.

Applied (practicing) anthropology   The branch of anthropology that concerns itself with applying anthropological knowledge to achieve practical goals, usually in the service of an agency outside the traditional academic setting.

Archaeology   The branch of anthropology that seeks to reconstruct the daily life and customs of peoples who lived in the past and to trace and explain cultural changes. Often lacking written records for study, archaeologists must try to reconstruct history from the material remains of human cultures. *See* **Historical archaeology**.

Avunculocal residence   A pattern of residence in which a married couple settles with or near the husband's mother's brother.

Balanced reciprocity   Giving with the expectation of a straightforward immediate or limited-time trade.

Band   A fairly small, usually nomadic local group that is politically autonomous.

Band organization   The kind of political organization where the local group or band is the largest territorial group in the society that acts as a unit.

Bilateral kinship   The type of kinship system in which individuals affiliate more or less equally with their mother's and father's relatives.

Bilocal residence   A pattern of residence in which a married couple lives with or near either the husband's parents or the wife's parents.

Biological (physical) anthropology   The study of humans as biological organisms, dealing with the emergence and evolution of humans and with contemporary biological variations among human populations.

Biomedicine   The dominant medical paradigm in Western countries today.

Bride price   A substantial gift of goods or money given to the bride's kin by the groom or his kin at or before the marriage. Also called *bride wealth*.

Bride service   Work performed by the groom for his bride's family for a variable length of time either before or after the marriage.

Caste   A ranked group, often associated with a certain occupation, in which membership is determined at birth and marriage is restricted to members of one's own caste.

Chief A person who exercises authority, usually on behalf of a multicommunity political unit. This role is generally found in rank societies and is usually permanent and often hereditary.

Chiefdom A political unit, with a chief at its head, integrating more than one community but not necessarily the whole society or language group.

Clan A set of kin whose members believe themselves to be descended from a common ancestor or ancestress but cannot specify the links back to that founder; often designated by a totem. Also called a *sib*.

Class A category of persons who have about the same opportunity to obtain economic resources, power, and prestige.

Class society A society containing social groups that have unequal access to economic resources, power, and prestige.

Clines Gradients of varying frequencies.

Codeswitching Using more than one language in the course of conversing.

Codified laws Formal principles for resolving disputes in heterogeneous and stratified societies.

Commercialization The increasing dependence on buying and selling, with money usually as the medium of exchange.

Compatibility-with-child-care theory An explanation for the gender division of labor that suggests that women's work will typically involve tasks that do not take women far from home for long periods, do not place children in potential danger if they are taken along, and can be stopped and resumed if an infant needs care.

Complementary opposition The occasional uniting of various segments of a segmentary lineage system in opposition to similar segments.

Core vocabulary Nonspecialist vocabulary.

Corvée A system of required labor.

Crime Violence not considered legitimate that occurs within a political unit.

Cross-cousins Children of siblings of the opposite sex. One's cross-cousins are father's sisters' children and mother's brothers' children.

Cross-cultural researcher An ethnologist who uses ethnographic data about many societies to test possible explanations of cultural variation to discover general patterns about cultural traits—what is universal, what is variable, why traits vary, and what the consequences of the variability might be.

Cultural anthropology The study of cultural variation and universals in the past and present.

Cultural relativism The attitude that a society's customs and ideas should be viewed within the context of that society's problems and opportunities.

Cultural resource management (CRM) The branch of applied anthropology that seeks to recover and preserve the archaeological record before programs of planned change disturb or destroy it.

Culture The set of learned behaviors and ideas (including beliefs, attitudes, values, and ideals) that are characteristic of a particular society or population.

Descriptive (structural) linguistics The study of how languages are constructed.

Dialect A variety of a language spoken in a particular area or by a particular social group.

Diffusion The borrowing by one society of a cultural trait belonging to another society as the result of contact between the two societies.

Divination Getting the supernatural to provide guidance.

Double descent A system that affiliates an individual with a group of matrilineal kin for some purposes and with a group of patrilineal kin for other purposes. Also called *double unilineal descent*.

Dowry A substantial transfer of goods or money from the bride's family to the bride.

Economic resources Things that have value in a culture, including land, tools and other technology, goods, and money.

Economy-of-effort theory An explanation for the gender division of labor that suggests that it may be advantageous for a gender to do tasks that follow in a production sequence (e.g., those who cut lumber make wooden objects; those who quarry stone make stone objects); it may also be advantageous for one gender to perform tasks that are located near each other (e.g., child care and other chores done in or near the home).

Egalitarian society A society in which all persons of a given age-sex category have equal access to economic resources, power, and prestige.

Ego In the reckoning of kinship, the reference point or focal person.

Endogamy The rule specifying marriage to a person within one's own group (kin, caste, community).

Ethnicity The process of defining ethnicity usually involves a group of people emphasizing common origins and language, shared history, and selected aspects of cultural difference such as a difference in religion. Since different groups are doing the perceiving, ethnic identities often vary with whether one is inside or outside the group.

Ethnocentric   Refers to judgment of other cultures solely in terms of one's own culture.

Ethnocentrism   The attitude that other societies' customs and ideas can be judged in the context of one's own culture.

Ethnogenesis   The process of the creation of a new culture.

Ethnographer   A person who spends some time living with, interviewing, and observing a group of people to describe their customs.

Ethnography   A description of a society's customary behaviors and ideas.

Ethnohistorian   An ethnologist who uses historical documents to study how a particular culture has changed over time.

Ethnology   The study of how and why recent cultures differ and are similar.

Ethnomedicine   The health-related beliefs, knowledge, and practices of a cultural group.

Exogamy   The rule specifying marriage to a person from outside one's own group (kin or community).

Expendability theory   An explanation for the gender division of labor that suggests that men, rather than women, will tend to do the dangerous work in a society because the loss of men is less disadvantageous reproductively than the loss of women.

Explanation   An answer to a why question. In science, there are two kinds of explanations that researchers try to achieve: associations and theories.

Extended family   A family consisting of two or more single-parent, monogamous, polygynous, or polyandrous families linked by a blood tie.

Extensive (shifting) cultivation   A type of horticulture in which the land is worked for short periods and then left to regenerate for some years before being used again.

Family   A social and economic unit consisting minimally of a parent and a child.

Feuding   A state of recurring hostility between families or groups of kin, usually motivated by a desire to avenge an offense against a member of the group.

Fieldwork   Firsthand experience with the people being studied and the usual means by which anthropological information is obtained. Regardless of other methods (e.g., censuses, surveys) that anthropologists may use, fieldwork usually involves participant-observation for an extended period of time, often a year or more. *See* **Participant-observation**.

Food collection   All forms of subsistence technology in which food-getting is dependent on naturally occurring resources—wild plants and animals.

Food production   The form of subsistence technology in which food-getting is dependent on the cultivation and domestication of plants and animals.

Foragers   People who subsist on the collection of naturally occurring plants and animals. Also referred to as *hunter-gatherers* or *food collectors*.

Forensic anthropology   The use of anthropology to help solve crimes.

Fossils   The hardened remains or impressions of plants and animals that lived in the past.

Gender differences   Differences between females and males that reflect cultural expectations and experiences.

Gender roles   Roles that are culturally assigned to genders.

Gender stratification   The degree of unequal access by the different genders to prestige, authority, power, rights, and economic resources.

General-purpose money   A universally accepted medium of exchange.

Generalized reciprocity   Gift giving without any immediate or planned return.

Ghosts   Supernatural beings who were once human; the souls of dead people.

Globalization   The ongoing spread of goods, people, information, and capital around the world.

Gods   Supernatural beings of nonhuman origin who are named personalities; often anthropomorphic.

Group marriage   Marriage in which more than one man is married to more than one woman at the same time; not customary in any known human society.

Headman   A person who holds a powerless but symbolically unifying position in a community within an egalitarian society; may exercise influence but has no power to impose sanctions.

Historical archaeology   A specialty within archaeology that studies the material remains of recent peoples who left written records.

Historical linguistics   The study of how languages change over time.

Holistic   Refers to an approach that studies many aspects of a multifaceted system.

Homo sapiens   All living people belong to one biological species, *Homo sapiens,* which means that all human populations on earth can successfully interbreed. The first *Homo sapiens* may have emerged 100,000 years ago.

Horticulture   Plant cultivation carried out with relatively simple tools and methods; nature is allowed to replace nutrients in the soil, in the absence of permanently cultivated fields.

Human paleontology The study of the emergence of humans and their later physical evolution. Also called *paleoanthropology.*

Human variation The study of how and why contemporary human populations vary biologically.

Hunter-gatherers People who collect food from naturally occurring resources, that is, wild plants, animals, and fish. The phrase "hunter-gatherers" minimizes sometimes heavy dependence on fishing. Also referred to as *foragers.*

Hypotheses Predictions, which may be derived from theories, about how variables are related.

Incest taboo Prohibition of sexual intercourse or marriage between mother and son, father and daughter, and brother and sister.

Indirect dowry Goods given by the groom's kin to the bride (or her father, who passes most of them to her) at or before her marriage.

Intensive agriculture Food production characterized by the permanent cultivation of fields and made possible by the use of the plow, draft animals or machines, fertilizers, irrigation, water-storage techniques, and other complex agricultural techniques.

Kindred A bilateral set of close relatives.

Laws (scientific) Associations or relationships that are accepted by almost all scientists.

Lexical content Vocabulary or lexicon.

Lexicon The words and morphs, and their meanings, of a language; approximated by a dictionary.

Lineage A set of kin whose members trace descent from a common ancestor through known links.

Magic The performance of certain rituals that are believed to compel the supernatural powers to act in particular ways.

Maladaptive customs Customs that diminish the chances of survival and reproduction in a particular environment. Usually applied to biological evolution, the term is often used by cultural anthropologists to refer to behavioral or cultural traits that are likely to disappear because they diminish reproductive success.

Mana A supernatural, impersonal force that inhabits certain objects or people and is believed to confer success and/or strength.

Manumission The granting of freedom to a slave.

Market (commercial) exchange Transactions in which the "prices" are subject to supply and demand, whether or not the transactions occur in a marketplace.

Marriage A socially approved sexual and economic union, usually between a man and a woman, that is presumed by both the couple and others to be more or less permanent, and that subsumes reciprocal rights and obligations between the two spouses and between spouses and their future children.

Matrifocal family A family consisting of a mother and her children.

Matrilineal descent The rule of descent that affiliates individuals with kin of both sexes related to them through women only.

Matrilocal residence A pattern of residence in which a married couple lives with or near the wife's parents.

Measure To describe how something compares with other things on some scale of variation.

Mediation The process by which a third party tries to bring about a settlement in the absence of formal authority to force a settlement.

Medical Anthropology The application of anthropological knowledge to the study of health and illness.

Medium Part-time religious practitioner who is asked to heal and divine while in a trance.

Moiety A unilineal descent group in a society that is divided into two such maximal groups; there may be smaller unilineal descent groups as well.

Monogamy Marriage to only one spouse at a time, usually one man and one woman.

Monotheistic Believing that there is only one high god and that all other supernatural beings are subordinate to, or are alternative manifestations of, this supreme being.

Morph The smallest unit of a language that has a meaning.

Morpheme One or more morphs with the same meaning.

Morphology The study of how sound sequences convey meaning.

Negotiation The process by which the parties to a dispute try to resolve it themselves.

Neolocal residence A pattern of residence whereby a married couple lives separately, and usually at some distance, from the kin of both spouses.

Nonsororal polygyny Marriage of a man to two or more women who are not sisters.

Norms Standards or rules about acceptable behavior in a society. The importance of a norm usually can be judged by how members of a society respond when the norm is violated.

Nuclear family A family consisting of a married couple and their young children.

Oath The act of calling upon a deity to bear witness to the truth of what one says.

Operational definition A description of the procedure that is followed in measuring a variable.

Ordeal   A means of determining guilt or innocence by submitting the accused to dangerous or painful tests believed to be under supernatural control.

Paleoanthropology   *See* **Human paleontology**.

Parallel cousins   Children of siblings of the same sex. One's parallel cousins are father's brothers' children and mother's sisters' children.

Participant-observation   Living among the people being studied—observing, questioning, and (when possible) taking part in the important events of the group. Writing or otherwise recording notes on observations, questions asked and answered, and things to check out later are parts of participant-observation.

Pastoralism   A form of subsistence technology in which food-getting is based directly or indirectly on the maintenance of domesticated animals.

Patrilineal descent   The rule of descent that affiliates an individual with kin of both sexes related to him or her through men only.

Patrilocal residence   A pattern of residence in which a married couple lives with or near the husband's parents.

Peasants   Rural people who produce food for their own subsistence but who must also contribute or sell their surpluses to others (in towns and cities) who do not produce their own food.

Phone   A speech sound in a language.

Phoneme   A sound or set of sounds that makes a difference in meaning to the speakers of the language.

Phonology   The study of the sounds in a language and how they are used.

Phratry   A unilineal descent group composed of a number of supposedly related clans (sibs).

Polyandry   The marriage of one woman to more than one man at a time.

Polygamy   Plural marriage; marriage to more than one spouse simultaneously.

Polygyny   The marriage of one man to more than one woman at a time.

Polytheistic   Recognizing many gods, none of whom is believed to be superordinate.

Postpartum sex taboo   Prohibition of sexual intercourse between a couple for a period of time after the birth of their child.

Power   The ability to make others do what they do not want to do or influence based on the threat of force.

Prehistory   The time before written records.

Prestige   Being accorded particular respect or honor.

Priest   Generally a full-time specialist, with very high status, who is thought to be able to relate to superior or high gods beyond the ordinary person's access or control.

Primary subsistence activities   All of the food-getting activities: gathering, hunting, fishing, herding, and agriculture.

Primate   A member of the mammalian order *Primates,* including prosimians, monkeys, apes, and humans.

Primatologists   Persons who study primates.

Protolanguage   A hypothesized ancestral language from which two or more languages seem to have derived.

Race   In biology, race refers to a subpopulation or variety of a species that differs somewhat in gene frequencies from other varieties of the species. All members of a species can interbreed and produce viable offspring. Many anthropologists do not think that the concept of race is usefully applied to humans because humans do not fall into geographic populations that can be easily distinguished in terms of different sets of biological or physical traits. Thus, "race" in humans is largely a culturally assigned category.

Racism   The belief that some "races" are inferior to others.

Raiding   A short-term use of force, generally planned and organized, to realize a limited objective.

Rank society   A society that does not have any unequal access to economic resources or power but with social groups that have unequal access to status positions and prestige.

Reciprocity   Giving and taking (not politically arranged) without the use of money.

Redistribution   The accumulation of goods (or labor) by a particular person or in a particular place and their subsequent distribution.

Religion   Any set of attitudes, beliefs, and practices pertaining to supernatural power, whether that power rests in forces, gods, spirits, ghosts, or demons.

Revitalization movement   A religious movement intended to save a culture by infusing it with a new purpose and life.

Revolution   A usually violent replacement of a society's rulers.

Rules of descent   Rules that connect individuals with particular sets of kin because of known or presumed common ancestry.

Secondary subsistence activities   Activities that involve the preparation and processing of food either to make it edible or to store it.

Segmentary lineage system   A hierarchy of more and more inclusive lineages; usually functions only in conflict situations.

Sex differences   The typical differences between females and males that are most likely due to biological differences.

Sexually dimorphic   Refers to a species in which males differ markedly from females in size and appearance.

Shaman   A religious intermediary, usually part time, whose primary function is to cure people through sacred songs, pantomime, and other means; sometimes called witch doctor by Westerners.

Siblings   A person's brothers and sisters.

Slash-and-burn   A form of shifting cultivation in which the natural vegetation is cut down and burned off. The cleared ground is used for a short time and then left to regenerate.

Slaves   A class of persons who do not own their own labor or the products thereof.

Society   A group of people who occupy a particular territory and speak a common language not generally understood by neighboring peoples. By this definition, societies do not necessarily correspond to nations.

Sociolinguistics   The study of cultural and subcultural patterns of speaking in different social contexts.

Sorcery   The use of certain materials to invoke supernatural powers to harm people.

Sororal polygyny   The marriage of a man to two or more sisters at the same time.

Spirits   Unnamed supernatural beings of nonhuman origin who are beneath the gods in prestige and often closer to the people; may be helpful, mischievous, or evil.

State   A political unit with centralized decision making affecting a large population. Most states have cities with public buildings; full-time craft and religious specialists; an "official" art style; a hierarchical social structure topped by an elite class; and a governmental monopoly on the legitimate use of force to implement policies.

State organization   A society is described as having state organization when it includes one or more states.

Statistical association   A relationship or correlation between two or more variables that is unlikely to be due to chance.

Strength theory   An explanation for the gender division of labor suggesting that men's work typically involves tasks (like hunting and lumbering) requiring greater strength and greater aerobic work capacity.

Subculture   The shared customs of a subgroup within a society.

Supernatural   Believed to be not human or not subject to the laws of nature.

Symbolic communication   An arbitrary (not obviously meaningful) gesture, call, word, or sentence that has meaning even when its *referent* is not present.

Syntax   The ways in which words are arranged to form phrases and sentences.

Taboo   A prohibition that, if violated, is believed to bring supernatural punishment.

Terrorism   The use or threat of violence to create terror in others, usually for political purposes.

Theoretical construct   Something that cannot be observed or verified directly.

Theories   Explanations of associations or laws.

Totem   A plant or animal associated with a clan (sib) as a means of group identification; may have other special significance for the group.

Tribal organization   The kind of political organization in which local communities mostly act autonomously but there are kin groups (such as clans) or associations (such as age-sets) that can temporarily integrate a number of local groups into a larger unit.

Tribe   A territorial population in which there are kin or nonkin groups with representatives in a number of local groups.

Unilineal descent   Affiliation with a group of kin through descent links of one sex only.

Unilocal residence   A pattern of residence (patrilocal, matrilocal, or avunculocal) that specifies just one set of relatives that the married couple lives with or near.

Variable   A thing or quantity that varies.

Warfare   Violence between political entities such as communities, districts, or nations.

Witchcraft   The practice of attempting to harm people by supernatural means, but through emotions and thought alone, not through the use of tangible objects.

NOTES

CHAPTER 1

1. Harrison 1975; Durham 1991: 228–37.
2. J. Cohen 2007.
3. Chambers 1989, as referred to in Kushner 1991.
4. Miracle 2004; Kushner 1991.
5. Hempel 1965: 139.
6. J. Whiting 1964.
7. Nagel 1961: 88–89.
8. Ibid., pp. 83–90.
9. Ibid., p. 85. See also McCain and Segal 1988: 75–79.
10. McCain and Segal 1988: 62–64.
11. Caws 1969: 1378.
12. McCain and Segal: 56–57, 131–32.
13. J. Whiting 1964: 519–20.
14. McCain and Segal 1988: 67–69.
15. Blalock 1972: 15–20 and Thomas 1986: 18–28. See also M. Ember 1970: 701–703.
16. Ogburn 1922: 200–280.

CHAPTER 2

1. Linton 1945: 30.
2. See, for example, Holland and Quinn 1987: 4.
3. Sapir 1938, cited by Pelto and Pelto 1975: 1.
4. Pelto and Pelto 1975: 14–15.
5. de Waal 2001: 269.
6. Hewlett 2004.
7. Miner 1956: 504–505, reproduced by permission of the American Anthropological Association. Miner is not a foreign visitor but he wrote this description to show how these behaviors might be viewed from an outside perspective.
8. Lee 1972.
9. Hatch 1997.
10. Durkheim 1938 [originally published 1895]: 3.

11. Asch 1956.
12. Hall 1966: 159–60.
13. Ibid., p. 120.
14. Wagley 1974.
15. R. Brown 1965: 549–609.
16. Bernard 2001: 323.
17. Peacock 1986: 54.
18. Lawless et al. 1983: xi–xxi; Peacock 1986: 54–65.
19. Romney et al. 1986.
20. Bernard 2001: 190.
21. American Anthropological Association 1991.
22. Szklut and Reed 1991.
23. K. Hill and Hurtado 2004.
24. See Murdock and White 1969 for a description of the SCCS sample; sets of the HRAF Collection of Ethnography in paper and microfiche are found in academic libraries in the United States and elsewhere. Many of the cultures in paper and microfiche (along with some additional cultures) can be found in eHRAF World Cultures, available at over 300 libraries. The HRAF Collections, which together now include indexed full-text on about 400 cultures, are described at http://www.yale.edu/hraf; for a description of the available cross-cultural samples see C. R. Ember and M. Ember 2001: 76–88.

CHAPTER 3

1. Keller 1974 [originally published 1902], p. 34.
2. Wilden 1987: 124, referred to in Christensen, Hockey, and James 2001.
3. Lambert 2001.
4. Ekman and Keltner 1997: 32.
5. von Frisch 1962.
6. King 1999a; Gibson and Jessee 1999: 189–90.
7. Seyfarth and Cheney 1982: 242, 246.

8. Hockett and Ascher 1964.

9. T. S. Eliot 1963.

10. Snowdon 1999: 81.

11. Pepperberg 1999.

12. Mukerjee 1996: 28.

13. Savage-Rumbaugh 1992: 138–41.

14. J. H. Hill 1978: 94; J. H. Hill 2004.

15. Ibid.

16. Senner 1989b.

17. Chomsky 1975.

18. Southworth and Daswani 1974: 312. See also Boas 1964: 121–23.

19. Bickerton 1983.

20. Ibid., p. 122.

21. B. Berlin 1992; Hays 1994.

22. G. Miller 2004.

23. Gleitman and Wanner 1982; Blount 1981.

24. R. Brown 1980: 93–94.

25. de Villiers and de Villiers 1979: 48; see also Wanner and Gleitman 1982.

26. Bickerton 1983: 122.

27. E. Bates and Marchman 1988 as referred to by Snowdon 1999: 88–91.

28. Crystal 1971: 168.

29. Ibid., pp. 100–101.

30. R. L. Munroe, R. H. Munroe, and Winters 1996; M. Ember and C. R. Ember 1999. The theory about the effect of baby-holding on consonant-vowel alternation is an extension of the theory that regular baby-holding encourages a preference for regular rhythm in music; see Ayres 1973.

31. Sapir and Swadesh 1964: 103.

32. Geoffrey Chaucer 1926: 8. Our modern English translation is based on the glossary in that book.

33. Akmajian, Demers, and Harnish 1984: 356.

34. Baldi 1983: 3.

35. Ibid., p. 12.

36. Greenberg 1972; see also Phillipson 1976: 71.

37. Phillipson 1976: 79.

38. Trudgill 1983: 34.

39. Weinreich 1968: 31.

40. But see Thomason and Kaufman 1988 for a discussion of how grammatical changes due to contact may be more important than was previously assumed.

41. Berlin and Kay 1969.

42. Ibid.

43. Ibid., pp. 5–6.

44. Ibid., p. 104; Witkowski and Brown 1978.

45. Bornstein 1973: 41–101.

46. M. Ember 1978: 364–67.

47. Ibid.

48. C. H. Brown 1977.

49. C. H. Brown 1979.

50. Witkowski and Burris 1981.

51. Ibid.

52. C. H. Brown and Witkowski 1980: 379.

53. C. H. Brown 1984: 106.

54. Webb 1977: 42–49; see also Rudmin 1988.

55. Sapir 1931: 578; see also J. B. Carroll 1956.

56. Wardhaugh 2002: 222.

57. Denny 1979: 97.

58. Friedrich 1986.

59. Guiora et al. 1982.

60. Ibid., pp. 85–148.

61. Hymes 1974: 83–117.

62. Fischer 1958; Wardhaugh 2002: 160–88.

63. R. Brown and Ford 1961.

64. Wardhaugh 2002: 315.

65. Shibamoto 1987: 28.

66. Holmes 2001: 153.

67. Robin Lakoff 1973; Robin Lakoff 1990b.

68. Wardhaugh 2002: 328; Holmes 2001: 158–59; Trudgill 1983: 87–88.

69. Keenan 1989.

70. Tannen 1990: 49–83.

71. Wardhaugh 2002: 100.

72. Heller 1988: 1.

73. Pfaff 1979.

74. Wardhaugh 2002: 108.

75. Gal 1988: 249–55.

76. Collins and Blot 2003: 1–3.

CHAPTER 4

1. Hitchcock and Beisele 2000: 5.

2. C. R. Ember 1978b.

3. Schrire 1984a; Myers 1988.

4. The discussion of the Australian aborigines is based on R. A. Gould 1969.

5. Burbank 1994: 23; Burbank 2004b.

6. Data from Textor 1967 and Service 1979.

7. Murdock and Provost 1973: 207.

8. Palsson 1988; Roscoe 2002.

9. Keeley 1991.

10. R. L. Kelly 1995: 293–315.

11. Mitchell 2004; Tollefson 2004.

12. R. B. Lee 1968; DeVore and Konner 1974.

13. C. R. Ember 1978b.

14. McCarthy and McArthur 1960.

15. R. B. Lee 1979: 256–58, 278–80.

16. D. Werner 1978.

17. Textor 1967.
18. This section is largely based on Hames 2004.
19. Chagnon 1987: 60.
20. S. S. King 1979.
21. Hickey 1964: 135–65.
22. C. R. Ember 1983: 289.
23. Textor 1967; Dirks 2004; Messer 1996: 244.
24. Barlett 1989: 253–91.
25. The farm population is now so small that the Bureau of the Census has stopped counting it.
26. Salzman 1996.
27. Lees and Bates 1974; A. L. Johnson 2002.
28. Whitaker 1955; Itkonen 1951.
29. Paine 1994.
30. Textor 1967.
31. Dirks 2004.
32. Boserup 1993 [1965].
33. R. C. Hunt 2000.
34. Janzen 1973.
35. Roosevelt 1992.
36. Hoebel 1968: 46–63.
37. Woodburn 1968.
38. Pryor 2005: 36.
39. Leacock and Lee 1982a: 8.
40. R. Murphy 1960: 69, 142–43.
41. Salzman 1996.
42. Not all pastoralists have individual ownership. For example, the Tungus of northern Siberia have kin group ownership of reindeer. See Dowling 1975: 422.
43. Salzman 2002.
44. Bodley 1990: 77–93; Wilmsen 1989: 1–14.
45. Salzman 1996: 904–905.
46. Plattner 1989b: 379–96.
47. Hage and Powers 1992.
48. Steward and Faron 1959: 122–25.
49. B. B. Whiting and Edwards 1988: 164.
50. Nag, White, and Peet 1978: 295–96.
51. Polanyi 1957.
52. Sahlins 1972: 188–96.
53. L. Marshall 1961: 239–41.
54. The // sign in the name for the G//ana people symbolizes a click sound not unlike the sound we make when we want a horse to move faster.
55. Cashdan 1980: 116–20.
56. H. Kaplan, Hill, and Hurtado 1990.
57. Winterhalder 1990.
58. Mooney 1978.
59. Balikci 1970 quoted in Mooney 1978: 392.
60. Mooney 1978: 392.
61. Fehr and Fischbacher 2003, Ensminger 2002a; Henrich et al. n.d., as cited by Ensminger 2002a.
62. Angier 2002: F1, F8.
63. Abler 2004.
64. Service 1962: 145–46.
65. M. Harris 1974: 118–21.
66. Plattner 1985: viii.
67. Plattner 1985: xii.

CHAPTER 5

1. In an analysis of many native societies in the New World, Feinman and Neitzel (1984: 57) argue that egalitarian and rank societies ("tribes" and "chiefdoms," respectively) are not systematically distinguishable.
2. Fried 1967: 33.
3. Boehm 1993: 230–31; Boehm 1999.
4. M. G. Smith 1966: 152.
5. D. Mitchell 2004.
6. Drucker 1965: 56–64.
7. Service 1978: 249.
8. Sahlins 1958: 80–81.
9. Betzig 1988.
10. Brittain 1978.
11. Higley 1995: 1–47.
12. Argyle 1994.
13. Stille 2001: A17, A19.
14. Treiman and Ganzeboom 1990: 117; Featherman and Hauser 1978: 4, 481.
15. Argyle 1994: 36–37, 178.
16. S. R. Barrett 1994: 17, 41.
17. K. Phillips 1990; U.S. Bureau of the Census 1993; *New York Times International* 1997: A26; Johnston 1999: 16.
18. Durrenberger 2001b, who refers to Goldschmidt 1999 and Newman 1988, 1993.
19. Scott and Leonhardt 2005.
20. S. R. Barrett 1994: 17, 41.
21. Klass 2004.
22. Ruskin 1963: 296–314.
23. O. Lewis 1958.
24. Kristof 1995: A18.
25. For more information about caste in Japan, see Berreman 1973 and 1972: 403–14.
26. Kristof 1995; Kristof 1997.
27. For more information about caste in Rwanda, see Berreman 1973 and 1972.
28. "Book of the Year (1995): World Affairs: RWANDA," and "Book of the Year (1995): Race and Ethnic Relations: Rwanda's Complex Ethnic History," *Britannica Online,* December 1997.
29. Berreman 1960: 120–27.

30. O. Patterson 1982: vii–xiii, 105.

31. Pryor 1977: 219.

32. Euripides 1937: 52.

33. Nadel 1942.

34. Lassiter et al. 2004: 49–50.

35. Ibid., pp. 59–67.

36. Pryor 1977: 217–47.

37. Marks 1994: 33; Shanklin 1991: 15–17.

38. Molnar 1998: 19.

39. Brace et al. 1993: 17–19.

40. Brooks, Jackson, and Grinker 1993: 11.

41. Brace et al. 1993: 19.

42. J. Cohen 2007.

43. M. D. Williams 2004.

44. S. S. Friedman 1980: 206.

45. M. H. Ross 2004a.

46. Marks 1994: 32.

47. Armelagos and Goodman 1998: 365.

48. O. Patterson 2000.

49. M. Nash 1989: 2.

50. Ibid., p.10.

51. Barth 1994: 27.

52. Yinger 1994: 169.

53. Ibid., pp. 169–71.

54. Ibid., pp. 216–17.

55. Benjamin 1991; see also M. D. Williams 2004.

56. Flannery 1972.

57. Data from Textor 1967.

58. Ibid.

59. Lenski 1984: 308–18.

60. Treiman and Ganzeboom 1990: 117; Cutright 1967: 564.

61. Sahlins 1958.

62. Ibid., p. 4.

63. Sahlins 1972.

64. Lenski 1984.

65. Gilman 1990.

66. Fried 1967: 201ff; and Harner 1975.

67. Meek 1940: 149–50.

CHAPTER 6

1. Leibowitz 1978: 43–44.

2. Schlegel 1989: 266; Epstein 1988: 5–6; Chafetz 1990: 28.

3. Jacobs and Roberts 1989.

4. Segal 2004; Segal also cites the work of W. Williams 1992.

5. Lang 1999: 93–94; Blackwood 1984b.

6. Wikan 1982: 168–86.

7. Stini 1971.

8. Frayer and Wolpoff 1985: 431–32.

9. For reviews of theories and research on sexual dimorphism and possible genetic and cultural determinants of variation in degree of dimorphism over time and place, see Frayer and Wolpoff 1985 and Gray 1985: 201–209, 217–25.

10. J. K. Brown 1970b: 1074.

11. Among the Aché hunter-gatherers of Paraguay, women collect the type of honey produced by stingless bees (men collect other honey); this division of labor is consistent with the compatibility theory. See Hurtado et al. 1985: 23.

12. Murdock and Provost 1973: 213; Byrne 1994.

13. R. O'Brian 1999.

14. D. R. White, Burton, and Brudner 1977: 1–24.

15. Mukhopadhyay and Higgins 1988: 473.

16. J. K. Brown 1970b: 1073–78; and D. R. White, Burton, and Brudner 1977.

17. Nerlove 1974.

18. N. E. Levine 1988.

19. M. J. Goodman et al. 1985.

20. Noss and Hewlett 2001.

21. C. R. Ember 1983: 288–89.

22. Mead 1950 [originally published 1935]: 180–84.

23. Rivers 1967 [originally published 1906]: 567.

24. M. Ember and C. R. Ember 1971: 573, table 1.

25. Schlegel and Barry 1986.

26. Boserup 1970: 22–25; see also Schlegel and Barry 1986: 144–45.

27. Boserup 1970: 22–25.

28. Ibid., pp. 31–34.

29. C. R. Ember 1983: 286–87; data from Murdock and Provost 1973: 212; Bradley 1995.

30. C. R. Ember 1983.

31. Ibid.

32. Ibid., pp. 287–93.

33. M. Ember and C. R. Ember 1971: 579–80.

34. Ibid., p. 581; see also Sanday 1973: 1684.

35. Nerlove 1974.

36. Schlegel and Barry 1986.

37. Whyte 1978a: 217.

38. Nussbaum 1995: 2, based on data from Human Development Report 1993.

39. Whyte 1978a; D. B. Adams 1983.

40. J. K. Brown 1970a.

41. Sanday 1974; and Divale and Harris 1976.

42. Quinn 1977: 189–90.

43. Graham 1979.

44. D. Werner 1982; and Stogdill 1974, cited in ibid.; see also Handwerker and Crosbie 1982.

45. Draper 1975: 103.
46. D. Werner 1984.
47. M. H. Ross 1986.
48. This description is based on the fieldwork of Elizabeth and Robert Fearnea (1956–1958), as reported in M. K. Martin and Voorhies 1975: 304–31.
49. Begler 1978.
50. Ibid. See also Whyte 1978a: 229–32.
51. Whyte 1978b: 95–120; see also Quinn 1977.
52. Whyte 1978b: 124–29, 145; see also Sanday 1973.
53. Whyte 1978b: 129–30.
54. J. K. Brown 1970.
55. Whyte 1978b: 135–36.
56. Ibid., p. 135.
57. Doyle 2005.
58. Quinn 1977: 85; see also Etienne and Leacock 1980: 19–20.
59. B. B. Whiting and Edwards 1973.
60. R. L. Munroe et al. 2000: 8–9.
61. Maccoby and Jacklin 1974.
62. For a more extensive discussion of behavior differences and possible explanations of them, see C. R. Ember 1981.
63. B. B. Whiting and Edwards 1973.
64. For references to this research, see C. R. Ember 1981: 559.
65. Rubin, Provenzano, and Haskett 1974.
66. For a discussion of this evidence, see Ellis 1986: 525–27; C. R. Ember 1981.
67. For example, Ellis 1986 considers the evidence for the biological view of aggression "beyond reasonable dispute."
68. For a discussion of other possibilities, see C. R. Ember 1981.
69. Rohner 1976.
70. B. B. Whiting and Whiting 1975; see also B. B. Whiting and Edwards 1988: 273.
71. C. R. Ember 1973: 424–39.
72. B. B. Whiting and Edwards 1973: 175–79; see also Maccoby and Jacklin 1974.
73. Burbank 1994.
74. Heise 1967.
75. C. S. Ford and Beach 1951: 191.
76. O. Lewis 1951: 397.
77. Farley 1996: 60.
78. C. S. Ford and Beach 1951: 23–25, 68–71.
79. Ibid., pp. 40–41, 73.
80. Broude 2004b.
81. C. S. Ford and Beach 1951: 82–83.
82. Broude and Greene 1976.
83. Kluckhohn 1948: 101.

84. M. Hunt 1974: 254–57; Lewin 1994.
85. Broude 1980: 184.
86. C. S. Ford and Beach 1951: 114.
87. Jankowiak, Nell, and Buckmaster 2002.
88. Lang 1999: 97, citing Thomas 1993.
89. J. Morris 1938: 191.
90. Underhill 1938: 117, 186.
91. 'Abd Allah 1917: 7, 20.
92. Cardoso and Werner 2004.
93. R. C. Kelly 1974.
94. Cardoso and Werner 2004.
95. Blackwood and Wieringa 1999: 49; Blackwood 1984a.
96. Data from Textor 1967.
97. W. N. Stephens 1972: 1–28.
98. Broude 1976: 243.
99. D. Werner 1979; D. Werner 1975.
100. D. Werner 1979: 345–62; see also D. Werner 1975: 36.
101. Data from Textor 1967.
102. Schlegel 1991.

CHAPTER 7

1. W. N. Stephens 1963: 5.
2. Murdock 1949: 8.
3. Murdock 1949: 7–8.
4. Ibid., pp. 9–10.
5. See, for example, Linton, 1936: 135–36.
6. M. Ember and C. R. Ember 1979.
7. Ibid.
8. Marlowe 2003: 221–23.
9. M. Ember and C. R. Ember 1979.
10. Schlegel and Eloul 1987: 119.
11. Schlegel and Eloul 1988: 295, table 1. We used the data to calculate the frequency of various types of economic transaction in a worldwide sample of 186 societies.
12. Schlegel and Eloul 1988: 298–99.
13. Pryor 1977: 363–64.
14. Ibid.
15. Schlegel and Eloul 1988: 296–97.
16. Ibid.
17. Ibid.
18. Radcliffe-Brown 1922: 73.
19. Murdock 1967; Goody 1973: 17–21.
20. Pryor 1977: 363–65; Schlegel and Eloul 1988: 296–99.
21. Schlegel and Eloul 1988, following Goody 1973: 20.
22. Middleton 1962: 606.

23. Durham 1991: 293–94, citing research by Hopkins 1980.
24. A. Howard and Rensel 2004.
25. Lingenfelter 2004.
26. MacDonald and Hewlett 1999: 504–506.
27. M. Ember 1975: 262, table 3.
28. Busby 2004.
29. M. Ember 1975: 260–69; see also Durham 1991: 341–57.
30. Oliver 1955: 352–53.
31. Ibid., pp. 223–24, quoted in W. Stephens 1963: 58.
32. The discussion of these customs is based on W. Stephens 1963: 63–67.
33. Kilbride and Kilbride 1990: 202–206.
34. C. Anderson 2000: 102–103.
35. J. W. M. Whiting 1964.
36. M. Ember 1974b.
37. M. Ember 1984–1985. The statistical relationship between late age of marriage for men and polygyny was first reported by Witkowski 1975.
38. M. Ember 1974: 202–205.
39. M. Ember 1984–1985. For other predictors of polygyny, see D. R. White and Burton 1988.
40. Sellen and Hruschka 2004.
41. Low 1990b.
42. Coult and Habenstein 1965; Murdock 1957.
43. M. C. Goldstein 1987: 39.
44. Stephens 1963: 45.
45. Hiatt 1980.
46. M. C. Goldstein 1987. Formerly, in feudal Tibet, a class of serfs who owned small parcels of land also practiced polyandry. Goldstein suggests that a shortage of land would explain their polyandry too. See M. C. Goldstein 1971.
47. Pasternak 1976: 96.
48. Coult and Habenstein 1965.
49. Mead 1928, quoted in Stephens 1963: 134–35.
50. Nimkoff and Middleton 1960.
51. Pasternak, C. R. Ember, and M. Ember 1976: 109–23.
52. Coult and Habenstein 1965; Murdock 1957.
53. Percentages calculated from Coult and Habenstein 1965.
54. L. Bohannan and P. Bohannan 1953.
55. J. D. Freeman 1961.
56. C. R. Ember, M. Ember, and Pasternak 1974: 84–89.
57. Pospisil 1963.
58. Schneider 1961a.
59. M. Ember and C. R. Ember 1971: 581.
60. Schneider 1961b.

61. Goodenough 1951: 145.
62. Coult and Habenstein 1965.
63. Data from Textor 1967.
64. Davenport 1959.
65. M. Ember 1967.
66. M. Ember and C. R. Ember. 1971. See also Divale 1974.
67. M. Ember and C. R. Ember 1971: 583–85; and Divale 1974.
68. M. Ember and C. R. Ember 1971. For a different theory—that matrilocal residence precedes, rather than follows, the development of purely external warfare—see Divale 1974.
69. Helms 2004; see also M. Ember and C. R. Ember 1971
70. Service 1962: 137.
71. C. R. Ember and M. Ember 1972.
72. C. R. Ember 1975.
73. M. Ember 1974a.
74. Data from Textor 1967.
75. C. R. Ember, M. Ember, and Pasternak 1974.
76. The importance of warfare and competition as factors in the formation of unilineal descent groups is also suggested by Service 1962 and Sahlins 1961: 332–45.

CHAPTER 8

1. Service 1962.
2. Schrire 1984b; see also Leacock and Lee 1982: 8.
3. Service 1962: 109.
4. Mathiassen 1928: 213.
5. Service 1962: 114–15.
6. Bohannan 1954: 3.
7. Sahlins 1961: 342.
8. Sahlins 1961: 345.
9. N. Dyson-Hudson 1966: chapters 5 and 6.
10. Sahlins 1962: 293–94.
11. Sahlins 1963: 295.
12. Sahlins 1983: 519.
13. Sahlins 1963: 297.
14. Carneiro 1970: 733.
15. Weber 1947: 154.
16. Wiberg 1983.
17. Finley 1983.
18. Carcopino 1940: 18–20.
19. M. Ember 1963.
20. Textor 1967.
21. M. Ember 1963.

22. Textor 1967.

23. Naroll 1961. See also Ross 1981.

24. M. Ember 1963: 244–46.

25. Service 1962; see also Braun and Plog 1982; Haas 1990a.

26. A. Johnson and Earle 1987: 158; Carneiro 1990.

27. Service 1962: 112, 145.

28. Feinman and Nietzel 1984.

29. For a more detailed description and evaluation of the available theories, see chapter 11 in C. R. Ember, M. Ember, and Peregrine 2007. See also Cohen and Service 1978.

30. McNeill 1976.

31. Carneiro 1978: 215.

32. Textor 1967.

33. Carneiro 1978; Hart 1948; Naroll 1967; Marano 1973: 35–40. See also Peregrine, M. Ember, and C. R. Ember 2004 and other articles in Graber 2004.

34. D. Werner 1982.

35. Kracke 1979: 232.

36. D. Werner 1982.

37. Sahlins 1963.

38. Kracke 1979: 41.

39. Brandewie 1991.

40. Lepowsky 1990.

41. Ross 1988: 73. The discussion in this section draws mostly from ibid., pp. 73–89, and from Ross 2004b.

42. For studies of international relations that support these conclusions, see the citations in footnotes 2 and 3 in C. R. Ember, M. Ember, and Russett 1992; see also chapter 3 in Russett and Oneal 2001.

43. C. R. Ember, M. Ember, and Russett 1992.

44. Rummel 2002b.

45. Scaglion 2004b.

46. Hoebel 1968: 4, quoting S. P. Simpson and Field 1946: 858.

47. Fry and Björkqvist 1997.

48. D. Black 1993: 79–83.

49. Ross 1988.

50. Boas 1888: 668.

51. Otterbein 1986: 107.

52. Archer and Gartner 1984: 118–39.

53. Scaglion 2004b; D. Black 1993: 83–86.

54. Ibid.

55. Evans-Pritchard 1940: 291. The discussion of the Nuer follows this source.

56. Hickson 1986.

57. Ibid.; and Koch et al. 1977: 279.

58. J. M. Roberts 1967: 169.

59. Roberts 1967: 192.

60. Hoebel 1968: chapter 9.

61. Schwartz 1954: 475.

62. Textor 1967.

63. Masumura 1977: 388–99.

64. Scaglion 2004b; Black 1993; Newman 1983: 131.

65. C. R. Ember and M. Ember 1994.

66. Newman 1983: 131.

67. Otterbein and Otterbein 1965: 1476.

68. D. R. White 1988.

69. Patterson 1982: 345–52.

70. Gat 1999: 373, as referred to in Wadley 2003.

71. Heider 1970: 105–11; Heider 1979: 88–99.

72. M. Ember and C. R. Ember 1992: 188–89.

73. C. R. Ember and M. Ember 1992; M. Ember 1982. For a discussion of how Dani warfare seems to be motivated mainly by economic considerations, see Shankman 1991. B. W. Kang 2000: 878–79 finds a strong correlation between environmental stress and warfare frequency in Korean history.

74. Otterbein 1970.

75. C. R. Ember and M. Ember 1992; see also Otterbein 1970 and Loftin 1971.

76. C. R. Ember 1974.

77. Otterbein 1968: 283; Ross 1985.

78. Divale and Harris 1976: 521–38; see also Gibbons 1993.

79. C. R. Ember and M. Ember 1992: 251–52.

80. Russett and Oneal 2001: 89.

81. Ibid., pp. 145–48.

CHAPTER 9

1. A. Wallace 1966: 60–61.

2. Malefijt 1968: 153.

3. Ray 1954: 172–89.

4. Rosenblatt, Walsh, and Jackson 1976: 51.

5. Ibid., p. 55.

6. Swanson 1969: 97–108; see also Sheils 1975.

7. Middleton 1971: 488.

8. Spiro and D'Andrade 1958.

9. Lambert, Triandis, and Wolf 1959; Rohner 1975: 108.

10. H. G. Barnett 1960: 79–85.

11. Swanson 1969: 56.

12. Ibid., pp. 55–81; see also W. D. Davis 1971. Peregrine (1996: 84–112) replicated Swanson's finding for North American societies.

13. Textor 1967; R. Underhill 1975.

14. Geertz 1966.

15. Swanson 1969: 153–74.
16. A. Wallace 1966: 52–67.
17. J. Middleton 1971
18. Winkelman 1986: 178–83.
19. Bourguignon 1973a.
20. Bourguignon and Evascu 1977; Winkelman 1986: 196–98.
21. Kehoe and Giletti 1981.
22. Raybeck 1998, referring to Raybeck, Shoobe, and Grauberger 1989.
23. Bourguignon 2004: 572.
24. Winkleman and Peck 2004.
25. O. K. Moore 1957.
26. Sheils 1980.
27. M. Adler 1989: 4–5.
28. Evans-Pritchard 1979: 362–66.
29. Swanson 1969: 150; see also H. R. Trevor-Roper 1971: 444–49.
30. Swanson 1969: 150–51.
31. Caporael 1976; Matossian 1982; and Matossian 1989: 70–80. For possible reasons to dismiss the ergot theory, see Spanos 1983.
32. Harner 1972b.
33. B. B. Whiting 1950: 36–37; see also Swanson 1969: pp. 137–52, 240–41.
34. Winkelman 1986a.
35. Ibid., pp. 28–29.
36. Knecht 2003: 11.
37. Harner and Doore 1987: 3, 8–9; Noll 1987: 49; Krippner 1987: 128.
38. de Laguna 1972: 701C.
39. See Krippner 1987: 126–27; Noll 1987: 49–50.
40. Boas 1930 as reported in Lévi-Strauss 1963a: 169.
41. Boas 1930: 1–41, reported in Lévi-Strauss 1963b: 169–73.
42. Winkelman 1986: 27–28.
43. Ibid., p. 27.
44. Ibid., pp. 35–37.
45. M. Harris 1966.
46. A. Wallace 1966: 30.
47. A. Wallace 1970: 239.
48. The Quakers, long-time neighbors and trusted advisers of the Seneca, took pains not to interfere with Seneca religion, principles, and attitudes.
49. D. O. Larson, Johnson, and Michaelsen 1994.
50. Discussion is based on Firth 1970.
51. Ibid., p. 387.
52. Ibid., p. 418.
53. Antoun 2001.
54. Nagata 2001.
55. Antoun 2001: 17–18.
56. Ibid., p. 45.
57. Stark 1985; Trompf 1990.

CHAPTER 10

1. Linton 1936: 306.
2. Ibid., pp. 310–11.
3. Silver 1981.
4. Greenfield, Maynard, and Childs 2000.
5. Rogers 1983: 263–69.
6. Valente 1995: 21.
7. Linton 1936: 326–27.
8. G. M. Foster 1962: 26.
9. Bodley 1990: 7.
10. Pelto and Müller-Wille 1987: 207–43.
11. Bodley 1990: 38–41.
12. Schrauf 1999.
13. The historical information we refer to comes from a book by Nevins 1927. For how radical the American Revolution was, see Wood 1992.
14. Paige 1975.
15. Boyd and Richerson 1996: 106.
16. Ibid., p. 135.
17. D. T. Campbell 1965. See also Boyd and Richerson 1996 and Durham 1991.
18. McNeill 1967: 283–87.
19. See, e.g., Gross et al. 1979.
20. The description of Tikopia is based on Firth 1959: chapters 5, 6, 7, and 9, passim.
21. Most of this discussion is based on R. F. Murphy and Steward 1956.
22. Burkhalter and Murphy 1989.
23. E. Wolf 1966: 3–4.
24. Gross and Underwood 1971.
25. Russett 1993: 10–11, 14, 138.
26. Bernard and Pelto 1987a: 367.
27. Pelto and Müller-Wille 1987: 237.
28. J. D. Hill 1996a: 1.
29. Sattler 1996: 42.
30. Ibid., pp. 50–51.
31. Ibid., p. 54.
32. Ibid., pp. 58–59.
33. Bestor 2001: 76.
34. Trouillot 2001: 128.
35. Durrenberger 2001a; see also Hannerz 1996.
36. Traphagan and Brown 2002.
37. Trouillot 2001: 128.
38. Bradsher 2002: 3.
39. Yergin 2002: A29.
40. G. Thompson 2002: A3.

41. Sengupta 2002: A3.
42. Conklin 2002.
43. Kottak 1996: 136, 153.
44. Roosens 1989: 9.
45. Cashdan 2001.
46. C. R. Ember and Levinson 1991.

CHAPTER 11

1. The discussion in this section draws extensively from Aptekar 1994.
2. Information collected during M. Ember's fieldwork in American Samoa, 1955–1956.
3. Mellor and Gavian 1987.
4. Dirks 1993.
5. Torry 1986.
6. Hardoy and Satterthwaite 1987.
7. Rodwin and Sanyal 1987.
8. Mangin 1967.
9. Rodwin and Sanyal 1987; for a critique of self-help programs, see Ward 1982a.
10. A. Cohen and Paul Koegel 2004.
11. U.S. Department of Housing and Urban Development 2007.
12. A. Cohen and Koegel 2004.
13. Baxter and Hopper 1981: 30–33, 50–74.
14. Ibid.
15. A. Cohen and Koegel 2004.
16. Herrman 1990.
17. Barak 1991: 63–65.
18. Aptekar 1991: 326.
19. Ibid., pp. 326–49; Aptekar 1988.
20. Korbin 1981b: 4.
21. Straus 2001: 195–96.
22. Straus and Kantor 1994.
23. Straus 1995: 30–33; Straus and Kantor 1995.
24. "Children as Victims," 2000; "Violent Crime," 1994; "Prevalence, Incidence, and Consequences of Violence against Women," 1998; and Straus 1991.
25. Levinson 1989: 11–12, 44.
26. Minturn and Stashak 1982. Using a sociobiological orientation, a study by Daly and Wilson (1988: 43–59) also suggests that infanticide is largely due to the difficulty of raising the infant successfully.
27. Levinson 1989: 26–28.
28. C. R. Ember and M. Ember 2005; see also Petersen, Lee, and Ellis 1982, as cited in Levinson 1989: 63.
29. Lareau 2003: 230.
30. Levinson 1989: 31.

31. Ibid., p. 71.
32. Gelles and Straus 1988: 78–88.
33. Erchak 2004; Levinson 1989: 44–45.
34. Straus 2001: 187.
35. Straus and Yodanis 1996.
36. Levinson 1989: 104–107.
37. Archer and Gartner 1984: 35.
38. Archer and Gartner 1984: 63–97.
39. Gurr 1989a: 47–48.
40. Russell 1972; Eckhardt 1975; Sipes 1973.
41. C. R. Ember and M. Ember 1994.
42. Archer and Gartner 1984: 118–39.
43. Bacon, Child, and Barry 1963; B. B. Whiting 1965.
44. Barber 2000.
45. C. R. Ember and M. Ember 1994: 625.
46. C. R. Ember and M. Ember 1993: 227.
47. C. A. Anderson and Bushman 2002: 2377; J. G. Johnson et al. 2002.
48. Loftin, McDowall, and Boudouris 1989; Krahn, Hartnagel, and Gartrell 1986, as referred to in Daly and Wilson, 1988: 287–88; Gartner 2004.
49. C. R. Ember and M. Ember 1997.
50. Most of the discussion in this section comes from M. Ember and C. R. Ember 1992: 204–206.
51. Meggitt 1977: 201; Gat 1999: 563–83.
52. Data from Korea is consistent with this explanation of war: More environmental stress strongly predicts higher frequencies of warfare in Korea between the first century B.C. and the eighth century A.D. B. W. Kang 2000: 878.
53. For the cross-cultural results suggesting the theory of war described here, see C. R. Ember and M. Ember 1992.
54. For the results on political participation and peace in the ethnographic record, see C. R. Ember, M. Ember, and Russett 1992. For the results on political participation and peace in the modern world, see the references in that essay.
55. Russett and Oneal 2001: 49.
56. Ibid., pp. 125ff.
57. Some of these examples are from Henderson 2001.
58. See the discussions in ibid., pp. 3–9, and S. K. Anderson and Sloan 2002: 1–5.
59. S. K. Anderson and Sloan 2002: 465.
60. This definition is adapted from Chomsky, who is quoted in Henderson 2001: 5.
61. S. K. Anderson and Sloan 2002: 6–7.
62. Ibid., pp. 6–8.
63. Suárez-Orozco 1992.
64. Rummel 2002a.
65. R. J. Rummel 2002c.

66. R. J. Rummel 2002d.
67. S. K. Anderson and Sloan 2002: 422.
68. "Crossroads for Planet Earth" 2005.

CHAPTER 12

1. Kushner 1991.
2. Mead 1978: 426–29.
3. Frankel and Trend 1991: 177.
4. Hackenberg 1988: 172.
5. Kushner 1991.
6. "Appendix C: Statements on Ethics . . . 2002" and "Appendix I: Revised Principles . . . 2002."
7. "Appendix A: Report of the Committee on Ethics . . . 2002" and "Appendix F: Professional and Ethical Responsibilities . . . 2002."
8. "Appendix H: National Association of Practicing Anthropologists' Ethical Guidelines . . . 2002."
9. Scudder 1978.
10. Ibid., pp. 204ff.
11. Picchi 1991: 26–38; for a more general description of the Bakairi, see Picchi 2004.
12. Niehoff 1966: 255–67.
13. G. M. Foster 1969: 8–9.
14. Jelliffe and Jelliffe 1975.
15. W. H. Fisher 1994.
16. G. M. Foster 1969: 122–23.
17. Coreil 1989: 149–50.
18. Rogers 1983: 321–31.
19. Bryant and Bailey 1990.
20. Niehoff 1966: 219–24.
21. Coreil 1989: 155.
22. Ravesloot 1997: 174.
23. Anyon and Ferguson 1995.
24. Zeder 1997.
25. Manhein 1999.
26. Joans 1997.
27. A. H. Goodman and Leatherman 1998; Kleinman, Das, and Lock 1997.
28. Rubel and Hass 1996: 120; Loustaunau and Sobo 1997: 80–81.
29. Loustaunau and Sobo 1997: 82–83, referring to Magner 1992: 93.
30. Loustaunau and Sobo 1997, referring to Gesler 1991: 16.
31. Loustaunau and Sobo 1997, referring to C. Leslie 1976: 4; and G. Foster 1994: 11.
32. Ahern 1975: 92–97, as appearing in eHRAF World Cultures on the Web.

33. Murdock 1980: 20.
34. C. C. Moore 1988.
35. T. Gladwin and Sarason 1953: 64–66.
36. Mahony 1971: 34–38, as seen in eHRAF World Cultures on the Web.
37. Gladwin and Sarason 1953: 65.
38. Hahn 1995: 133–39.
39. For an exhaustively documented presentation of the more universalistic approach, see E. A. Berlin and Berlin 1996; see also Browner 1985; and Rubel, O'Nell, and Collado-Ardón 1984.
40. E. A. Berlin 1996.
41. Browner 1985; Ortiz de Montellano and Browner 1985.
42. Etkin and Ross 1997.
43. Loustaunau and Sobo 1997: 98–101.
44. Winkelman 1986a.
45. Torrey n.d.
46. Loustaunau and Sobo 1997: 101–102; and Moerman 1997.
47. Loustaunau and Sobo 1997: 102.
48. Dow 1986: 6–9, 125.
49. Hahn 1995: 131–72.
50. Ibid., p. 165.
51. For a discussion of some of the relevant research, see ibid., pp. 80–82.
52. Mascie-Taylor 1990: 118–21.
53. See references in Hahn 1995: 82–87; National Center for Health Statistics 2006.
54. A. Cohen 1999.
55. Herdt 1997: 3–22.
56. Bolton 1989.
57. Reported in Carey et al. 2004: 462.
58. Bolton 1989.
59. Carrier and Bolton 1991; Schoepf 1988: 625, cited in Carrier and Bolton 1991.
60. Simmons, Farmer, and Schoepf 1996: 64.
61. Schoepf 1988: 637–38.
62. Bolton 1992.
63. Farmer 1997: 414. Married men in Thailand are gradually turning away from commercial sex and having affairs with married women who are believed to be safe; see Lyttleton 2000: 299.
64. Quandt 1996.
65. McElroy and Townsend 2000.
66. Gross and Underwood 1971.
67. McElroy and Townsend 2002: 187, referring to Harvey and Heywood 1983: 27–35.
68. Quandt 1996: 277.
69. McKee 1984: 96.

REFERENCES

'Abd Allah, Mahmud M. 1917. "Siwan Customs." *Harvard African Studies,* 1: 1–28.

Abler, Thomas S. 2004. "Iroquois: The Tree of Peace and the War Kettle." In *Portraits of Culture,* in C. R. Ember, M. Ember, and N. Peregrine, eds., *New Directions in Anthropology.* Upper Saddle River, NJ: Prentice Hall, CD-ROM.

Adams, David B. 1983. "Why There Are So Few Women Warriors." *Behavior Science Research,* 18: 196–212.

Adler, Mortimer. 1986. *Drawing Down the Moon.* Boston: Beacon.

Ahern, Emily M. 1975. "Sacred and Secular Medicine in a Taiwan Village: A Study of Cosmological Disorders." In A. Kleinman et al., eds., *Medicine in Chinese Cultures: Comparative Studies of Health Care in Chinese and Other Societies.* Washington, D.C.: U.S. Department of Health, Education, and Welfare, National Institutes of Health, as seen in eHRAF World Cultures on the Web.

Akmajian, Adrian, Richard A. Demers, and Robert M. Harnish. 1984. *Linguistics: An Introduction to Language and Communication.* 2nd ed. Cambridge, MA: MIT Press.

Akmajian, Adrian, Richard A. Demers, and Robert M. Harnish. 2001. *Linguistics: An Introduction to Language and Communication.* 5th ed. Cambridge, MA: MIT Press.

Allen, John S., and Susan M. Cheer. 1996. "The Non-Thrifty Genotype." *Current Anthropology,* 37: 831–42.

Alvarez, Lizette. 2003. "Arranged Marriages Get a Little Rearranging," *The New York Times,* June 22, 2003, p. 1.3.

American Anthropological Association. 1991. "Revised Principles of Professional Responsibility, 1990." In C. Fluehr-Lobban, ed, *Ethics and the Profession of Anthropology: Dialogue for a New Era.* Philadelphia: University of Pennsylvania Press, pp. 274–79.

Anderson, Connie M. 2000. "The Persistence of Polygyny as an Adaptive Response to Poverty and Oppression in Apartheid South Africa." *Cross-Cultural Research,* 34: 99–112.

Anderson, J. L., C. B. Crawford, J. Nadeau, and T. Lindberg. 1992. "Was the Duchess of Windsor Right? A Cross-Cultural Review of the Socioecology of Ideal Female Body Shape." *Ethnology and Sociobiology,* 13: 197–227.

Anderson, Sean K., and Stephen Sloan. 2002. *Historical Dictionary of Terrorism.* 2nd ed. Lanham, MD: Scarecrow Press.

Angier, Natalie. 2002. "Why We're So Nice: We're Wired to Cooperate." Science Times in *The New York Times,* July 23, 2002, pp. F1, F8.

Antoun, Richard T. 2001. *Understanding Fundamentalism: Christian, Islamic, and Jewish Movements.* Walnut Creek, CA: AltaMira Press.

Anyon, Roger, and T. J. Ferguson. 1995. "Cultural Resources Management at the Pueblo of Zuni, New Mexico, USA." *Antiquity,* 69: 913–30.

"Appendix A: Report of the Committee on Ethics, Society for Applied Anthropology." 2002. In C. Fluehr-Lobban, ed., *Ethics and the Profession of Anthropology.* Philadelphia: University of Pennsylvania Press.

"Appendix C: Statements on Ethics: Principles of Professional Responsibility, Adopted by the Council of the American Anthropological Association, May 1971." 1991. In C. Fluehr-Lobban, ed., *Ethics and the Profession of Anthropology.* Philadelphia: University of Pennsylvania Press.

"Appendix F: Professional and Ethical Responsibilities, SfAA." 2002. In C. Fluehr-Lobban, ed., *Ethics and the Profession of Anthropology.* Philadelphia: University of Pennsylvania Press.

"Appendix H: National Association of Practicing Anthropologists' Ethical Guidelines for Practitioners, 1988."

1991. In C. Fluehr-Lobban, ed., *Ethics and the Profession of Anthropology.* Philadelphia: University of Pennsylvania Press.

Aptekar, Lewis. 1988. *Street Children of Cali.* Durham, NC: Duke University Press.

Aptekar, Lewis. 1991. "Are Colombian Street Children Neglected? The Contributions of Ethnographic and Ethnohistorical Approaches to the Study of Children." *Anthropology and Education Quarterly,* 22: 326–49.

Aptekar, Lewis. 1994. *Environmental Disasters in Global Perspective.* New York: G. K. Hall/Macmillan.

Archer, Dane, and Rosemary Gartner. 1984. *Violence and Crime in Cross-National Perspective.* New Haven, CT: Yale University Press.

Argyle, Michael. 1994. *The Psychology of Social Class.* New York: Routledge.

Armelagos, George J., and Alan H. Goodman. 1998. "Race, Racism, and Anthropology." In A. H. Goodman and T. L. Leatherman, eds., *Building a New Biocultural Synthesis: Political-Economic Perspectives on Human Biology.* Ann Arbor: University of Michigan Press.

Armstrong, Robert P. 1982. *The Powers of Presence.* Philadelphia: University of Pennsylvania Press.

Asch, Solomon. 1956. "Studies of Independence and Conformity: A Minority of One against a Unanimous Majority." *Psychological Monographs,* 70: 1–70.

"Association Business: Clyde Snow, Forensic Anthropologist, Works for Justice." *Anthropology News* (October 2000): 12.

Bacon, Margaret, Irvin L. Child, and Herbert Barry, III. 1963. "A Cross-Cultural Study of Correlates of Crime." *Journal of Abnormal and Social Psychology,* 66: 291–300.

Bailey, Robert C., Genevieve Head, Mark Jenike, Bruce Owen, Robert Rectman, and Elzbieta Zechenter. 1989. "Hunting and Gathering in Tropical Rain Forest: Is It Possible?" *American Anthropologist,* 91: 59–82.

Baldi, Philip. 1983. *An Introduction to the Indo-European Languages.* Carbondale, IL: Southern Illinois University Press.

Balikci, Asen. 1970. *The Netsilik Eskimo.* Garden City, NY: Natural History Press.

Banton, Michael, ed. 1966. *Anthropological Approaches to the Study of Religion.* Association of Social Anthropologists of the Commonwealth, Monograph No. 3. New York: Praeger.

Barak, Gregg. 1991. *Gimme Shelter: A Social History of Homelessness in Contemporary America.* New York: Praeger.

Barber, Nigel. 2000. "The Sex Ratio as a Predictor of Cross-National Variation in Violent Crime." *Cross-Cultural Research,* 34: 264–82.

Barber, Nigel. 2003. "Paternal Investment Prospects and Cross-National Differences in Single Parenthood." *Cross-Cultural Research,* 37: 163–77.

Barlett, Peggy F. 1989. "Industrial Agriculture." In S. Plattner, ed., *Economic Anthropology.* Stanford, CA: Stanford University Press.

Barnett, H. G. 1960. *Being a Palauan.* New York: Holt, Rinehart & Winston.

Barrett, Stanley R. 1994. *Paradise: Class, Commuters, and Ethnicity in Rural Ontario.* Toronto: University of Toronto Press.

Barth, Fredrik. 1994. "Enduring and Emerging Issues in the Analysis of Ethnicity." In H. Vermeulen and C. Govers, eds., *The Anthropology of Ethnicity.* Amsterdam: Het Spinhuis.

Bates, E., and V. A. Marchman. 1988. "What Is and Is Not Universal in Language Acquisition." In F. Plum, ed., *Language, Communication, and the Brain.* New York: Raven Press, pp. 19–38.

Baxter, Ellen, and Kim Hopper. 1981. *Private Lives/Public Spaces: Homeless Adults on the Streets of New York City.* New York: Community Service Society of New York.

Beattie, John. 1960. *Bunyoro: An African Kingdom.* New York: Holt, Rinehart & Winston.

Begler, Elsie B. 1978. "Sex, Status, and Authority in Egalitarian Society." *American Anthropologist,* 80: 571–88.

Benjamin, Lois. 1991. *The Black Elite: Facing the Color Line in the Twilight of the Twentieth Century.* Chicago: Nelson-Hall.

Berlin, Brent. 1992. *Ethnobiological Classification: Principles of Categorization of Plants and Animals in Traditional Societies.* Princeton, NJ: Princeton University Press.

Berlin, Brent, and Paul Kay. 1969. *Basic Color Terms: Their Universality and Evolution.* Berkeley: University of California Press.

Berlin, E. A. 1996. "General Overview of Maya Ethnomedicine." In E. A. Berlin and B. Berlin, *Medical Ethnobiology of the Highland Maya of Chiapas, Mexico.* Princeton, NJ: Princeton University Press, pp. 52–53.

Berlin, Elois Ann, and Brent Berlin. 1996. *Medical Ethnobiology of the Highland Maya of Chiapas, Mexico: The Gastrointestinal Diseases.* Princeton, NJ: Princeton University Press.

Bernard, H. Russell. 1994. *Research Methods in Cultural Anthropology: Qualitative and Quantitative Approaches.* 2nd ed. Newbury Park, CA: Sage.

Bernard, H. Russell, and Pertti J. Pelto. 1987a. "Technology and Anthropological Theory: Conclusions." In H. R. Bernard and P. J. Pelto, eds., *Technology and Social Change.* 2nd ed. Prospect Height, IL: Waveland.

Bernard, H. Russell, and Pertti J. Pelto, eds. 1987b. *Technology and Social Change*. 2nd ed. Prospect Heights, IL: Waveland.

Berreman, Gerald D. 1960. "Caste in India and the United States." *American Journal of Sociology,* 66: 120–27.

Berreman, Gerald D. 1972. "Race, Caste and Other Invidious Distinctions in Social Stratification." *Race,* 13: 403–14.

Berreman, Gerald D. 1973. *Caste in the Modern World.* Morristown, NJ: General Learning Press.

Bestor, Theodore C. 2001. "Supply-Side Sushi: Commodity, Market, and the Global City." *American Anthropologist,* 103: 76–95.

Betzig, Laura. 1988. "Redistribution: Equity or Exploitation?" In L. Betzig, M. Borgerhoff Mulder, and P. Turke, eds., *Human Reproductive Behavior.* Cambridge: Cambridge University Press, pp. 49–63.

Bickerton, Derek. 1983. "Creole Languages." *Scientific American* (July): 116–22.

Bindon, James R., and Douglas E. Crews. 1993. "Changes in Some Health Status Characteristics of American Samoan Men: Preliminary Observations from a 12-Year Follow-up Study." *American Journal of Human Biology,* 5: 31–37.

Bindon, James R., Amy Knight, William W. Dressler, and Douglas E. Crews. 1997. "Social Context and Psychosocial Influences on Blood Pressure among American Samoans." *American Journal of Physical Anthropology,* 103: 7–18.

Binford, Lewis R. 1971. "Post-Pleistocene Adaptations." In S. Struever, ed., *Prehistoric Agriculture.* Garden City, NY: Natural History Press.

Black, Donald. 1993. *The Social Structure of Right and Wrong.* San Diego, CA: Academic Press.

Blackwood, Evelyn. 1984a. *Cross-Cultural Dimensions of Lesbian Relations.* Master's thesis, San Francisco State University. As referred to in Blackwood and Wieringa 1999.

Blackwood, Evelyn. 1984b. "Sexuality and Gender in Certain Native American Tribes: The Case of Cross-Gender Females." *Signs,* 10: 27–42.

Blackwood, Evelyn and Saskia E. Wieringa. 1999. "Sapphic Shadows: Challenging the Silence in the Study of Sexuality." In E. Blackwood and S. E. Weiringa, eds., *Female Desires: Same-Sex Relations and Transgender Practices Across Cultures.* New York: Columbia University Press, pp. 39–63.

Blalock, Hubert M., Jr. 1972. *Social Statistics.* 2nd ed. New York: McGraw-Hill.

Blount, Ben G. 1981. "The Development of Language in Children." In R. H. Munroe, R. L. Munroe, and B. B. Whiting, eds., *Handbook of Cross-Cultural Human Development.* New York: Garland.

Blount, Ben G., ed. 1995. *Language, Culture, and Society; A Book of Readings.* 2nd ed. Prospect Heights, IL: Waveland.

Blumler, Mark A., and Roger Byrne. 1991. "The Ecological Genetics of Domestication and the Origins of Agriculture." *Current Anthropology,* 32: 23–35.

Boas, Franz. 1888. *Central Eskimos.* Bureau of American Ethnology Annual Report No. 6. Washington, D.C.

Boas, Franz. 1930. *The Religion of the Kwakiutl.* Columbia University Contributions to Anthropology, vol. 10, pt. 2. New York: Columbia University.

Boas, Franz. 1964 [1911]. "On Grammatical Categories." In D. Hymes, ed., *Language in Culture and Society.* New York: Harper & Row.

Bodley, John H. 1990. *Victims of Progress.* 3rd ed. Mountain View, CA: Mayfield.

Boehm, Christopher. 1993. "Egalitarian Behavior and Reverse Dominance Hierarchy." *Current Anthropology,* 34: 230–31.

Boehm, Christopher. 1999. *Hierarchy in the Forest: The Evolution of Egalitarian Behavior.* Cambridge, MA: Harvard University Press.

Bogoras, Waldemar. 1909. "The Chukchee." Pt. 3. *Memoirs of the American Museum of Natural History,* 2.

Bohannan, Laura, and Paul Bohannan. 1953. *The Tiv of Central Nigeria.* London: International African Institute.

Bohannan, Paul. 1954. "The Migration and Expansion of the Tiv." *Africa,* 24: 2–16.

Bolton, Ralph. 1989. "Introduction: The AIDS Pandemic, a Global Emergency." *Medical Anthropology,* 10: 93–104.

Bolton, Ralph. 1992. "AIDS and Promiscuity: Muddled in the Models of HIV Prevention." *Medical Anthropology,* 14: 145–223.

"Book of the Year (1995): World Affairs: RWANDA," and "Book of the Year (1995): Race and Ethnic Relations: Rwanda's Complex Ethnic History." *Brittanica Online,* December.

Bornstein, Marc H. 1973. "The Psychophysiological Component of Cultural Difference in Color Naming and Illusion Susceptibility." *Behavior Science Notes,* 8: 41–101.

Boserup, Ester. 1993 [1965]. *The Conditions of Agricultural Growth: The Economics of Agrarian Change under Population Pressure.* Toronto: Earthscan Publishers.

Boserup, Ester. 1970. *Woman's Role in Economic Development.* New York: St. Martin's Press.

Bourguignon, Erika. 1973. "Introduction: A Framework for the Comparative Study of Altered States of Consciousness." In E. Bourguignon, *Religion, Altered*

States of Consciousness, and Social Change. Columbus: Ohio State University Press.

Bourguignon, Erika. 2004. "Suffering and Healing, Subordination and Power: Women and Possession Trance." *Ethos,* 32: 557–74.

Bourguignon, Erika, and Thomas L. Evascu. 1977. "Altered States of Consciousness within a General Evolutionary Perspective: A Holocultural Analysis." *Behavior Science Research,* 12: 197–216.

Boyd, Robert, and Peter J. Richerson. 1996. [1985]. *Culture and the Evolutionary Process.* Chicago: University of Chicago Press.

Brace, C. Loring, David P. Tracer, Lucia Allen Yaroch, John Robb, Kari Brandt, and A. Russell Nelson. 1993. "Clines and Clusters versus 'Race': A Test in Ancient Egypt and the Case of a Death on the Nile." *Yearbook of Physical Anthropology,* 36: 1–31.

Bradley, Candice. 1995. "Keeping the Soil in Good Heart: Weeding, Women and Ecofeminism." In K. Warren, ed., *Ecofeminism.* Bloomington: Indiana University Press.

Bradsher, Keith. 2002. "Pakistanis Fume as Clothing Sales to U.S. Tumble." *The New York Times,* June 23, p. 3.

Brandewie, Ernest. 1991. "The Place of the Big Man in Traditional Hagen Society in the Central Highlands of New Guinea." In F. McGlynn and A. Tuden, eds., *Anthropological Approaches to Political Behavior.* Pittsburgh, PA: University of Pittsburgh Press, pp. 62–82.

Braun, David P., and Stephen Plog. 1982. "Evolution of 'Tribal' Social Networks: Theory and Prehistoric North American Evidence." *American Antiquity,* 47: 504–25.

Bringa, Tone. 1995. *Being Muslim the Bosnian Way: Identity and Community in a Central Bosnian Village.* Princeton, NJ: Princeton University Press, as examined in eHRAF World Cultures on the Web.

Brittain, John A. 1978. *Inheritance and the Inequality of Material Wealth.* Washington, D.C.: Brookings Institution.

Brooks, Alison S., Fatimah Linda Collier Jackson, and R. Richard Grinker. 1993. "Race and Ethnicity in America." *Anthro Notes* (National Museum of Natural History Bulletin for Teachers), 15, no. 3: 1–3, 11–15.

Broude, Gwen J. 1976. "Cross-Cultural Patterning of Some Sexual Attitudes and Practices." *Behavior Science Research,* 11: 227–62.

Broude, Gwen J. 1980. "Extramarital Sex Norms in Cross-Cultural Perspective." *Behavior Science Research,* 15: 181–218.

Broude, Gwen J. 2004. "Variations in Sexual Attitudes, Norms, and Practices." In *Cross-Cultural Research for Social Science,* in C. R. Ember, M. Ember, and P. N. Peregrine, eds., *New Directions in Anthropology.* Upper Saddle River, NJ: Prentice Hall, CD-ROM.

Broude Gwen J., and Sarah J. Greene. 1976. "Cross-Cultural Codes on Twenty Sexual Attitudes and Practices." *Ethnology,* 15: 409–29.

Brown, Cecil H. 1977. "Folk Botanical Life-Forms: Their Universality and Growth." *American Anthropologist,* 79: 317–42.

Brown, Cecil H. 1979. "Folk Zoological Life-Forms: Their Universality and Growth." *American Anthropologist,* 81: 791–817.

Brown, Cecil H. 1984. "World View and Lexical Uniformities." *Reviews in Anthropology,* 11: 99–112.

Brown, Cecil H., and Stanley R. Witkowski. 1980. "Language Universals." Appendix B in D. Levinson and M. J. Malone, eds., *Toward Explaining Human Culture.* New Haven, CT: HRAF Press.

Brown, Donald E. 1991. *Human Universals.* Philadelphia: Temple University Press.

Brown, Judith K. 1970a. "Economic Organization and the Position of Women among the Iroquois." *Ethnohistory,* 17: 151–67.

Brown, Judith K. 1970b. "A Note on the Division of Labor by Sex." *American Anthropologist,* 72: 1073–78.

Brown, Peter J. 1999. "Culture and the Evolution of Obesity." In A. Podolefsky and P. J. Brown, eds., *Applying Cultural Anthropology: An Introductory Reader.* Mountain View, CA: Mayfield.

Brown, Roger. 1965. *Social Psychology.* New York: Free Press.

Brown, Roger. 1980. "The First Sentence of Child and Chimpanzee." In T. A. Sebeok and J. Umiker-Sebeok, eds., *Speaking of Apes.* New York: Plenum Press.

Brown, Roger, and Marguerite Ford. 1961. "Address in American English." *Journal of Abnormal and Social Psychology,* 62: 375–85.

Browner, C. H. 1985. "Criteria for Selecting Herbal Remedies." *Ethnology,* 24: 13–32.

Bryant, Carol A., and Doraine F. C. Bailey. 1990. "The Use of Focus Group Research in Program Development." In J. van Willigen and T. L. Finan, eds., *Soundings.* NAPA Bulletin No. 10. Washington, D.C.: American Anthropological Association, pp. 24–39.

Burbank, Victoria K. 1994. *Fighting Women: Anger and Aggression in Aboriginal Australia.* Berkeley: University of California Press.

Burbank, Victoria K. 2004. "Australian Aborigines: An Adolescent Mother and Her Family." In *Portraits of Culture,* in C. R. Ember, M. Ember, and P. N. Peregrine, eds., *New Directions in Anthropology.* Upper Saddle River, NJ: Prentice Hall, CD-ROM.

Burkhalter, S. Brian, and Robert F. Murphy. 1989. "Tappers and Sappers: Rubber, Gold and Money among the Mundurucú." *American Ethnologist,* 16: 100–116.

Burns, Alisa, and Cath Scott. 1994. *Mother-Headed Families and Why They Have Increased.* Hillsdale, NJ: Lawrence Erlbaum Associates.

Busby, Annette. 2004. "Kurds: A Culture Straddling National Borders." In *Portraits of Culture,* in C. R. Ember, M. Ember and P. N. Peregrine, eds., *New Directions in Anthropology.* Upper Saddle River, NJ: Prentice Hall, CD-ROM.

Byrne, Bryan. 1994. "Access to Subsistence Resources and the Sexual Division of Labor among Potters." *Cross-Cultural Research,* 28: 225–50.

Campbell, Donald T. 1965. "Variation and Selective Retention in Socio-Cultural Evolution." In H. Barringer, G. Blankstein, and R. Mack, eds., *Social Change in Developing Areas.* Cambridge, MA: Schenkman, pp. 19–49.

Caporael, Linnda R. 1976. "Ergotism: The Satan Loosed in Salem?" *Science* (April 2): 21–26.

Carcopino, Jerome. 1940. *Daily Life in Ancient Rome: The People and the City at the Height of the Empire.* Edited with bibliography and notes by Henry T. Rowell. Translated from the French by E. O. Lorimer. New Haven, CT: Yale University Press.

Cardoso, Fernando Luis, and Dennis Werner. 2004. "Homosexuality." In C. R. Ember and M. Ember, eds., *Encyclopedia of Sex and Gender: Men and Women in the World's Cultures.* New York: Kluwer Academic/Plenum, vol. 1, pp. 204–15.

Carey, James W., Erin Picone-DeCaro, Mary Spink Neumann, Devorah Schwartz, Delia Easton, and Daphne Cobb St. John. 2004. "HIV/AIDS Research and Prevention." In C. R. Ember and M. Ember, eds., *Encyclopedia of Medical Anthropology: Health and Illness in the World's Cultures,* 2 vols. New York: Kluwer Academic/Plenum, vol. 1, pp. 462–79.

Carneiro, Robert L. 1970. "A Theory of the Origin of the State." *Science* (August 21): 733–38.

Carneiro, Robert L. 1978. "Political Expansion as an Expression of the Principle of Competitive Exclusion." In R. Cohen and E. R. Service, eds., *Origins of the State.* Philadelphia: Institute for the Study of Human Issues.

Carneiro, Robert L. 1990. "Chiefdom-Level Warfare as Exemplified in Fiji and the Cauca Valley." In J. Haas, ed., *The Anthropology of War.* New York: Cambridge University Press, pp. 190–211.

Carrier, Joseph, and Ralph Bolton. 1991. "Anthropological Perspectives on Sexuality and HIV Prevention." *Annual Review of Sex Research,* 2: 49–75.

Carroll, John B., ed. 1956. *Language, Thought, and Reality: Selected Writings of Benjamin Lee Whorf.* New York: Wiley.

Cashdan, Elizabeth A. 1980. "Egalitarianism among Hunters and Gatherers." *American Anthropologist,* 82: 116–20.

Cashdan, Elizabeth. 2001. "Ethnic Diversity and Its Environmental Determinants: Effects of Climate, Pathogens, and Habitat Diversity." *American Anthropologist,* 103: 968–91.

Caulkins, D. Douglas. 1997. "Welsh." In D. Levinson and M. Ember, eds., *American Immigrant Cultures: Builders of a Nation,* 2 vols. New York: Macmillan, vol. 2, pp. 935–41.

Caws, Peter. 1969. "The Structure of Discovery." *Science* (December 12): 1375–80.

Chafetz, Janet Saltzman. 1990. *Gender Equity: An Integrated Theory of Stability and Change.* Sage Library of Social Research No. 176. Newbury Park, CA: Sage.

Chagnon, Napoleon. 1983. *Yanomamö: The Fierce People.* 3rd ed. New York: Holt, Rinehart & Winston.

Chambers, Erve. 1989. *Applied Anthropology: A Practical Guide.* Rev. ed. Prospect Heights, IL: Waveland.

Chaucer, Geoffrey. 1926. *The Prologue to the Canterbury Tales, the Knights Tale, the Nonnes Prestes Tale.* Ed. Mark H. Liddell. New York: Macmillan.

Chayanov, Alexander V. 1966. *The Theory of Peasant Economy.* Ed. Daniel Thorner, Basile Kerblay, and R. E. F. Smith. Homewood, IL: Richard D. Irwin.

Chen, F. C., and W. H. Li. 2001. "Genomic Divergences between Humans and Other Hominoids and the Effective Population Size of the Common Ancestor of Humans and Chimpanzees." *American Journal of Human Genetics,* 68: 445–56.

"Children as Victims." 2000. *Juvenile Justice Bulletin.* 1999 National Report Series. Washington, D.C.: U.S. Department of Justice, May 2000.

Chomsky, Noam. 1975. *Reflections on Language.* New York: Pantheon.

Christensen, Pia, Jenny Hockey, and Allison James. 2001. "Talk, Silence and the Material World: Patterns of Indirect Communication among Agricultural Farmers in Northern England." In J. Hendry and C. W. Watson, eds., *An Anthropology of Indirect Communication.* London: Routledge, pp. 68–82.

Clifford, James. 1986. "Introduction: Partial Truths." In J. Clifford and G. E. Marcus, eds., *Writing Culture: The Poetics and Politics of Ethnography.* Berkeley: University of California Press.

Clifton, James H., ed. 1968. *Introduction to Cultural Anthropology.* Boston: Houghton Mifflin.

Cohen, Alex. 1999. *The Mental Health of Indigenous Peoples: An International Overview.* Geneva: Department of Mental Health, World Health Organization.

Cohen, Alex, and Paul Koegel. 2004. "Homelessness." In *Research Frontiers,* in C. R. Ember, M. Ember, and P. N. Peregrine, eds., *New Directions in Anthropology.* Upper Saddle River, NJ: Prentice Hall, CD-ROM.

Cohen, Jon. 2007. "Relative Differences: The Myth of 1%." *Science* (June 29): 1836.

Cohen, Mark N. 1977a. *The Food Crisis in Prehistory: Overpopulation and the Origins of Agriculture.* New Haven, CT: Yale University Press.

Cohen, Mark N. 1977b. "Population Pressure and the Origins of Agriculture." In C. A. Reed, ed., *Origins of Agriculture.* The Hague: Mouton.

Cohen, Mark Nathan. 1998. *Culture of Intolerance: Chauvinism, Class, and Racism in the United States.* New Haven, CT: Yale University Press.

Cohen, Ronald, and Elman R. Service, eds. 1978. *Origins of the State: The Anthropology of Political Evolution.* Philadelphia: Institute for the Study of Human Issues.

Collins, James, and Richard Blot. 2003. *Literacy and Literacies.* Cambridge: Cambridge University Press.

Conklin, Beth A. 2002. "Shamans versus Pirates in the Amazonian Treasure Chest." *American Anthropologist,* 104: 1050–61.

Coreil, Jeannine. 1989. "Lessons from a Community Study of Oral Rehydration Therapy in Haiti." In J. van Willigen, B. Rylko-Bauer, and A. McElroy, eds., *Making Our Research Useful.* Boulder, CO: Westview.

Coult, Allan D., and Robert W. Habenstein. 1965. *Cross Tabulations of Murdock's World Ethnographic Sample.* Columbia, MO: University of Missouri Press.

"Crossroads for Planet Earth." 2005. *Scientific American.* Special Issue, September.

Crystal, David. 1971. *Linguistics.* Middlesex, UK: Penguin.

Cutright, Phillips. 1967. "Inequality: A Cross-National Analysis." *American Sociological Review,* 32: 562–78.

Daly, Martin, and Margo Wilson. 1988. *Homicide.* New York: Aldine.

Davenport, William. 1959. "Nonunilinear Descent and Descent Groups." *American Anthropologist,* 61: 557–72.

Davis, William D. 1971. "Societal Complexity and the Nature of Primitive Man's Conception of the Supernatural." Ph.D. dissertation, University of North Carolina, Chapel Hill.

DeLaguna, Frederica. 1972. *Under Mount Saint Elias: The History and Culture of the Yakutat Tlingit.* Washington, D.C.: Smithsonian Institution Press, as seen in eHRAF World Cultures on the Web.

DeMallie, Raymond, and Alfonzo Ortiz, eds., 1994. *North American Indian Anthropology: Essays on Society and Culture.* Norman, OK: University of Oklahoma Press.

Denny, J. Peter. 1979. "The 'Extendedness' Variable in Classifier Semantics: Universal Features and Cultural Variation." In M. Mathiot, ed., *Ethnolinguistics.* The Hague: Mouton.

Dentan, Robert K. 1968. *The Semai: A Nonviolent People of Malaya.* New York: Holt, Rinehart & Winston.

Deutsch, A., ed. 1948. *Sex Habits of American Men.* Upper Saddle River, NJ: Prentice Hall.

De Villiers, Peter A., and Jill G. de Villiers. 1979. *Early Language.* Cambridge, MA: Harvard University Press.

De Vita, Philip, and James D. Armstrong, eds. 1993. *Distant Mirrors: America as a Foreign Culture.* Belmont, CA: Wadsworth.

DeVore, Irven, and Melvin J. Konner. 1974. "Infancy in Hunter-Gatherer Life: An Ethological Perspective." In N. F. White, ed., *Ethology and Psychiatry.* Toronto: Ontario Mental Health Foundation and University of Toronto Press.

de Waal, Frans. 2001. *The Ape and the Sushi Master: Cultural Reflections of a Primatologist.* New York: Basic Books.

Diament, Michelle. 2005. "Diversifying Their Crops: Agriculture Schools, Focusing on Job Prospects, Reach out to Potential Students from Cities and Suburbs," *The Chronicle of Higher Education,* May 6, 2005, pp. A32–34.

Diamond, Norma. 1975. "Collectivization, Kinship, and the Status of Women in Rural China." In R. R. Reiter, ed., *Toward an Anthropology of Women.* New York: Monthly Review Press.

Dickson, D. Bruce, Jeffrey Olsen, P. Fred Dahm, and Mitchell S. Wachtel. 2005. "Where Do You Go When You Die? A Cross-Cultural Test of the Hypothesis That Infrastructure Predicts Individual Eschatology." *Journal of Anthropological Research,* 1: 53–79.

Dirks, Robert. 2004. "Hunger and Famine." In *Research Frontiers,* in C. R. Ember, M. Ember, and P. N. Peregrine, eds., *New Directions in Anthropology.* Upper Saddle River, NJ: Prentice Hall, CD-ROM.

Dirks, Robert. 1993. "Starvation and Famine." *Cross-Cultural Research,* 27: 28–69.

Divale, William T. 1974. "Migration, External Warfare, and Matrilocal Residence." *Behavior Science Research,* 9: 75–133.

Divale, William T., and Marvin Harris. 1976. "Population, Warfare, and the Male Supremacist Complex." *American Anthropologist,* 78: 521–38.

Divale, William, and Clifford Zipin. 1977. "Hunting and the Development of Sign Language: A Cross-Cultural Test." *Journal of Anthropological Research,* 33: 185–201.

Donaldson, Peter. 1971. *Worlds Apart: The Economic Gulf between Nations.* London: British Broadcasting Corporation.

Dow, James. 1986. *The Shaman's Touch: Otomi Indian Symbolic Healing.* Salt Lake City: University of Utah Press.

Dowling, John H. 1975. "Property Relations and Productive Strategies in Pastoral Societies." *American Ethnologist,* 2: 419–26.

Doyle, Rodger. 2005. "Leveling the Playing Field: Economic Development Helps Women Pull Even with Men." *Scientific American* (June): 32.

Draper, Patricia. 1975. "!Kung Women: Contrasts in Sexual Egalitarianism in Foraging and Sedentary Contexts." In R. R. Reiter, ed., *Toward an Anthropology of Women.* New York: Monthly Review Press.

Drucker, Philip. 1965. *Cultures of the North Pacific Coast.* San Francisco: Chandler.

Du, Shanshan. 2003. "Is Buddha a Couple: Gender-Unitary Perspectives from the Lahu of Southwest China." *Ethnology,* 42: 253–71.

Duane, Daniel. 2003. "Turning Garbage into Oil." *New York Times Magazine,* December 14, p. 100.

Durham, William H. 1991. *Coevolution: Genes, Culture and Human Diversity.* Stanford, CA: Stanford University Press.

Durkheim, Émile. 1938 [1895]. *The Rules of Sociological Method.* 8th ed. Trans. Sarah A. Soloway and John H. Mueller. Ed. George E. Catlin. New York: Free Press.

Durrenberger, E. Paul. 2001a. "Anthropology and Globalization." *American Anthropologist,* 103: 531–35.

Durrenberger, E. Paul. 2001b. "Explorations of Class and Consciousness in the United States." *Journal of Anthropological Research,* 57: 41–60.

Dyson-Hudson, Neville. 1966. *Karimojong Politics.* Oxford: Clarendon Press.

Eckhardt, William. 1975. "Primitive Militarism." *Journal of Peace Research,* 12: 55–62.

Ekman, Paul, and Dachner Keltner. 1997. "Universal Facial Expressions of Emotion: An Old Controversy and New Findings." In U. Segerstrale and P. Molnar, eds., *Nonverbal Communication: Where Nature Meets Culture.* Mahwah, NJ: Lawrence Erlbaum.

Eliot, T. S. 1963. "The Love Song of J. Alfred Prufrock." In *Collected Poems, 1909–1962.* New York: Harcourt, Brace & World.

Ellis, Lee. 1986. "Evidence of Neuroandrogenic Etiology of Sex Roles from a Combined Analysis of Human, Nonhuman Primate and Nonprimate Mammalian Studies." *Personality and Individual Differences,* 7: 519–52.

Ember, Carol R. 1973. "Feminine Task Assignment and the Social Behavior of Boys." *Ethos,* 1: 424–39.

Ember, Carol R. 1974. "An Evaluation of Alternative Theories of Matrilocal versus Patrilocal Residence." *Behavior Science Research,* 9: 135–49.

Ember, Carol R. 1975. "Residential Variation among Hunter-Gatherers." *Behavior Science Research,* 9: 135–49.

Ember, Carol R. 1978. "Myths about Hunter-Gatherers." *Ethnology,* 17: 439–48.

Ember, Carol R. 1981. "A Cross-Cultural Perspective on Sex Differences." In R. H. Munroe, R. L. Munroe, and B. B. Whiting, eds., *Handbook of Cross-Cultural Human Development.* New York: Garland, pp. 531–80.

Ember, Carol R. 1983. "The Relative Decline in Women's Contribution to Agriculture with Intensification." *American Anthropologist,* 85: 285–304.

Ember, Carol R., and Melvin Ember. 1972. "The Conditions Favoring Multilocal Residence." *Southwestern Journal of Anthropology,* 28: 382–400.

Ember, Carol R., and Melvin Ember. 1992. "Resource Unpredictability, Mistrust, and War: A Cross-Cultural Study." *Journal of Conflict Resolution,* 36: 242–62.

Ember, Carol R., and Melvin Ember. 1993. "Issues in Cross-Cultural Studies of Interpersonal Violence." *Violence and Victims,* 8: 217–33.

Ember, Carol R., and Melvin Ember. 1994. "War, Socialization, and Interpersonal Violence: A Cross-Cultural Study." *Journal of Conflict Resolution,* 38: 620–46.

Ember, Carol R., and Melvin Ember. 1997. "Violence in the Ethnographic Record: Results of Cross-Cultural Research on War and Aggression." In D. Frayer and D. Martin, eds., *Troubled Times.* Langhorne, PA: Gordon and Breach, pp. 1–20.

Ember, Carol R., and Melvin Ember. 2001. *Cross-Cultural Research Methods.* Walnut Creek, CA: AltaMira Press.

Ember, Carol R., and Melvin Ember. 2005. "Explaining Corporal Punishment of Children: A Cross-Cultural Study." *American Anthropologist,* 107: 609–19.

Ember, Carol R., Melvin Ember, and Peter N. Peregrine. 2007. *Anthropology.* 12th ed. Upper Saddle River, NJ: Prentice Hall.

Ember, Carol R., Melvin Ember, Andrey Korotayev, and Victor de Munck. 2005. "Valuing Thinness or Fatness in Women: Reevaluating the Effect of Resource Scarcity." *Evolution and Human Behavior,* 26: 257–70.

Ember, Carol R., Melvin Ember, and Burton Pasternak. 1974. "On the Development of Unilineal Descent." *Journal of Anthropological Research,* 30: 69–94.

Ember, Carol R., Melvin Ember, and Bruce Russett. 1992. "Peace between Participatory Polities: A Cross-Cultural Test of the 'Democracies Rarely Fight Each Other' Hypothesis." *World Politics,* 44: 573–99.

Ember, Carol R., and David Levinson. 1991. "The Substantive Contributions of Worldwide Cross-Cultural Studies Using Secondary Data." *Behavior Science Research* (special issue, "Cross-Cultural and Comparative Research: Theory and Method"), 25: 79–140.

Ember, Melvin. 1963. "The Relationship between Economic and Political Development in Nonindustrialized Societies." *Ethnology,* 2: 228–48.

Ember, Melvin. 1967. "The Emergence of Neolocal Residence." *Transactions of the New York Academy of Sciences,* 30: 291–302.

Ember, Melvin. 1970. "Taxonomy in Comparative Studies." In R. Naroll and R. Cohen, eds., *A Handbook of Method in Cultural Anthropology.* Garden City, NY: Natural History Press.

Ember, Melvin. 1974a. "The Conditions That May Favor Avunculocal Residence." *Behavior Science Research,* 9: 203–209.

Ember, Melvin. 1974b. "Warfare, Sex Ratio, and Polygyny." *Ethnology,* 13: 197–206.

Ember, Melvin. 1975. "On the Origin and Extension of the Incest Taboo." *Behavior Science Research,* 10: 249–81.

Ember, Melvin. 1978. "Size of Color Lexicon: Interaction of Cultural and Biological Factors." *American Anthropologist,* 80: 364–67.

Ember, Melvin. 1984–1985. "Alternative Predictors of Polygyny." *Behavior Science Research,* 19: 1–23.

Ember, Melvin, and Carol R. Ember. 1971. "The Conditions Favoring Matrilocal versus Patrilocal Residence." *American Anthropologist,* 73: 571–94.

Ember, Melvin, and Carol R. Ember. 1979. "Male-Female Bonding: A Cross-Species Study of Mammals and Birds." *Behavior Science Research,* 14: 37–56.

Ember, Melvin, and Carol R. Ember. 1992. "Cross-Cultural Studies of War and Peace: Recent Achievements and Future Possibilities." In S. P. Reyna and R. E. Downs, eds., *Studying War.* New York: Gordon and Breach.

Ember, Melvin, and Carol R. Ember. 1999. "Cross-Language Predictors of Consonant-Vowel Syllables." *American Anthropologist,* 101: 730–42.

Ember, Melvin, and Carol R. Ember, eds. 2002. *Encyclopedia of Urban Cultures: Cities and Cultures around the World,* 4 vols. Danbury, CT: Grolier/Scholastic.

Ember, Melvin, Carol R. Ember, and Ian Skoggard, eds. 2004. *Encyclopedia of Diasporas: Immigrant and Refugee Cultures Around the World,* 2 vols. New York: Kluwer Academic/Plenum.

Ensminger, Jean. 2002a. "Experimental Economics: A Powerful New Method for Theory Testing in Anthropology." In J. Ensminger, ed., *Theory in Economic Anthropology.* Walnut Creek, CA: AltaMira Press, pp. 59–78.

Ensminger, Jean, ed. 2002b. *Theory in Economic Anthropology.* Lanham, MD: AltaMira Press.

Epstein, Cynthia Fuchs. 1988. *Deceptive Distinctions: Sex, Gender, and the Social Order.* New York: Russell Sage Foundation.

Erchak, Gerald M. 2004. "Family Violence." In *Research Frontiers,* in C. R. Ember, M. Ember, and P. N. Peregrine, eds., *New Directions in Anthropology.* Upper Saddle River, NJ: Prentice Hall, CD-ROM.

Etienne, Mona, and Eleanor Leacock, eds. 1980. *Women and Colonization: Anthropological Perspectives.* New York: Praeger.

Etkin, Nina L., and Paul J. Ross 1997. "Malaria, Medicine, and Meals: A Biobehavioral Perspective." In L. Romanucci-Ross, D. E. Moerman, and L. R. Tancredi, eds., *The Anthropology of Medicine.* Westport, CT: Bergin & Garvey, pp. 169–209.

Euripides. 1937. "The Trojan Women." In E. Hamilton, trans., *Three Greek Plays.* New York: Norton.

Evans-Pritchard, E. E. 1940. "The Nuer of the Southern Sudan." In M. Fortes and E. E. Evans-Pritchard, eds., *African Political Systems.* New York: Oxford University Press.

Evans-Pritchard, E. E. 1971. "Witchcraft Explains Unfortunate Events." In W. A. Lessa and E. Z. Vogt, eds., *Reader in Comparative Religion.* 4th ed. New York: Harper & Row.

Fagan, B. M. 1997. *People of the Earth: An Introduction to World Prehistory.* 9th ed. New York: HarperCollins.

Fagan, Brian. M. 2001. *People of the Earth: An Introduction to World Prehistory.* 10th ed. Upper Saddle River: Prentice Hall.

Farley, Reynolds. 1996. *The New American Reality: Who We Are, How We Got Here, Where We Are Going.* New York: Russell Sage Foundation.

Farmer, Paul. 1997. "Ethnography, Social Analysis, and the Prevention of Sexually Transmitted HIV Infection among Poor Women in Haiti." In M. C. Inhorn and P. J. Brown, eds., *The Anthropology of Infectious Disease.* Amsterdam: Gordon and Breach, pp. 413–38.

Fearnea, Elizabeth, and Robert Fearnea. 1975. As reported in M. Kay Martin and Barbara Voorhies, *Female of the Species.* New York: Columbia University Press,.

Featherman, David L., and Robert M. Hauser. 1978. *Opportunity and Change.* New York: Academic Press,.

Fehr, Ernst, and Urs Fischbacher. 2003. "The Nature of Human Altruism." *Nature,* 23: 785–91.

Feinman, Gary, and Jill Neitzel. 1984. "Too Many Types: An Overview of Sedentary Prestate Societies in the Americas." In M. B. Schiffer, ed., *Advances in Archaeological Methods and Theory.* Vol. 7. Orlando, FL: Academic Press, pp. 39–102.

Ferguson, R. Brian, and Neil L. Whitehead. 1992. "The Violent Edge of Empire." In R. B. Ferguson and N. Whitehead, eds., *War in the Tribal Zone.* Santa Fe, NM: School of American Research Press, pp. 1–30.

Fields, Jason. 2003. *America's Families and Living Arrangements, 2003.* Current Population Reports, P20–553. Washington, D.C.: U.S. Census Bureau.

Finley, M. I. 1983. *Politics in the Ancient World.* Cambridge: Cambridge University Press.

Firth, Raymond. 1959. *Social Change in Tikopia.* New York: Macmillan.

Firth, Raymond. 1970. *Rank and Religion in Tikopia.* Boston: Beacon Press.

Fischer, John L. 1958. "Social Influences on the Choice of a Linguistic Variant." *Word,* 14: 47–56.

Fisher, William H. 1994. "Megadevelopment, Environmentalism, and Resistance: The Institutional Context of Kayapo Indigenous Politics in Central Brazil." *Human Organization,* 53: 220–32.

Flannery, Kent V. 1971. "The Origins and Ecological Effects of Early Domestication in Iran and the Near East." In S. Struever, ed., *Prehistoric Agriculture.* Garden City, NY: Natural History Press.

Flannery, Kent V. 1972. "The Cultural Evolution of Civilizations." *Annual Review of Ecology and Systematics,* 3: 399–426.

Flannery, Kent V. 1973. "The Origins of the Village as a Settlement Type in Mesoamerica and the Near East: A Comparative Study." In R. Tringham, ed., *Territoriality and Proxemics.* Andover, MA: Warner.

Flannery, Kent V., ed. 1986a. *Guila Naquitz: Archaic Foraging and Early Agriculture in Oaxaca, Mexico.* Orlando, FL: Academic Press.

Flannery, Kent V. 1986b. "The Research Problem." In K. V. Flannery, ed., *Guila Naquitz.* Orlando, FL: Academic Press.

Ford, Clellan S., and Frank A. Beach. 1951. *Patterns of Sexual Behavior.* New York: Harper.

Foster, George M. 1962. *Traditional Cultures and the Impact of Technological Change.* New York: Harper & Row.

Foster, George M. 1969. *Applied Anthropology.* Boston: Little, Brown.

Foster, George M. 1994. *Hippocrates' Latin American Legacy: Humoral Medicine in the New World.* Amsterdam: Gordon and Breach.

Foster, Philips. 1992. *The World Food Problem: Tackling the Causes of Undernutrition in the Third World.* Boulder, CO: Lynne Rienner.

Frake, Charles O. 1960. "The Eastern Subanun of Mindanao." In G. P. Murdock, ed., *Social Structure in Southeast Asia.* Chicago: Quadrangle, pp. 51–64.

Frankel, Barbara, and M. G. Trend. 1991. "Principles, Pressures and Paychecks: The Anthropologist as Employee." In C. Fluehr-Lobban, ed., *Ethics and the Profession of Anthropology.* Philadelphia: University of Pennsylvania Press.

Frayer, David, and Debra Martin, eds. 1995. *Troubled Times: Osteological and Archaeological Evidence of Violence.* Langhorne, PA: Gordon and Breach.

Frayer, David W., and Milford H. Wolpoff. 1985. "Sexual Dimorphism." *Annual Review of Anthropology,* 14: 429–73.

Freeman, J. D. 1961. "On the Concept of the Kindred." *Journal of the Royal Anthropological Institute,* 91: 192–220.

Fried, Morton H. 1967. *The Evolution of Political Society: An Essay in Political Anthropology.* New York: Random House.

Friedman, Jeffrey M. 2003. "A War on Obesity, Not the Obese." *Science* (February 7): 856–58.

Friedman, Saul S. 1980. "Holocaust." In *Academic American* [now Grolier] *Encyclopedia.* Vol. 10. Princeton, NJ: Arete.

Friedrich, Paul. 1986. *The Language Parallax.* Austin: University of Texas Press.

Fry, Douglas P., and Kaj Björkqvist, eds. 1997. *Cultural Variation in Conflict Resolution: Alternatives to Violence.* Mahwah, NJ: Lawrence Erlbaum.

Gal, Susan. 1988. "The Political Economy of Code Choice." In M. Heller, ed., *Codeswitching.* Berlin: Mouton de Gruyter, pp. 345–64.

Gartner, Rosemary. 2004. "Crime Variations across Cultures and Nations." In *Cross-Cultural Research for Social Science,* in C. R. Ember, M. Ember, and P. N. Peregrine, eds., *New Directions in Anthropology.* Upper Saddle River, NJ: Prentice Hall, CD-ROM.

Gat, Azar. 1999. "The Pattern of Fighting in Simple, Small-Scale, Prestate Societies." *Journal of Anthropological Research,* 55: 563–83.

Geertz, Clifford. 1966. "Religion as a Cultural System." In M. Banton, ed., *Anthropological Approaches to the Study of Religion.* New York: Praeger, pp. 1–46.

Gelles, Richard J., and Murray A. Straus. 1988. *Intimate Violence.* New York: Simon & Schuster.

Gesler, W. 1991. *The Cultural Geography of Health Care.* Pittsburgh, PA: University of Pittsburgh Press.

Gibbons, Ann. 1993. "Warring over Women." *Science* (August 20): 987–88.

Gibbs, James L., Jr., ed. 1965. *Peoples of Africa.* New York: Holt, Rinehart & Winston.

Gibson, Kathleen R., and Stephen Jessee. 1999. "Language Evolution and Expansions of Multiple Neurological Processing Areas." In B. J. King, ed., *The Origins of Language.* Santa Fe, NM: School of American Research Press, pp. 189–227.

Gilliland, Mary Kay. 1995. "Nationalism and Ethnogenesis in the Former Yugoslavia." In L. Romanucci-Ross and G. A. De Vos, eds., *Ethnic Identity: Creation, Conflict, and Accommodation.* 3rd ed. Walnut Creek, CA: AltaMira Press, pp. 197–221.

Gilman, Antonio. 1990. "The Development of Social Stratification in Bronze Age Europe." *Current Anthropology,* 22: 1–23.

Gladwin, Thomas, and Seymour B. Sarason. 1953. *Truk: Man in Paradise.* New York: Wenner-Gren Foundation for Anthropological Research, 1953, as seen in eHRAF World Cultures on the Web, 2000.

Gleitman, Lila R., and Eric Wanner. 1982. "Language Acquisition: The State of the State of the Art." In E. Wanner and L. R. Gleitman, eds., *Language Acquisition.* Cambridge: Cambridge University Press.

Goldschmidt, Walter. 1999. "Dynamics and Status in America." *Anthropology Newsletter* 40(5): 62, 64.

Goldstein, Joshua S. 2004. "War and Gender." In C. R. Ember and M. Ember, eds., *Encyclopedia of Sex and Gender: Men and Women in the World's Cultures.* Vol. 1. New York: Kluwer Academic/Plenum, pp. 107–16.

Goldstein, Melvyn C. 1971. "Stratification, Polyandry, and Family Structure in Central Tibet." *Southwestern Journal of Anthropology,* 27: 65–74.

Goldstein, Melvyn C. 1987. "When Brothers Share a Wife." *Natural History* (March): 39–48.

Goodenough, Ward H. 1951. *Property, Kin, and Community on Truk.* New Haven, CT: Yale University Press.

Goodman, Madeleine J., P. Bion Griffin, Agnes A. Estioko-Griffin, and John S. Grove. 1985. "The Compatibility of Hunting and Mothering among the Agta Hunter-Gatherers of the Philippines." *Sex Roles,* 12: 1199–209.

Goody, Jack. 1973. "Bridewealth and Dowry in Africa and Eurasia." In J. Goody and S. H. Tambiah, eds., *Bridewealth and Dowry.* Cambridge: Cambridge University Press.

Goody, Jack, and S. H. Tambiah, eds. 1973. *Bridewealth and Dowry.* Cambridge: Cambridge University Press.

Graber, Robert Bates, ed. 2004. "The Future State of the World: An Anthropological Symposium." Special issue of *Cross-Cultural Research,* 38: 95–207.

Graham, Susan Brandt. 1979. "Biology and Human Social Behavior: A Response to van den Berghe and Barash." *American Anthropologist,* 81: 357–60.

Gray, J. Patrick. 1985. *Primate Sociobiology.* New Haven, CT: HRAF Press.

Greenberg, Joseph H. 1972. "Linguistic Evidence Regarding Bantu Origins." *Journal of African History,* 13: 189–216.

Greenfield, Patricia M., Ashley E. Maynard, and Carla P. Childs. 2000. "History, Culture, Learning, and Development." *Cross-Cultural Research,* 34: 351–74.

Gross, Daniel R., George Eiten, Nancy M. Flowers, Francisca M. Leoi, Madeline Lattman Ritter, and Dennis W. Werner. 1979. "Ecology and Acculturation among Native Peoples of Central Brazil." *Science* (November 30): 1043–50.

Gross, Daniel R., and Barbara A. Underwood. 1971. "Technological Change and Caloric Costs: Sisal Agriculture in Northeastern Brazil." *American Anthropologist,* 73: 725–40.

Guiora, Alexander Z., Benjamin Beit-Hallahmi, Risto Fried, and Cecelia Yoder. 1982. "Language Environment and Gender Identity Attainment." *Language Learning,* 32: 289–304.

Gurr, Ted Robert. 1989a. "Historical Trends in Violent Crime: Europe and the United States." In T. R. Gurr, ed., *Violence in America,* Vol. 1: *The History of Crime.* Newbury Park, CA: Sage.

Gurr, Ted Robert. 1989b. "The History of Violent Crime in America: An Overview." In T. R. Gurr, ed., *Violence in America,* Vol. 1: *The History of Crime.* Newbury Park, CA: Sage.

Haas, Jonathan. 1990a. "Warfare and the Evolution of Tribal Polities in the Prehistoric Southwest." In J. Haas, ed., *The Anthropology of War.* New York: Cambridge University Press, pp. 171–89.

Haas, Jonathan, ed. 1990b. *The Anthropology of War.* New York: Cambridge University Press.

Hackenberg, Robert A. 1988. "Scientists or Survivors? The Future of Applied Anthropology under Maximum Uncertainty." In R. T. Trotter, II, ed., *Anthropology for Tomorrow.* Washington, D.C.: American Anthropological Association.

Hage, Jerald, and Charles H. Powers. 1992. *Post-Industrial Lives: Roles and Relationships in the 21st Century.* Newbury Park, CA: Sage.

Hahn, Robert A. 1995. *Sickness and Healing: An Anthropological Perspective.* New Haven, CT: Yale University Press.

Hall, Edward T. 1966. *The Hidden Dimension.* Garden City, NY: Doubleday.

Hames, Raymond. 2004. "Yanomamö: Varying Adaptations of Foraging Horticulturalists." In *Portraits of Culture,* in C. R. Ember, M. Ember, and P. N. Peregrine, eds., *New Directions in Anthropology.* Upper Saddle River, NJ: Prentice Hall, CD-ROM.

Handwerker, W. Penn, and Paul V. Crosbie. 1982. "Sex and Dominance." *American Anthropologist,* 84: 97–104.

Hannerz, Ulf. 1996. *Transnational Connections: Culture, People, Places.* London: Routledge.

Hardoy, Jorge, and David Satterthwaite. 1987. "The Legal and the Illegal City." In L. Rodwin, ed., *Shelter, Settlement, and Development.* Boston: Allen & Unwin, pp. 304–38.

Harner, Michael. 1972. "The Role of Hallucinogenic Plants in European Witchcraft." In M. Harner, ed., *Hallucinogens and Shamanism.* New York: Oxford University Press, pp. 127–50.

Harner, Michael J. 1975. "Scarcity, the Factors of Production, and Social Evolution." In S. Polgar, ed., *Population, Ecology, and Social Evolution.* The Hague: Mouton, pp. 123–38.

Harner, Michael, and Gary Doore. 1987. "The Ancient Wisdom in Shamanic Cultures." In S. Nicholson, comp., *Shamanism.* Wheaton, IL: Theosophical Publishing House, pp. 3–16.

Harris, Marvin. 1966. "The Cultural Ecology of India's Sacred Cattle." *Current Anthropology,* 7: 51–63.

Harris, Marvin. 1975. *Cows, Pigs, Wars and Witches: The Riddles of Culture.* New York: Random House, Vintage.

Harrison, Gail G. 1975. "Primary Adult Lactase Deficiency: A Problem in Anthropological Genetics." *American Anthropologist,* 77: 812–35.

Hart, Hornell. 1948. "The Logistic Growth of Political Areas." *Social Forces,* 26: 396–408.

Harvey, Philip W., and Peter F. Heywood. 1983. "Twenty-five Years of Dietary Change in Simbu Province, Papua New Guinea." *Ecology of Food and Nutrition,* 13: 27–35.

Hatch, Elvin. 1997. "The Good Side of Relativism." *Journal of Anthropological Research,* 53: 371–81.

Hays, Terence E. 1994. "Sound Symbolism, Onomatopoeia, and New Guinea Frog Names." *Journal of Linguistic Anthropology,* 4: 153–74.

Heider, Karl. 1970. *The Dugum Dani.* Chicago: Aldine.

Heider, Karl. 1979. *Grand Valley Dani: Peaceful Warriors.* New York: Holt, Rinehart & Winston.

Heise, David R. 1967. "Cultural Patterning of Sexual Socialization." *American Sociological Review,* 32: 726–39.

Heller, Monica, ed. 1988. *Codeswitching: Anthropological and Sociolinguistic Perspectives.* Berlin: Mouton de Gruyter.

Helms, Mary W. 2004. "Miskito: Adaptations to Colonial Empires, Past and Present." In *Portraits of Culture,* in C. R. Ember, M. Ember, and P. N. Peregrine, eds., *New Directions in Anthropology.* Upper Saddle River, NJ: Prentice Hall, CD-ROM.

Hempel, Carl G. 1965. *Aspects of Scientific Explanation.* New York: Free Press.

Henderson, Harry. 2001. *Global Terrorism: The Complete Reference Guide.* New York: Checkmark Books.

Henry, Donald O. 1989. *From Foraging to Agriculture: The Levant at the End of the Ice Age.* Philadelphia: University of Pennsylvania Press.

Herdt, Gilbert. 1997. "Sexual Cultures and Population Movement: Implications for AIDS/STDs." In G. Herdt, ed., *Sexual Cultures and Migration in the Era of AIDS: Anthropological and Demographic Perspectives.* Oxford: Oxford University Press, pp. 3–22.

Herrman, Helen. 1990. "A Survey of Homeless Mentally Ill People in Melbourne, Australia." *Hospital and Community Psychiatry,* 41: 1291–92.

Hewlett, Barry. 2004. "Diverse Contexts of Human Infancy." In *Cross-Cultural Research for Social Science,* in C. R. Ember, M. Ember, and P. N. Peregrine, eds., *New Directions in Anthropology.* Upper Saddle River, NJ: Prentice Hall, CD-ROM.

Hiatt, L. R. 1980. "Polyandry in Sri Lanka: A Test Case for Parental Investment Theory." *Man,* 15: 583–98.

Hickey, Gerald Cannon. 1964. *Village in Vietnam.* New Haven, CT: Yale University Press.

Hickson, Letitia. 1986. "The Social Contexts of Apology in Dispute Settlement: A Cross-Cultural Study." *Ethnology,* 25: 283–94.

Higley, Stephen Richard. 1995. *Privilege, Power, and Place: The Geography of the American Upper Class.* Lanham, MD: Roman & Littlefield.

Hill, Jane H. 1978. "Apes and Language." *Annual Review of Anthropology,* 7: 89–112.

Hill, Jane H. 2004. "Do Apes Have Language?" In *Research Frontiers,* in C. R. Ember, M. Ember, and P. N. Peregrine, eds., *New Directions in Anthropology.* Upper Saddle River, NJ: Prentice Hall, CD-ROM.

Hill, Jonathan D. 1996a. "Introduction: Ethnogenesis in the Americas, 1492–1992." In J. D. Hill, ed., *Ethnogenesis in the Americas, 1492–1992.* Iowa City, IA: University of Iowa Press, pp. 1–19.

Hill, Jonathan D., ed. 1996b. *Ethnogenesis in the Americas, 1492–1992.* Iowa City, IA: University of Iowa Press.

Hill, Kim, and A. Magdalena Hurtado. 2004. "The Ethics of Anthropological Research with Remote Tribal

Populations." In F. M. Salzano and A. M. Hurtado, eds., *Lost Paradises and the Ethics of Research and Publication.* Oxford: Oxford University Press, pp. 193–210.

Hitchcock, Robert K., and Megan Beisele. 2000. "Introduction." In P. P. Schweitzer, M. Biesele, and R. K. Hitchcock, eds., *Hunters and Gatherers in the Modern World: Conflict, Resistance, and Self-Determinations.* New York: Berghahn Books, pp. 1–27.

Hockett, C. F., and R. Ascher. 1964. "The Human Revolution." *Current Anthropology,* 5: 135–68.

Hoebel, E. Adamson. 1968 [1954]. *The Law of Primitive Man.* New York: Atheneum.

Holland, Dorothy, and Naomi Quinn, eds. 1987. *Cultural Models in Language and Thought.* Cambridge: Cambridge University Press.

Holmes, Janet. 1992. *An Introduction to Sociolinguistics.* London: Longman.

Holmes, Janet. 2001. *An Introduction to Sociolinguistics.* 2nd ed. London: Longman.

Hopkins, K. 1980. "Brother-Sister Marriage in Roman Egypt." *Comparative Studies in Society and History,* 22: 303–54.

Howard, Alan, and Jan Rensel. 2004. "Rotuma: Interpreting a Wedding." In *Portraits of Culture,* in C. R. Ember, M. Ember, and P. N. Peregrine, eds., *New Directions in Anthropology.* Upper Saddle River, NJ: Prentice Hall, CD-ROM.

"Human Development Report 2001." 2001. United Nations Development Programme. New York: Oxford University Press, pp. 9–25.

Hunt, Morton. 1974. *Sexual Behavior in the 1970s.* Chicago: Playboy Press.

Hunt, Robert C. 2000. "Labor Productivity and Agricultural Development: Boserup Revisited." *Human Ecology,* 28: 251–77.

Hurtado, Ana M., Kristen Hawkes, Kim Hill, and Hillard Kaplan. 1985. "Female Subsistence Strategies among the Aché Hunter-Gatherers of Eastern Paraguay." *Human Ecology,* 13: 1–28.

Hymes, Dell. 1974. *Foundations in Sociolinguistics: An Ethnographic Approach.* Philadelphia: University of Pennsylvania Press.

Itkonen, T. I. 1951. "The Lapps of Finland." *Southwestern Journal of Anthropology,* 7: 32–68.

Jacobs, Sue-Ellen, and Christine Roberts. 1989. "Sex, Sexuality, Gender and Gender Variance." In S. Morgen, ed., *Gender and Anthropology.* Washington, D.C.: American Anthropological Association, pp. 438–62.

Jankowiak, William, M. Diane Nell, and Ann Buckmaster. 2002. "Managing Infidelity: A Cross-Cultural Perspective." *Ethnology,* 41: 85–101.

Janzen, Daniel H. 1973. "Tropical Agroecosystems." *Science* (December 21): 1212–19.

Jelliffe, Derrick B., and E. F. Patrice Jelliffe. 1975. "Human Milk, Nutrition, and the World Resource Crisis." *Science* (May 9): 557–61.

Joans, Barbara. 1984. "Problems in Pocatello: A Study in Linguistic Misunderstanding." *Practicing Anthropology,* 6; reprinted in Podolefsky and Brown, eds., *Applying Cultural Anthropology: An Introductory Reader.* 3rd ed. Mountain View, CA: Mayfield, 1997, pp. 51–54.

Johnson, Allen, and Timothy Earle. 1987. *The Evolution of Human Societies: From Foraging Group to Agrarian State.* Stanford, CA: Stanford University Press.

Johnson, Amber Lynn. 2002. "Cross-Cultural Analysis of Pastoral Adaptations and Organizational States: A Preliminary Study." *Cross-Cultural Research,* 36: 151–80.

Johnson, Jeffrey G., Patricia Cohen, Elizabeth M. Smailies, Stephanie Kasen, and Judith S. Brook. 2002. "Television Viewing and Aggressive Behavior During Adolescence and Adulthood." *Science* (March 29): 2468–70.

Johnston, David Cay. 1999. "Gap Between Rich and Poor Found Substantially Wider." *The New York Times,* September 5, 1999, p. 16.

Jones, Steve, Robert Martin, and David Pilbeam, eds. 1992. *The Cambridge Encyclopedia of Human Evolution.* New York: Cambridge University Press.

Kang, Bong W. 2000. "A Reconsideration of Population Pressure and Warfare: A Protohistoric Korean Case." *Current Anthropology,* 4: 873–81.

Kaplan, Hillard, Kim Hill, and A. Magdalena Hurtado. 1990. "Risk, Foraging and Food Sharing among the Aché." In E. Cashdan, ed., *Risk and Uncertainty in Tribal and Peasant Economies.* Boulder, CO: Westview.

Keeley, Lawrence H. 1991. "Ethnographic Models for Late Glacial Hunter-Gatherers." In N. Barton, A. J. Roberts, and D. A. Roe, eds., *The Late Glacial in North-West Europe: Human Adaptation and Environmental Change at the End of the Pleistocene.* CBA Research Report 77, London: Council for British Archaeology, pp. 179–90.

Keenan, Elinor. 1989. "Norm-Makers, Norm-Breakers: Uses of Speech by Men and Women in a Malagasy Community." In R. Bauman and J. Sherzer, eds., *Explorations in the Ethnography of Speaking.* 2nd ed. New York: Cambridge University Press.

Kehoe, Alice B., and Dody H. Giletti. 1981. "Women's Preponderance in Possession Cults: The Calcium-Deficiency Hypothesis Extended." *American Anthropologist,* 83: 549–61.

Keller, Helen. 1974 [1902]. *The Story of My Life.* New York: Dell.

Kelly, Raymond C. 1974. "Witchcraft and Sexual Relations: An Exploration in the Social and Semantic Implications of the Structure of Belief." Paper presented at the annual meeting of the American Anthropological Association, Mexico City.

Kelly, Raymond C. 1985. *The Nuer Conquest: The Structure and Development of an Expansionist System.* Ann Arbor, MI: University of Michigan Press.

Kilbride, Philip L., and Janet C. Kilbride. 1990. *Changing Family Life in East Africa: Women and Children at Risk.* University Park, PA: Pennsylvania State University Press.

King, Barbara J. 1999. "Introduction." In B. J. King, ed., *The Origins of Language.* Santa Fe, NM: School of American Research Press, pp. 3–19.

King, Seth S. 1979. "Some Farm Machinery Seems Less than Human." *The New York Times,* April 8, 1979, p. E9.

Klass, Morton. 2004. "Is There 'Caste' Outside of India?" In *Cross-Cultural Research for Social Science,* in C. R. Ember, M. Ember, and P. N. Peregrine, eds., *New Directions in Anthropology.* Upper Saddle River, NJ: Prentice Hall, CD-ROM.

Kleinman, Arthur, Veena Das, and Margaret Lock, eds. 1997. *Social Suffering.* Berkeley: University of California Press.

Kluckhohn, Clyde. 1948. "As an Anthropologist Views It." In A. Deutsch, ed., *Sex Habits of American Men.* Upper Saddle River, NJ: Prentice Hall.

Knecht, Peter. 2003. "Aspects of Shamanism: An Introduction." In C. Chilson and P. Knecht, eds., *Shamans in Asia.* London: RoutledgeCurzon, pp. 1–30.

Koch, Klaus-Friedrich, Soraya Altorki, Andrew Arno, and Letitia Hickson. 1977. "Ritual Reconciliation and the Obviation of Grievances: A Comparative Study in the Ethnography of Law." *Ethnology,* 16: 269–84.

Korbin, Jill E. 1981a. "Introduction." In J. E. Korbin, ed., *Child Abuse and Neglect.* Berkeley: University of California Press.

Korbin, Jill E., ed. 1981b. *Child Abuse and Neglect: Cross-Cultural Perspectives.* Berkeley: University of California Press.

Kottak, Conrad P. 1983. *Assault on Paradise: Social Change in a Brazilian Village.* New York: Random House.

Kottak, Conrad P. 1999. "The New Ecological Anthropology." *Current Anthropology,* 101: 23–35.

Kracke, Waud H. 1979. *Force and Persuasion: Leadership in an Amazonian Society.* Chicago: University of Chicago Press.

Krahn, H., T. F. Hartnagel, and J. W. Gartrell. 1986. "Income Inequality and Homicide Rates: Cross-National Data and Criminological Theories." *Criminology,* 24: 269–95.

Krippner, Stanley. 1987. "Dreams and Shamanism." In S. Nicholson, comp., *Shamanism.* Wheaton, IL: Theosophical Publishing House, pp. 125–32.

Kristof, Nicholas D. 1995. "Japan's Invisible Minority: Better Off Than in Past, but Still Outcasts." *New York Times International,* November 30, 1995, p. A18.

Kristof, Nicholas D. 1997. "Japan's Invisible Minority: Burakumin," *Brittanica Online,* December.

Kushner, Gilbert. 1991. "Applied Anthropology." In W. G. Emener and M. Darrow, eds., *Career Explorations in Human Services.* Springfield, IL: Charles C. Thomas.

LaBarre, Weston. 1945. "Some Observations on Character Structure in the Orient: The Japanese." *Psychiatry,* 8: 326–42.

Lakoff, Robin. 1973. "Language and Woman's Place." *Language in Society,* 2: 45–80.

Lakoff, Robin. 1990a. *Talking Power: The Politics of Language in Our Lives.* New York: Basic Books.

Lakoff, Robin. 1990b. "Why Can't a Woman Be Less Like a Man?" In R. Lakoff, *Talking Power.* New York: Basic Books.

Lambert, Helen. 2001. "Not Talking about Sex in India: Indirection and the Communication of Bodily Intention." In J. Hendry and C. W. Watson, eds., *An Anthropology of Indirect Communication.* London: Routledge, pp. 51–67.

Lambert, William W., Leigh Minturn Triandis, and Margery Wolf. 1959. "Some Correlates of Beliefs in the Malevolence and Benevolence of Supernatural Beings: A Cross-Societal Study." *Journal of Abnormal and Social Psychology,* 58: 162–69.

Lang, Sabine. 1999. "Lesbians, Men-Women and Two-Spirits: Homosexuality and Gender in Native American Cultures." In E. Blackwood and S. E. Weiringa, eds., *Female Desires: Same-Sex Relations and Transgender Practices Across Cultures.* New York: Columbia University Press, pp. 91–116.

Lareau, Annette. 2003. *Unequal Childhoods: Class, Race, and Family Life.* Berkeley, CA: University of California Press.

Larson, Daniel O., John R. Johnson, and Joel C. Michaelsen. 1994. "Missionization among the Coastal Chumash of Central California: A Study of Risk Minimization Strategies." *American Anthropologist,* 96: 263–99.

Lassiter, Luke Eric, Hurley Goodall, Elizabeth Campbell, and Michelle Natasya Johnson, eds. 2004. *The Other Side of Middletown: Exploring Muncie's African American Community.* Walnut Creek, CA: AltaMira Press.

Lawless, Robert. 2004. "Haitians: From Political Repression to Chaos." In *Portraits of Culture,* in C. R. Ember, M. Ember, and P. N. Peregrine, eds., *New Directions in*

Anthropology. Upper Saddle River, NJ: Prentice Hall, CD-ROM.

Lawless, Robert, Vinson H. Sutlive, Jr., and Mario D. Zamora, eds. 1983. *Fieldwork: The Human Experience.* New York: Gordon and Breach.

Leacock, Eleanor, and Richard Lee. 1982a. "Introduction." In E. Leacock and R. Lee, eds., *Politics and History in Band Societies.* Cambridge: Cambridge University Press.

Leacock, Eleanor, and Richard Lee, eds. 1982b. *Politics and History in Band Societies.* Cambridge: Cambridge University Press.

Lee, Richard B. 1968. "What Hunters Do for a Living, or, How to Make Out on Scarce Resources." In R. B. Lee and I. DeVore, eds., *Man the Hunter.* Chicago: Aldine.

Lee, Richard B. 1972. "Population Growth and the Beginnings of Sedentary Life among the !Kung Bushmen." In B. Spooner, ed., *Population Growth.* Cambridge, MA: MIT Press.

Lee, Richard B. 1979. *The !Kung San: Men, Women, and Work in a Foraging Society.* Cambridge: Cambridge University Press.

Lees, Susan H., and Daniel G. Bates. 1974. "The Origins of Specialized Nomadic Pastoralism: A Systemic Model." *American Antiquity,* 39: 187–93.

Leibowitz, Lila. 1978. *Females, Males, Families: A Biosocial Approach.* North Scituate, MA: Duxbury.

Lenski, Gerhard. 1984. *Power and Privilege: A Theory of Social Stratification.* Chapel Hill, NC: University of North Carolina Press. First published 1966.

Lepowsky, Maria. 1990. "Big Men, Big Women and Cultural Autonomy." *Ethnology,* 29: 35–50.

Leslie, C. 1976. "Introduction." In C. Leslie, ed., *Asian Medical Systems: A Comparative Study.* Los Angeles: University of California Press.

Lessa, William A., and Evon Z. Vogt, eds. 1971. *Reader in Comparative Religion: An Anthropological Approach.* 3rd ed. New York: Harper & Row.

Lessa, William A., and Evon Z. Vogt, eds. 1979. *Reader in Comparative Religion: An Anthropological Approach.* 4th ed. New York: Harper & Row.

Lett, James. 1996. "Scientific Anthropology." In D. Levinson and M. Ember, eds., *Encyclopedia of Cultural Anthropology.* New York: Henry Holt.

Levine, James A., Robert Weisell, Simon Chevassus, Claudio D. Martinez, and Barbara Burlingame. "The Distribution of Work Tasks for Male and Female Children and Adults Separated by Gender" in "Looking at Child Labor," *Science* (May 10): 1025.

Levine, Nancy E. 1988. "Women's Work and Infant Feeding: A Case from Rural Nepal." *Ethnology,* 27: 231–51.

Levinson, David. 1989. *Family Violence in Cross-Cultural Perspective.* Newbury Park, CA: Sage.

Levinson, David, and Melvin Ember, eds. 1997. *American Immigrant Cultures: Builders of a Nation.* 2 vols. New York: Macmillan Reference.

Lévi-Strauss, Claude. 1963a. "The Sorcerer and His Magic." In C. Lévi-Strauss, *Structural Anthropology.* New York: Basic Books.

Lévi-Strauss, Claude. 1963b. *Structural Anthropology.* Trans. Claire Jacobson and Brooke Grundfest Schoepf. New York: Basic Books.

Lewin, Tamar. 1994. "Sex in America: Faithfulness in Marriage Is Overwhelming." *The New York Times,* October 7, 1994, pp. A1, A18.

Lewis, Oscar. 1951. *Life in a Mexican Village: Tepoztlan Revisited.* Urbana, IL: University of Illinois Press.

Lewis, Oscar (with the assistance of Victor Barnouw). 1958. *Village Life in Northern India.* Urbana, IL: University of Illinois Press.

Lichter, Daniel T., Diane K. McLaughlin, George Kephart, and David J. Landry. 1992. "Race and the Retreat from Marriage: A Shortage of Marriageable Men?" *American Sociological Review,* 57: 781–99.

Lingenfelter, Sherwood G. 2004. "Yap: Changing Roles of Men and Women." In *Portraits of Culture,* in C. R. Ember, M. Ember, and P. N. Peregrine, eds., *New Directions in Anthropology.* Upper Saddle River, NJ: Prentice Hall, CD-ROM.

Linton, Ralph. 1936. *The Study of Man.* New York: Appleton-Century-Crofts.

Linton, Ralph. 1945. *The Cultural Background of Personality.* New York: Appleton-Century-Crofts.

Loftin, Colin K. 1971. "Warfare and Societal Complexity: A Cross-Cultural Study of Organized Fighting in Preindustrial Societies." Ph.D. dissertation, University of North Carolina at Chapel Hill.

Loftin, Colin, David McDowall, and James Boudouris. 1989. "Economic Change and Homicide in Detroit, 1926–1979." In T. R. Gurr, ed., *Violence in America,* Vol. 1: *The History of Crime.* Newbury Park, CA: Sage, pp. 163–77.

Loustaunau, Martha O., and Elisa J. Sobo. 1997. *The Cultural Context of Health, Illness, and Medicine.* Westport, CT: Bergin & Garvey.

Low, Bobbi. 1990. "Marriage Systems and Pathogen Stress in Human Societies." *American Zoologist,* 30: 325–39.

Low, Bobbi S. 2004. "Behavioral Ecology, 'Sociobiology,' and Human Behavior." In *Research Frontiers,* in C. R. Ember, M. Ember, and P. N. Peregrine, eds., *New Directions in Anthropology.* Upper Saddle River, NJ: Prentice Hall, CD-ROM.

Lyttleton, Chris. 2000. *Endangered Relations: Negotiating Sex and AIDS in Thailand.* Bangkok: White Lotus Press.

Maccoby, Eleanor E., and Carol N. Jacklin. 1974. *The Psychology of Sex Differences.* Stanford, CA: Stanford University Press.

MacDonald, Douglas H. and Barry S. Hewlett. 1999. "Reproductive Interests and Forager Mobility." *Current Anthropology,* 40: 501–23.

Magner, L. 1992. *A History of Medicine.* New York: Marcel Dekker.

Mahony, Frank Joseph. 1971. *A Trukese Theory of Medicine.* Ann Arbor, MI: University Microfilms, 1070, as seen in eHRAF World Cultures on the Web.

Malefijt, Annemarie De Waal. 1968. *Religion and Culture: An Introduction to Anthropology of Religion.* New York: Macmillan.

Mangin, William. 1967. "Latin American Squatter Settlements: A Problem and a Solution." *Latin American Research Review,* 2: 65–98.

Manhein, Mary H. 1999. *The Bone Lady: Life as a Forensic Anthropologist.* Baton Rouge: Louisiana State University Press.

Marano, Louis A. 1973. "A Macrohistoric Trend toward World Government." *Behavior Science Notes,* 8: 35–40.

Marks, Jonathan. 1994. "Black, White, Other: Racial Categories Are Cultural Constructs Masquerading as Biology." *Natural History* (December): 32–35.

Marshall, Lorna. 1961. "Sharing, Talking and Giving: Relief of Social Tensions among !Kung Bushmen." *Africa,* 31: 239–42.

Martin, M. Kay, and Barbara Voorhies. 1975. *Female of the Species.* New York: Columbia University Press.

Mascie-Taylor, C. G. Nicholas. 1990. "The Biology of Social Class." In C. G. N. Mascie-Taylor, ed., *Biosocial Aspects of Social Class.* Oxford: Oxford University Press, pp. 117–42.

Masumura, Wilfred T. 1977. "Law and Violence: A Cross-Cultural Study." *Journal of Anthropological Research,* 33: 388–99.

Mathiassen, Therkel. 1928. *Material Culture of Iglulik Eskimos.* Copenhagen: Glydendalske.

Matossian, Mary K. 1982. "Ergot and the Salem Witchcraft Affair." *American Scientist,* 70: 355–57.

Matossian, Mary K. 1989. *Poisons of the Past: Molds, Epidemics, and History.* New Haven, CT: Yale University Press.

McCain, Garvin, and Erwin M. Segal. 1988. *The Game of Science.* 5th ed. Monterey, CA: Brooks/Cole.

McCarthy, Frederick D., and Margaret McArthur. 1960. "The Food Quest and the Time Factor in Aboriginal Economic Life." In C. P. Mountford, ed., *Records of the Australian-American Scientific Expedition to Arnhem Land,* Vol. 2: *Anthropology and Nutrition.* Melbourne: Melbourne University Press.

McCorriston, Joy, and Frank Hole. 1991. "The Ecology of Seasonal Stress and the Origins of Agriculture in the Near East." *American Anthropologist,* 93: 46–69.

McGarvey, Stephen T. 1994. "The Thrifty Gene Concept and Adiposity Studies in Biological Anthropology." *Journal of the Polynesian Society,* 103: 29–42.

McKee, Lauris A. 1984. "Sex Differentials in Survivorship and the Customary Treatment of Infants and Children." *Medical Anthropology,* 8: 91–108.

McNeill, William H. 1967. *A World History.* New York: Oxford University Press.

McNeill, William H. 1976. *Plagues and Peoples.* Garden City, NY: Doubleday/Anchor.

McNeill, William H. 1992. *Plagues and Peoples.* Magnolia, MA: Peter Smith.

Mead, Margaret. 1950 [1935]. *Sex and Temperament in Three Primitive Societies.* New York: Mentor.

Mead, Margaret. 1961 [1928]. *Coming of Age in Samoa.* 3rd ed. New York: Morrow.

Mead, Margaret. 1978. "The Evolving Ethics of Applied Anthropology." In E. M. Eddy and W. L. Partridge, eds., *Applied Anthropology in America.* New York: Columbia University Press.

Meek, C. K. 1940. *Land Law and Custom in the Colonies.* London: Oxford University Press.

Meggitt, Mervyn. 1977. *Blood Is Their Argument: Warfare among the Mae Enga Tribesmen of the New Guinea Highlands.* Palo Alto, CA: Mayfield.

Mellor, John W., and Sarah Gavian. 1987. "Famine: Causes, Prevention, and Relief." *Science* (January 30): 539–44.

Messer, Ellen. 1996. "Hunger Vulnerability from an Anthropologist's Food Systems Perspective." In E. F. Moran, ed., *Transforming Societies, Transforming Anthropology.* Ann Arbor, MI: University of Michigan Press.

Middleton, John. 1971. "The Cult of the Dead: Ancestors and Ghosts." In W. A. Lessa and E. Z. Vogt, eds., *Reader in Comparative Religion.* 3rd ed. New York: Harper & Row.

Middleton, Russell. 1962. "Brother-Sister and Father-Daughter Marriage in Ancient Egypt." *American Sociological Review,* 27: 603–11.

Milanovic, Branko. 1994. *State of the World 1994: A Worldwatch Institute Report on Progress toward a Sustainable Society.* New York: Norton.

Milanovic, Branko. 2002. "True World Income Distribution, 1988 and 1993: First Calculation Based on

Household Surveys Alone." *The Economic Journal,* 112: 51–92.

Miller, Greg. 2004. "Listen, Baby." *Science* (November).

Miner, Horace. 1956. "Body Rituals among the Nacirema." *American Anthropologist,* 58: 504–505.

Minturn, Leigh, and Jerry Stashak. 1982. "Infanticide as a Terminal Abortion Procedure." *Behavior Science Research,* 17: 70–85.

Miracle, Andrew W. 2004. "A Shaman to Organizations." In *Research Frontiers,* in C. R. Ember, M. Ember, and P. N. Peregrine, eds., *New Directions in Anthropology.* Upper Saddle River, NJ: Prentice Hall, CD-ROM.

Mitchell, Donald. 2004. "Nimpkish: Complex Foragers on the Northwest Coast of North America." In *Portraits of Culture,* in C. R. Ember, M. Ember, and P. N. Peregrine, eds., *New Directions in Anthropology.* Upper Saddle River, NJ: Prentice Hall, CD-ROM.

Moerman, Daniel E. 1997. "Physiology and Symbols: The Anthropological Implications of the Placebo Effect." In L. Romanucci-Ross, D. E. Moerman, and L. R. Tancredi, eds., *The Anthropology of Medicine.* 3rd ed. Westport, CT: Bergin & Garvey, pp. 240–53.

Molnar, Stephen. 1998. *Human Variation: Races, Types, and Ethnic Groups.* 4th ed. Upper Saddle River, NJ: Prentice Hall.

Mooney, Kathleen A. 1978. "The Effects of Rank and Wealth on Exchange among the Coast Salish." *Ethnology,* 17: 391–406.

Moore, Carmella Caracci. 1988. "An Optimal Scaling of Murdock's Theories of Illness Data—An Approach to the Problem of Interdependence." *Behavior Science Research,* 22: 161–79.

Moore, Carmella C., A. Kimball Romney, Ti-Lien Hsia, and Craig D. Rusch. 1999. "The Universality of the Semantic Structure of Emotion Terms: Methods for the Study of Inter- and Intra-Cultural Variability." *American Anthropologist,* 101: 529–46.

Moore, John H., and Janis E. Campbell. 2002. "Confirming Unilocal Residence in Native North America." *Ethnology,* 41: 175–88.

Moore, Omar Khayyam. 1957. "Divination: A New Perspective." *American Anthropologist,* 59: 69–74.

Moran, Emilio F. 1993. *Through Amazon Eyes: The Human Ecology of Amazonian Populations.* Iowa City, IA: University of Iowa Press.

Moran, Emilio F., ed. 1996. *Transforming Societies, Transforming Anthropology.* Ann Arbor, MI: University of Michigan Press.

Morris, John. 1938. *Living with Lepchas: A Book about the Sikkim Himalayas.* London: Heinemann.

Mukerjee, Madhusree. 1996. "Field Notes: Interview with a Parrot." *Scientific American* (April).

Mukhopadhyay, Carol C., and Patricia J. Higgins. 1988. "Anthropological Studies of Women's Status Revisited: 1977–1987." *Annual Review of Anthropology,* 17: 461–95.

Munroe, Robert L., Robert Hulefeld, James M. Rodgers, Damon L. Tomeo, and Steven K. Yamazaki. 2000. "Aggression Among Children in Four Cultures." *Cross-Cultural Research,* 34: 3–25.

Munroe, Robert L., Ruth H. Munroe, and Stephen Winters. 1996. "Cross-Cultural Correlates of the Consonant-Vowel (CV) Syllable." *Cross-Cultural Research,* 30: 60–83.

Munroe, Ruth H., Robert L. Munroe, and Harold S. Shimmin. 1984. "Children's Work in Four Cultures: Determinants and Consequences." *American Anthropologist,* 86: 369–79.

Munroe, Ruth H., Robert L. Munroe, and Beatrice B. Whiting, eds. 1981. *Handbook of Cross-Cultural Human Development.* New York: Garland.

Murdock, George P. 1949. *Social Structure.* New York: Macmillan.

Murdock, George P. 1967. "Ethnographic Atlas: A Summary." *Ethnology,* 6: 109–236.

Murdock, George Peter. 1980. *Theories of Illness: A World Survey.* Pittsburgh, PA: University of Pittsburgh Press.

Murdock, George P., and Caterina Provost. 1973. "Factors in the Division of Labor by Sex: A Cross-Cultural Analysis." *Ethnology,* 12: 203–25.

Murdock, George P., and Douglas R. White. 1969. "Standard Cross-Cultural Sample." *Ethnology,* 8: 329–69.

Murphy, Robert F. 1960. *Headhunter's Heritage: Social and Economic Change among the Mundurucú.* Berkeley: University of California Press.

Murphy, Robert F., and Julian H. Steward. 1956. "Tappers and Trappers: Parallel Process in Acculturation." *Economic Development and Cultural Change,* 4 (July): 335–55.

Myers, Fred R. 1988. "Critical Trends in the Study of Hunter-Gatherers." *Annual Review of Anthropology,* 17: 261–82.

Nadel, S. F. 1935. "Nupe State and Community." *Africa,* 8: 257–303.

Nadel, S. F. 1942. *A Black Byzantium: The Kingdom of Nupe in Nigeria.* London: Oxford University Press.

Nag, Moni, Benjamin N. F. White, and R. Creighton Peet. 1978. "An Anthropological Approach to the Study of the Economic Value of Children in Java and Nepal." *Current Anthropology,* 19: 293–301.

Nagata, Judith. 2001. "Beyond Theology: Toward an Anthropology of 'Fundamentalism'." *American Anthropologist,* 103: 481–98.

Nagel, Ernest. 1961. *The Structure of Science: Problems in the Logic of Scientific Explanation.* New York: Harcourt, Brace & World.

Naroll, Raoul. 1961. "Two Solutions to Galton's Problem." *Philosophy of Science,* 28 (January): 15–39.

Naroll, Raoul. 1967. "Imperial Cycles and World Order." *Peace Research Society: Papers,* 7: 83–101.

Nash, Manning. 1989. *The Cauldron of Ethnicity in the Modern World.* Chicago: University of Chicago Press.

National Center for Health Statistics. 2006. *Health, United States, 2006, with Chartbook on Trends in the Health of Americans.* Hyattsville, MD.

Nerlove, Sara B. 1974. "Women's Workload and Infant Feeding Practices: A Relationship with Demographic Implications." *Ethnology,* 13: 207–14.

Nevins, Allan. 1927. *The American States during and after the Revolution.* New York: Macmillan.

Newman, Katherine S. 1983. *Law and Economic Organization: A Comparative Study of Preindustrial Societies.* Cambridge, MA: Cambridge University Press.

New York Times International, September 30, 1997, p. A26.

Niehoff, Arthur H. 1966. *A Casebook of Social Change.* Chicago: Aldine.

Nimkoff, M. F., and Russell Middleton. 1960. "Types of Family and Types of Economy." *American Journal of Sociology,* 66: 215–25.

Noll, Richard. 1987. "The Presence of Spirits in Magic and Madness." In S. Nicholson, comp., *Shamanism.* Wheaton, IL: Theosophical Publishing House, pp. 47–61.

Noss, Andrew J., and Barry S. Hewlett. 2001. "The Contexts of Female Hunting in Central Africa." *American Anthropologist,* 103: 1024–40.

Nussbaum, Martha C. 1995. "Introduction." In M. C. Nussbaum and J. Glover, *Women, Culture, and Development: A Study of Human Capabilities.* Oxford: Clarendon Press.

O'Brian, Robin. 1999. "Who Weaves and Why? Weaving, Loom Complexity, and Trade." *Cross-Cultural Research,* 33: 30–42.

Oerlemans, J. 2005. "Extracting a Climate Signal from 169 Glacial Records." *Science,* 38 (April 28): 675–77.

Ogburn, William F. 1922. *Social Change.* New York: Huebsch.

Oliver, Douglas L. 1955. *A Solomon Island Society.* Cambridge, MA: Harvard University Press.

Ortiz de Montellano, B. R., and C. H. Browner. 1985. "Chemical Bases for Medicinal Plant Use in Oaxaca, Mexico." *Journal of Ethnopharmacology,* 13: 57–88.

Otterbein, Keith. 1968. "Internal War: A Cross-Cultural Study." *American Anthropologist,* 70: 277–89.

Otterbein, Keith. 1970. *The Evolution of War.* New Haven, CT: HRAF Press.

Otterbein, Keith. 1986. *The Ultimate Coercive Sanction: A Cross-Cultural Study of Capital Punishment.* New Haven, CT: HRAF Press.

Otterbein, Keith, and Charlotte Swanson Otterbein. 1965. "An Eye for an Eye, a Tooth for a Tooth: A Cross-Cultural Study of Feuding." *American Anthropologist,* 67: 1470–82.

Paige, Jeffery M. 1975. *Agrarian Revolution: Social Movements and Export Agriculture in the Underdeveloped World.* New York: Free Press.

Paine, Robert. 1994. *Herds of the Tundra.* Washington, D.C.: Smithsonian Institution Press.

Palsson, Gisli. 1988. "Hunters and Gatherers of the Sea." In T. Ingold, D. Riches, and J. Woodburn, eds., *Hunters and Gatherers. 1. History, Evolution and Social Change.* New York: St. Martin's Press.

"Paper." 1980. *Academic American Encyclopedia.* Princeton, NJ: Areté.

Pasternak, Burton. 1976. *Introduction to Kinship and Social Organization.* Upper Saddle River, NJ: Prentice Hall.

Pasternak, Burton, Carol R. Ember, and Melvin Ember. 1976. "On the Conditions Favoring Extended Family Households." *Journal of Anthropological Research,* 32: 109–23.

Patterson, Orlando. 1982. *Slavery and Social Death: A Comparative Study.* Cambridge, MA: Harvard University Press.

Patterson, Orlando. 2000. Review of *One Drop of Blood: The American Misadventure of Race* by Scott L. Malcomson. *New York Times Book Review,* October 22, 2000, pp. 15–16.

Peacock, James L. 1986. *The Anthropological Lens: Harsh Light, Soft Focus.* Cambridge: Cambridge University Press.

Pearson, J. D., Gary D. James, and Daniel E. Brown. 1993. "Stress and Changing Lifestyles in the Pacific: Physiological Stress Responses of Samoans in Rural and Urban Settings." *American Journal of Human Biology,* 5: 49–60.

Pelto, Pertti J., and Ludger Müller-Wille. 1987. "Snowmobiles: Technological Revolution in the Arctic." In H. R. Bernard and P. J. Pelto, eds., *Technology and Social Change.* 2nd ed. Prospect Heights, IL: Waveland Press, pp. 207–43.

Pelto, Pertti J., and Gretel H. Pelto. 1975. "Intra-Cultural Diversity: Some Theoretical Issues." *American Ethnologist,* 2: 1–18.

Pepperberg, Irene Maxine. 1999. *The Alex Studies: Cognitive and Communicative Abilities of Grey Parrots.* Cambridge, MA: Harvard University Press.

Peregrine, Peter. 1996. "The Birth of the Gods Revisited: A Partial Replication of Guy Swanson's (1960) Cross-Cultural Study of Religion." *Cross-Cultural Research,* 30: 84–112.

Peregrine, Peter N., Carol R. Ember, and Melvin Ember, eds. 2002. *Archaeology: Original Readings in Method and Practice.* Upper Saddle River, NJ: Prentice Hall.

Peregrine, Peter N., Melvin Ember, and Carol R. Ember. 2004. "Predicting the Future State of the World Using Archaeological Data: An Exercise in Archaeomancy. *Cross-Cultural Research,* 38: 133–46.

Petersen, L. R., G. R. Lee, and G. J. Ellis. 1982. "Social Structure, Socialization Values, and Disciplinary Techniques: A Cross-Cultural Analysis." *Journal of Marriage and the Family,* 44: 131–42.

Pfaff, C. 1979. "Constraints on Language Mixing." *Language,* 55: 291–318, as cited in Wardhaugh, *An Introduction to Sociolinguistics.* 2nd ed.

Phillipson, D. W. 1976. "Archaeology and Bantu Linguistics." *World Archaeology,* 8: 65–82.

Picchi, Debra. 1991. "The Impact of an Industrial Agricultural Project on the Bakairí Indians of Central Brazil." *Human Organization,* 50: 26–38.

Picchi, Debra. 2004. "Bakairí: The Death of an Indian." In *Portraits of Culture* in C. R. Ember, M. Ember, and P. N. Peregrine, eds., *New Directions in Anthropology.* Upper Saddle River, NJ: Prentice Hall, CD-ROM.

Plattner, Stuart, ed. 1985. *Markets and Marketing.* Monographs in Economic Anthropology, No. 4. Lanham, MD: University Press of America.

Plattner, Stuart. 1989. "Marxism." In S. Plattner, ed., *Economic Anthropology.* Stanford, CA: Stanford University Press.

"Plundering Earth Is Nothing New." *Los Angeles Times* News Service, as reported in the *New Haven Register,* June 12, 1994, pp. A18–A19.

Podolefsky, Aaron, and Peter J. Brown. 1997. *Applying Cultural Anthropology: An Introductory Reader.* 3rd ed. Mountain View, CA: Mayfield.

Podolefsky, Aaron, and Peter J. Brown. 1999. *Applying Cultural Anthropology: An Introductory Reader.* 4th ed. Mountain View, CA: Mayfield.

Poggie, John J., Jr., Billie R. DeWalt, and William W. Dressler, eds. 1991. *Anthropological Research: Process and Application.* Albany, NY: State University of New York Press.

Poggie, John J., Jr., and Richard B. Pollnac. 1988. "Danger and Rituals of Avoidance among New England Fishermen." *MAST: Maritime Anthropological Studies,* 1: 66–78.

Poggie, John J., Jr., Richard B. Pollnac, and Carl Gersuny. 1976. "Risk as a Basis for Taboos among Fishermen in Southern New England." *Journal for the Scientific Study of Religion,* 15: 257–62.

Polanyi, Karl. 1957. "The Economy as Instituted Process." In K. Polanyi, C. M. Arensberg, and H. W. Pearson, eds., *Trade and Market in the Early Empires.* New York: Free Press.

Polanyi, Karl, Conrad M. Arensberg, and Harry W. Pearson, eds. 1957. *Trade and Market in the Early Empires.* New York: Free Press.

Popenoe, David. 1988. *Disturbing the Nest: Family Change and Decline in Modern Societies.* New York: Aldine.

Popenoe, Rebecca. 2004. *Feeding Desire: Fatness, Beauty, and Sexuality Among a Saharan People.* London: Routledge.

Pospisil, Leopold. 1963. *The Kapauku Papuans of West New Guinea.* New York: Holt, Rinehart & Winston.

Prevalence, Incidence, and Consequences of Violence against Women: Findings from the National Violence against Women Survey. 1998. Washington, D.C.: U.S. Department of Justice, November 1998.

Pryor, Frederic L. 1977. *The Origins of the Economy: A Comparative Study of Distribution in Primitive and Peasant Economies.* New York: Academic Press.

Pryor, Frederic L. 2005. *Economic Systems of Foraging, Agricultural, and Industrial Societies.* Cambridge: Cambridge University Press.

Quandt, Sara A. 1996. "Nutrition in Anthropology." In C. F. Sargent and T. M. Johnson, eds., *Handbook of Medical Anthropology.* Rev. ed. Westport, CT: Greenwood Press, pp. 272–89.

Quinn, Naomi. 1977. "Anthropological Studies on Women's Status." *Annual Review of Anthropology,* 6: 181–225.

Radcliffe-Brown, A. R. 1922. *The Andaman Islanders: A Study in Social Anthropology.* Cambridge: Cambridge University Press.

Rathje, William L. 1971. "The Origin and Development of Lowland Classic Maya Civilization." *American Antiquity,* 36: 275–85.

Ravesloot, John. 1997. "Changing Native American Perceptions of Archaeology and Archaeologists." In N. Swidler et al., eds., *Native Americans and Archaeologists.* Walnut Creek, CA: AltaMira Press.

Ray, Verne F. 1954. *The Sanpoil and Nespelem: Salishan Peoples of Northeastern Washington.* New Haven, CT: HRAF Press.

Raybeck, Douglas. 1998. "Toward More Holistic Explanations: Cross-Cultural Research and Cross-Level Analysis." *Cross-Cultural Research,* 32: 123–42.

Raybeck, Douglas, J. Shoobe, and J. Grauberger. 1989. "Women, Stress and Participation in Possession Cults: A Reexamination of the Calcium Deficiency Hypothesis." *Medical Anthropology Quarterly,* 3: 139–61.

Revkin, Andrew C. 2005. "Tracking the Imperiled Bluefin From Ocean to Sushi Platter." *The New York Times,* May 3, 2005, pp. F1, F4.

Rivers, W. H. R. 1967 [1906]. *The Todas.* Oosterhout, N.B., The Netherlands: Anthropological Publications.

Roberts, John M. 1967. "Oaths, Autonomic Ordeals, and Power." In C. S. Ford, ed., *Cross-Cultural Approaches.* New Haven, CT: HRAF Press.

Rodwin, Lloyd, and Bishwapriya Sanyal. 1987. "Shelter, Settlement, and Development: An Overview." In L. Rodwin, ed., *Shelter, Settlement, and Development.* Boston: Allen & Unwin, pp. 3–31.

Rogers, Everett M. 1983. *Diffusion of Innovations.* 3rd ed. New York: Free Press.

Rogers, Everett M. 1995. *Diffusion of Innovations.* 4th ed. New York: Free Press.

Rogers, Everett M. 2003. *Diffusion of Innovations.* 5th ed. New York: Simon & Schuster.

Rogoff, Barbara. 2002. *The Cultural Nature of Human Development.* New York: Oxford University Press.

Rohner, Ronald P. 1975. *They Love Me, They Love Me Not: A Worldwide Study of the Effects of Parental Acceptance and Rejection.* New Haven, CT: HRAF Press.

Rohner, Ronald P. 1976. "Sex Differences in Aggression: Phylogenetic and Enculturation Perspectives." *Ethos,* 4: 57–72.

Romney, A. Kimball, Susan C. Weller, and William H. Batchelder. 1986. "Culture as Consensus: A Theory of Culture and Informant Accuracy." *American Anthropologist,* 88: 313–38.

Roosens, Eugeen E. 1989. *Creating Ethnicity: The Process of Ethnogenesis.* Newbury Park, CA: Sage Publications.

Roosevelt, A. C. 1992. "Secrets of the Forest." *The Sciences* (November/December): 22–28.

Rosaldo, Michelle Z., and Louise Lamphere, eds. 1974. *Woman, Culture, and Society.* Stanford, CA: Stanford University Press.

Roscoe, Paul. 2002. "The Hunters and Gatherers of New Guinea." *Current Anthropology,* 43: 153–62.

Rosenblatt, Paul C., R. Patricia Walsh, and Douglas A. Jackson. 1976. *Grief and Mourning in Cross-Cultural Perspective.* New Haven, CT: HRAF Press.

Ross, Marc Howard. 1981. "Socioeconomic Complexity, Socialization, and Political Differentiation: A Cross-Cultural Study." *Ethos,* 9: 217–47.

Ross, Marc Howard. 1985. "Internal and External Conflict and Violence." *Journal of Conflict Resolution,* 29: 547–79.

Ross, Marc Howard. 1988. "Political Organization and Political Participation: Exit, Voice, and Loyalty in Preindustrial Societies." *Comparative Politics,* 21: 73–89.

Ross, Marc Howard. 2004a. "Ethnocentrism and Ethnic Conflict." In *Research Frontiers,* in C. R. Ember, M. Ember, and P. N. Peregrine, eds., *New Directions in Anthropology.* Upper Saddle River, NJ: Prentice Hall, CD-ROM.

Ross, Marc Howard. 2004b. "Political Participation." In *Cross-Cultural Research for Social Science,* in C. R. Ember, M. Ember, and P. N. Peregrine, eds., *New Directions in Anthropology.* Upper Saddle River, NJ: Prentice Hall, CD-ROM.

Rubel, Arthur J., and Michael R. Hass. 1996. "Ethnomedicine." In T. M. Johnson and C. F. Sargent, *Medical Anthropology.* Westport, CT: Praeger, pp. 115–31; reprinted in Sargent and Johnson, *Handbook of Medical Anthropology.*

Rubel, Arthur J., Carl O. Nell, and Rolando Collado-Ardón (with the assistance of John Krejci and Jean Krejci). 1984. *Susto: A Folk Illness.* Berkeley: University of California Press.

Rubin, J. Z., F. J. Provenzano, and R. F. Haskett. 1974. "The Eye of the Beholder: Parents' Views on the Sex of New Borns." *American Journal of Orthopsychiatry,* 44: 512–19.

Rudmin, Floyd Webster. 1988. "Dominance, Social Control, and Ownership: A History and a Cross-Cultural Study of Motivations for Private Property." *Behavior Science Research,* 22: 130–60.

Rummel, R. J. 2002a. *Death by Government.* Chapter 1. Accessed at http://www.hawaii.edu/powerkills/DBG. CHAP1.HTM

Rummel, R. J. 2002b. "Democracies Are Less Warlike Than Other Regimes." Accessed at http://www.hawaii. edu/powerkills/DP95.HTM

Rummel, R. J. 2002c. *Statistics of Democide.* Chapter 17. Accessed at http://www.hawaii.edu/powerkills/SOD. CHAP17.HTM

Rummel, R. J. 2002d. *Statistics of Democide.* Chapter 21. Accessed at http://www.hawaii.edu/powerkills/SOD. CHAP21.HTM

Ruskin, John. 1963. "Of King's Treasures." In J. D. Rosenberg, ed., *The Genius of John Ruskin.* New York: Braziller.

Russell, Elbert W. 1972. "Factors of Human Aggression." *Behavior Science Notes,* 7: 275–312.

Russett, Bruce (with the collaboration of William Antholis, Carol R. Ember, Melvin Ember, and Zeev Maoz). 1993. *Grasping the Democratic Peace: Principles for a Post–Cold War World.* Princeton, NJ: Princeton University Press.

Russett, Bruce, and John R. Oneal. 2001. *Triangulating Peace: Democracy, Interdependence, and International Organizations.* New York: Norton.

Sahlins, Marshall D. 1958. *Social Stratification in Polynesia.* Seattle: University of Washington Press.

Sahlins, Marshall D. 1961. "The Segmentary Lineage: An Organization of Predatory Expansion." *American Anthropologist,* 63: 332–45.

Sahlins, Marshall D. 1962. *Moala: Culture and Nature on a Fijian Island.* Ann Arbor, MI: University of Michigan Press.

Sahlins, Marshall D. 1963. "Poor Man, Rich Man, Big-Man, Chief: Political Types in Melanesia and Polynesia." *Comparative Studies in Society and History,* 5: 285–303.

Sahlins, Marshall. 1983. "Other Times, Other Customs: The Anthropology of History." *American Anthropologist,* 85: 517–44.

Sahlins, Marshall D. 1972. *Stone Age Economics.* Chicago: Aldine.

Sahlins, Marshall, and Elman Service. 1960. *Evolution and Culture.* Ann Arbor, MI: University of Michigan Press.

Salzman, Philip Carl. 1996. "Pastoralism." In D. Levinson and M. Ember, eds., *Encyclopedia of Cultural Anthropology.* New York: Henry Holt, vol. 3, pp. 899–905.

Salzman, Philip Carl. 2002. "Pastoral Nomads: Some General Observations Based on Research in Iran." *Journal of Anthropological Research,* 58: 245–64.

Sanday, Peggy R. 1973. "Toward a Theory of the Status of Women." *American Anthropologist,* 75: 1682–700.

Sanday, Peggy R. 1974. "Female Status in the Public Domain." In M. Z. Rosaldo and L. Lamphere, eds., *Woman, Culture, and Society.* Stanford, CA: Stanford University Press, pp. 189–206.

Sapir, Edward. 1938. "Why Cultural Anthropology Needs the Psychiatrist." *Psychiatry,* 1: 7–12.

Sapir, Edward. 1949 [1921]. *Language: An Introduction to the Study of Speech.* New York: Harcourt Brace Jovanovich.

Sapir, Edward, and M. Swadesh. 1964. "American Indian Grammatical Categories." In D. Hymes, ed., *Language in Culture and Society.* New York: Harper & Row.

Sargent, Carolyn F., and Thomas M. Johnson, eds. 1996. *Handbook of Medical Anthropology: Contemporary Theory and Method.* Rev. ed. Westport, CT: Greenwood Press, pp. 272–89.

Sattler, Richard A. 1996. "Remnants, Renegades, and Runaways: Seminole Ethnogenesis Reconsidered." In J. D. Hill, *Ethnogenesis in the Americas.* Iowa City: University of Iowa Press, pp. 36–69.

Savage-Rumbaugh, E. S. 1992. "Language Training of Apes." In S. Jones, R. Martin, and D. Pilbeam, eds., *The Cambridge Encyclopedia of Human Evolution.* New York: Cambridge University Press.

Scaglion, Richard. 2004. "Law and Society." *Cross-Cultural Research for Social Science,* in C. R. Ember, M. Ember, and P. N. Peregrine, eds., *New Directions in Anthropology.* Upper Saddle River, NJ: Prentice Hall, CD-ROM.

Schiffer, Michael B., ed. 1984. *Advances in Archaeological Method and Theory.* Vol. 7. Orlando, FL: Academic Press.

Schlegel, Alice. 1972. *Male Dominance and Female Autonomy.* New Haven, CT: HRAF Press.

Schlegel, Alice, ed. 1977. *Sexual Stratification: A Cross-Cultural View.* New York: Columbia University Press.

Schlegel, Alice. 1989. "Gender Issues and Cross-Cultural Research." *Behavior Science Research,* 23: 265–80.

Schlegel, Alice. 1991. "Status, Property, and the Value on Virginity." *American Ethnologist,* 18: 719–34.

Schlegel, Alice, and Herbert Barry, III. 1986. "The Cultural Consequences of Female Contribution to Subsistence." *American Anthropologist,* 88: 142–50.

Schlegel, Alice, and Rohn Eloul. 1987. "A New Coding of Marriage Transactions." *Behavior Science Research,* 21: 118–40.

Schlegel, Alice, and Rohn Eloul. 1988. "Marriage Transactions: Labor, Property, and Status." *American Anthropologist,* 90: 291–309.

Schneider, David M. 1961a. "The Distinctive Features of Matrilineal Descent Groups." In D. M. Schneider and K. Gough, eds., *Matrilineal Kinship.* Berkeley: University of California Press, pp. 1–35.

Schneider, David M. 1961b. "Truk." In D. M. Schneider and K. Gough, eds., *Matrilineal Kinship.* Berkeley: University of California Press, pp. 202–33.

Schneider, David M., and Kathleen Gough, eds. 1961c. *Matrilineal Kinship.* Berkeley: University of California Press.

Schoepf, B. 1988. "Women, AIDS and Economic Crisis in Central Africa." *Canadian Journal of African Studies,* 22: 625–44.

Schrauf, Robert W. 1999. "Mother Tongue Maintenance Among North American Ethnic Groups." *Cross-Cultural Research,* 33: 175–92.

Schrire, Carmel, ed. 1984a. *Past and Present in Hunter-Gatherer Studies.* Orlando, FL: Academic Press.

Schrire, Carmel. 1984b. "Wild Surmises on Savage Thoughts." In C. Schrire, ed., *Past and Present in Hunter-Gatherer Studies.* Orlando, FL: Academic Press, pp. 1–25.

Scott, Janny, and David Leonhardt. 2005. "Class in America: Shadowy Lines That Still Divide." *The New York Times,* May 15, 2005, pp. 1, 26.

Scudder, Thayer. 1978. "Opportunities, Issues and Achievements in Development Anthropology since the Mid-1960s: A Personal View." In E. M. Eddy and W. L. Partridge, eds., *Applied Anthropology in America.* 2nd ed. New York: Columbia University Press.

Segal, Edwin S. 2004. "Cultural Constructions of Gender." In C. R. Ember and M. Ember, eds., *Encyclopedia of Sex and Gender: Men and Women in the World's Cultures.* Vol 1. New York: Kluwer Academic/Plenum, pp. 3–10.

Sellen, Daniel W., and Daniel J. Hruschka. 2004. "Extracted-Food Resource-Defense Polygyny in Native Western North American Societies at Contact." *Current Anthropology,* 45: 707–14.

Sengupta, Somini. 2002. "Money From Kin Abroad Helps Bengalis Get By." *The New York Times,* June 24, p. A3.

Senner, Wayne M. 1989. "Theories and Myths on the Origins of Writing: A Historical Overview." In W. M. Senner, ed., *The Origins of Writing.* Lincoln, NE: University of Nebraska Press.

Service, Elman R. 1962. *Primitive Social Organization: An Evolutionary Perspective.* New York: Random House.

Service, Elman R. 1975. *Origins of the State and Civilization: The Process of Cultural Evolution.* New York: Norton.

Service, Elman R. 1978. *Profiles in Ethnology.* 3rd ed. New York: Harper & Row.

Service, Elman R. 1979. *The Hunters.* 2nd ed. Upper Saddle River, NJ: Prentice Hall.

Seyfarth, Robert M., and Dorothy L. Cheney. 1982. "How Monkeys See the World: A Review of Recent Research on East African Vervet Monkeys." In C. T. Snowdon, C. H. Brown, and M. R. Petersen, eds., *Primate Communication.* New York: Cambridge University Press.

Shanklin, Eugenia. 1991. *Anthropology and Race.* Belmont, CA: Wadsworth, 1994.

Shankman, Paul. 1991. "Culture Contact, Cultural Ecology, and Dani Warfare." *Man,* 26: 299–321.

Sheils, Dean. 1975. "Toward a Unified Theory of Ancestor Worship: A Cross-Cultural Study." *Social Forces,* 54: 427–40.

Sheils, Dean. 1980. "A Comparative Study of Human Sacrifice." *Behavior Science Research,* 15: 245–62.

Shibamoto, Janet S. 1987. "The Womanly Woman: Japanese Female Speech." In S. U. Philips, S. Steele, and C. Tanz, eds., *Language, Gender, and Sex in Comparative Perspective.* Cambridge: Cambridge University Press.

Silver, Harry R. 1981. "Calculating Risks: The Socioeconomic Foundations of Aesthetic Innovation in an Ashanti Carving Community." *Ethnology,* 20: 101–14.

Simmons, Janie, Paul Farmer, and Brooke G. Schoepf. 1996. "A Global Perspective." In P. Farmer, M. Connors, and J. Simmons, eds., *Women, Poverty, and AIDS: Sex, Drugs, and Structural Violence.* Monroe, ME: Common Courage Press, pp. 39–90.

Simpson, S. P., and Ruth Field. 1946. "Law and the Social Sciences." *Virginia Law Review,* 32: 858.

Sipes, Richard G. 1973. "War, Sports, and Aggression: An Empirical Test of Two Rival Theories." *American Anthropologist,* 75: 64–86.

Smedley, Audrey. 2004. *Women Creating Patrilyny.* Walnut Creek, CA: AltaMira.

Smith, Michael G. 1966. "Pre-Industrial Stratification Systems." In N. J. Smelser and S. M. Lipset, eds., *Social Structure and Mobility in Economic Development.* Chicago: Aldine.

Snowdon, Charles T. 1999. "An Empiricist View of Language Evolution and Development." In B. J. King, ed., *The Origins of Language.* Santa Fe, NM: School of American Research Press, pp. 79–114.

Southworth, Franklin C., and Chandler J. Daswani. 1974. *Foundations of Linguistics.* New York: Free Press.

Spanos, Nicholas P. 1983. "Ergotism and the Salem Witch Panic: A Critical Analysis and an Alternative Conceptualization." *Journal of the History of the Behavioral Sciences,* 19: 358–69.

Speth, John D., and Katherine A. Spielmann. 1983. "Energy Source, Protein Metabolism, and Hunter-Gatherer Subsistence Strategies." *Journal of Anthropological Archaeology,* 2: 1–31.

Spiro, Melford E. 1982. *Oedipus in the Trobriands.* Chicago: University of Chicago Press.

Spiro, Melford E., and Roy G. D'Andrade. 1958. "A Cross-Cultural Study of Some Supernatural Beliefs." *American Anthropologist,* 60: 456–66.

Stark, Rodney. 1985. *The Future of Religion: Secularization, Revival and Cult Formation.* Berkeley: University of California Press.

State of the World: A Worldwatch Institute Report on Progress toward a Sustainable Society. New York: Norton, 1994.

Stephens, William N. 1963. *The Family in Cross-Cultural Perspective.* New York: Holt, Rinehart & Winston.

Stephens, William N. 1972. "A Cross-Cultural Study of Modesty." *Behavior Science Research,* 7: 1–28.

Steward, Julian H., and Louis C. Faron. 1959. *Native Peoples of South America.* New York: McGraw-Hill.

Stille, Alexander. 2001. "Grounded by an Income Gap." *New York Times Arts & Ideas,* December 15.

Stini, William A. 1971. "Evolutionary Implications of Changing Nutritional Patterns in Human Populations." *American Anthropologist,* 73: 1019–30.

Stogdill, Ralph M. 1974. *Handbook of Leadership: A Survey of Theory and Research.* New York: Macmillan.

Straus, Murray A. 1991. "Physical Violence in American Families: Incidence Rates, Causes, and Trends." In D. D. Knudsen and J. L. Miller, eds., *Abused and Battered.* New York: Aldine, pp. 17–34.

Straus, Murray A. 1995. "Trends in Cultural Norms and Rates of Partner Violence: An Update to 1992." In S. M. Stith and M. A. Straus, eds., *Understanding Partner Violence: Prevalence, Causes, Consequences, and Solutions.* Minneapolis, MN: National Council on Family Relations, pp. 30–33, accessed at http://pubpages.unh.edu/-mas2/v56.pdf/, August 2002.

Straus, Murray A. 2001. "Physical Aggression in the Family: Prevalence Rates, Links to Non-Family Violence, and Implications for Primary Prevention of Societal Violence." In M. Martinez, ed., *Prevention and Control of Aggression and the Impact on Its Victims.* New York: Kluwer Academic/Plenum, pp. 181–200.

Straus, Murray A., and Glenda Kaufman Kantor. 1995. "Trends in Physical Abuse by Parents from 1975 to 1992: A Comparison of Three National Surveys." Paper presented at the annual meeting of the American Society of Criminology, Boston, November 18, 1995, accessed at http://pubpages.unh.edu/-mas2/v57.pdf/, August 2002.

Straus, Murray A., and Carrie L. Yodanis. 1996. "Corporal Punishment in Adolescence and Physical Assaults on Spouses in Later Life: What Accounts for the Link?" *Journal of Marriage and the Family,* 58: 825–41.

Suárez-Orozco, Marcelo. 1992. "A Grammar of Terror: Psychocultural Responses to State Terrorism in Dirty War and Post-Dirty War Argentina." In C. Nordstrom and J. Martin, eds., *The Paths to Domination, Resistance, and Terror.* Berkeley, CA: University of California Press, pp. 219–59.

Swanson, Guy E. 1969. *The Birth of the Gods: The Origin of Primitive Beliefs.* Ann Arbor, MI: University of Michigan Press.

Szklut, Jay, and Robert Roy Reed. 1991. "Community Anonymity in Anthropological Research: A Reassessment." In C. Fluehr-Lobban, ed., *Ethics and the Profession of Anthropology: Dialogue for a New Era.* Philadelphia: University of Pennsylvania Press, pp. 97–116.

Tannen, Deborah. 1990. *You Just Don't Understand: Women and Men in Conversation.* New York: William Morrow.

Textor, Robert B., comp. 1967. *A Cross-Cultural Summary.* New Haven, CT: HRAF Press.

Thomas, David H. 1986. *Refiguring Anthropology: First Principles of Probability and Statistics.* Prospect Heights, IL: Waveland.

Thomas, Elizabeth Marshall. 1959. *The Harmless People.* New York: Knopf.

Thomas, Wesley. 1993. "A Traditional Navajo's Perspectives on the Cultural Construction of Gender in the Navajo World." Paper presented at the University of Frankfurt, Germany. As referred to in Lang 1999.

Thomason, Sarah Grey, and Terrence Kaufman. 1988. *Language Contact, Creolization, and Genetic Linguistics.* Berkeley: University of California Press.

Thompson, Ginger. 2002. "Mexico Is Attracting a Better Class of Factory in Its South." *The New York Times,* June 29, p. A3.

Thompson, Stith. 1965. "Star Husband Tale." In A. Dundes, ed., *The Study of Folklore.* Upper Saddle River, NJ: Prentice Hall.

Timpane, John. 1991. "Essay: The Poetry of Science." *Scientific American* (July): 128.

Tollefson, Kenneth D. 2004. "Tlingit: Chiefs Past and Present." In *Portraits of Culture,* in C. R. Ember, M. Ember, and P. N. Peregrine, eds., *New Directions in Anthropology.* Upper Saddle River, NJ: Prentice Hall, CD-ROM.

Torrey, E. Fuller. n.d. *The Mind Game: Witchdoctors and Psychiatrists.* New York: Emerson Hall.

Torry, William I. 1986. "Morality and Harm: Hindu Peasant Adjustments to Famines." *Social Science Information,* 25: 125–60.

Traphagan, John W., and L. Keith Brown. 2002. "Fast Food and Intergenerational Commensality in Japan: New Styles and Old Patterns." *Ethnology,* 41: 119–34.

Treiman, Donald J., and Harry B. G. Ganzeboom. 1990. "Cross-National Comparative Status-Attainment Research." *Research in Social Stratification and Mobility,* 9: 117.

Trevor-Roper, H. R. 1971. "The European Witch-Craze of the Sixteenth and Seventeenth Centuries." In W. A. Lessa and E. Z. Vogt, eds., *Reader in Comparative Religion.* 3rd ed. New York: Harper & Row.

Trouillot, Michel-Rolph. 2001. "The Anthropology of the State in the Age of Globalization: Close Encounters of the Deceptive Kind." *Current Anthropology,* 42: 125–38.

Trudgill, Peter. 1983. *Sociolinguistics: An Introduction to Language and Society.* Rev. ed. New York: Penguin.

Underhill, Ralph. 1975. "Economic and Political Antecedents of Monotheism: A Cross-Cultural Study." *American Journal of Sociology,* 80: 841–61.

Underhill, Ruth M. 1938. *Social Organization of the Papago Indians.* New York: Columbia University Press.

United Nations Development Programme. 1994. *Human Development Report 1994*. New York: Oxford University Press.

Urban Institute. 2000. "America's Homeless II: Populations and Services." Washington, D.C.: Urban Institute, February 1, 2000. Accessed at http://www.urban.org/housing/homeless/numbers/index.htm

U.S. Department of Housing and Urban Development, 2007. "Hud Releases Landmark Homeless Study." http://www.hud.gov/news/release.cfm?CONTENT=pr07-220.cfm.

Valente, Thomas W. 1995. *Network Models of the Diffusion of Innovations*. Cresskill, NJ: Hampton Press.

Vanneman, Reeve, and Lynn Weber Cannon. 1987. *The American Perception of Class*. Philadelphia: Temple University Press.

Van Willigen, John. 1986. *Applied Anthropology: An Introduction*. South Hadley, MA: Bergin & Garvey.

Van Willigen, John. 1993. *Applied Anthropology: An Introduction*. Rev. ed. Westport, CT: Bergin & Garvey.

Van Willigen, John, and Timothy L. Finan, eds. 1990. *Soundings: Rapid and Reliable Research Methods for Practicing Anthropologists*. NAPA Bulletin No. 10. Washington, D.C.: American Anthropological Association.

Van Willigen, John, Barbara Rylko-Bauer, and Ann McElroy, eds. 1989. *Making Our Research Useful: Case Studies in the Utilization of Anthropological Knowledge*. Boulder, CO: Westview.

"Violent Crime." NCJ-147486. Washington, D.C.: U.S. Department of Justice, April 1994.

Von Frisch, Karl. 1962. "Dialects in the Language of the Bees." *Scientific American* (August): 78–87.

Wadley, Reed L. 2003. "Lethal Treachery and the Imbalance of Power in Warfare and Feuding." *Journal of Anthropological Research*, 59: 531–54.

Wagley, Charles. 1974. "Cultural Influences on Population: A Comparison of Two Tupi Tribes." In P. J. Lyon, ed., *Native South Americans*. Boston: Little, Brown, pp. 377–84.

Wald, Matthew L. 2000. "Hybrid Cars Show Up in M.I.T.'s Crystal Ball." *The New York Times*, November 3, 2000, p. F1; and the special advertisement produced by energy companies, "Energy: Investing for a New Century," *The New York Times*, October 30, 2000, pp. EN1–EN8.

Wallace, Anthony. 1966. *Religion: An Anthropological View*. New York: Random House.

Wallace, Anthony. 1970. *The Death and Rebirth of the Seneca*. New York: Knopf.

Wanner, Eric, and Lila R. Gleitman, eds. 1982. *Language Acquisition: The State of the Art*. Cambridge: Cambridge University Press.

Ward, Peter M., ed. 1982. *Self-Help Housing: A Critique*. London: Mansell.

Wardhaugh, Ronald. 1992. *An Introduction to Sociolinguistics*. 2nd ed. Oxford: Blackwell.

Wardhaugh, Ronald. 1997. *An Introduction to Sociolinguistics*. 3rd ed. Oxford: Blackwell.

Wardhaugh, Ronald. 2002. *An Introduction to Sociolinguistics*. 4th ed. Oxford: Blackwell.

Warner, John Anson. 1986. "The Individual in Native American Art: A Sociological View." In E. L. Wade, ed., *The Arts of the North American Indian*. New York: Hudson Hills Press.

Webb, Karen E. 1977. "An Evolutionary Aspect of Social Structure and a Verb 'Have'." *American Anthropologist*, 79: 42–49.

Weber, Max. 1947. *The Theory of Social and Economic Organization*. Trans. A. M. Henderson and Talcott Parsons. New York: Oxford University Press.

Weinreich, Uriel. 1968. *Languages in Contact*. The Hague: Mouton.

Weisner, Thomas S., and Ronald Gallimore. 1977. "My Brother's Keeper: Child and Sibling Caretaking." *Current Anthropology*, 18: 169–90.

Werner, Dennis. 1975. "On the Societal Acceptance or Rejection of Male Homosexuality." M.A. thesis, Hunter College of the City University of New York.

Werner, Dennis. 1978. "Trekking in the Amazon Forest." *Natural History* (November): 42–54.

Werner, Dennis. 1979. "A Cross-Cultural Perspective on Theory and Research on Male Homosexuality." *Journal of Homosexuality*, 4: 345–62.

Werner, Dennis. 1982. "Chiefs and Presidents: A Comparison of Leadership Traits in the United States and among the Mekranoti-Kayapo of Central Brazil." *Ethos*, 10: 136–48.

Whitaker, Ian. 1955. *Social Relations in a Nomadic Lappish Community*. Oslo: Utgitt av Norsk Folksmuseum.

White, Douglas R. 1988. "Rethinking Polygyny: Co-Wives, Codes, and Cultural Systems." *Current Anthropology*, 29, 529–88.

White, Douglas R., and Michael L. Burton. 1988. "Causes of Polygyny: Ecology, Economy, Kinship, and Warfare." *American Anthropologist*, 90: 871–87.

White, Douglas R., Michael L. Burton, and Lilyan A. Brudner. 1977. "Entailment Theory and Method: A Cross-Cultural Analysis of the Sexual Division of Labor." *Behavior Science Research*, 12: 1–24.

Whiting, Beatrice B. 1950. *Paiute Sorcery*. Viking Fund Publications in Anthropology No. 15. New York: Wenner-Gren Foundation.

Whiting, Beatrice B. 1965. "Sex Identity Conflict and Physical Violence." *American Anthropologist,* 67: 123–40.

Whiting, Beatrice B., and Carolyn Pope Edwards. 1973. "A Cross-Cultural Analysis of Sex Differences in the Behavior of Children Aged Three through Eleven." *Journal of Social Psychology,* 91: 171–88.

Whiting, Beatrice B., and Carolyn Pope Edwards (in collaboration with Carol R. Ember, Gerald M. Erchak, Sara Harkness, Robert L. Munroe, Ruth H. Munroe, Sara B. Nerlove, Susan Seymour, Charles M. Super, Thomas S. Weisner, and Martha Wenger). 1988. *Children of Different Worlds: The Formation of Social Behavior.* Cambridge, MA: Harvard University Press.

Whiting, Beatrice B., and John W. M. Whiting (in collaboration with Richard Longabaugh). 1975. *Children of Six Cultures: A Psycho-Cultural Analysis.* Cambridge, MA: Harvard University Press.

Whiting, John W. M. 1964. "Effects of Climate on Certain Cultural Practices." In W. H. Goodenough, ed., *Explorations in Cultural Anthropology.* New York: McGraw-Hill, pp. 511–44.

Whyte, Martin K. 1978a. "Cross-Cultural Codes Dealing with the Relative Status of Women." *Ethnology,* 17: 211–37.

Whyte, Martin K. 1978b. *The Status of Women in Preindustrial Societies.* Princeton, NJ: Princeton University Press.

Wiberg, Hakan. 1983. "Self-Determination as an International Issue." In I. M. Lewis, ed., *Nationalism and Self-Determination in the Horn of Africa.* London: Ithaca Press, pp. 43–65.

Wikan, Unni. 1982. *Beyond the Veil in Arabia.* Baltimore: Johns Hopkins University Press.

Williams, Melvin D. 2004. "Racism: The Production, Reproduction, and Obsolescence of Social Inferiority." In *Research Frontiers,* in C. R. Ember, M. Ember, and P. N. Peregrine, eds., *New Directions in Anthropology.* Upper Saddle River, NJ: Prentice Hall, CD-ROM.

Williams, Walter L. 1992. *The Spirit and the Flesh.* Boston: Beacon Press.

Wilmsen, Edwin N., ed. 1989. *We Are Here: Politics of Aboriginal Land Tenure.* Berkeley: University of California Press.

Winkelman, Michael James. 1986a. "Magico-Religious Practitioner Types and Socioeconomic Conditions." *Behavior Science Research,* 20: 17–46.

Winkelman, Michael. 1986b. "Trance States: A Theoretical Model and Cross-Cultural Analysis." *Ethos,* 14: 174–203.

Winkleman, Michael, and Philip M. Peck, eds. 2004. *Divination and Healing: Potent Vision.* Tucson: University of Arizona Press.

Winterhalder, Bruce. 1990. "Open Field, Common Pot: Harvest Variability and Risk Avoidance in Agricultural and Foraging Societies." In E. Cashdan, ed., *Risk and Uncertainty in Tribal and Peasant Economies.* Boulder, CO: Westview.

Witkowski, Stanley R. 1975. "Polygyny, Age of Marriage, and Female Status." Paper presented at the annual meeting of the American Anthropological Association, San Francisco.

Witkowski, Stanley R., and Cecil H. Brown. 1978. "Lexical Universals." *Annual Review of Anthropology,* 7: 427–51.

Witkowski, Stanley R., and Harold W. Burris. 1981. "Societal Complexity and Lexical Growth." *Behavior Science Research,* 16: 143–59.

Wolf, Eric. 1966. *Peasants.* Upper Saddle River, NJ: Prentice Hall.

Wolf, Naomi. 1991. *The Beauty Myth: How Images of Beauty Are Used against Women.* New York: Morrow.

Wood, Gordon S. 1992. *The Radicalism of the American Revolution.* New York: Knopf.

Woodburn, James. 1968. "An Introduction to Hadza Ecology." In R. B. Lee and I. DeVore, eds., *Man the Hunter.* Chicago: Aldine, pp. 49–55.

World Bank. 1995. *World Development Report 1995. Workers in an Integrating World.* Oxford: Oxford University Press.

World Bank. 2001. *2001 World Development Indicators.* Washington, D.C.: World Bank.

Worldwatch Institute. 1994. *State of the World 1994: A Worldwatch Institute Report on Progress toward a Sustainable Society.* New York: Norton.

Wright, Gary A. 1971. "Origins of Food Production in Southwestern Asia: A Survey of Ideas." *Current Anthropology,* 12: 447–78.

Yergin, Daniel. 2002. "Giving Aid to World Trade," *The New York Times,* June 27, p. A29.

Yinger, J. Milton. 1994. *Ethnicity: Source of Strength? Source of Conflict?* Albany, NY: State University Press.

Zeder, Melinda. 1997. *The American Archaeologist: A Profile.* Walnut Creek, CA: AltaMira.

PHOTO CREDITS

CHAPTER 1

Page 1: Doranne Jacobson/International Images; page 5: Spooner/Redmond-Callow/ZUMA Press–Gamma; page 8: Peggy and Yoram Kahana/Peter Arnold, Inc.; page 10: Robert Brenner/PhotoEdit Inc.; page 15 (left): Victor Englebert/Photo Researchers, Inc.; page 15 (right): Bildarchiv Okapia/Photo Researchers, Inc.; page 16: Corbis Royalty Free; page 19: © Mark Peterson/Corbis SABA.

CHAPTER 2

Page 22: © Mark A. Johnson/CORBIS, All Rights Reserved; page 25: © Cameron/CORBIS, All Rights Reserved; page 27 (left): N. Martin Haudrich/Photo Researchers, Inc.; page 27 (right): James L. Stanfield/National Geographic Image Collection; page 30 (left): © Ariel Skelley/CORBIS, All Rights Reserved; page 30 (right): © Rolf Bruderer/CORBIS, All Rights Reserved; page 32 (left): Jeremy Horner/Corbis/Bettmann; page 32 (right): Jonathan Blair/Corbis/Bettmann; page 36: © Christel Gerstenberg/CORBIS, All Rights Reserved; page 38: Dagli Orti/The Art Archive/Musée Lapérouse Albi.

CHAPTER 3

Page 43: © Anthony Bannister/Gallo Images/CORBIS, All Rights Reserved; page 46 (left): © Peter Steiner/CORBIS, All Rights Reserved; page 46 (right): Susan Kuklin/Science Source/Photo Researchers, Inc.; page 49: Roy Morsch/Corbis/Bettmann; page 55: © Philip Spruyt/Stapleton Collection/CORBIS, All Rights Reserved; page 59: Vince Streano/Corbis/Bettmann; page 61 (left): Rhoda Sidney; page 61 (right): Renate Hiller; page 65: © Caroline Penn/CORBIS, All Rights Reserved.

CHAPTER 4

Page 68: © Keren Su/CORBIS, All Rights Reserved; page 73: Victor Englebert/Photo Researchers, Inc.; page 75: © Keren Su/CORBIS, All Rights Reserved; page 77: Tiziana Baldizzone/Corbis/Bettmann; page 78: © Richard Hamilton Smith/CORBIS, All Rights Reserved; page 82: James P. Blair/NGS Image Collection; page 84: © Jeremy Horner/CORBIS, All Rights Reserved; page 85: © Bernard Annebicque/Corbis Sygma; page 86: John Roberts/Corbis/Stock Market; page 89: John Eastcott/Yva Momatiuk/Woodfin Camp & Associates, Inc.

CHAPTER 5

Page 94: © Andrew Holbrooke; page 97: Wendy Stone/CORBIS–NY; page 99: Wendy Stone/Odyssey/Chicago/Odyssey Productions, Inc.; page 100: Mike Dobel/Masterfile Corporation; page 103: © Sherwin Crasto/Reuters/Corbis; page 107: Photograph provided courtesy of Syracuse University, All rights reserved; page 110 (left): © Kevin Fleming/CORBIS, All Rights Reserved; page 110 (right): David de Lossy, Ghislain & Marie/Getty Images Inc.–Image Bank.

CHAPTER 6

Page 115: Marc Romanelli/Getty Images Inc.–Image Bank; page 117: Pete Saloutos/Corbis/Stock Market; page 120: Jorgen Shytte/Peter Arnold, Inc.; page 122: Laurence Fordyce/Corbis/Bettmann; page 126: Ann Mohs/Bruce Miller; page 127: © Setboun/CORBIS, All Rights Reserved; page 130 (left): © Kevin Cozad/O'Brien Productions/CORBIS, All Rights Reserved; page 130 (right): © Michael Newman/PhotoEdit, Inc.; page 132: Charles Lenars/Corbis/Bettmann.

CHAPTER 7

Page 137: Don Mason/Corbis/Stock Market; page 138: © Lindsay Hebberd/CORBIS, All Rights Reserved; page 140: © Punch/Rothco; page 142: © Caroline Penn/CORBIS, All Rights Reserved; page 144: © Lindsay Hebberd/CORBIS, All Rights Reserved; page 146: Nik Wheeler/Corbis/Bettmann; page 149: © Hamid Sardar/CORBIS, All Rights Reserved; page 152: Toshifumi Kiramura/Agence France Presse/Getty Images; page 157: Harvey Lloyd/Getty Images, Inc.–Taxi; page 162: Eric Smith/Art Directors & Trip Photo Library.

CHAPTER 8

Page 165: Lionel Bonaventure/Corbis/Sygma; page 170: Katz/Anthro-Photo File; page 173: Peter Andrews/Reuters/Corbis/Reuters America LLC; page 175: © European Commission/Handout/Reuters/CORBIS, All Rights Reserved; page 177: Maria Lepowsky; page 181: David Austen/Woodfin Camp & Associates, Inc.

CHAPTER 9

Page 187: © Dallas and John Heaton/Free Agents Limited/CORBIS, All Rights Reserved; page 190: ScienceCartoonsPlus.com; page 191: © Reuters/Jorge Silva/Corbis; page 194: Mike Yamashita/Woodfin Camp & Associates, Inc.; page 197: © Catherine Karnow/CORBIS, All Rights Reserved; page 201: Ogallala Sioux performing the Ghost Dance at the Pine Ridge Indian Agency, South Dakota, Illustration by Frederic Remington, 1890, The Granger Collection.

CHAPTER 10

Page 206: Greg Girard/Contact Press Images Inc.; page 209: Getty Images, Inc.; page 211: © Bettmann/CORBIS, All Rights Reserved; page 213: Currier & Ives, "Give Me Liberty or Give Me Death!" 1775, Lithograph, 1876, © The Granger Collection, New York; page 216: Peter Bowater/Photo Researchers, Inc.; page 219: Wolfgang Kaehler Photography; page 221: AP Wide World Photos; page 222: Peter Turnley/Corbis/Bettmann.

CHAPTER 11

Page 227: David Greedy/Getty Images, Inc.–Liaison; page 229: Rick Wilking/Corbis/Reuters America LLC; page 231: Sucheta Das/Corbis/Reuters America LLC; page 237: Edouard Berne/Getty Images Inc.–Stone Allstock; page 238: Peter Glass/Peter Glass Photography; page 241: Peter Chen/The Image Works; page 242: © Dusko Despotovic/Bettmann/CORBIS, All Rights Reserved.

CHAPTER 12

Page 245: Richard Lord/The Image Works; page 246: © Reuters/Diario El Pais/Corbis; page 250: Kamal Kishore/Corbis/Reuters America LLC; page 252: © Yannis Kontos/Corbis Sygma; page 255: Jeffrey Aaronson/Still Media; page 256: Henning Christoph/DAS FOTOARCHIV/Peter Arnold, Inc.; page 259: Martha Cooper/Peter Arnold, Inc.; page 261: © Gideon Mendel for The International HIV/AIDS Alliance/CORBIS, All Rights Reserved; page 264: Michael J. Balick/Peter Arnold, Inc.

INDEX

Page numbers followed by *t* indicate tables. Page numbers in bold type indicate glossary entries.

A

Aborigines, Australian, 70–71
Abuse, family, 234–35
Accent, **267**
Accidental juxtaposition, 207–208
Acculturation, 210–12
Acquired immune deficiency syndrome, 260–62, **267**
Acquisition, language, 45–50
Adaptive customs, 34–35, 214–15, **267**. *See also* Change, cultural
Adaptivity, religious, 199–204
Adjudication, 181, **267**. *See also* Codified laws
Adoption, innovative, 208
Age, labor and, 86–87. *See also* Children
Age-set systems, 169
Aggression, gender and, 129–32, 237–38
Agriculture, intensive. *See* Intensive agriculture
AIDS, 260–62, **267**
Air pollution, 232
Allocation, resource, 81–84. *See also* Resources, economic
Ambilineal descent, 155, 160–62, **267**
Ancestor spirits, 191–92, **267**
Androgen, 130
Animals, words for, 58–59
Anthropological linguistics. *See* Linguistics, anthropological
Anthropology, definition of, **267**
Apology, ritual, 180
Applied anthropology, 9–10, 246–65, **267**
Archaeology, 6–7, 246, 251–53, **267**. *See also* Cultural anthropology
Arranged marriages, 143–44

Assimilation, 212
Associations, explanatory, 11. *See also* Explanation
Australian aborigines, 70–71
Avoidance, conflict, 179
Avoidance, rituals of, 189
Avunculocal residence, 153, 162, **267**

B

Balance, concept of, 255
Balanced reciprocity, 90, **267**
Band, society as, 167, **267**
Barriers, change-acceptance, 250–51
Basic research, 9
Beauty, culture and, 263
Behavior, 24–25, 29–30, 129–32. *See also* Customs, cultural
Beings, supernatural, 190–93
Bell-shaped curve, 32–33
Benefits, innovative, 208–209
Benefits, religious, 199–204
Berdache, 116
Big status, tribal, 176–77
Bilateral kinship, 156–57, **267**
Bilocal residence, 152, 161, **267**
Biological anthropology, 4–6, **267**
Biology, race and, 107–108
Biomedicine, 254, 256–57, 259, **267**
Biopiracy, 224
Bride price, 141–42, **267**
Bride service, 142, **267**
Burakumin, 103

C

Cali, Colombia, 233
Capital punishment, 179, 236
Capitoes, 217
Cash crop, 217–18
Caste, 102–104, **267**
Change, cultural, 36–37, 207–26. *See also* Adaptive customs
Change, religious. *See* Revitalization movement
Character traits, supernatural, 192
Chiefdom, society as, 168*t*, 170–71, **268**
Child-care theory. *See* Compatibility-with-child-care theory
Children
    gender and, 118–20, 121, 129–30, 139–41
    labor and, 86–87
    language acquisition by, 49–50
    marriage and, 139
    religion and, 192
    violence against, 234–35
Chuuk, 256
Cities, growth of, 172
Clan, 157, **268**
Class, 61, 96, 99–106, **268**. *See also* Stratification, social
Classification, anthropological, 15
Climate, food production and, 79
Clines, 108, **268**
Closed class systems. *See* Caste
Closed system, communicative, 46
Codeswitching, 63, **268**
Codified laws, 178–79, 181–82, **268**
Collection, food. *See* Food
Colonialism, land and, 83–84
Colors, words for, 57–58
Combat. *See* Warfare
Commercialization, 76, 90–91, 151, 215–18, **268**
Communication, definition of, 44. *See also* Linguistics, anthropological
Community action conflict resolution, 179
Compatibility-with-child-care theory, 118–20, 121, **268**
Compensation, informant, 39
Competition, sexual, 139–40
Complementary opposition, 169, **268**
Computerized production mode, 85
Conflict, resolution of, 178–85. *See also* Warfare
Conformity, 31. *See also* Patterns, cultural
Consensus model, cultural, 38

Constraints, cultural, 31. *See also* Norms, cultural; Patterns, cultural
Construct, theoretical, 13, **272**
Content, lexical, 57–59
Contingency table, 16–17
Contract archaeology. *See* Cultural resource management
Conversion, religious, 200–202
Conversion, resource. *See* Labor
Cooperation. *See* Reciprocity
Core vocabulary, 59, **268**
Corporal punishment, 234–35
Corvée, 86, **268**
Costs, innovative, 208–209
Courts. *See* Adjudication
Cousin marriages, 144–45
Creator gods, 190
Creole languages, 48–49
Crime, 182–83, 236–38, **268**
CRM. *See* Cultural resource management
Crops, cash, 217–18, **267**
Cross-cousins, 145, **268**
Cross-cultural research, 9, 40–41, **268**
Cultivation, shifting. *See* Horticulture
Cultural anthropology, 6–10, 37–41, **268**
Cultural barriers, 250
Cultural relativism, 27–29, **268**
Cultural resource management, 246, 251–53, **268**
Culture
    adaptivity of, 207–26
    customs and, 29–30, 34–35, 214–15
    definition of, 6, 23–24, **268**
    language and, 57–63
    medicine and, 254–57
    study of, 6–10, 23–42
Curve, bell-shaped, 32–33
Customs, cultural, 29–30, 34–35, 214–15. *See also* Behavior

D

Delinquency, juvenile, 236–37
Democide, 243
Democracy, culture and, 220, 239–41
dependency, infant, 139
Descent, family, 153–63, 169. *See also* Family
Descriptive linguistics, 7, 50–54, **268**. *See also* Linguistics, anthropological

Diabetes, 219
Dialect, 56, **268**
Diaspora, cultural, 28. *See also* Migration
Diffusion, 209–10, **268**
Dimorphism, sexual, 117–18, **272**
Disasters, natural, 228–30
Discovery, innovative, 207
Disease, treatment of, 257–59. *See also* Medical
     anthropology
Distribution, economic, 88–91
Distribution, frequency, 32–33
Divergence, linguistic, 54–57
Diversity, cultural, 28, 224–25
Divination, 194–95, **268**
Division of labor, 86–87, 118–24, 139
Doctors. *See* Practitioners, medical
Domestic production mode, 84
Double descent, 156, **268**
Dowry, 142–43, **268**
Draft, military, 86

E

Economics
     crime and, 237–38
     culture and, 215–18
     distribution and, 88–91
     food and, 69–80
     health and, 260
     labor and, 84–87, 118–24, 139, 215–16
     marriage and, 141–43
     resources and, 81–87, **268**
     stratification and, 95, 97, 98–99, 101, 105
     unilineal descent and, 159
Economy-of-effort theory, 120, **268**
Egalitarian society, 95, 96–98, **268**. *See also*
     Reciprocity
Ego, 156–57, **268**
Endogamy, 144, **268**
Equilibrium, concept of, 255
Ergot, 196
Eta, 103
Ethics, 39, 247–51
Ethnicity, 95, 106–11, 240, **268**
Ethnocentrism, 26–27, **269**
Ethnogenesis, 220–21, **269**
Ethnography, 37–39, 60–63, **269**
Ethnohistory, 41, **269**
Ethnology, 8–9, **269**. *See also* Cultural anthropology

Ethnomedicine, 254–57, **269**
Evidence, anthropological, 14–18
Exchange, economic. *See* Commercialization; Market
     exchange
Exchange, female, 142
Exchange, premarital gift, 142
Exogamy, 144, **269**
Expectations, patient, 258
Expendability theory, 120, **269**
Explanation, 11–14, **269**
Extended family, 148–51, **269**
Extensive cultivation, **269**. *See also* Horticulture
Extramarital sex, 133–34

F

Falsification, theoretical, 14
Families, linguistic, 55–56
Family, 148–63, 234–35, **269**. *See also* Children;
     Marriage
Famine, 229–30
Fatness, female, 263
Females, exchange of, 142
Feuding, 183, **269**
Fields, anthropological, 4–10
Fieldwork, anthropological, 37–39, **269**
Food
     collection, 69–72, 81–82, **269**
     production, 71*t*, 72–80, 83, 123, **269**
Foragers, 69–72, 81–82, **269**
Forced labor, 85–86. *See also* Labor
Forensic anthropology, 246, 253–54, **269**
Fossil fuels, dependence on, 232
Fossils, 4–5, **269**
Fraternal polyandry, 147–48
Frequency distribution, 32–33
Fundamentalism, 202–203

G

Gaiwiio, 200
Gathering, food. *See* Food
Gender, 62, 86–87, 116–36, 139, **269**
Generalized reciprocity, 88–89, **269**
General-purpose money, 91, **269**
Ghosts, 191–92, **269**
Gift exchange, premarital, 142
Globalization, 221–24, **269**

Global warming, 232
Gods, 190, **269**. *See also* Beings, supernatural
Goods, distribution of, 88–91
Grammar, linguistic, 50–51
Group marriage, 145, **269**
Groups, unilineal, 157–60

H

Handsome Lake, 200
Headman, **269**
Healers. *See* Practitioners, medical
Health, modernization and, 219. *See also* Medical
    anthropology
Herding. *See* Pastoralism
Historical archaeology, 6, **269**
Historical linguistics, 7, 54–56, **269**. *See also*
    Linguistics, anthropological
Historical research. *See* Ethnohistory
HIV, 260–62
Holism, anthropological, 3, **269**
Homelessness, 231–33
Homicide, 236
Homo sapiens, **269**
Homosexuality, 134–35
Horticulture, 71*t*, 72–74, 82, **269**. *See also* Food
Housing, 230–33
Human immunodeficiency virus, 260–62
Humanism, anthropological, 12
Human paleontology, 4–5, **270**. *See also* Biological
    anthropology
Human sacrifice, 195
Human variation, 5–6, 29–30, **270**. *See also* Biological
    anthropology
Hunter-gatherers, **270**. *See also* Food
Hypertension, 219
Hypotheses, theoretical, 14, **270**

I

Ideals, cultural. *See* Patterns, cultural
Immigration. *See* Migration
Incest taboo, 143, **270**
Indirect dowry, 143, **270**
Individuals, culture and, 29–30
Indo-European, 55–56

Industrial agriculture, 76, 218. *See also* Intensive
    agriculture
Industrial production mode, 84
Inequality, economic, 101, 105. *See also* Stratification,
    social
Infant dependency, prolonged, 139
Infanticide, 234
Influence, channels of, 251
Informants, anthropological, 38
Innovation, culture and, 207–209
Integration, cultural, 35
Intensive agriculture. *See also* Food
    characteristics of, 71*t*, 74–76
    definition of, **270**
    gender and, 123
    industrial, 218
    land and, 83
Intentional innovation, 208
Intercultural research. *See* Cross-cultural research
Intervention, divine, 193
Intracultural comparison. *See* Within-culture
    comparison
Invention, culture and, 207–209

J

Joking, cross-cousin, 145
Juvenile delinquency, 236–37
Juxtaposition, accidental, 207–208

K

Kindred, bilateral, 156–57, **270**
Kinship, 153–63, 169. *See also* Family
Kosciusko, 212

L

Labor, 84–87, 118–24, 139, 215–16
Lag, cultural, 18
Land, allocation of, 81–84. *See also* Resources,
    economic
Language. *See* Linguistics, anthropological
Lapps, the, 77–78
Laws, codified. *See* Codified laws

Laws, scientific, 11, **270**
Leadership, political, 176–77. *See also* Politics
Learning, cultural, 24–25
Lexicon, 53, **270**
Life-forms, words for, 58–59
Lineage, 157, 169, **270**. *See also* Kinship
Linguistics, anthropological, 7, 25, 44–66, **267**. *See also* Cultural anthropology
Literacy, 63–65

M

Magic, 195–97, **270**. *See also* Religion
Maladaptive customs, 34, **270**
Malnutrition, 262–65
Mana, 170–71, 188–90, **270**
Manumission, **270**
Market exchange, **270**. *See also* Commercialization
Marriage, 132–34, 138–48, 150–51, 159, **270**. *See also* Children; Family
Material culture, 23
Matrifocal family, 148, **270**
Matrilineal descent, 155, 158–59, **270**
Matrilocal residence, 152–53, 160–61, 163, **270**
Meals, sacred, 195
Measurement, evidentiary, 15–16, **270**
Mechanization, 76, 218
Mediation, conflict, 180, **270**
Medical anthropology, 246, 254–65, **270**
Mediums, spiritual, 198, **270**
Mekong Delta, the, 75
Migration
    cities and, 172
    culture and, 28, 224
    food and, 80
    labor and, 215–16
    language and, 64
Military activity. *See* Warfare
Missionaries. *See* Conversion, religious
Mitigation plan, CRM, 252
Mobility, social, 100–102
Mode, statistical, 32
Moiety, 158, **270**
Money. *See* General-purpose money
Monogamy, **270**
Monotheism, 192–93, **270**
Morphology, 51, 52–53, **270**
Mother tongues, 64

Multilingualism, 63
Mundurucú, 216–17

N

Naming process, disease, 258
Natural disasters, 228–30
Negotiation, conflict, 180, **270**
Neolocal residence, 151–52, 153, 160, **270**
Nonagricultural commercial production, 216–17
Nonfraternal polyandry, 147–48
Nonhuman communication, 45–47
Nonsororal polygyny, 146, **270**
Nonverbal communication, 44–47
Norms, cultural, 31, **270**. *See also* Patterns, cultural
Nuclear family, 148, **270**
Nupe, the, 104–106

O

Oaths, 180–81, **270**
Obesity, 219, 263
Objectivity, scientific, 12
Observation, participant. *See* Participant-observation
Oil, dependence on, 232
One-parent families, 150–51
Open class systems, 100–102
Open system, communicative, 46
Operational definition, 14–15, **270**. *See also* Evidence, anthropological
Opposition, complementary. *See* Complementary opposition
Ordeal, 180–81, **271**
Organization, political, 166–74. *See also* Politics

P

Paleoanthropology. *See* Human paleontology
Parallel cousins, 145, **271**
Participant-observation, 37–39, **271**
Participation, political, 177–78. *See also* Democracy, culture and
Pastoralism, 71t, 76–78, 83, **271**. *See also* Food
Patrilineal descent, 154, 158, **271**
Patrilocal residence, 152–53, 160–61, 163, **271**

Pattern, modal, 32
Patterns, cultural, 31–33
Peasants, 91, 217–18, **271**
Permissiveness, sexual, 132–35
Personality, 129–32, 258
Phonology, 51–52, **271**
Phratry, 158, **271**
Physical anthropology. *See* Biological anthropology
Physician. *See* Practitioners, medical
Physiology, gender, 117–18
Pidgin, 48
Placebo effect, 258–59
Plants, words for, 58–59
Plow agriculture, 123
Politics, 124–26, 159–60, 166–85, 220, 260
Pollution, 232
Polyandry, 145, 147–48, **271**
Polygamy, 145–48, **271**
Polygyny, 145–47, **271**
Polytheism, 192, **271**
Population, food production and, 79
Possession, religious, 194, 198
Postindustrial production mode, 85
Postpartum requirements, animal, 140–41
Postpartum sex taboo, 146–47, **271**
Power, 95–96, 97–98, **271**. *See also* Politics
p-value. *See* Probability value
Practices, religious, 193–99
Practicing anthropology. *See* Applied anthropology
Practitioners, medical, 258–59
Prehistory, **271**
Premarital sex, 132–33
Prestige, 96–97, 98–99, **271**. *See also* Stratification, social
Price, bride, 141–42, **267**
Priests, 198–99, **271**
Primary subsistence activities, 121–24, **271**
Primatology, 5, **271**
Private property, 81
Probability value, 17
Process, political, 175–78. *See also* Politics
Production, economic. *See* Labor
Production, food. *See* Food
Production, nonagricultural, 216–17
Prolonged infant dependency, 139
Property, private, 81
Protolanguage, 55, **271**
Psychological barriers, 250–51
Punishment, physical, 234–35

R

Racism, 95, 106–109, **271**. *See also* Ethnicity
Raiding, 183, **271**
Rank society, 96, 98–99, **271**
Reciprocity, 88–90, **271**. *See also* Egalitarian society
Reconciliation, ritual, 180
Redistribution, 90, **271**
Referent, symbolic, 45
Regional comparison, 40
Relationships, explanatory, 11. *See also* Explanation
Relativism, cultural, 27–29, **268**
Religion, 160, 188–204, **271**. *See also* Supernatural, the
Required labor, 85–86. *See also* Labor
Research, basic, 9
Research, cultural, 37–41
Residence, marital, 151–53, 160–63
Resolution, conflict, 178–85. *See also* Warfare
Resource management, cultural, 246, 251–53, **268**
Resources, economic
    allocation of, 81–84
    conversion of, 84–87
    definition of, **268**
    stratification and, 95, 97, 98–99, 101, 105
Restrictions, marital, 143–48
Restrictions, sexual, 132–35
Revitalization movement, 200, **271**
Revolution, 212–13, **271**
Ritual reconciliation, 180
Roles, gender, 118–21, **269**
Rules of descent, 154, **271**

S

Saami, the. *See* Lapps, the
Sacrifices, religious, 195
Sampling, anthropological, 16, 33
Sapir–Whorf hypothesis, 59–60
Science, anthropology and, 12
Secondary subsistence activities, 121, **271**
Segmentary lineage system, 169, **271**
Seminole, the, 221
Seneca, the, 200
Service, bride, 142, **267**
Services, distribution of, 88–91
Sets, anthropological, 15
Sex differences, 117–18, **271**
Sexual dimorphism, 73–74, **272**

Sexuality, 132–35, 139–40
Shamans, 197–98, 224, 258–59, **272**
Sharing. *See* Reciprocity
Shifting cultivation. *See* Horticulture
Sib. *See* Clan
Siblings, **272**
Significance, statistical, 17–18
Six Cultures project, 129, 131
Slash-and-burn, **272**. *See also* Horticulture
Slavery, 86, 104–106, **272**
Slums, 230–31
Social barriers, 250–51
Social status. *See* Stratification, social
Society, definition of, 23–24, **272**. *See also* Culture
Sociolinguistics, 7, 60–63, **272**. *See also* Linguistics, anthropological
Sorcery, 196–97, 198, **272**
Sororal polygyny, 146, **272**
Specialization, labor, 86–87, 118–24, 139
Spirits, supernatural, 191–92, **272**
Spouse abuse, 234–35
Squatter settlements, 230–31
State, society as, 168*t*, 171–73, 174–75, **272**
State terrorism, 243
Statistical association, 11, **272**
Statistics, anthropological, 16–18
Stratification, social
    culture and, 95–113, 220
    gender and, 127–29, **269**
    health and, 260
    language and, 61
    religion and, 192–93
    sexuality and, 135
Strength theory, 118, 120, **272**
Structural linguistics. *See* Descriptive linguistics
Structure, kinship. *See* Kinship
Subculture, definition of, 24, **272**
Subsistence work, 121–24, **271**
Supernatural, the, 188, 255–56, **272**. *See also* Religion
Superstition, 188–90. *See also* Religion
Symbolic communication, 45, **272**
Syntax, 51, 53–54, **272**

T

Taboo, 143, 146–47, 189, 190, **272**
Taxation, 85–86
Techniques, curing, 258

Telecommuting, 85
Terrorism, 241–43, **272**
Theoretical construct, 13, **272**
Theories, anthropological, 11–14, **272**. *See also* Explanation
Thinness, female, 263
Thrifty gene, the, 219
Tikopia, 201–202, 215–16
Totems, clan, 157, **272**
Trances, religious, 194, 198
Treatment, medical, 257–59. *See also* Medical anthropology
Tribe, society as, 168–69, **272**
Tributary production mode, 84–85
Truk, 256
Two-spirit gender, 116

U

Unconscious invention, 207–208
Undernutrition, 262–65
Unilineal descent, 154–60, 162–63, **272**
Unilocal residence patterns, 153, **272**
Urban anthropology, 172
Usufruct, 81

V

Variable, 11, **272**
Variation, human, 5–6, 29–30, **270**. *See also* Biological anthropology
Vietnam, agriculture in, 75
Violence, 182–85, 234–35. *See also* Warfare
Vocabulary, culture and, 57–59

W

Warfare. *See also* Conflict, resolution of
    causes of, 238–41
    as conflict resolution, 178, 182–85
    definition of, **272**
    gender and, 124–26
    homicide and, 236
    marriage and, 147, 161–63

Warming, global, 232
Wealth. *See* Resources, economic
Wife abuse, 234–35
Witchcraft, 196–97, 198, **272**
Within-culture comparison, 39–41
Women. *See* Gender
Work. *See* Labor

Writing, 63–65
Wua nium, 176

X

Xanith, 116–17